D1290153

From Deterrence to Engagement

From Deterrence to Engagement

The U.S. Defense Commitment to South Korea

Terence Roehrig

LEXINGTON BOOKS

A division of
ROWMAN & LITTLEFIELD PUBLISHERS, INC.
Lanham • Boulder • New York • Toronto • Oxford

LEXINGTON BOOKS

A division of Rowman & Littlefield Publishers, Inc.
A wholly owned subsidiary of The Rowman & Littlefield Publishing Group, Inc.
4501 Forbes Boulevard, Suite 200
Lanham, MD 20706

PO Box 317
Oxford
OX2 9RU, UK

British Library Cataloguing in Publication Information Available

Library of Congress Cataloging-in-Publication Data

Roehrig, Terence, 1955–
  From deterrence to engagement : the U.S. defense commitment to South Korea /
Terence Roehrig.
      p. cm.
  Includes bibliographical references and index.
  ISBN: 978-0-7391-0560-3
  1. United States—Military relations—Korea (South) 2. Korea (South)—Military
relations—United States. I. Title.
  E183.8.K6R64 2006
  327.7305195'09045—dc22   2005029531

Printed in the United States of America

♾™ The paper used in this publication meets the minimum requirements of American
National Standard for Information Sciences—Permanence of Paper for Printed Library
Materials, ANSI/NISO Z39.48–1992.

For Amy.

Contents

List of Tables   ix

Acknowledgments   xi

Introduction   1

1   Deterrence, Compellence, and Korean Security   11

2   The Threat: North Korea, China, and the Soviet Union,   29
       1948-1990

3   The North Korean Threat: 75
       Conventional and Nuclear Weapons,
       1991 to the Present

4   U.S. Interests in Korea   111

5   U.S. Security Policy: Deterrence   161

6   U.S. Security Policy: Engagement and Compellence   201

Conclusion   231

Selected Bibliography   263

Index   279

About the Author   285

Tables

1.1	Types of Deterrence Situations	17
2.1	North and South Korean Military Personnel 1961 and 1969	39
2.2	North and South Korean Military Personnel 1970 and 1979	52
2.3	North and South Korean Military Equipment 1970 and 1979	53
2.4	North and South Korean Combat Aircraft 1970 and 1979	54
2.5	North and South Korean Military Personnel 1989-1990	61
2.6	North and South Korean Military Equipment 1989-1990	62
3.1	North and South Korean Military Personnel 2003-2004	81
3.2	North and South Korean Military Equipment 2003-2004	82
3.3	North and South Korean Military Capabilities 1960-2003	102
5.1	U.S. Economic Aid and Military Assistance to Korea 1955-1967	174
5.2	CINC, U.S.-ROK Combined Forces Command	185

Acknowledgments

The completion of this book has been a long time coming. A good portion of what you will read is based on research conducted for my PhD dissertation that I completed at the University of Wisconsin-Madison in 1995. Then, the manuscript sat for a few years as I worked on other research tasks that were more pressing. After finishing a different book in 2002 along with several other pieces on Korean security issues, I returned to this project. Much had happened in Korea since 1994/95 and so considerable work was needed to reflect the changes in the region and make the book relevant to these events. Hopefully, this book will be helpful in understanding this crucial region in global politics.

I am grateful to several people who have read various portions of the manuscript at different times and provided valuable comments and suggestions. These include David Tarr, my advisor, Robert McCalla, Wayne Patterson, and Neil Richardson who read this work in the mid-1990s as my dissertation at the University of Wisconsin-Madison. Eric Pullin, and an anonymous reader have been very generous in their feedback on later versions. However, any errors are my responsibility.

I would also like to express my thanks for the support I received from Cardinal Stritch University through faculty development grants to help defray some of the research costs. I also want to thank the staff at the Cardinal Stritch University library, especially Ly Nghiem, for the constant help in obtaining materials. Their assistance in finishing this effort was priceless.

Finally, I want to thank my family and friends for their patience with me throughout this endeavor. My constant lament of "but I have to work on my book" no doubt became tiresome. Most importantly, I want to acknowledge the support and encouragement given by my wife Amy, to whom this book is dedicated, along with my parents Richard and Shirley and my daughter Ann.

INTRODUCTION

For more than fifty years, the United States has provided a security guarantee to protect the Republic of Korea (ROK) from invasion. Prior to the Korean War in 1950, the guarantee was informal and often unclear, based on an uncertain appraisal of U.S. interests in the region. Following the end of the war in 1953, the United States and South Korea formalized the commitment with the signing of the U.S.-ROK Mutual Defense Treaty. In the years since, the United States has sought to deter an attack on South Korea by each or any of the following: North Korea, also known by its official name of the Democratic People's Republic of Korea (DPRK); China; and the Soviet Union. According to deterrence theory, the U.S.-ROK relationship is an example of extended deterrence. In contrast to deterring an attack on one's homeland, known as primary deterrence, in this case, U.S. policy is deterring an attack on an ally. Throughout the Cold War, deterrence in Korea held. Despite an immense buildup of arms and several occasions of increased tension, there is little indication that North Korea or its allies ever considered challenging the U.S. defense commitment after the Korean War.

The end of the Cold War and the breakup of the Soviet Union brought great change to international security relations. The world community looked forward to a significant relaxation of global tension and movement towards a more peaceful world. Despite these hopes, on the Korean peninsula, the confrontation with its roots in the Cold War remained. While relations between North and South Korea have improved, both sides remain well armed and divided by the 2.5-kilometer-wide demilitarized zone separating the peninsula. The U.S. deterrence commitment to its ally remains a cornerstone for security on the peninsula, demonstrated by the security treaty, the presence of U.S. military personnel, and regular presidential affirmation of the importance of the alliance. Though one can never be certain U.S. policy was the deciding factor, it has been an important contribution in helping to maintain peace in the region.

Despite the absence of war on the Korean peninsula, new concerns began to take center stage in the 1980s. Policy makers in Seoul and Washington became increasingly concerned with the North's production, testing, and export of ballistic missiles and its efforts to develop nuclear weapons. Though the U.S. deter-

1

rence posture remained firm and resolute, it became increasingly apparent to several administrations that deterrence alone was insufficient to address the problems of weapons proliferation. As a result, U.S. policy makers turned to another approach, that of compellence. Under compellence, U.S. officials faced the more difficult task of halting two weapons programs already in operation. To do so, Washington used a sometimes haphazard combination of efforts to engage North Korea and threats to compel Pyongyang into giving up these programs. While deterrence was adequate in addressing the conventional threat posed by the North for the first 40-odd years of the alliance, in the last 15 years, deterrence alone was not sufficient to address the proliferation threat of the DPRK. As a result, the security situation in Korea over the past ten to fifteen years has been an interesting mix of deterrence, compellence, and engagement.

Since the end of the Cold War and the U.S.-Soviet nuclear confrontation, there has been less interest among policy makers, academics, and the public with deterrence. Some may question whether a study of this sort has any relevance. However, dismissing further understanding of deterrence is misplaced. So long as there is international conflict, states will use deterrence to discourage war and protect their interests. Moreover, while the Cold War nuclear threat has abated, substantial nuclear arsenals remain and the danger of weapons proliferation, not only to other states but to terrorists as well, remains an ever-present threat.

This book is also an examination of an important case study in extended deterrence. Most theoretical work on this topic focused on the U.S. security guarantee to Western Europe. With the end of the Cold War, concern for deterrence in Europe has ended, but tension rooted in the Cold War remains on the Korean Peninsula. Moreover, deterrence has also been important in addressing other regional threats such as pre-war Iraq, Iran, and other so-called rogue states. This book examines the U.S. defense commitment to South Korea from 1953 to the present as a case study of extended deterrence. The Korean case, however, exists in a very different context and points to some different considerations for the implementation of an extended deterrence policy than indicated by previous work. With a changed international climate since 1991, and in part, because of the changes brought about by September 11th, the context for the security relationship is different. Thus, there are elements of the Korean case, both before and after the Cold War that provide important insights into extended deterrence theory. Using deterrence theory as the analytical framework, this book focuses on four questions: What is the nature of the threat faced by South Korea and the United States in Korea and how has it changed? What U.S. interests have been at stake in Korea? How has the United States implemented its deterrence policy to deter aggression against its ally South Korea? How has U.S. policy addressed the proliferation threat and why has it failed here while deterrence has been successful?

Alliances

Since the end of World War II, the United States maintained a number of extended deterrence commitments throughout the world. Most of these commitments were formalized with security treaties such as the bilateral alliances with Japan, South Korea, Taiwan, and the Philippines, and the multilateral alliances of NATO, SEATO, CENTO, and the Rio Pact. However a commitment need not have a formal treaty or presence of troops, as is the case with U.S.-Israeli relations. While a formal commitment may aid in signaling the defender's pledge to a challenger, there may be reasons—domestic opposition to a formal guarantee or complications with other states—that prohibit a formally declared commitment. Though there may be a variety of means to do so, the defender must clearly communicate to the challenger its deterrent objectives and threats to respond. Without such communication, it is difficult to conclude whether a deterrence relationship existed at all. The U.S.-ROK security relationship is an example of a formal extended deterrence commitment.

The alliance structure within which the South Korean security guarantee operates has some important dynamics. The U.S. commitment to Western Europe occurred within NATO, a multilateral alliance. In the Pacific, the alliance structure has consisted of a series of separate agreements with South Korea, Japan, the Philippines, Australia, and New Zealand (ANZUS). American officials wished to develop a more unified alliance system, but South Korea was hostile to any security cooperation that included Japan. In discussions with the United States in 1953 concerning the security pact, South Korean President Syngman Rhee wanted it clarified that the United States would also defend Korea against an attack from Japan.[1] This resentment, developed during Tokyo's colonial rule of Korea from 1910 to 1945, has continued, and made multilateral security cooperation in East Asia difficult. Though the United States would have preferred a more formal NATO-type alliance structure in Asia, American leaders had to be content with the bilateral system that developed.[2]

Deterrence and U.S.-South Korean Security Relations: The Literature

A case study of extended deterrence in Korea intersects two large groups of literature in national security studies. The first of these is deterrence theory, or more specifically, extended deterrence. The literature on deterrence theory is vast and too extensive to review here in its entirety. Many of these studies grew out of an effort to examine the role nuclear weapons played in national security strategy and international relations along with understanding the nuclear dynamics of the U.S.-Soviet conflict. One of the topics within this literature that has received considerable attention is that of extended deterrence.

A number of studies in this body of literature have been done exclusively on the concept of extended deterrence.[3] Most of the work in this area deals either with the analysis of a data base of "immediate" extended deterrence cases where there is an imminent danger of attack or are studies of extended deterrence in the context of the U.S. commitment to Western Europe. In both instances, the U.S.-ROK case from 1953 to the present is excluded. A study by William T. Tow examines extended deterrence, but does so from a broad regional perspective, without a focus on the Korean case.[4] Despite being an important example of extended deterrence, the U.S.-ROK relationship has escaped detailed analysis from this theoretical perspective.

The second portion of literature addressed in this book is the work done on the U.S.-South Korean alliance. Many good studies examine the alliance, or U.S.-ROK-Japan security ties, but do not use the framework of extended deterrence, relying mostly on policy description and prescription.[5] Several of these works argue for the United States to reassess its Korea policy given the ROK's economic and political success during the 1970s and 1980s and the end of the Cold War. Accordingly, U.S. policy makers should deal with South Korea more as an equal partner with shared interests than as a client state. These works usually include a requisite analysis of the military balance in Korea and examine whether U.S. troops should remain or be removed.

Other studies have focused on security relations in East Asia or Northeast Asia more broadly and include Korea as one of the components.[6] This research also addresses issues such as: the degree to which a continued U.S. presence in the Pacific is necessary to support U.S. interests; and the need for greater cooperation among the United States and its allies in the Pacific, particularly considering the changed global power structure and the economic and political success of Asia. While including Korea in these regional studies is important, they fail to analyze the Korean case through the lens of, and contribute to a better understanding of, extended deterrence theory.

In the last ten years, several studies have examined the political and economic circumstances of North Korea, particularly assessments following the passing of longtime leader Kim Il Sung and the North Korean nuclear problem.[7] Other recent studies have made an important contribution to the debate over how to solve the nuclear impasse.[8] Likewise, these works do not take a comprehensive look at the role of extended deterrence in U.S. policy in addressing these issues. This book provides a link between extended deterrence theory and the subject of U.S.-South Korea security relations, another long-term case study for the analysis of this important theoretical framework. In addition, this book will also examine the use of engagement and compellence to supplement deterrence in dealing with the North Korean nuclear problem.

A study of U.S. extended deterrence policy in Korea since 1953 is essentially a study of a "deterrence success"; since 1953, there has been no war on the Korean Peninsula. Yet this approach raises a number of methodological problems. Is the absence of war ipso facto evidence that deterrence has "succeeded"? Was U.S. deterrence policy the crucial variable or would peace have resulted regardless of U.S. actions? These are important concerns, particularly when combined with the paucity of information from North Korea on how its leaders perceived U.S. policy. Yet, while we cannot be as certain of the causes of deterrence success as we might be in the analysis of deterrence failures, analyses of successful deterrence cases can provide insights—though of a more tentative nature—on the workings of deterrence policy in practice.

Overview

As an examination of the U.S. defense commitment to South Korea, the organization of this book mirrors the basic ingredients of that policy. After addressing the theoretical issues of deterrence and compellence that frame this study, the book will move to an analysis of the threat.

The Threat

Threat perception is an important starting point for analyzing the U.S. defense commitment to South Korea. As a study of U.S. policy, this chapter will focus on the threat perceptions of American policy makers. To what degree North Korea was a threat in any "objective" sense is not important here. The crucial factors that drive the security commitment are the perceptions of U.S. leaders. The purpose here is not to evaluate the accuracy of their judgments. Instead, the goal is to determine how these assessments and perceptions affected U.S. actions in Korea, leading to a clearer understanding of the U.S. security guarantee in Korea and the theories of extended deterrence and compellence.

Two types of threats drive extended deterrence commitments. In one type of threat, the challenger and the threat of attack are obvious; the adversary brandishes dangerous military power and a clear intent to use it when an opportunity arises. The other type is based on uncertainty where the challenger possesses significant military strength, but its intentions are ambiguous. The U.S. commitment to South Korea is based on the latter where the threat emanates from doubt and fear of what North Korea and its patrons might do. North Korea has consistently maintained its intention to reunify the peninsula, but it was not clear what the North would be willing to do to achieve that goal. For most of the period since 1953, there has not been an impending fear of attack. However, on a few occasions, the threat was feared to be more definite, requiring specific counterthreats from the United States and South Korea.

Who did the United States perceive to be a threat to South Korea? North Korea, China, and the Soviet Union were the three main concerns. Yet each of these was not viewed to be equally threatening and these perceptions changed over time. The military capabilities and intentions of each shifted on a number of occasions and relations between these three states varied. The occurrence of Sino-Soviet animosity and the effect it had on their extended deterrence guarantee for North Korea is one example of these changes. U.S. actions would likely be different when the threat emanated from a non-nuclear North Korea—though possibly supported by its nuclear patrons—than if the threat were primarily from the Soviet Union or China in conjunction with the North Koreans. As a result, the "threat" to South Korea and U.S. interests in the region have been more complex and not the single entity usually assumed by deterrence theory.

In addition to sources of the threat, it will also be important to understand the nature of the threat. This analysis will examine the military balance in Korea since 1953 as well as U.S. estimates of the intentions of the three challengers. To measure intent, three criteria will be utilized: (1) the objectives of the challenger and the degree to which those objectives conflicted with those of the defender and protégé;[9] (2) the "value" the challenger placed on achieving those objectives; and (3) the willingness of the challenger to assume the risks necessary to the achieve the goals.

For most of the U.S. defense commitment, the chief threat was subversion and a direct, conventional attack from the North, a possible repeat of the Korean War. In the 1980s, the nature of the DPRK threat took on an added and potentially more ominous dimension—the acquisition of nuclear weapons and the ballistic missiles to deliver them. This prospect was dangerous for regional security as it put nuclear weapons in the hands of a regime already heavily armed with conventional weapons and might spark others in the region—South Korea and Japan—to acquire a similar capability to address this menace. A nuclear North Korea also damaged U.S. nonproliferation goals globally and raised the possibility Pyongyang might choose to sell material, technology, or a completed weapon to another country or terrorist group.

U.S. Interests in Korea

An important foundation for any defense commitment is the interests the defender sees at stake in the ally and the region more generally. This chapter addresses one question. Why did the United States come to South Korea's rescue in 1950 and remain the South's defender and ally for over 50 years? U.S. interests began with Cold War security and political concerns, yet as South Korea's economic, military, and political prowess grew, new interests emerged while political and security concerns diminished. Security interests have moved to the forefront once again regarding proliferation worries with North Korea's nuclear and ballistic missile potential. Most important here is that these proliferation issues were more difficult to address solely with a deterrence policy. As a result, the United States under the Bush I, Clinton, and Bush II administrations included a compellence and engagement component with its continued deterrence posture. Thus, U.S. interest assessments had a dynamic character that affected security relations and U.S. policy.

The assessment of interests and stakes influences the defender's decision to protect a protégé in danger. A defender will not undertake the necessary preparations to support a protégé if that ally is not sufficiently valuable to its goals and objectives. However, the assessment of value hinges on more than whether a list of interests is sufficiently long. Interests are also closely linked to stakes— the costs and benefits of securing those interests. Leaders assess their interests *and* the stakes so that a state may have any number of interests but the stakes may vary. In general, the greater the stakes, the more likely a defender will be to implement a credible security guarantee.

The interests at stake in a protégé may take many different forms. A protégé may be important for economic reasons such as the possession of resources or its trade links to the defender. These trade links need not be significant for the defender alone, but may be of importance for other allies of the defender, or an important part of regional economic and trade relationships. A protégé may also be an important interest because of its ties to other security interests. The territorial integrity of the protégé may or may not be the crucial factor, however, the protégé's link to regional stability or the status quo more generally may make the defense of the protégé a priority. A defender may lend its support simply because it cannot tolerate any alteration of the status quo by a challenger, or a challenger's patron, even if the protégé has little or no intrinsic value. Finally, geopolitical worth may be a notable attribute of a protégé state. The location of the protégé may give the area strategic importance, making it necessary for the area to remain in the defender's camp or, at least, not fall under the challenger's control.

These remarks indicate how interests may be "interconnected" in any number of ways. For example, consider a possible link between security and trade issues in a particular region. A defender may have substantial trade relations with its protégé, and the protégé may hold an important position in the regional balance of power. Though the security interests may tend to dominate, there is a complex interplay between security and trade interests. The relative importance of these interests may change over time, producing a web of interests that may be difficult to separate.

Interests may also have ties across geographical locations. The defense of a protégé may be bound to other security interests in the region or globally. In fact, concern for the protégé may be driven more by security interests in other areas than for any interest in that particular protégé. The "connectedness" of these concerns points to some important questions for U.S. interests in Korea. To what degree has U.S. policy in Korea been driven by interests in Korea? How much of U.S. policy has been driven by U.S. interests elsewhere? How does this "connectedness" affect extended deterrence? Korea's link to U.S. interests in Japan has an important bearing on these questions. Yet, it does not provide all the answers concerning U.S. interests in Korea. One of the goals in chapter 4 will be to examine Korea's relationship to other U.S. interests and the effect these relationships have on extended deterrence.

Assessments of interests and stakes exert a strong influence on the defender's decision to support the protégé. Greater stakes may mean a greater effort by the defender to protect its ally. Moreover, the presence and declaration of important interests makes a patron's commitment to its protégé more credible and less likely to be seen as a bluff by the attacker.

U.S. Security Policy

Throughout the years of the security commitment to South Korea, the United States has relied on a policy of deterrence to prevent an attack on its ally. The United States utilized four techniques to fashion its deterrence policy: declarations of support including a Mutual Defense Treaty; infusions of economic and military aid; the positioning of U.S. troops in South Korea; and the deployment of tactical nuclear weapons. This book argues that the U.S. commitment, given the difficulties of Vietnam and the length of time the alliance has existed, has been largely credible and consistent despite some changes in the specific components of the deterrence policy. However, deterrence has not been the only element of U.S. policy in the region. Beginning in the 1980s, U.S. policy makers pursued simultaneously a policy of compellence and engagement that culminated in the Agreed Framework to prevent the DPRK from developing nuclear weapons. The Clinton administration also undertook efforts to curtail the production, testing, and export of ballistic missiles but was unsuccessful. As a result, this book will also examine the following questions: Why did the United States shift to a policy that utilized deterrence along with compellence and engagement? How has the United States managed this more complex policy configuration and what have been the results?

In addition to conclusions about the U.S.-ROK security relationship, this book also contains analysis on two important security issues that have broader impact. First, deterrence theory, long a staple of Cold War security analysis, has received less attention in the post-1991 world.[10] Yet, U.S. policy makers continue to be concerned with containing certain problem countries such as Iran, Iraq, and North Korea. Thus, while classical deterrence theory has been of diminishing interest, policy makers continue to utilize deterrence in their effort to address important security concerns. A case study of U.S. deterrence policy in Korea provides an important example to study the application of deterrence to small states in the post-Cold War world.

Second, deterrence theory provides clear direction for how a state should prevent an adversary from attacking either itself or an ally. Yet, deterrence theory gives little guidance nor suggests any likelihood for states in a deterrence relationship to move beyond the hostility implicit in a situation such as this. One of the interesting developments in post-Cold War Korea is not only how Cold War tension has persisted but also how it has evolved into a situation where a firm deterrence policy has included efforts to engage the adversary. Peace and stability have long been the goal of U.S. policy in the region and policy makers relied on deterrence to achieve those objectives. However, concern for nuclear and ballistic missile proliferation in North Korea along with a deteriorating economic situation were not adequately addressed by a deterrence policy and have led U.S. leaders to engage in greater dialogue with the North.

Notes

1. "The President of the Republic of Korea (Rhee) to the Secretary of State," 26 July 1953, *Foreign Relations of the United States, 1952-1954*, XV, part 2, 1440. Hereafter referred to as *FRUS*.

2. "Second Progress Report by the Operations Coordinating Board to the National Security Council on NSC 170/1," 29 December 1954, *FRUS, 1952-1954*, XV, part 2, 1953.

3. See Stephen Cimbala, *Extended Deterrence: The U.S. and NATO Europe* (Lexington: Lexington Books, 1987); Paul Huth, *Extended Deterrence and the Prevention of War* (New Haven: Yale University Press, 1988) and "The Extended Deterrent Value of Nuclear Weapons," *Journal of Conflict Resolution* 34, no. 2 (June 1990): 270-290; Alexander George and Richard Smoke, *Deterrence in American Foreign Policy* (New York: Columbia University Press, 1974); Bruce Russett, "Extended Deterrence with Nuclear Weapons: How Necessary, How Acceptable?," *The Review of Politics* 50, no. 2 (Spring 1988): 282-302; David Garnham, "Extending Deterrence with German Nuclear Weapons," *International Security* 10, no. 1 (Summer 1985): 96-110; William T. Tow, *Encountering the Dominant Player: U.S. Extended Deterrence Strategy in the Asia-Pacific* (New York: Columbia University Press, 1991); and John Arquilla and Paul K. Davis, *Extended Deterrence, Compellence and the "Old World Order,"* N-3482-JS (Rand Corporation, 1992); Suzanne Werner, "Deterring Intervention: The Stakes of War and Third-Party Involvement," *American Journal of Political Science* 44, no. 4 (October 2000): 720-732; Charles T. Allan, "Extended Conventional Deterrence: In from the Cold and out of the Nuclear Fire?," *The Washington Quarterly* 17, no. 3 (Summer 1994): 203-233; and Holger H. Mey, "Nuclear Norms and German Nuclear Interests," *Comparative Strategy* 20, no. 3 (July-September 2000): 241-249.

4. William T. Tow, *Encountering the Dominant Player: U.S. Extended Deterrence Strategy in the Asia-Pacific* (New York: Columbia University Press, 1991).

5. See Ralph Clough, *Deterrence and Defense in Korea* (Washington D.C.: The Brookings Institution, 1976); Gerald L. Curtis and Sung-joo Han, eds., *The U.S.-South Korean Alliance* (Lexington: D.C. Heath, 1983); Edward A. Olsen, *U.S. Policy and the Two Koreas* (Boulder: Westview Press, 1988); Manwoo Lee, Ronald D. McLaurin and Chung-In Moon, *Alliance Under Tension: The Evolution of South Korean-U.S. Relations* (Boulder: Westview Press, 1988); Tong Whan Park, "From Extended Deterrence to Global Interdependence: The Future of U.S. South Korean Security Relations," *Korea 1991: The Road to Peace*, eds. Michael J. Mazarr, et al. (Boulder: Westview Press, 1991); Claude A. Buss, *The United States and the Republic of Korea: Background for Policy* (Stanford: Hoover Institution Press, 1982); Richard T. Detrio, *Strategic Partners: South Korea and the United States* (Washington D.C.: National Defense University, 1989); Yur-Bok Lee and Wayne Patterson, eds., *Korean-American Relations: 1866-1997* (Albany, NY: State University of New York Press, 1999); Ralph A. Cossa, ed., *U.S.-Korea-Japan Relations: Building Toward a "Virtual Alliance"* (Washington, D.C.: Center for Strategic and International Studies, 1999); Victor D. Cha, *Alignment Despite Antagonism: The United States-Korea-Japan Security Triangle* (Stanford: Stanford University Press, 1999); Jonathan D. Pollack and Young Koo Cha, *A New Alliance for the Next Century: The Future of U.S.-Korean Security Cooperation* (Santa Monica, CA: RAND, 1995); Young Whan Kihl, ed., *Korea and the World: Beyond the Cold War* (Boulder: Westview Press, 1994); Robert D. Blackwill and Paul Dibb, eds., *America's Asian Alliance* (Cambridge, MA: MIT Press, 2000); Ilpyong J. Kim, ed., *Korean Challenges and American Policy* (New York: Paragon House, 1991); and Nicholas Eberstadt and Richard J. Ellings, eds., *Korea's Future and the Great Powers* (Seattle:

University of Washington Press, 2001); Michael H. Armacost and Daniel I. Okimoto, eds., *The Future of America's Alliances in Northeast* Asia (Stanford, CA: Asia-Pacific Research Center, 2004); and Edward A. Olsen, *Toward Normalizing U.S.-Korea Relations: In Due Course?* (Boulder: Lynne Rienner: 2002).

6. See Ronald D. McLaurin and Chung-in Moon, *The United States and the Defense of the Pacific* (Boulder: Westview Press, 1989); Yosikazu Sakamoto, ed., *Asia: Militarization and Regional Conflict* (London: Zed Books, 1988); Stuart E. Johnson and Joseph A. Yager, *The Military Equation in Northeast Asia* (Washington, D.C.: Brookings Institution, 1979); Sheldon W. Simon, ed., *East Asian Security in the Post-Cold War Era* (Armonk, NY: M.E. Sharpe, 1993); Young Whan Kihl and Lawrence E. Grinter, ed., *Security, Strategy and Policy Responses in the Pacific Rim* (Boulder: Lynne Rienner Publishers, 1989); A. James Gregor and Maria Hsia Chang, *The Iron Triangle* (Stanford: Hoover Institution Press, 1984); and Young Whan Kihl and Peter Hayes, eds., *Peace and Security in Northeast Asia: The Nuclear Issue and the Korean Peninsula* (Armonk, NY: M.E. Sharpe, 1997); and Uk Heo and Shale A. Horowitz, eds., *Conflict in Asia* (Westport CT: Praeger, 2003).

7. See Andrew S. Natsios, *The Great North Korean Famine* (Washington, D.C.: US Institute of Peace, 2001); Thomas H. Henriksen and Jongryn Mo, eds., *North Korea After Kim Il Sung: Continuity or Change* (Stanford, CA: Hoover Institution, 1997); Dae-Sook Suh and Chae-Jin Lee, eds., *North Korea After Kim Il Sung* (Boulder, CO: Lynne Rienner, 1998); Samuel S. Kim and Tai Hwan Lee, eds., *North Korea and Northeast Asia* (Lanham, MD: Rowman & Littlefield); Marcus Noland, *Avoiding the Apocalpyse* (Washington, D.C.: Institute for International Economics, 2000); Kondan Oh and Ralph C. Hassig, *North Korea Through the Looking Glass* (Washington, D.C.: Brookings Institution, 2000); Joel S. Wit, Daniel B. Poneman, and Robert L. Gallucci, *Going Critical: The First North Korean Nuclear Crisis* (Washington, D.C.: Brookings Institution, 2004); Michael J. Mazarr, *North Korea and the Bomb* (New York: St. Martin's Press, 1995); Richard Saccone, *To the Brink and Back: Negotiating with North Korea* (Elizabeth, NJ: Hollym, 2003) and Scott Snyder, *Negotiating on the Edge: North Korean Negotiating Behavior* (Washington, D.C.: US Institute of Peace Press, 1999).

8. Michael O'Hanlon and Mike Mochizuki, *Crisis on the Korean Peninsula: How to Deal with a Nuclear North Korea* (New York: McGraw-Hill, 2003); Victor D. Cha and David C. Kang, *Nuclear North Korea: A Debate on Engagement Strategies* (New York: Columbia University Press, 2003); James M. Minnich, *The Denuclearization of North Korea* (Bloomington, IN: 1st Books, 2002); and James T. Laney and Jason T. Shaplen, "How to Deal With North Korea," *Foreign Affairs* 82, no. 2 (March/April 2003): 16-30.

9. George and Smoke, *Deterrence in American Foreign Policy*, 99-100.

10. Three important exceptions to this include Max G. Manwaring, ed., *Deterrence in the 21st Century* (London: Frank Cass, 2001), Patrick M. Morgan, *Deterrence Now* (Cambridge: Cambridge University Press, 2003), and Lawrence Freedman, *Deterrence* (Cambridge, UK: Polity Press, 2004).

Chapter 1

DETERRENCE, COMPELLENCE, AND KOREAN SECURITY

Deterrence theory, a subject that has received considerable attention from scholars and analysts, provides the analytical framework for this study. The literature on deterrence is extensive and used widely to explain security issues generally and those in Korea. However, while this theoretical framework has been dominant, and appropriately so, in explaining Korean security, use of it alone misses some important aspects of the security relationship. As a result, it is necessary to employ a second theoretical approach, namely compellence. Both approaches, deterrence and compellence, can be grouped under the label of coercive diplomacy and share some similarities. In fact, the two may be so intermingled that separating them may be very difficult.[1] However, they are sufficiently different and provide alternative explanations to warrant separate treatment as theoretical approaches.

Deterrence and compellence are premised on an adversarial relationship between two hostile sides. There is little guidance or hope provided by either theory for moving beyond a relationship based on conflict and tension. Instead the adversaries are locked into a continuing relationship of military preparedness and mistrust. Yet in a dynamic relationship that has lasted as long as that of the United States, South Korea, and North Korea, there is a possibility that the relationship can move towards a policy that utilizes greater engagement. In addition, deterrence and compellence have proven ineffective in preventing North Korean efforts to acquire nuclear weapons. This chapter will explain the basic tenets of each theoretical approach and provide an initial application of the theories to Korean security.

11

Deterrence Theory and Korean Security

Deterrence is commonly defined as "the use of threats of harm to prevent someone from doing something you do not want him to."[2] The core of deterrence is a
threat by the defender to raise the costs of a challenger's action to such a level
that the challenger will refrain from the action. The defender must pose the prospect that whatever the challenger seeks, the costs of achieving the objective will
offset the gain. If the costs outweigh the benefits, deterrence theory maintains the
challenger is likely to be deterred.

Deterrence, as distinguished from defense, involves the dissuasion of an
attack. Once deterrence fails, the defender employs active resistance to prevent
the challenger from achieving its goals. However, deterrence and defense are
closely linked in terms of military postures since the existence of a formidable
defense capability may also help to deter.

There are three important distinctions in deterrence threats: deterrence by
denial, deterrence by punishment, and deterrence by reward.[3] Throughout much
of history, states operationalized deterrence by possessing sufficient military
resources to prevent an opponent from obtaining its desired territorial objectives.
Under deterrence by denial, a defender has the ability to defeat an attack, or
make an attack so costly that the enemy would refrain from assault. In *Conventional Deterrence*, John Mearsheimer asserted that the most successful deterrence by denial is one that can deny the aggressor a quick, "blitzkrieg" type victory, turning an attack into a long war of attrition.[4]

The advent of air power began to change some of these strategies. Strategic
bombardment allowed an adversary to bypass the ground forces of an opponent
and strike directly at civilian or industrial targets. For the first time, a country
could implement deterrence by threatening punishing air strikes without first
having to defeating the opposition's military.[5]

Nuclear weapons, particularly those delivered with ballistic missiles, further
enhanced the ability of a nuclear state to unleash devastating attacks on an enemy's homeland. In the nuclear age, a defender can raise tremendously the costs
of an attack by threatening nuclear retaliation. As Kenneth Waltz notes, "with
nuclear weapons, stability and peace rest on easy calculations of what one country can do to another."[6] Furthermore, Stephen Cimbala has argued that the potential for horrendous nuclear destruction evokes caution in leaders who seek to
avoid these types of situations. As Cimbala suggests wryly, "leaders will be staring into Nietzsche's abyss, and the abyss will be staring back."[7]

Deterrence by denial is relative, based on the military capabilities of each
side. If the defender maintains a certain level of military preparedness while the
attacker drastically increases its military capabilities, deterrence by denial may
no longer be successful. Thus, the defender's ability to deter is relative to the
attacker's military strength. Conversely, nuclear punishment is absolute. The
military balance does not affect the defender's ability to launch a retaliatory nuclear strike so long as it possesses even a small number of survivable nuclear

weapons.[8] As a result, even relatively large differences in the nuclear capabilities of adversaries may not alter one side's ability to punish its adversary.

Finally, an adversary can also be persuaded from taking certain actions by providing incentives—deterrence by reward. A state need not rely solely on threats to achieve its goals in a deterrence situation. Moreover, once the incentives are provided, say economic aid or foreign investment, they become part of the status quo that can be used as a lever to be withdrawn should it become necessary. This book assumes that deterrence may utilize both threats and rewards to dissuade an adversary from taking a course of action deemed unacceptable.

Rationality

Successful deterrence depends on the defender issuing a credible threat that raises the challenger's costs to unacceptable levels and outweighs the potential benefits of the action. Implicit here is the ability of the decision makers in the challenger state to make rational calculations. Rational decision making occurs in a three step process: (1) collect all necessary information available regarding options and the costs and benefits associated with each; (2) evaluate the information and options by making the needed cost/benefit calculations; and (3) choose the option that carries the greatest benefit for the least cost. Though no one assumes that leaders and governments act with "perfect rationality," theorists have argued that the assumption of rationality helps to produce intellectually coherent and parsimonious theory.

Scholars have criticized the utility of the rationality assumption on several grounds. Patrick Morgan identified four factors that limit the ability of states to be fully rational. First, the decision makers are human and have limited ability to store, recall, and analyze information. Second, values and goals are difficult to convert into and weigh with precise numerical measures of costs and benefits. Third, decision makers may have competing notions of costs, benefits, and rationality. For example, one member within a leadership circle may believe the costs of a particular decision to uphold human rights standards are intolerable while another member of the group may regard such costs as meaningless. Finally, Morgan asserts that the information available to decision makers is often incomplete, which further impedes the development and evaluation of potential courses of action.[9] Intelligence may be incomplete or certain options might never reach the leadership. Moreover, these concerns apply as well to estimating the opponent's calculations.[10] Thus, working within a deterrence framework, adversaries must deal with information deficiencies and imperfect rational calculations in order to make their own cost-benefit analysis and then that of their adversary.

Robert Jervis, Richard Ned Lebow, and Janice Gross Stein warn that "rationality" may vary with the motivations held by each side in a conflict. For example, country A may believe that it possesses sufficient military strength so that country B could not possibly conclude that the benefits to be gained in attacking outweigh the costs. However, country B, as the authors argued was the case when Argentina attacked the British-held Falkland Islands, may be driven by its own set of domestic pressures that compel it to attack in the face of potentially grave military costs. In fact, the leaders of country B may know that their chances of winning are small. To country A, B is being "irrational" when it attacks in the face of A's superior military capability. However, the domestic political costs to country B of not attacking and accepting the status quo may be far greater, prompting country B to attack despite a substantial risk of military defeat.[11]

In Korea, U.S. leaders have often questioned the rationality of North Korean leaders Kim Il Sung and Kim Jong Il and their apparent willingness to absorb costs and risks beyond the potential benefits. In 1970, U.S. Ambassador to South Korea William Porter commented that North Korea "is one of the world's most intractable and potentially dangerous problems. The North Koreans remain both belligerent and unpredictable."[12] In 1976, the Defense Department lamented "our intelligence does not pretend to understand the convolutions of Kim Il Sung's mind."[13] Twenty-five years later, little had changed about U.S. assessments of the North Korean leadership. Speaking about the North Korean leader, President George W. Bush declared "I loathe Kim Jong Il! I've got a visceral reaction to this guy, because he is starving his people. And I have seen intelligence of these prison camps—they're huge—that he uses to break up families, and to torture people. I am appalled."[14]

Over the years, U.S. leaders were often uncertain of North Korea's rationality, yet they assumed the North was capable of some level of rational cost-benefit calculation, and that the United States could influence those calculations with a robust deterrence policy. As a case study of extended deterrence, this book will utilize the rationality assumption since it is both parsimonious and central to the logic of deterrence theory and U.S. policy in Korea.

Immediate and General Deterrence

States use deterrence to help ensure their security. Thus, deterrence is a policy that governments implement to protect their countries from attack. In an important refinement of deterrence theory, Patrick Morgan noted that there were two different situations within which deterrence policies occur: immediate and general deterrence.[15]

According to Morgan, four basic conditions characterize a situation of immediate deterrence:

(1) In a relationship between two hostile states the officials in at least one of them are seriously considering attacking the other or attacking some area of the world the other deems important.
(2) Key officials of the other state realize this.
(3) Realizing that an attack is a distinct possibility, the latter set of officials threaten the use of force in retaliation, attempting to prevent the attack.

(4) Leaders of the state planning to attack decide to desist primarily because of the retaliatory threat(s). [16]

Immediate deterrence occurs in crisis situations. The defender believes an attack is likely and responds by issuing specific counterthreats of retaliation to deter the challenger's assault. If the challenger state does desist, the deterrence policy is successful. However, the deterrence policy in an immediate deterrence situation could also fail with the challenger attacking despite the threat of force.

It is important to note here that deterrence is inextricably linked to perceptions. Whether an action will occur in some objective sense is not essential. What is crucial is that either state believes something will happen. Thus, a defender need only believe an attack is probable or forthcoming to issue counterthreats to retaliate. Likewise, the challenger need not be objectively certain that the defender will retaliate; the challenger need only believe retaliation with unacceptable damage will follow for deterrence to be successful.

Morgan identified the second type of situation as general deterrence noting three conditions:

(1) Relations between opponents are such that leaders in at least one would consider resorting to force if the opportunity arose.
(2) The other side, precisely because it believes the opponent would be willing to consider resort to force, maintains forces of its own and offers warnings to respond in kind to attempts to use force contrary to its interests.
(3) The decision makers at whom the general deterrent threat is aimed do not go beyond preliminary consideration of resorting to force because of the expectation that such a policy would result in a corresponding resort to force of some sort by leaders of the opposing state. [17]

The two states are adversaries, but there is no immediate crisis or imminent danger of attack in a situation of general deterrence. While the threatened state believes that an adversary might attack, its general defense preparations are not a response to a specific crisis. Nevertheless, relations between the two adversaries are strained and filled with hostility and suspicion.

Achieving successful deterrence under conditions of general deterrence requires different responses than under conditions of immediate deterrence. Under immediate deterrence, the challenger has already made or is about to make a decision to attack; a defender must dissuade the challenger from attacking with specific and immediate counterthreats. Under general deterrence, specific counterthreats are not necessary since an attack is not imminent, though a state may still choose to issue these threats. Instead, a nation undertakes preparations that may include the buildup of military forces and issues general warnings of its intent to respond should the adversary's behavior become more ominous. Successful general deterrence preparations forestall a crisis and prevent the movement to the more dangerous situation of immediate deterrence. [18]

The concept of a deterrence situation "moving" from general to immediate deterrence is an important one requiring further discussion. These two situations are not categorical positions whereby a particular deterrence case is classified as either a general or immediate deterrence situation. They are best conceptualized as positions along a continuum, where deterrence situations are fluid, moving from one to the other. Thus, a deterrence situation may pass through any number of stages—growing antagonism and increasing possibility of attack—as it escalates from general deterrence to a crisis of immediate deterrence.

On occasion, a state may believe that, despite its preparations, an adversary has perceived an opportunity to attack and actively considers the option. Consequently, the threatened nation perceives the deterrence situation to have begun shifting from general to immediate deterrence. To ensure that deterrence remains robust, the threatened nation must adjust its deterrence policy to include the specific counterthreats needed to deter in a situation of immediate deterrence. Constant vigilance is necessary to ensure that a deterrence policy makes the proper adjustments to maintain peace and stability.

Primary and Extended Deterrence

Nations experience security threats not only to themselves, but also to their allies. This difference points to another important distinction in deterrence theory. Attempting to prevent an attack on oneself is known as "primary" deterrence while seeking to deter an attack on an ally is "extended" deterrence.[19]

Integrating these concepts of deterrence—primary and extended deterrence—with the deterrence situations Morgan identified—general and immediate situations—produces four specific types of deterrence situations: primary immediate; primary general; extended immediate; and extended general.[20]

United States-South Korean security relations have been primarily an example of an extended general deterrence situation, though on some occasions, it has resembled a situation of extended immediate deterrence. Initially motivated by the fear of another attack, the American guarantee to South Korea has been driven by the uncertain intentions and military buildup of the DPRK. Fear of imminent attack has been infrequent. On a few occasions since 1953, the United States and South Korea, anticipating an attack from the North, made specific counterthreats to reinforce deterrence. President Johnson's reaction to the seizure of the USS *Pueblo* in January 1968 and President Carter's response to the assassination of South Korean President Park Chung Hee in October 1979 are two examples of these efforts to reinforce deterrence. Overall, however, the relationship has resembled a situation of extended general deterrence.

Table 1.1

TYPES OF DETERRENCE SITUATIONS

Type	Description	Example
Primary Immediate	Imminent threat of direct attack against your homeland.	China-India border dispute in 1962.
Primary General	Enmity exists, but no immediate danger of attack.	U.S.-Soviet conflict during the Cold War.
Extended Immediate	Attack on an ally is likely; a defender attempts to deter the challenger with specific counterthreats.	U.S. measures to dissuade a Chinese move on Taiwan in 1950.
Extended General	Defender provides security guarantees for an ally, but the threat of attack is not imminent.	U.S.-South Korean Defense Commitment.

A few words are needed regarding the roles played by the states in their deterrence relationships in Korea. In this case study of the U.S. extended deterrence policy, I have chosen to use the following labels: "challenger" for North Korea, the Soviet Union, and China; "defender" for the United States; and "protégé" for South Korea. For the United States and South Korea, the DPRK's role of challenger was fixed during the Korean War—North Korea, which the Truman administration judged to be a proxy of the Soviets, invaded the South, joined six months later by Chinese forces. The three challenger states also had a deterrence relationship among themselves, as Moscow and Beijing were defenders for their protégé North Korea. These states certainly viewed the United States and South Korea as the "challengers" and would object to being given that label. However, as a study of U.S. deterrence policy, these labels are appropriate and will cause the least confusion.

Credibility

Credibility is an important requisite for a deterrence policy. In *The Requirements of Deterrence*, William Kaufmann identified three components of a credible deterrence policy: capability, cost, and resolve.[21] First, the defender must persuade the challenger that it has the capability to carry out the threats. It is not necessary for the defender actually to have the necessary means; the defender need only "convince" the challenger it has the capability. If the challenger does not believe the defender has sufficient military power to support the threat, even if it does, deterrence theory maintains war will be more likely. Second, the defender's military capability must be sufficient to impose costs that are unacceptable to the challenger. Finally, the defender must demonstrate the resolve to carry out the threat. A clear commitment and sufficient military capability do not ensure implementation; the defender must show it is willing to follow through should deterrence fail.

What degree of certainty must accompany the threat for deterrence to be credible? Suppose a nation's threat to retaliate was certain. The challenger might still attack, believing the costs of that retaliation are acceptable. Conversely, an uncertain or even unlikely threat might be sufficient to deter if that threat poses a dramatic increase in costs. Thomas Schelling described this condition as the "threat that leaves something to chance." Schelling argued "a response that carries some risk of war can be plausible, even reasonable, at a time when a final, ultimate decision to have a general war would be implausible or unreasonable. A country can threaten to stumble into a war even if it cannot credibly threaten to invite one."[22] Thus, resolve does not rest solely on precise calculations of the probability of retaliation. Rather, it is a constantly shifting balance of the costs and likelihood of retaliation.

Analyses of deterrence policies have often employed Kaufmann's criteria. However, the application of these criteria to situations of extended general deterrence requires further elaboration. In extended general deterrence, the defender undertakes military preparations—attention to the military balance—and issues general declarations of warning of its intent to support the protégé. The defender's objective is to discourage a challenge to the status quo through a favorable military balance that prevents the rivalry from escalating to a crisis. Thus, under a situation of general deterrence, "possessing sufficient capability to exact unacceptable cost" translates into maintaining ample military preparation by both the defender and the protégé to dissuade the challenger from even considering an attack.

The preparations of the defender and protégé in a situation of general deterrence can cause an unintended result. These preparations might alter the challenger's perceptions and provoke an escalation of preparations. A classic misperception may occur in which each side believes its preparations are obviously "defensive," but are actually perceived by the opposition as threatening. Richard Ned Lebow labeled this "miscalculated escalation" where an adversary crosses the "threshold" of acceptable behavior, believing the enemy will tolerate its actions. Rather than being tolerated, these actions incite a vigorous counterresponse.[23] Morgan noted that situations of general deterrence often lead to a spiraling arms race between the two sides.[24] Consequently, the defender and protégé must be careful that their preparations not cause the perceptions of the challenger to shift and increase tension among the adversaries.

How much preparation is necessary to deter? This question precludes a precise answer, but suggests that convincing an adversary there is "no opportunity to attack" is a less demanding task than that of convincing an adversary to reverse its active consideration of an attack. Once consideration of an attack has begun, a challenger is demonstrating its willingness to use determined means to change the status quo. If a challenger has come to this point, its discontent with current relations is considerable and will be more difficult to reverse.

Convincing an adversary there is "no opportunity to attack" is similar to Mearsheimer's argument regarding conventional deterrence.[25] He maintained that deterrence is most likely to succeed when the defender and protégé have the capability to deny the challenger a quick victory. Sufficient preparation must demonstrate to the challenger the prospect of a long, costly war should it decide to attack. These preparations require close attention to the military balance in the region. Seeing "no opportunity" for an attack, the adversary is less likely to consider challenging the status quo. Determining there is "no opportunity" for attack is another conceptualization of the challenger's cost-benefit calculus. So long as the costs out weigh the benefits, deterrence theory maintains that the opportunity to successfully challenge the status quo will not be present.

One last aspect of "sufficient preparation" requires attention. As noted earlier, a situation of general deterrence may shift towards a crisis of immediate deterrence where an attack appears imminent. To deter this attack, the defender and protégé must issue the counterthreats necessary to dissuade the challenger from attempting to alter the status quo. The "sufficient preparation" of the defender and protégé must allow for issuing these threats should a crisis develop. For example, a defender's threat to deploy troops and deliver military equipment to a threatened protégé may not be effective if the troops and equipment will take a long time to arrive. The necessary military assets must be deliverable in a timely manner in order to affect the cost-benefit calculations of the challenger.

Resolve is the final and most difficult requirement of a credible deterrence policy. The threat to retaliate for an attack on your homeland is very credible because the stakes are obvious. However, a defender's willingness to risk damage for the sake of an ally is inherently less credible. There is no guarantee that a nation will decide to honor a commitment in the face of a crisis that might bring destruction to its homeland.[26] For example, the U.S. security commitment to Western Europe always carried the danger of direct conflict with the Soviet Union. That policy, especially since it included the potential use of nuclear weapons, meant that the U.S. homeland might become a target of Soviet retaliation. Would the United States really launch a retaliatory strike on the Soviet Union in response to a Soviet attack in Europe, knowing Moscow would be likely to launch a counter-strike on the United States? In a 1979 speech to NATO defense ministers, Henry Kissinger noted this problem and called on the European allies not to keep "asking us to multiply strategic assurances that we cannot possibly mean or if we do mean, we should not want to execute because if we execute, we risk the destruction of civilization."[27] Thus, the U.S. pledge to respond to Soviet aggression in Europe raised some daunting questions regarding Washington's resolve. When the Soviets developed their own robust nuclear capability, the U.S. commitment to Europe entailed even greater risks.

In Korea, once the Soviets and Chinese were judged not to be the main threat, a U.S. response to aggression from the North entailed little danger to the American homeland. It is possible that the Soviets or Chinese, as Pyongyang's defenders, might have come to the aid of North Korea, but any large-scale response by Moscow or Beijing brought the same kind of danger to their homelands as the United States faced in Europe. In short, it became problematic that the Soviets and Chinese would risk retaliation by the United States over North Korea.

U.S. policy makers were also risk averse. No Americans relished involvement in "another Korea" that could lead to a recurrent draining ground war in Asia. Yet, the United States was less concerned that a conflict in Korea would lead to an attack on the U.S. homeland. Thus, U.S. officials could employ deterrence threats without risking an attack on the continental United States, making credibility less of a problem.

States often demonstrate resolve through declarations of determination, or treaties and alliances of support. Yet, in times of crisis, these demonstrations of commitment may not be honored. Since extended deterrence declarations do not guarantee an automatic response, Thomas Schelling argued these need to be fashioned with "The Art of Commitment."[28] According to Schelling, the most convincing declaration of resolve is one that demonstrates to your adversary that your response will be automatic should deterrence fail. Borrowing from the game of chicken, Schelling argued that, ideally, a defender should structure its commitment to foreclose all options except retaliation. Only the challenger is given the choice to "swerve or collide." Under this circumstance, deterrence is fully credible.[29]

The defender can enhance credibility by deploying its military forces on the ally's territory. Placing troops in harm's way as a "trip wire" makes the defender's involvement more plausible. Once blood has been spilled, the defender is more likely to stay the course. Moreover, this type of commitment is more difficult to reverse in a crisis and provides a direct link to the other military resources of the defender. In *The Strategy of Conflict*, Schelling enumerated other techniques to enhance credibility. For example, a nation could feign irrationality and appear oblivious to the costs of retaliation, or turn the decision to retaliate over to the protégé.[30] Finally, Schelling asserts that staking your reputation on the commitment is another way to convince an adversary of the seriousness and irreversibility of your pledge.[31]

The defender's interests at stake in its relationship with the protégé also affect the security commitment. The stakes—the costs and benefits of pursuing those interests—may be significant for several reasons, such as the protégé's mineral wealth, geostrategic location, and links to other interests of the defender. As Paul Huth and Bruce Russett note, "resolve is . . . a function of the interests at stake. . . . Presumably . . . the willingness to run risks or pay costs to defend a protégé will be greater the greater the objective or intrinsic value of the protégé."[32] Commenting on situations of immediate deterrence, Robert Jervis adds that the side with the greater interests at stake is able to make threats that are more credible.[33]

According to George and Smoke, the defender's interests in the protégé, as perceived by the challenger, are a decisive factor in the challenger's calculations. They note that, "the opponent [challenger] is likely to pay more attention to strategic, political, economic, and ideological factors determining the nature and magnitude of those interests than to rhetorical and other signaling devices the defending power may employ to enhance credibility."[34] Thus, emphasis on "giving the right signal"—declaratory statements, economic aid—may be misplaced; despite a strong signal, the challenging state may still believe that its interests outweigh the defender's.[35]

Russett makes a related argument maintaining economic, political, and military ties between the defender and the protégé are central to a credible commitment. In particular, Russett believes "economic interdependence may be virtually essential to successful deterrence."[36] These ties may not be sufficient to guarantee successful deterrence, but success will be almost impossible without them. Since policy decisions can strengthen these ties, Russett believes they are important mechanisms for nations to reinforce deterrence. However, the efficacy of economic, political, and military ties has its critics. Huth maintains that these ties are superseded by past bargaining behavior that is more indicative of a defender's willingness to maintain an extended deterrence commitment.[37] Specifically, Huth notes, "the past behavior of the defender in the most recent confrontation with the potential attacker had a significant effect on deterrence outcomes," and, in turn "reflects the importance of the interests at stake for the defender."[38] Yet, concern for reputation may take on a life of its own, becoming an important interest in itself and skewing the assessment of other interests at stake.

Huth's conclusion came from a study of immediate extended deterrence crises. Yet the situation in Korea since 1953 has been largely a situation of general deterrence, characterized by different dynamics than those of immediate deterrence. It is probable that the presence of strong ties between the defender and protégé may be more important in general deterrence and prevent a general deterrence situation from deteriorating into a crisis of immediate deterrence. Strong ties may not be decisive, as Huth maintains, once the two sides move towards war. Nevertheless, these ties may be very helpful in deterring the onset of a crisis.

Huth's conclusions about past behavior may also apply to situations of extended general deterrence. Though not necessarily more important than ties between the defender and protégé, past behavior likely affects the challenger's perception of how the defender will respond next time. This is especially true if the leadership of the challenging state has remained the same throughout a number of crises. In North Korea, the leadership remained essentially unchanged from

1945 when Kim Il Sung became premier until his death on 8 July 1994. In 1993, before Kim Il Sung's passing, reports indicated that his son, Kim Jong Il, gradually assumed control of the regime, even as the elder Kim continued to play an important role in policy.[39]

Compellence and Korean Security

In order to complete the theoretical picture of security relations in Korea, it is necessary to examine the concept of compellence. Compellence differs from deterrence in two important ways. First, compellence uses threats or an actual use of force (by the initiator) to persuade an adversary (target state) to halt an act already in progress or undo an act that has been completed. In contrast, deterrence utilizes threats to prevent an action from occurring. Thus, deterrence seeks to maintain the status quo while compellence attempts to alter it.[40]

Patrick Morgan notes an important dilemma when states actually utilize deterrence and compellence. Two adversaries may have different perceptions of a conflict whereby one sees it as a problem of deterrence while the other sees it as the more threatening predicament of compellence. Take U.S. efforts to stop North Korea from developing nuclear weapons as an example. Morgan maintains there are serious complications if the United States views this dilemma as a deterrence problem (halting a DPRK action), while North Korea sees it as compellence (reversing its efforts to acquire nuclear weapons). According to Morgan, "if compellence is harder than deterrence then it matters what the opponent thinks is the situation since that is crucial to his reaction to the threat."[41] A threat that may be sufficient to deter may not be sufficient to compel. In fact, the United States was not always sure whether North Korea's nuclear weapons program was a problem of deterrence or compellence, further compounding the difficulty of the task.

Second, implementing deterrence is easier since compliance requires only that the target state do nothing. However, to comply with a compellent demand, the target must take an action that stops or reverses something already done, a much more difficult task. As Schelling notes, "it is that the very act of compliance—of doing what is demanded—is more conspicuously compliant, more recognizable as submission under duress, than when an act is merely withheld in the face of a deterrent threat."[42] States will be hesitant because they may have to explain their acquiescence or perceived surrender to the public, political opponents, or other key players in the system such as military leaders. Thus, Morgan argues, "people tend to be more reluctant . . . to take a loss—to give up a benefit in hand—than to forgo seeking an additional benefit of equivalent value."[43] Deterrence and compellence can become intertwined because once deterrence fails and the defender chooses to implement its deterrence threats, the actions become those of compellence in an effort to halt this challenge to the deterrence commitment.

To implement a compellence strategy, the initiator must clearly state its demand, articulate the punishment that will commence if the target state chooses non-compliance, and declare a time frame within which the target state must comply. Without a firm timeline, the target state will feel no urgency to satisfy the initiator's demands, and perhaps will never comply.[44] The target state must also know that its compliance will stop the threats, or it will have no incentive to comply. However, Schelling notes that target states face serious problems even if they do comply with the initiator's demands. If it complies with the demands, it runs the risk of encouraging the initiator to issue additional ultimatums, thereby "upping the ante." Thus, Schelling notes the adage, "if you can get one mile, why not try for two?"[45] Generally, a compellence situation will have a shorter timeframe expecting more prompt compliance while deterrence often expects the target to refrain from an action indefinitely.

Compellence threats may take two different forms.[46] First, threats may be diplomatic where the initiator warns a specific response if the target does not halt or reverse the problematic deed. However, no immediate action is taken until the target state has an opportunity to respond. The threatened responses can run a gamut of actions from the imposition of sanctions or a blockade to a limited use of force, or even full-scale war. In addition to imposing some specified action, the response could also entail withholding something valuable from the target state. Robert Art dismisses actions such as economic sanctions or the withholding of benefits as "coercive attempts" because they do not involve the use of force.[47] However, these have been important features of U.S. actions in Korea, particularly in the post-Cold War period and fit within a broad definition of coercive measures utilized to influence North Korean behavior. Similar to deterrence, compellence threats must be credible. The target must believe that whatever threats are made, the initiator has the capability and resolve to carry them out so that acceding to the demands are preferable. Patrick Morgan notes an important complication here for the initiator to actually carry out the threats in that "using force to maintain the status quo often seems psychologically more legitimate (to the parties involved and observers) than trying to change it."[48] Implementing a deterrence threat appears far more "defensive" in nature whereas compellence threats seem more "offensive," creating a potential political cost or international backlash in response to these actions.

A second form of compellence is a demonstrative use of force but one that is well short of war. This may be implemented at two different levels. The first is an "exemplary" demonstration of force that not only shows how the specific compellent action will appear but also indicates the initiator's willingness to use force. Troop mobilizations or deployments, the imposition of economic sanctions, or a naval blockade are options at this level. If this exemplary demonstration does not achieve the desired action, the initiator can ratchet up the response to a second level that entails a limited use of force directed at the target state. Possible actions might include limited air strikes or brief incursions by ground forces into the target's territory. These two levels of demonstration should employ actions that convince the target state that the use of force is the next step or that more drastic measures will follow if it does not accede to the demands.[49] However, in all instances of a demonstrative use of force, the initiator stops well short of a full-scale military operation to force the target state's hand. It is also important to note that whatever threats are implemented, they must be tolerable for the initiator and sustainable for a relatively long period of time.[50]

Should these efforts fail, the initiator may resort to an unrestrained military operation that forces acquiescence to the initiator's demands. This action explicitly demonstrates that compellence has failed and that the initiator has made the decision to use blunt force to achieve its goals.

While the use of force in one area may indicate diplomacy has failed, these actions may also have an impact on diplomacy in other regions. In April 2003, the United States invaded Iraq in an effort to force Saddam Hussein's compliance with UN weapons inspections and to drive the regime from power. In this instance, coercive diplomacy failed and the United States resorted to a major military operation. However, concerning U.S.-DPRK relations, the invasion of Iraq had the demonstrative effect of indicating Washington's willingness to use force in an effort to stop Pyongyang's acquisition of nuclear weapons. Recall, in January 2002, President George W. Bush included North Korea in the "axis of evil" along with Iraq and Iran. There is considerable evidence that North Korean leaders believed once Iraq was taken down that they might be next. Thus, while war indicated a failure of diplomacy in U.S.-Iraqi relations, it likely had a demonstration effect on diplomatic efforts with North Korea.

Though often focusing on the use of threats, a compellent strategy can also include positive inducements to encourage compliance. Possible "carrots" include economic aid or concessions in another issue area such as arms control or trade negotiations. It is important to note that these inducements may be relatively minor but have what Alexander George refers to as a "face-saving character."[51] The target state is in a potentially humiliating position if it backs down and any ability it has to "claim" some sort of victory may be important in reaching a settlement. The need for a face-saving gesture is significant not only for democratic target states that might need to justify their actions to voters but also authoritarian regimes that might have to placate a conservative military establishment. Because threats alone might not induce compliance, "carrots" allow for a degree of bargaining and can be crucial in obtaining a resolution of the problem.[52] Moreover, once a carrot is given and becomes part of a negotiated agreement, it can later be withdrawn, providing another stick that can be used at a later date should the target state renege on its commitment.

Similar to threats, inducements must also be credible so that the target is convinced these will follow with the desired behavior. Credibility means demonstrating the will to carry out not only a one-time pay-off of carrots but also the willingness to implement a long-term commitment. Thus, if a five-year economic aid package is promised in return for compliance, the aid must be delivered on time for the full time period or the target may renege on its share of the deal.

While theoretically possible to include "carrots" in resolving a strategic crisis, there might be significant restrictions, possibly based on domestic politics or the views of allies involved, that prevent the inclusion of certain carrots, or at least the valuable ones, that might best encourage the target to comply. In U.S.-North Korean negotiations, the United States could dangle a formal, bilateral security guarantee that North Korea claims to want desperately, but such an agreement would have little chance of passing in the Senate. The range of threats may be similarly constrained based on military realities or ally forebodings of actions that may spark a larger regional conflict. South Korea has been reluctant to endorse the Bush administration's efforts to pressure North Korea, which, in turn, has moderated Washington's more aggressive approach toward the North.

The primary goal of compellent threats is "to create in the opponent the ex-pectation of costs of sufficient magnitude to erode his motivation to continue what he is doing."[53] However, the initiator often underestimates the target state's costs for giving in to the demands. Thus, the initiator must be careful to choose demands where the stakes are high for it—willing to bear the costs of the threats—but low for the target state.[54] If not, the initiator will encounter a target state determined to hold on to what it has despite huge costs.

Though most of U.S.-ROK security relations are best characterized as deter-rence, there have also been some elements of compellence present. In particular, recent U.S. actions to persuade North Korea to comply with the Nuclear Nonpro-liferation Treaty (NPT) are best viewed as a strategy of compellence. The Clin-ton administration used compellent threats—economic sanctions, sending more troops to the South—along with positive inducements of economic aid and dip-lomatic relations. The North Korean nuclear weapons problem will be discussed in greater detail in subsequent parts of this book.

North Korea itself utilized a compellent strategy at various times. For exam-ple, during the late 1960s, North Korea, in an effort to force the United States to abandon its commitment to the South, pursued compellence by drastically in-creasing its infiltration and subversion campaign against the South, seizing the USS *Pueblo*, and shooting down an EC-121 spy plane over international waters. While the United States was involved in Vietnam, the North tried to raise the potential costs for a continued American commitment to the ROK with implied threats of another costly Asian conflict.

Conclusion

Deterrence and compellence have been useful in explaining security rela-tions in Korea. However, as policy prescriptions, they point to two chief difficul-ties. First, both theoretical approaches are premised on a hostile, adversarial rela-tionship. Traditionally, though it is possible to use positive inducements to coax the desired behavior, both deterrence and compellence rely on the use of threats to achieve policy goals. The problem here is that neither approach provides much guidance for how to move beyond a relationship based on threats and ten-sion. As George and Smoke note, deterrence is "only a formula for frustrating the perceived aggressive intent" and must "be supplemented with attempts to reduce the motivation underlying the intention, and/or provide alternative goals."[55] Somehow, states must figure out ways to move beyond the hostility of a deterrence situation or the region will be locked into a long-term adversarial relationship.

Second, deterrence and compellence may be problematic in addressing one of the United States' chief foreign policy goals: halting the proliferation of nuclear, chemical, and biological weapons. If states acquire these weapons to address perceived security threats, policies of deterrence and compellence that are based largely on intimidation are likely to be counterproductive. U.S. actions to end North Korea's nuclear weapons program is a good example of how threats have produced a state that may be more paranoid about its security and less likely to give up its nuclear capability. Thus, the use of threats to curtail the acquisition of nuclear weapons only worsens the threat perceptions of the target state. This may not be the case in all circumstances, as some states can be coerced into giving up their nuclear ambitions. However, with North Korea, this has not been the case.

In part, the Clinton administration began to recognize the ineffectiveness of coercion to prevent nuclear proliferation, the chief problem in U.S.-North Korean relations. Instead, it began to move in the direction of engaging the North along with maintaining a firm deterrence posture. The Bush administration continues the struggle to induce North Korea to give up its nuclear ambitions but with theoretical constructs that are less useful in achieving the desired goals.

In the end, the theoretical picture in Korean security has moved toward a more complex mixture that includes the continued use of deterrence and compellence but increasingly calls for greater engagement and less reliance on direct or implicit threats. Deterrence, compellence, and engagement will remain important in understanding Korean security, but engagement along with a reduction of coercive threats must be utilized to a greater degree by future administrations while maintaining a robust deterrence posture.

Notes

1. Morgan, *Deterrence Now*, 2.

2. Patrick M. Morgan, *Deterrence: A Conceptual Analysis*, 2nd ed. (Beverly Hills: SAGE Publications, 1983), 19.

3. Glenn Snyder, *Deterrence and Defense* (Princeton: Princeton University Press, 1961), 9-16 and Robert H. Dorff and Joseph R. Cerami, "Deterrence and Competitive Strategies: A New Look at an Old Concept," in Max G. Manwaring, ed., *Deterrence in the 21st Century* (London: Frank Cass, 2001), 109-123.

4. John J. Mearsheimer, *Conventional Deterrence* (Ithaca: Cornell University Press, 1983), 28-30.

5. George H. Quester, *Deterrence Before Hiroshima: The Airpower Background of Modern Strategy* (New York: Wiley, 1966).

6. Kenneth N. Waltz, "Nuclear Myths and Political Realities," *American Political*

Science Review 84, no. 3 (September 1990): 734.

7. Stephen J. Cimbala, *Nuclear Strategizing: Deterrence and Reality* (New York: Praeger Publishers, 1988), 7.

8. Robert Jervis, *The Meaning of the Nuclear Revolution: Statecraft and the Prospect of Armageddon* (Ithaca: Cornell University Press, 1989), 18.

9. Morgan, *Deterrence: A Conceptual Analysis*, 104-105.

10. Alexander L. George and Richard Smoke, *Deterrence in American Foreign Policy: Theory and Practice* (New York: Columbia University Press, 1974), 75.

11. Robert Jervis, Richard Ned Lebow, and Janice Gross Stein, *Psychology and Deterrence* (Baltimore: Johns Hopkins University Press, 1985).

12. U.S. Senate, "Statement of Hon. William J. Porter, Ambassador to the Republic of Korea," Appendix I, *United States Security Agreements and Commitments Abroad: Republic of Korea*, Hearings before the Subcommittee on U.S. Security Agreements and Commitments Abroad of the Committee on Foreign Relations, 91st Congress, 2nd Session, Part 6, 24, 25, and 26 February 1970 (Washington, D.C.: Government Printing Office, 1970): 1709. Hereafter noted as *Security Agreements Hearings* (1970).

13. James R. Schlesinger, Secretary of Defense, U.S. Department of Defense, *Annual Report, FY 1977* (Washington, D.C.: Government Printing Office, 1976): III-11.

14. Bob Woodward, *Bush at War* (New York: Simon & Schuster, 2002), 340.

15. Morgan, *Deterrence: A Conceptual Analysis*, 27-47.

16. Morgan, *Deterrence: A Conceptual Analysis*, 38.

17. Morgan, *Deterrence: A Conceptual Analysis*, 42-44.

18. Morgan, *Deterrence: A Conceptual Analysis*, 44.

19. For definitions of extended deterrence, see Paul Huth, *Extended Deterrence and the Prevention of War* (New Haven: Yale University Press, 1988), 16, William T. Tow, *Encountering the Dominant Player* (New York: Columbia University Press, 1991), 2, and David W. Tarr, *Nuclear Deterrence and International Security: Alternative Nuclear Regimes* (New York: Longman Press, 1991), 69-73.

20. Paul Huth uses these designations in a matrix in *Extended Deterrence and the Prevention of War*, 15-20. See also Allen Whiting, *The Chinese Calculus of Deterrence: India and Indochina* (Ann Arbor: University of Michigan Press, 1975).

21. William W. Kaufmann, *The Requirements of Deterrence* (Princeton: Center for International Studies, 1954), 19.

22. Thomas Schelling, *Arms and Influence* (New Haven: Yale University Press, 1966), 97-98.

23. Richard Ned Lebow, *Nuclear Crisis Management: A Dangerous Illusion* (Ithaca: Cornell University Press, 1987), 26.

24. Morgan, *Deterrence: A Conceptual Analysis*, 43.

25. Mearsheimer, *Conventional Deterrence*, 28-30.

26. In Bruce M. Russett, "The Calculus of Deterrence," *Journal of Conflict Resolution* II, no. 2 (June 1963), he looked at 17 cases of extended deterrence and only 1 successful case had an oath or promise of help from a defender.

27. Henry Kissinger, *For the Record: Selected Statements, 1977-1980* (Boston: Little, Brown, 1981), 240.

28. Schelling, *Arms and Influence*, 35-91.

29. Schelling, *Arms and Influence*, 43-44.

30. David Garnham in "Extending Deterrence with German Nuclear Weapons," *In-*

ternational Security 10, no. 1 (Summer 1985), makes this argument for giving nuclear weapons to the West Germans.

31. Schelling, *The Strategy of Conflict*, 35-39.

32. Paul Huth and Bruce Russett, "What Makes Deterrence Work?," *World Politics* XXXVI, no. 4 (July 1984), 502.

33. Robert Jervis, *The Meaning of the Nuclear Revolution*, 30.

34. George and Smoke, *Deterrence in American Foreign Policy*, 561.

35. George and Smoke, *Deterrence in American Foreign Policy*, 558-561.

36. Bruce Russett, "The Calculus of Deterrence," 105.

37. Paul Huth, "Extended Deterrence and the Outbreak of War," *American Political Science Review* 82, no. 2 (June 1988): 436.

38. Huth, "Extended Deterrence and the Outbreak of War," 436-437.

39. David E. Sanger, "Son of North Korean Leader May Be Succeeding to Power," *New York Times*, 19 March 1993, A1. Speculation of Kim Jong Il's succession began in 1974. In 1991, the younger Kim was named supreme commander of the military, indicating to some that the transition to power was approaching its final stages. "North Korea Heir To Head The Army," *New York Times*, 26 December 1991, A8.

40. Schelling, *Arms and Influence*, 69.

41. Morgan, *Deterrence Now*, 3.

42. Schelling, *Arms and Influence*, 82.

43. Morgan, *Deterrence Now*, 2.

44. Alexander George, *Forceful Persuasion: Coercive Diplomacy as an Alternative to War* (Washington D.C.: United States Institute of Peace Press, 1991), 7.

45. Schelling, *Arms and Influence*, 74.

46. Robert J. Art, "Introduction," in Robert J. Art and Patrick M. Cronin (eds.), *The United States and Coercive Diplomacy* (Washington, D.C.: United States Institute of Peace Press, 2003), 9.

47. See Art, "Introduction," 7.

48. Morgan, *Deterrence Now*, 2.

49. George, *Forceful Persuasion*, 5-6.

50. Schelling, *Arms and Influence*, 76.

51. George, *Forceful Persuasion*, 11.

52. George, *Forceful Persuasion*, 10-11.

53. George, *Forceful Persuasion*, 11.

54. George, *Forceful Persuasion*, 12-13.

55. George and Smoke, *Deterrence in American Foreign Policy*, 63.

Chapter 2

THE THREAT: North Korea, China, and the Soviet Union, 1948-1990

The threat perception of the defender is an important starting point for analyzing an extended deterrence security relationship. The nature of the threat helps determine the preparations taken to implement the policy. The focus here is on three specific aspects of U.S. threat assessments. First, who was the threat to South Korea? During the past fifty to sixty years, the challenger to U.S. deterrence policy in Korea consisted of three states, North Korea, the Soviet Union, and China, rather than a single entity, an assumption often made by deterrence theory to simplify calculations. Relations among the three challenger states further complicated threat assessments. For example, the Soviet Union and China were defenders for their protégé North Korea. However, by the late 1950s, Sino-Soviet relations had soured, and North Korea began to doubt the reliability of its two defenders. In 1991, the end of the Cold War and the disintegration of the Soviet Union along with concerns for North Korea's development of nuclear weapons and ballistic missiles added more uncertainty. Thus, the threat in Korea for U.S. policy makers was a complex configuration of three states with evolving capabilities that made assessing the source and nature of the threat more difficult. Second, what military capabilities did the threat possess and how did these affect the military balance in Korea? Third, what were the intentions of the challengers with respect to the use of military force in Korea? These three aspects of the threat—source, capabilities, and intent—are applied here to five specific time periods of the U.S.-ROK security relationship: 1953 to 1961; 1961 to 1969; 1969 to 1979; 1980 to 1990; and 1991 to the present. These divisions provide a useful periodization of U.S. threat assessments and mark chronologically significant changes made to those evaluations. This chapter will examine the first four periods up to 1990 and the end of the Cold War that were defined largely by the North's conventional military capability. Chapter 3 will address the post-Cold War period when the North Korean threat included the development and proliferation of ballistic missiles and nuclear weapons.

For most of the time since 1953, the threat to South Korea has been uncertain. The perceived danger of imminent attack was generally low, but had the potential to change quickly. U.S. and ROK officials also feared communist efforts to destabilize the South Korean government through infiltration and subversion. The challengers—North Korea, China, and the Soviet Union—all possessed threatening military capabilities, but their intent was unclear. However, from time to time the United States and South Korea sensed that North Korea might believe there was an "opportunity" to strike and took specific countermeasures to dissuade the North from acting. Thus, the threat to South Korea has, on occasion, possessed the characteristics of an immediate deterrence problem, which required specific counterthreats. However, for most of the security relationship the threat to South Korea has been consistent with that of an extended general deterrence relationship. There has been no immediate threat of hostilities, but rather a more generalized danger where a challenger might attack if the opportunity arose. Today, North Korea remains the chief threat to U.S. interests in Korea, more dangerous still should the DPRK continue to export ballistic missiles and develop a nuclear weapons capability.

1953-1961: The Global Communist Threat

Source

On 25 June 1950, North Korean forces launched an invasion of South Korea to forcibly reunify the peninsula. Prior to that point, the Truman administration had believed that the primary threat to South Korea was subversion and infiltration. The use of armed force came as a shock. In his memoirs, Dean Rusk, who was Assistant Secretary of State for Far Eastern Affairs when the Korean War broke out, noted: "The North Korean invasion came as a complete surprise. Only four days before, I had told a congressional committee we saw no evidence of war brewing in Korea."[1] A CIA document released in 1993 confirmed that only six days prior to the invasion, Director of Central Intelligence Walter Bedell Smith approved a report that North Korea would not invade but rather had opted for subversion and destabilization of the South.[2] Immediately, U.S. leaders judged the attack to be dramatic evidence that world communism was far more determined in its drive for domination than previously believed. In a statement released shortly after the war, President Truman maintained the North Korean attack made "it plain beyond all doubt that Communism has passed beyond the use of subversion . . . and will now use armed invasion and war."[3] After the war, Secretary of State Dean Acheson observed, "I think we can sum it up this way, that Korea moved a great many things from the realm of theory and brought them right into . . . the realm of urgency." Moreover, Korea "confirmed in our minds the correctness of the analysis of NSC 68" and that "the USSR was willing to use forces in battle to achieve objectives."[4]

While North Korea initiated the hostilities, American officials believed from the outset that the Soviet Union and China were the instigators.[5] However, they were not sure if the attack was an isolated incident or a prelude/diversion for communist aggression elsewhere. Dean Rusk recalled later, "when the North Koreans first attacked, we didn't know if this was a single offensive or the opening shot in a much broader communist offensive in Asia."[6] Soon after the attack, President Truman directed the National Security Council to conduct a review of "what other points the USSR or its satellites might attack."[7] The review, completed in NSC 73/4 in August 1950, speculated that "in causing the attack to be launched in Korea, the Kremlin did not intend to bring about a global war. . . . The probable aim of the Kremlin was simply to gain control of the entire Korean peninsula and thus to strengthen materially its strategic position in Northern Asia with global political and military results."[8] However, the report continued that the Soviet Union might be willing to launch "local armed attacks"[9] or encourage "piecemeal attacks by present or created satellite forces against Yugoslavia, Iran, Greece, Turkey, or other states around the Soviet periphery."[10] In deliberations that preceded the formulation of NSC 73/4, George Kennan argued, "the USSR intended to avoid open involvement and did not intend to launch a general war." However, "the Soviet intention of exploiting the Asiatic satellites against us was more probable because there was no risk involved for the USSR."[11] Concerning the Chinese, the report concluded that their forces might intervene in Korea or Southeast Asia and that an attack on Formosa might be forthcoming.[12] The fears of Russian adventurism in the wake of Korea did not come to pass, but on 26 November 1950, Chinese "volunteers" intervened in support of the North.

By January 1951, the Chinese assault had ground to a halt around the 38th parallel, and soon after, the war became a stalemate. At this point, the Truman administration sought to "avoid the extension of hostilities in Korea into a general war with the Soviet Union, or with Communist China," and the top priority became conclusion of an armistice.[13] NSC 118/2 also noted that while an armistice was "the first step in reaching a minimum settlement. The greatest danger . . . will be renewal of the aggression."[14] Preventing future incursions by the Soviets and Chinese will require a "powerful deterrent" whereby "the renewal of the aggression will bring prompt and certain retaliation, not only in Korea but upon China itself."[15] China and North Korea were the most immediate military threat since their soldiers did the fighting in the Korean War. Yet, the Soviet Union remained the leader of the global, communist menace. In a 1952 memorandum to President Eisenhower on the war, Secretary Dulles outlined the following:

1. It is probable that the dominant will with which we have to deal is that of the Soviet Union. The Kremlin cannot impose its will on Communist China in the same arbitrary way that it imposes its will upon Poland, Rumania [sic], etc. Nevertheless the Chinese Communist Party accepts the dominance of the Soviet Communist Party as leader of the world proletariat.

2. If this conclusion is sound the considerations which determine whether or not the Communists will continue the war are global considerations and not considerations limited merely to the battle line in Korea or the desires of the North Koreans or Chinese Communists. There is no doubt that Moscow looks on the Korean war as only one of many fronts. What it does there will be determined not by local considerations alone, but by other situations in Asia, Europe and the Middle East.[16]

On 21 July 1953, the war ended with an armistice, but for U.S. leaders the threat of communist aggression in Korea remained. The United States began implementing the "powerful deterrent" by concluding the "Greater Sanctions" declaration with the other fifteen nations that fought in Korea—Australia, Canada, New Zealand, United Kingdom, Belgium, Luxembourg, Colombia, Ethiopia, France, Greece, the Netherlands, the Philippines, Thailand, Turkey, and South Africa. The agreement stated that any further unprovoked Communist aggression on the peninsula would not be tolerated and "the consequences of such a breach of the armistice would be so grave that, in all probability, it would not be possible to confine hostilities within the frontiers of Korea."[17]

After the Korean War, U.S. policy makers continued to view the threat in Korea emanating from monolithic communism. President Eisenhower noted: "Our safety depends upon recognition of the fact that the Communist design for such encirclement must be stopped . . . before it is again too late to save peace. We must maintain a common world-wide defense against the menace of International Communism."[18] North Korea, China, and the Soviet Union would play varying roles if hostilities were renewed in Korea but a renewal of aggression in Korea would come from decisions by the "bloc leaders" in Moscow and Beijing.[19] The Chinese and North Koreans were the most likely to send troops, but American leaders believed they would all undoubtedly be acting in concert.

To counter the global communist threat, U.S. defense strategy relied on the doctrine of massive retaliation. Rather than maintaining costly conventional forces to deter communist aggression, the United States relied on its ability to respond with nuclear strikes. In the 1954 speech that outlined the massive retaliation doctrine, Secretary of State Dulles maintained that U.S. policy would "depend primarily upon a great capacity to retaliate, instantly, by means and at places of our choosing."[20] In a meeting with President Rhee and other South Korean leaders in 1954, Dulles argued, "As new weapons are developed, not so much manpower is needed at the front. We can not afford both to develop new weapons and to maintain the old-fashioned forces."[21] As a result the Eisenhower administration hoped to reduce American troops in Korea, and lessen U.S. aid since a large ROK military force would not be necessary. U.S. leaders believed that deterrence could be maintained in Korea largely through the threat of nuclear retaliation. As Secretary Dulles concluded, "the real deterrent to a renewed Communist attack on South Korea was the nuclear power which the United States had and our ability to use this power to destroy the bulk of Chinese Communist industry."[22] China was the main target of retaliation because U.S. leaders believed it was more likely to commit troops to an invasion than the Soviets. Yet, Eisenhower still viewed the "communist threat" as a partnership between the USSR and China that threatened Korea and other regions in Asia. Commenting on the Chinese shelling of Quemoy and Matsu in 1958, Eisenhower lamented:

> So, aggression by ruthless despots again imposes a clear danger to the United States and the free world. In this effort the Chinese Communists and the Soviet Union appear to be working hand in hand. Last Monday, I received a long letter on this subject from Prime Minister Khrushchev. He warned the United States against helping its allies in the Western Pacific. He said that we should not support the Republic of China and the Republic of Korea. He contended that we should desert them, return all of our naval forces to our home bases, and leave our friends in the Far East to face, alone, the combined military power of the Soviet Union and Communist China. Does Mr. Khrushchev think that we have so soon forgotten Korea? I must say to you very frankly and soberly, my friends, the United States cannot accept the result that the Communists seek. Neither can we show, now, a weakness of purpose—a timidity—which would surely lead them to move more aggressively against us and our friends in the Western Pacific area.[23]

While the United States saw the threat to South Korea as part of the communist drive for world domination, a variety of "threat scenarios" existed that concerned U.S. and ROK officials. These possibilities ranged from subversion and infiltration to a general war that would include fighting in Korea. As South Korea struggled in the 1950s to develop a stable economy and democratic government, Eisenhower feared that South Korea would be ripe for communist subversion. In a special message to Congress upon the conclusion of the Korean War armistice, President Eisenhower argued that

> the government has been constantly aware that all that has been won by this valiant struggle [in Korea] could be imperiled and lost by an economic collapse. Poverty and despair could inflict wounds beyond the power of enemy guns. . . . I am convinced that the security interests of the United States clearly indicate the need to act promptly not only to meet immediate relief needs but also to begin the long-range work of restoring the Korean economy to health and strength.[24]

This had, in fact, been the chief worry before the Korean War, and remained a concern during the rebuilding that followed the armistice in 1953. In a 1957 speech, Eisenhower stated, "our Communist antagonists are resourceful and cunning. Their aggression is not limited to the use of force or the threat of its use. They are doing their best to take advantage of poverty and need in the developing nations, and so turn them against the free world."[25] In response to these concerns, the United States developed an extensive military and economic aid package to rebuild South Korea.

Despite the fear of communist subversion, a 1955 report prepared by the U.S. Embassy in Korea on the counter-subversive capacity of the ROK stated that the "threat of Communist control of the ROK through subversion is at present a potential, rather than an actual danger."[26] Policy makers did not view subversion as a serious threat because there was little communist sympathy in the South, and "there are at present relatively few manifestations of internal Communist activity in South Korea."[27] However, the report continued, a potentially dangerous situation could result when Rhee dies or if he becomes incapacitated. The political upheaval following the many years of Rhee's "personal rule" could be "fertile ground for Communist subversive activities."[28] Thus, Rhee's advancing age made it imperative for the Eisenhower administration to strengthen South Korea's economic and political stability.

Military Capabilities

The threat of armed attack by the communist side was a serious concern. If another war pitted U.S.-ROK-UN forces against only North Korea, U.S. leaders were confident ROK forces could stop the North. A 1956 U.S. intelligence estimate noted, "the ROK army is superior in both offensive and defensive capabilities to the North Korean army alone."[29] The North's armed forces stood at 350,000, well below ROK forces that were 650,000.[30] The ROK and DPRK also possessed reserve forces that ranged from 400,000 to 450,000. The ROK military was also confident of its ability to stop a North Korean attack. In a briefing by the ROK Army Chief of Staff, General Chung Il Kwon, he noted: "The ROK is not concerned about the North Korean forces, which they believe they could easily handle."[31]

Three years of intense fighting during the Korean War wrecked North Korea's armed forces. In 1950, believing that a U.S. response would be late or nonexistent, the North had hoped to conquer South Korea before any action might be taken against them. In his memoirs, Khrushchev recalled Stalin "was worried that the Americans would jump in, but we were inclined to think that if the war were fought swiftly—and Kim Il-sung was sure that it could be won swiftly—then intervention by the USA could be avoided."[32] However, Kim Il Sung badly miscalculated and the war turned into a military disaster. If not for Chinese intervention, the U.S. decision to advance to the Yalu River would have eliminated the North Korean regime. When the war ended in July 1953, Kim Il Sung faced the daunting task of rebuilding a war torn country, devastated by three years of ground combat, and naval and aerial bombardment. According to a report issued during the war by the United Nations Bomber Command in the Far East, "there are no more targets in Korea."[33]

Although precise numbers are not available, the war killed close to 700,000 North Korean soldiers and civilians with almost an equal number missing. The war severely damaged the North Korean economy, destroying industry and farmland while demolishing homes, hospitals, and schools. In a 1953 National Intelligence Estimate, officials noted:

A critical food situation apparently exists in North Korea. Although the regime has claimed a bumper crop for 1952, food production and distribution have apparently not met civilian and military requirements, and substantial assistance from Communist China has been necessary. North Korean housing, industry, and electric power have all been severely curtailed by UNC operations. In addition, major shortages exist in consumer goods and in agricultural manpower.[34]

When Pyongyang rebuilt its factories, many were constructed further inland to lessen vulnerability to shelling from offshore naval forces.[35] From 1949 to 1953, some estimates indicate that North Korea lost 1.13 million people from a total in 1949 of 9.62 million, and the population of Pyongyang, the Northern capital, fell from 400,000 to 80,000. The resulting labor shortage hurt the North Korean economy for many years.[36]

Following the war, Kim Il Sung also confronted an internal struggle for political power. The strife created by the war gave Kim's political opponents an opportunity to oust him. Though he eventually subdued his rivals, the struggle left its mark and pointed to potential problems should he initiate another attack on South Korea and fail again. As one scholar noted, "his country lay in ruins. . . . If the war taught him nothing else, it surely must have brought home the point that military invasion was not a suitable means of bringing about Korean unity."[37]

Though U.S. and ROK officials were sanguine about the ROK-DPRK military balance on the ground, these officials worried about a growing imbalance in air power between the two Koreas. Estimates of the DPRK air force included 310 jet fighters and 65 light jet bombers.[38] ROK planes were obsolete, propeller-driven F-51s that were no match for North Korean MiG 15s.[39] The imbalance in air power was due largely to Communist violations of subparagraph 13-d in the 1953 Armistice.[40] This provision prohibited the introduction of "reinforcing" military equipment not present in Korea at the time of the signing of the Armistice. Equipment that was "destroyed, damaged, wornout, or used up" could be "replaced on the basis of piece-for-piece of the same effectiveness and the same type." In violation of this provision, Pyongyang's allies rebuilt the North Korean air force with jet fighters as well as other modern weapons that were not previously in Korea. If the Communist side continued to violate 13-d, the United States believed that the ROK Army might lose its capability to stop a North Korean attack.[41] To address this concern, in June 1957, the United States announced that it would suspend subparagraph 13-d and begin providing modern equipment to South Korea, including all weather fighters (F-86D and F-102), tactical jet bombers (B-57), and jet fighters (F-100).[42]

While both the United States and ROK were confident of the South's ability to repel a DPRK assault, a joint Chinese-North Korean invasion was a different matter. Constrained by budget considerations, U.S. aid was insufficient to build up the ROK military to withstand a Chinese-DPRK attack. Consequently, "immediate and substantial U.S. military assistance" would be necessary "to resist successfully a Chinese Communist-North Korean attack if Chinese reinforcements, immediately available from Manchuria and Northeast China, were moved into Korea."[43]

China's proximity to Korea was foremost among U.S.-ROK worries. Despite continued withdrawals after the Korean War, China could redeploy to Korea substantial numbers of soldiers without opposition in 10 to 14 days.[44] However, U.S. and ROK officials believed that these movements would be detected, providing a degree of warning.[45] Most importantly, the ROK, along with American units in Korea, must be able to hold long enough for the United States to intervene in strength.[46]

The remaining component of the threat was the Soviet Union. Moscow's military strength was an important concern to U.S. officials, especially when linked to China through the Sino-Soviet alliance. Initial U.S. plans to "hit China hard" and "wherever it would hurt the most"[47] should the Chinese invade Korea were later modified because it might force Soviet intervention. U.S. planners believed that if an American response to Chinese aggression in Korea threatened China itself, the Soviet Union would be apt join the conflict. Events might then escalate to a general war and threaten U.S. interests in Europe.[48] Instead, the Joint Chiefs of Staff (JCS) and the State Department concluded that the United States should strike only those Chinese assets directly supporting a war in Korea. This would be less likely to provoke a large-scale Soviet response.[49] So long as the United States did not arouse the Soviet Union, the Eisenhower administration believed Moscow would not send its own troops to a war in Korea, barring a general war with the United States.

Intentions

Since Kim Il Sung assumed control of the DPRK in 1948, the North Korean regime had proclaimed one overriding objective: the reunification of the two Koreas under communist rule. Concerning the Soviets and the Chinese, "the objective of the Communists continues to be the gaining of control over the entire peninsula."[50] When reunification talks stalled, U.S. officials believed "it was evident that the Communists would not agree to any unification that did not permit continuance of the Communist regime."[51] In contrast, U.S. policy was "to bring about the unification of Korea with a self-supporting economy and under a free, independent, and representative government, friendly toward the U.S. and other countries of the free world."[52] U.S. officials doubted that any agreement would be reached concerning unification in the foreseeable future and the result was likely to be a continuing "situation of tension and instability."[53]

Stalin's motivations here are interesting. Initially, he agreed with the goal of reuniting Korea under Kim's control, but was reluctant to give his approval for fear of the costs that could follow if the United States came to the South's aid. Instead, he believed the North should continue its efforts to destabilize the Rhee regime and work to bring about an uprising in the South. After several attempts by Kim to convince Stalin, the Soviet leader finally assented when Kim assured him the victory could be achieved quickly. Stalin's approval came on 30 January 1950, and may have been influenced by Secretary of State Acheson's speech on January 12th that excluded South Korea from the U.S. defense perimeter. Stalin also insisted Kim obtain Mao Zedong's approval, which was forthcoming. Given North Korea's economic dependency, Kim Il Sung needed Moscow's approval for the attack, but it was Kim Il Sung that was the driving force behind the invasion.[54]

Yet, U.S. assessments of the challengers' risk calculus mollified their concern. Though the North remained committed to reunification and had demonstrated in 1950 its willingness to use force to obtain this objective, a 1956 intelligence estimate noted, "we believe that they will not resort to force to obtain this objective, at least so long as the U.S. remains committed to the defense of the ROK."[55] A Department of State memorandum quotes from this same intelligence estimate that "a renewal of aggression by north Korean forces acting alone . . . is extremely unlikely, especially in view of the role played by the Soviet Union in directing north Korea's external policies."[56] In turn, Eisenhower "did not believe . . . that the USSR was going to let itself get involved in full-scale warfare in the Far East. The risks were just too great and the distances for supply too extended."[57] Finally, a 1954 National Intelligence Estimate maintained "the Chinese Communists will not deliberately undertake courses of action which they believe would involve serious risk of U.S. action against the Chinese mainland. We have also estimated and still believe that the Communists will try to avoid courses of action which clearly involve substantial risk of general war."[58] Consistent with the characteristics of general deterrence, U.S. officials did not believe an attack was imminent. So long as the American commitment remained firm, the Eisenhower administration concluded that China and the Soviet Union "will not utilize military force in Korea short of a decision to embark on global war."[59]

While considering it unlikely that the communist side would risk an invasion, U.S. leaders certainly believed they would exploit any potential opportunity to gain control of the South by other means. In a letter to South Korean President Syngman Rhee, Eisenhower stated, "we intend to do all that we can to prevent Korea from falling prey to Communist aggression whether that aggression is by open acts of hostility or by subversion."[60] U.S. leaders believed a strong commitment to South Korea was necessary to address this danger as well, a danger that became more serious in the 1960s.

1961-1969: Subversion and Infiltration

Source

By 1961, U.S. threat perceptions started to change, altering Washington's view of the challenger configuration in Korea. The Sino-Soviet rift that began in the late 1950s eroded the notion of a monolithic communist threat. Though the Soviets remained a serious menace, for U.S. policy makers, the newly emerging power of China posed a more critical danger in Asia. President Kennedy noted:

Our problem now, of course, is that with the rise of the Communist powers in China combined with an expansionist, Stalinist philosophy, our major problem, is how we can contain the expansion of communism in Asia so that we do not find the Chinese moving out into a dominant position in all of Asia, with its hundreds and hundreds of millions of people in Asia.[61]

In 1966, President Johnson noted that Chinese aggression had to be stopped or the United States would have to "abandon much of Asia to the domination of the Communists."[62] Later in the year, a joint statement by Johnson and South Korean President Park Chung Hee confirmed the "growing strength" of the Sino-DPRK threat.[63]

By the 1960s, Pyongyang had completed a large share of its rebuilding efforts and had increased its military strength significantly. American military officials did not believe the North's capabilities were overwhelming should they attack alone. By now, the DPRK was pursuing fully a policy Kim Il Sung called "*juche*"—self-reliance—which entailed the North undertaking a more independent foreign policy. Furthermore, North Korean actions became more threatening, including a dramatic rise in infiltration efforts, incidents along the DMZ, and proclamations of revolutionary rhetoric. All of these were dangerous indications of North Korea's growing hostile intent. Thus, U.S. deterrence policy in the 1960s became most concerned with the threat from North Korea and China.

Military Capabilities[64]

Pyongyang made some significant advances during the 1960s to improve its military capabilities. During this period, North Korean armed forces personnel rose from 338,000 to 384,500, a 10.2 percent increase. These totals remained well short of the 600,000 to 620,000 total military personnel maintained by the ROK. The bulk of DPRK forces were in the army where ground forces grew from 280,000 to 350,000. The North also had 15,000 soldiers in special commando units that could be airlifted into South Korea or sent ashore along the many miles of ROK coastline. The DPRK had reserve forces of 110,000 and a civilian militia of 1.2 million that supplemented the regular army.

The ROK Army numbered approximately 580,000 during the 1960s, though there was some variation in different years. From 1965 to 1972, the ROK had 2 infantry divisions fighting with U.S. forces in Vietnam. These forces numbered over 47,000 and are included in this total. South Korea's ground forces included 25,000 to 30,000 Marines and 10,000 Koreans serving in the U.S. Army. These Koreans, designated as Koreans attached to the U.S. Army (KATUSA), were fully integrated into American units. Reserves and a civilian militia numbering two million further augmented ROK forces.

The ROK military possessed significant numerical advantages, were well-trained, and as personnel rotated to Korea from Vietnam, also gained important combat experience. However, one area of concern for ROK forces was their equipment, particularly rifles. During this period, the ROK had yet to develop its own indigenous arms industries and relied heavily on U.S. aid. Congressional hearings noted that even as late as 1970 a large portion of ROK ground units still used the World War II vintage M-1 carbine as the standard infantry weapon instead of the M-16 used by U.S. units. Pentagon testimony noted that budgetary factors were the primary reasons for ROK units not having the more advanced rifle, but planning was underway for the South to manufacture its own M-16 rifles.[65]

The twenty-five-mile distance that separates Seoul from the DMZ also complicates U.S.-ROK military planning. As occurred in 1950, a rapid assault spearheaded by tanks and other armored vehicles could overrun Seoul before the ROK and United States fully mobilized their forces. Thus, the number and types of DPRK tanks and armored personnel carriers (APC) was an important concern since these forces indicated the North's potential for a quick strike against the South Korean capital.

Table 2.1

NORTH AND SOUTH KOREAN MILITARY PERSONNEL, 1961 and 1969

| | 1961 | | 1969 | |
	North	South	North	South
Total Armed Forces	338,000	600,000	384,500	620,000
Ground Forces	280,00	550,000	350,000	580,000*

Source: *The Communist Bloc and Western Alliances*, 1961-1963 and *Military Balance*, 1964-1969.

By 1966, North Korea had a total of 430 tanks in its arsenal. However, these numbers rose quickly to 900 by 1969. Among the North's tank units were the PT-76, a light amphibious tank, the T-34, T-54, and T-55. In contrast, South Korea had ten tank battalions made up of the American-built M-47 and M-48 Patton tanks. By 1969, the entire ROK tank force consisted of M-48s. While the North had a quantitative advantage, ROK tanks had a qualitative edge. The T-34, a large part of DPRK tank units, was actually a light tank, and inferior in speed and armament to the M-48.[66] The PT-76, a light amphibious tank, was also likely to be inferior to the M-48.

North Korean APCs numbered 900 by 1968, including the BTR-40 and BTR-152. The BTR-152 was the largest of the APCs and capable of carrying nineteen to twenty riflemen.[67] One analyst noted that an even larger number of APCs (1,000) would still be insufficient to motorize a significant number of DPRK forces.[68]

The force levels for North Korean artillery indicate an advantage here as well. By 1969, Pyongyang had 200 self-propelled guns, Su-76, Su-100, and ZSu-57 and 6,000 other guns and mortars up to 152mm. *The Military Balance* gives no breakdown of the types or numbers of most of these artillery pieces, and it is difficult to make a more accurate assessment. Seoul's proximity to the border puts it well within range of these guns, giving Pyongyang the capability to strike without launching an invasion. From 1966 to 1968, South Korea possessed 40 independent artillery battalions. However, in 1968, the ROK added the firepower of an Honest John rocket battalion and in 1969 doubled their artillery units, bringing the total to 80 artillery battalions of guns up to 155mm.

Both North and South also had small naval forces. In particular, U.S. leaders feared the four Soviet submarines delivered to the DPRK between 1963 and 1967 and four Komar-class missile patrol boats.[69] Three destroyers and four frigates were the main ships in the South Korean Navy. The North used its navy primarily for coastal defense, though the submarines could blockade South Korea if war broke out. However, U.S. naval forces could break the blockade, and Washington concluded that North Korean vessels would not play a major role in another conflict in Korea.[70]

The most troubling concern for U.S.-ROK planners in the 1960s, as it had been in the previous decade, was North Korean air power. Secretary of State Dean Rusk noted in his memoirs that "South Korean ground forces were more than a match for North Korean, but the latter had clear superiority in the air, with their large contingent of Soviet MiGs."[71] The DPRK had a significant numerical advantage with 500 to 590 combat aircraft. By the late 1960s, the North possessed more than 400 MiG-15s and MiG-17s. By the end of the decade, the DPRK air force included more modern planes—80 IL-28s, 20 MiG-19s, and 60 MiG-21s—to complement the older MiGs.

During this period, the South had approximately 200 combat planes. For the first half of the decade, ROK aircraft units consisted of the F-86 D and E. During the mid-1960s, the South added 45 F-5s, in addition to the 160 F-86s. For the first half of the 1960s, ROK F-86s and F-5s faced primarily MiG-15s and MiG-17s from the North. Though the MiGs could outperform the F-86 at altitude during the Korean War, an earlier version of the F-86 had a 10 to 1 combat exchange ratio against MiG-15s and MiG-17s. Defense officials also believed the F-5 was superior to the MiG-15s and 17s and superior in air combat to the MiG-19 and SU-7.[72]

Qualitative problems became evident in the latter half of the decade with the introduction of the MiG-21 into the DPRK. According to the Pentagon, the "F-5 performance limitations in speed and altitude seriously limit its counter-MiG-21 capability," except at low altitudes.[73] In 1969, partially to redress the imbalance created by the MiG-21 and partially as a show of American determination following the seizure of the USS *Pueblo*, Washington provided the ROK with the more advanced F-4. The F-4 provided air interdiction or ground support capability, and according to one analyst, "North Korea has no aircraft as modern and versatile" as the F-4.[74] Though the performance of the South's planes offset some of the North's numerical superiority, the U.S. military believed that the ROK Air Force was "at a decided qualitative disadvantage compared with the North Korean Air Force."[75]

Despite the DPRK advantages in air power, U.S. assessments of the overall military balance were positive. A 1970 statement by the Commander of U.S. forces in Korea noted "ROK forces are well trained, equipped with aging equipment and, at present, are capable, with U.S. assistance, of defending and containing a NK attack."[76] With U.S. forces included—two U.S. infantry divisions, U.S. air and naval units, and the presence of tactical nuclear weapons—there was a high degree of confidence that ROK and U.S. forces could repel a North Korean attack.

As in the 1950s, U.S. and ROK planners were more concerned for a joint North Korean-Chinese attack. China's border with North Korea and its ability to send large numbers of conventional forces into Korea to support a DPRK invasion remained problematic. In 1964, China exploded its first atomic device and by 1967, had exploded a hydrogen bomb. China's sheer size in population and area, and its potential as a nuclear power made it a significant military threat in Asia. In a 1967 news conference, Secretary of State Dean Rusk cautioned, "there will be a billion Chinese on the mainland, armed with nuclear weapons, with no certainty about what their attitude toward the rest of Asia will be."[77] The ROK would not have the capability to resist a combined Sino-DPRK invasion as "defense against a NK attack, reinforced by the ChiComs [Chinese Communists] could be sustained for only a short time by the ROK forces."[78]

The military capabilities of North Korea increased in both numbers and quality with the help of Soviet and Chinese aid. China was also becoming a greater military threat to South Korea and other U.S. interests in Asia. These capabilities became more menacing with growing indications of North Korean and Chinese hostility and an apparent willingness to risk a confrontation with the United States. However, it was unclear if Pyongyang and Beijing were willing to risk a war in Korea that could bring in the United States.

Intentions

During the 1960s, the United States became deeply involved in Vietnam in an effort to halt the spread of communism. However, Vietnam was only one of several areas in Asia threatened by communism. Laos, Korea, and Thailand were a few of the other countries the United States believed to be at risk. The main instigator of this unrest in Asia, according to U.S. estimates, was Communist China. In deliberations before the UN concerning China's admission to that organization in 1965, U.S. Representative Arthur Goldberg argued that China had no interest in peaceful coexistence and "openly espouses and practices the doctrine that 'political power grows out of the barrel of a gun,' that the seizure of power by armed force, the settlement of the issue by war, is the central task and highest form of revolution."[79]

U.S. leaders were particularly concerned about Chinese aid and subversion in third world conflicts. In a news conference, Secretary of State Rusk noted: "the other side [China] must realize that the use of militancy, of men and arms across frontiers in pursuit of what they call 'wars of liberation,' also is dangerous."[80] Two years later, Rusk maintained, "we are not picking out Peking as some sort of special enemy. Peking has nominated itself by proclaiming a militant doctrine of the world revolution and doing something about it. This is not a theoretical debate; they are doing something about it."[81] Chinese aggression had to be stopped or the United States would have to concede much of Asia to Chinese domination. In talks with Japanese Prime Minister Sato in 1965, Johnson noted "his grave concern that Communist China's militant policies and expansionist pressures against its neighbors endanger the peace in Asia."[82] Though these statements focused primarily on Vietnam, the Chinese threat to South Korea also worried U.S. leaders. In the joint statement of Presidents Johnson and Park in 1966, "they agreed that the growing strength of the Communist forces in the northern part of Korea and of the Chinese Communists remained a major threat to the security of the Republic of Korea and neighboring areas."[83] The proximity of Chinese military power was troublesome, but U.S. leaders did not believe China would risk a direct confrontation with the United States in Korea. Rather, China was likely to continue its pressure on the South through its protégé, North Korea.

While the Chinese posed a formidable threat, the United States also began to view North Korea as more autonomous from Moscow and Beijing and a greater danger in its own right. In a statement given to a congressional committee in 1970, U.S. Ambassador to Korea William Porter maintained:

> In October, 1966, Premier Kim Il-sung declared North Korea's neutrality in the Sino-Soviet dispute and its independence of either side. Neither can claim North Korea as a satellite. Relations tend to be closer with the Soviet Union from which the North receives much greater economic and military assistance. Correct but cool relations with Communist China have warmed noticeably since mid-1969, but not at the expense of relations with the Soviets.[84]

Thus, while China remained a serious regional threat, the DPRK was no longer viewed as a puppet of either Moscow or Beijing. North Korea was pursuing a more independent foreign policy and maintained reasonably cordial relations with both the Soviet Union and China.

By 1961, North Korea had successfully rebuilt a large portion of its economy, and actually surpassed South Korea in gross national product per capita.[85] Kim Il Sung remained firmly in control, allowing more direct attention to his goal of unification. There was no indication that U.S. troops would leave anytime soon, which made a direct assault on the South a risky option. For a variety of reasons that will be discussed shortly, North Korea embarked on a new course of subversion and infiltration in its attempt to destabilize South Korea. Though the North also sent contradictory signals indicating a desire for peaceful reunification, their increasing hostility and violent acts alarmed U.S. and ROK leaders.

To begin analyzing North Korean strategy in the 1960s, it is necessary to review the political turmoil in South Korea that preceded it. After the end of the Korean War, South Koreans became increasingly dissatisfied with their government under President Syngman Rhee. Despite large amounts of U.S. aid, economic development in the South remained minimal, and Rhee's government became exceedingly corrupt and authoritarian. The last straw came in 1960 when government officials blatantly rigged national elections. The leading opposition candidate against Rhee, Cho Pyong Ok, died shortly before the election so that Rhee's presidential victory was almost assured. However, Rhee's advancing age (85 years old) and the possibility of his death in office focused attention on the vice presidential race, which was voted on a separate ballot. Rhee's Liberal Party vice presidential candidate, Yi Ki-bung, defeated the incumbent vice president, Chang Myon, with massive fraud perpetrated by the police and ministry of internal affairs.[86] A rapid succession of events—massive student demonstrations, public outrage over the discovery of a 17-year-old boy's body killed during a demonstration and dumped into Masan Bay by police, the army's refusal to shoot at student demonstrators, further demonstrations joined by university professors, and a shift in U.S. policy from toleration to condemnation of the president—lead to Rhee's resignation on 27 April 1960.[87]

With Rhee gone, South Korea adopted a parliamentary system of government that shifted power from the executive branch to the National Assembly. However, a proliferation of factions within the ruling Democratic Party, as well as within other parties, made it difficult to formulate and implement policy. This prevented the nation from moving on a number of serious problems, particularly the enactment of measures to stimulate economic development. Furthermore, the students, who had been the main catalyst for Rhee's removal, continued their activism and attempted to deal with other pressing national issues, the most important being reunification. Student groups proposed meeting with their North Korean counterparts to hold a conference to resolve the reunification question.[88]

The political chaos and economic woes that followed Rhee's departure disturbed many South Koreans, especially those in the military. With the purpose of restoring order and preventing radical students from making hasty overtures to the North, the ROK military seized power in May 1961. Major General Park Chung Hee led the coup and established a regime based on tight political control that will "lay down anticommunism as the first national policy."[89]

The political environment in South Korea now presented Kim Il Sung with different challenges. The South Korean regime under Park Chung Hee was militantly anti-communist and took measures to eliminate any communist activity in the South.[90] ROK authorities suppressed political dissent, particularly student protest, so that further opportunities for North Korea to organize support in the South diminished greatly. It is likely that Kim Il Sung regretted not having taken advantage of the fluid political situation in South Korea during Rhee's ouster and the short-lived government that followed.[91] Later actions by Kim Il Sung to develop a stronger Communist movement in the South were, in part, a reaction to the perceived errors of this time. Furthermore, the new South Korean government was not interested in negotiations to reunify the peninsula.

Within two months of Park's coup, North Korea signed security agreements with the Soviet Union and China. The rapid conclusion of these deals, according to some analysts, indicated North Korea's fear of this new regime.[92] The operative clause in these pacts stated "in case one party of the pact is in a state of war, the other party will provide, without delay, military and other assistance, employing all measures in its power."[93] This is the exact wording in the agreement with the Soviet Union (signed 6 July 1961), and the language in the agreement with China is similar (signed 11 July 1961). In remarks following the signing, Premier Khrushchev argued that the Soviet Union does not believe in military pacts, but "we had to sign this treaty of a defensive nature because the Governments of the United States, Japan and other powers have turned down all our proposals toward the relaxation of tension and insuring of security in the Far East."[94] Kim Il Sung's post-signing remarks further condemned the United States, declaring "the American imperialists are the most rabid enemies of the Asian peoples as well as of the other nations that are fighting for peace and social progress."[95] The State Department noted the Soviet-DPRK pact was another "military link in the Communist colonial empire."[96]

After concluding their treaty with the North Koreans five days later, Chinese officials noted that the agreements were a sign of the unity and solidarity of the Communist bloc.[97] U.S. officials reached a similar conclusion. A press report noted that the State Department "branded the Chinese Communist-North Korean mutual assistance pact today as a sign of 'militancy' shown by the Communists throughout the world."[98]

Despite signing these security agreements, Kim Il Sung probably questioned his allies' reliability, in part due to the growing Sino-Soviet rift and the Soviet retreat during the Cuban missile crisis. Consequently, Kim Il Sung embarked on a more self-reliant defense posture.[99] In 1962, he announced a four-point program to build up the military capabilities of North Korea, a signal that indicated a shift towards a Maoist version of people's war and away from a conventional war strategy.

1. Upgrade the political and technical training of the Korean People's Army so that all KPA soldiers may become "cadres."
2. Modernize arms and equipment.
3. Arm the entire people.
4. Turn the entire country into a fortress.[100]

A little over a year later, Kim Il Sung further refined the North Korean strategy in a February 1964 speech to the Korean Worker's Party titled "Let Us Strengthen in Every Way Revolutionary Forces for the Realization of the Great Task of Fatherland Unification." According to the speech, three stages were necessary to reunify Korea. First, North Korea had to build up its own "revolutionary base" by educating and training its own people with the proper doctrine as well as further strengthening the economic prosperity and military power of the nation. Kim noted that North Korea needed its military power to "preserve the fruits of revolution against aggression by the enemy nor protect, let alone strengthen, its political and economic capabilities."[101]

The second stage called for fostering the revolutionary forces within South Korea. Borrowing from Marxist doctrine, Kim believed the South Korean masses suffered from false consciousness and did not realize the extent of their oppression under the U.S. imperialists and their South Korean lackeys. To remedy this situation, Kim wanted greater organization of the masses through a vanguard party in the South.

Finally, Kim Il Sung directed that international forces also needed to be strengthened. By this he meant that North Korea needed to pursue friendly relations with other third world states while exploiting the conflicts that existed between the countries of the West. Kim hoped to isolate and force the United States to halt its "imperialist posture" in Korea and elsewhere in the world.

While Kim Il Sung proposed revolutionary measures, he also sent conflicting messages that called for peaceful unification. In September 1960, North Korean Foreign Minister Chung Il-Hyung announced that his country renounced the policy of liberating the South by force.[102] Later, in 1962, Kim Il Sung stated further that "unification must be attained gradually through a series of intermediate steps."[103] In the same statement, Kim asserted that communism would not be imposed on South Korea and that "the question of unifying our country is not one of who wins and who loses but one of completely liberating the previously unified people from the yoke of imperialism and restoring national unification."[104] Whether these proposals were a smokescreen or a sincere effort is not clear. Later actions would indicate to U.S. leaders that Kim Il Sung did not see peaceful unification as a likely possibility, and he was not afraid to risk operations that probed the limits of U.S. and ROK tolerance.

Events in Vietnam also affected North Korean policy as the Communist insurgency there impressed Kim Il Sung.[105] He hoped the establishment of a similar movement in South Korea would further the North's ambitions as well as provide the revolutionary base from which to exploit any instability similar to events in 1960. Apparently, Kim surmised that since the United States was already involved in Vietnam, he could probe the potential for insurgency in the South and the limits of U.S. resolve with less risk of provoking a strong U.S. response.[106]

Did Kim Il Sung really believe that U.S. involvement in Vietnam lessened the credibility of the American commitment to the ROK? Though we cannot be certain, it is unlikely that the U.S. deterrent posture would have led Kim Il Sung to reach this conclusion. Throughout the Vietnam War, U.S. declaratory support for South Korea remained strong and there was no discussion of removing U.S. troops from Korea. Upon visiting Korea in 1966, President Johnson "reaffirmed the readiness and determination of the United States to render prompt and effective assistance to defeat an armed attack against the Republic of Korea."[107] By 1965, the ROK had sent the first of two infantry divisions to Vietnam, for which the United States was very thankful. In a letter to President Park, Johnson stated that he was "deeply gratified" for the decision to send troops to Vietnam and that "the American people welcome this further demonstration of the devotion of Korea to the spirit of liberty and independence."[108] On the contrary, the DPRK strategy of infiltration and subversion was evidence that, in spite of the Vietnam War, Kim Il Sung was still reluctant to challenge the U.S. security guarantee more directly. While Kim Il Sung remained committed to reunification, a military confrontation with the United States—particularly without the certain support of his defenders—carried risks he was unwilling to take. A strategy of subversion and infiltration allowed Pyongyang much greater control of the risks while trying to push the United States out of Korea.

It is possible to argue that infiltration and subversion were merely a prelude to an invasion. In fact, Mao Zedong's writings suggest that infiltration and subversion were important preparatory measures before a larger assault.[109] Therefore, Kim Il Sung may have been laying the groundwork for an invasion rather than being deterred from it.

While this explanation is plausible, it is incorrect for two reasons. First, Kim Il Sung had already exercised the option of a direct attack in 1950 and failed miserably. There was little reason for him to conclude his chances had improved. As opposed to 1950, ROK military capabilities had grown and were augmented by U.S. forces and the U.S. security guarantee. It is likely that Kim Il Sung concluded a North Korean attack, whether preceded by infiltration and subversion or not, was destined to fail. Second, by the mid-1960s, Kim Il Sung had begun to question the commitment of his defenders, China and the Soviet Union. The DPRK perceived its allies to be unreliable, and Kim could not consider a direct challenge to the United States. However, North Korea could "ratchet up" its pressure while allowing itself room to back down should the United States or South Korea respond in an unacceptable manner. The North's strategy provided a way to manipulate and contain the risks of challenging the U.S. commitment. Also, the U.S. security guarantee did not give Kim Il Sung an "opportunity" to use more direct means; subversion and infiltration were most probably his way of "working around" a very credible commitment.[110]

North Korean efforts to destabilize the South had been a concern ever since the Korean War ended. As noted earlier, U.S. officials recognized the threat, but believed there was little sympathy in the South for communism and ROK authorities had taken the appropriate steps to control covert North Korean activities. In answer to a question in congressional hearings regarding communist insurgency in the ROK, U.S. Ambassador to Korea William Porter answered, there is "practically none. There may be an isolated sympathizer here or there who is contacted when an agent comes down, but the bulk of the population, and certainly the rural population, has given every evidence of anti-Communist sentiment." [111] However, in the late 1960s, North Korea drastically escalated its attempts to infiltrate the South, reaching its peak in 1967 and 1968 with bolder and more numerous acts of violence. According to Dae-Sook Suh there were two key turning points that marked the increased militancy of the North. The first is a Central Committee meeting held in July 1967 where North Korean leaders rededicated themselves to unifying Korea. The second turning point was the rise to prominent positions within the DPRK regime of a number of generals that advocated a more aggressive approach to reunification.[112]

A November 1967 UN Command report stated that incidents along the Demilitarized Zone (DMZ) and within South Korea initiated by the DPRK increased from 50 in 1966 to 543 for the first nine and one-half months of 1967. During 1967, North Korea had 224 infiltrators killed while on missions in the South. The report continues to note that these actions "raise serious doubts about (North Korea's) attitude toward the promotion of peace and stability in the area."[113]

The level of incidents at the DMZ reached a peak in 1968 at 629. In November 1968, 120 North Korean commandos infiltrated South Korea along the East Coast. However, most of these infiltrators were either killed or captured, causing little damage in the South. In 1969, incidents along the DMZ decreased to 111, but still more than twice 1966 levels.[114]

The most serious infiltration occurred on 21 January 1968 when a 31-man commando squad attempted to assassinate South Korean President Park at his residence in Seoul. President Park was unharmed, but the event pointed to weak areas in South Korean counter-infiltration capability. Two days later, North Korea seized the U.S. intelligence ship *Pueblo* in an area that the U.S. maintained was international waters and held the ship and crew for more than a year. To U.S. officials, North Korean motives for the seizure were unclear, but they feared the event might be part of a larger DPRK move against the South. Secretary of State Dean Rusk noted, "although we didn't know why North Korea had seized the *Pueblo*, we feared that North Korea would move against South Korea, possibly believing that the United States was tied down in Vietnam and would not respond."[115] According to one scholar the seizure of USS *Pueblo* was not planned. The "success" of the *Pueblo* seizure offset many of the failed infiltration adventures, and Kim Il Sung was delighted to embarrass the United States. However, he and his generals "knew the price they had paid for such military adventurism" and realized they were fortunate to have avoided a direct confrontation with the United States.[116]

North Korean provocations, particularly those of 1968, were warning signs to U.S. and ROK officials and "pointed to the possibility that North Korea might be entering a new and more aggressive phase of the confrontation."[117] In response, the United States shifted from the preparations appropriate for a situation of general deterrence to more specific measures to demonstrate U.S. resolve. After the *Pueblo* seizure, President Johnson activated 15,000 reservists, increased U.S. combat and transport aircraft in Korea by 372 and deployed a large naval task force in the Sea of Japan.[118] The United States rushed specialists and key spare parts to U.S. troops in Korea, while ROK forces received shipments of new military hardware. The American government also believed it necessary to send a contingent of F-4 jets to the ROK Air Force, a plane capable of countering the recently introduced MiG-21, to "present dramatic evidence of the support of the United States Government to the Republic of Korea."[119]

President Johnson pledged $100 million in special military aid and reaffirmed the American commitment to defend South Korea. The ROK greatly strengthened its military capabilities with the acquisition of new equipment, undertook new and stronger measures to better their counter-infiltration capability, and established the Homeland Defense Reserve Force of more than two million men.[120]

By 1969, North Korea began to retreat from its militant strategy of infiltration and subversion. In congressional testimony, Ambassador Porter gave his assessment for the decrease in these operations after 1968. "I think initially they were losing too many trained men to go on the way they were. I think that probably somebody had to account in North Korea for the loss of the 120, and then, of course, the 31 who participated in the Blue House raid. . . . No doubt, someone had advocated that kind of program and someone had to explain the lack of success."[121] After the downing of an EC-121 spy plane, Kim Il Sung quietly removed a number of the generals that had urged more militant actions towards the United States and South Korea because they, according to one scholar, "were taking him to the brink too often and too recklessly."[122] In addition, North Korea became less caustic in its rhetoric and displayed a willingness to enter into negotiations with the ROK and the United States. Kim Il Sung had hoped that the infiltrations would organize and fire the revolutionary zeal of supporters in the South. U.S. Ambassador William Porter argued other reasons for these actions may include "an effort to impress the North Vietnamese that they were exerting pressure on the South, an effort also, perhaps, to destroy investor confidence inasmuch as the economy of the South at that time was beginning to show real strength and expansion."[123] The infiltrations were largely unsuccessful and the attempts to organize the South Korean populace made little progress.[124] Moreover, North Korean attempts at destabilization intensified fear and disdain in the South for Kim Il Sung's regime, making it more difficult to establish a foothold among the South Korean people.[125] Ultimately, North Korean agitation during the 1960s increased ROK vigilance to the North's provocations and strengthened the U.S. commitment to remain in the region.[126]

Whether Kim Il Sung was actually considering an attack in the late 1960s is unknown. Yet, U.S. leaders believed that the DPRK's actions, particularly the increased infiltration and subversion of the late 1960s, indicated that Kim might be considering an assault. In response, the United States made important adjustments in its extended deterrence policy as conditions appeared to be shifting from a situation of general deterrence towards immediate deterrence. By going beyond the previous preparations and making more specific demonstrations of U.S. resolve, American policy makers hoped they were persuading North Korea that any contemplation of invasion would be unwise. Though it is not certain whether U.S. policy was the determining factor, Kim Il Sung reevaluated his strategy of the 1960s and shifted to a different approach in the decade to follow.

1950s and 1960s: An Assessment

Deterrence theory often assumes the challenger to be a single entity. During the 1950s, that assumption fit U.S. assessments since the threat was perceived to be monolithic communism controlled from Moscow. However, the 1960s demonstrated that "the challenger" can be more complicated, composed of several challenger states possessing different goals, objectives, and capabilities. The threat was no longer monolithic; the two defenders, the Soviet Union and China, squabbled between themselves, and North Korea pursued an independent foreign policy that steered a course between the feuding patrons. Kim Il Sung began to have serious doubts concerning the reliability of his two defenders. U.S. leaders assumed that all three challengers maintained the goal of reunifying the peninsula. However, American assessments concluded that the Soviets and Chinese were less willing to take substantial risks to achieve reunification. Thus, "the challenger" was separating into distinct entities, making threat assessment more complicated.

While the United States was implementing a deterrence policy, North Korea appears to have been utilizing another strategy of coercive diplomacy, compellence. By the 1960s, the American defense commitment, especially the presence of U.S. troops, was a permanent fixture in Korea. With the United States already involved in a costly ground war in Vietnam, North Korean actions to destabilize the South tried to demonstrate the costs and possible risks of continued U.S. support for the ROK. By raising the potential costs—the prospect of fighting another war in Asia—Pyongyang hoped to compel the United States to abandon its support of the South. North Korea could turn up the pressure if the compellence strategy proved successful or turn it down if the United States or the ROK responded unfavorably. In either case, it is likely that North Korea viewed compellence as a strategy where they could manage carefully the level of risk to achieve reunification without starting a war.

To the North's dismay, the U.S. commitment remained firm. By 1969, Pyongyang's costs for continuing a compellence strategy were becoming unacceptably high—numerous failed commando raids, growing international isolation, and anti-communist sentiment in the South—while providing few benefits. Furthermore, it was unlikely Pyongyang could escalate the pressure without provoking an unacceptable U.S. response. Indeed, during the *Pueblo* incident, North Korea believed it had come dangerously close to an armed confrontation with the United States, and Washington had taken a number of measures to strengthen its commitment to the South. In the face of a determined U.S. commitment and fears that it could no longer be certain of controlling the risks involved, North Korea backed off its compellence strategy to pursue other courses of action.

1969-1979: The Buildup

Source

By 1969, Kim Il Sung adopted a more conciliatory approach, including a series of negotiations to reduce tension and move towards peaceful unification. Discussions between the two Koreas produced an agreement in July 1972 that declared three principles upon which both North and South Korea would strive for reunification. The joint communiqué stated:

> First, unification shall be attained independently, without reliance upon or interference from an external power. Second, unification shall be realized through peaceful means rather than the use of force. Third, both sides shall promote a great national unity as homogenous people, transcending differences in ideas, ideologies, and systems.[127]

Despite the potential improvement in North-South relations indicated by the communiqué, little in the agreement was ever implemented.

Although Kim Il Sung began these negotiations, he also initiated a major buildup of his military forces and began digging tunnels under the DMZ. U.S. intelligence agencies did not immediately recognize the extent of the buildup. However, by 1978-1979, the intelligence community was crediting North Korea with the fifth largest military in the world.[128]

The U.S. presence in Korea under conditions of general deterrence was based on the uncertainty of North Korean intentions and the fear engendered by sizable DPRK military capabilities. During the 1970s, North Korean actions did little to allay U.S. and ROK concerns about the North's intentions. By 1979, the DPRK military buildup and the assassination of South Korean President Park had U.S. leaders worried again that the situation in Korea was in danger of shifting from general towards immediate deterrence. Soon after the assassination, the State Department announced that the United States "will react strongly" to a North Korean attempt to exploit the political turmoil in the South.[129] The United States and ROK took other important steps such as sending additional aircraft, artillery, and other military equipment to bolster deterrence and dissuade the DPRK from contemplating an attack.[130]

As the North Korean threat became more troublesome in the 1970s, important changes had taken place in the support the DPRK received from its defenders. Moscow's backing for North Korea had already been lukewarm in the early 1960s. In 1962, the Soviets criticized North Korean economic policy and cut off all economic aid. Kim Il Sung responded by accusing the Soviets of "arrogance," "xenophobia," and "big-power chauvinism."[131] However, a few years later the North's dependence on sophisticated Soviet military equipment and Khrushchev's ouster in 1964 induced North Korea to repair relations. Despite these efforts, the Soviet Union provided little advanced weaponry to the North.

Kim Il Sung had other reasons to question the depth of Soviet support. After World War II, Stalin had made a virtual colony out of the North, but when the Korean War commenced, he quickly evacuated Soviet advisors. Khrushchev addressed this decision in his memoirs.

> It's absolutely incomprehensible to me why he [Stalin] did it, but when Kim Il-sung was preparing for his march, Stalin called back all our advisors who were with the North Korean divisions and regiments, as well as all the advisors who were serving as consultants and helping to build up the army. I asked Stalin about this, and he snapped back at me, "It's too dangerous to keep our advisors there. They might be taken prisoner. We don't want there to be evidence for accusing us of taking part in this business. It's Kim Il-sung's affair." So our advisors were recalled. As a result, the North Korean army was in trouble from the very start.[132]

Later, both Khrushchev and Brezhnev utilized political and economic pressure to coerce DPRK behavior.[133] Ever since October 1962, when the Soviets backed down from the United States over missiles in Cuba, Kim Il Sung doubted the reliability of Soviet support.

Although the Chinese continued to support North Korea, Kim also believed they were becoming less dependable. As Sino-U.S. relations began to thaw,

North Korea realized that its interests in unification were likely subordinate to Chinese interests in rapprochement.[134] In April 1975, Kim Il Sung traveled to Beijing with three senior military leaders, arousing suspicion that he was trying to obtain Chinese support for another invasion of South Korea. Though Kim Il Sung's motives were not certain, he apparently was not convincing since Chinese statements and the joint communiqué that followed the meeting stressed the need for "independent and peaceful reunification" of the peninsula.[135] Moreover, the Sino-Soviet split had become exceedingly tense, leading Kim to believe that henceforth, he could not count on either one for support, and would need to steer an independent course.

For North Korea, all of these events—the Sino-Soviet dispute, Soviet acquiescence in the Cuban missile crisis, Soviet-U.S. détente, and Sino-U.S. rapprochement—demonstrated that its allies were unreliable. Most likely Kim Il Sung believed his allies were very willing to "torpedo" North Korean reunification desires for the sake of their own interests. As a result, North Korea embarked on an extensive military buildup of its own to address these concerns.

The U.S. assessment of Soviet and Chinese intentions in Korea was not unlike that of the DPRK. American policy makers had believed for some time that the Soviet Union would not begin a conflict in Korea, and by the 1970s, concluded that both the Soviet Union and China had little interest in starting another war. In January 1979, the Secretary of Defense, Harold Brown, noted in a report that "the geopolitical situation of the North has changed substantially since 1950. . . . As far as we can tell, neither the Chinese nor the Soviets seem willing to lend support to any North Korean impulse for adventurous aggressive action."[136] This was an important change for U.S. threat assessments; now, U.S. leaders viewed North Korea as the chief threat to stability. U.S. policy makers recognized that a conflict in Korea could drag in China and the Soviets as the DPRK defenders, but they were no longer the chief worry to begin another war. The 1979 Defense Department report notes again that, "North Korea remains unpredictable: its military capabilities have grown, and it could disrupt the peace on the peninsula and embroil the great powers."[137] U.S.-Soviet and U.S.-Chinese relations had improved to the point where Washington believed that Moscow and Beijing were "prudent powers."[138] However, the military capability of North Korea and its belligerent behavior continued to be a serious concern.

Capabilities

During the 1970s, North Korea embarked on a substantial buildup of its conventional military forces. Intelligence estimates noted significant increases in several categories including troop strength, tanks, and artillery pieces. While the defense and intelligence communities had expected this rise, they seriously underestimated the magnitude of the buildup. In September 1976, when General Vessey assumed command of U.S. Forces in Korea, he received a briefing that pointed to a dramatic increase in North Korean armored strength.[139] After receiving other briefings that presented similar North Korean force estimates, in

January 1978, Vessey asked for a new evaluation of North Korean army strength. By May 1978, the CIA and DIA also began independent studies of the DPRK armed forces. In January 1979, some of the results of these studies became public. The new estimates indicated that DPRK ground force strength was 25 percent higher than previously believed.[140] North Korean tanks had increased by 35 percent while artillery tubes and APCs rose by about 20 percent.[141]

In previous estimates, North Korea was superior in air power, but the ROK was stronger on the ground. When U.S. forces in Korea were included, the military balance reflected a rough equivalence between the two sides. In 1976, the Pentagon's annual report noted "the 2nd Division in South Korea, along with the ROK forces on line, assures a solid front and a sufficiently favorable ratio of manpower and firepower to provide reasonable assurance that we could repulse any sudden attack from North Korea alone."[142] However, following the intelligence reassessments, the Pentagon was less sanguine about the military balance. In the FY 1980 Annual Report, the Defense Department noted that North Korean ground forces were "near parity" with the ROK. The report continued: "Given a strong defense by South Korean ground forces, however, and a heavy commitment of U.S. airpower, the North Koreans could not be assured of achieving decisive results in the initial days of their offensive."[143] The 1982 Defense Department Report concluded that the military balance between North and South Korea alone had shifted in favor of the North. However, "U.S. air and ground forces in the South produce a rough overall balance" but the DPRK buildup deserves "close watching to ensure that their short-term advantages do not tempt them into aggression and war."[144]

Table 2.2

NORTH AND SOUTH KOREAN MILITARY PERSONNEL, 1970 and 1979

	1970		1979	
	North	South	North	South
Total Armed Forces	413,000	645,000	632,000–672,000	619,000
Ground Forces	370,000	570,000	560,000–600,000	540,000

Source: *The Military Balance*, 1970-1971 and 1979-1980
Note: The 1979-1980 edition of *The Military Balance* gives DPRK force levels as a range

Across almost every category DPRK force levels rose from 20 percent to 30 percent. During the 1970s, North Korean troop levels rose somewhere between 53 and 63 percent, surpassing total South Korean forces for the first time. Most of these increases occurred in ground force personnel that showed a similar rise of between 51 percent and 62 percent. By 1980, North Korea also maintained 22 brigades of special forces, well-trained and capable of subversion and disruption behind enemy lines.[145] However, an analysis by Joseph Bermudez Jr. in *Jane's Defence Weekly* questions the effectiveness of these units, noting "a shortage of supply capabilities, lack of heavy weapons, and paucity of popular support."[146]

The North's growing troop strength was accompanied by increases in the number of tanks, APCs, artillery pieces, and rockets. By the late 1970s, the DPRK was producing its own modified version of the T-62. These additions gave North Korea significant advantages in firepower and mobility though many of the additions were "based largely on dated Soviet technology with retrofitted indigenous improvements."[147]

Table 2.3

NORTH AND SOUTH KOREAN MILITARY EQUIPMENT, 1970 and 1979

	1970	1979
Tanks		
North Korea	750: 600 T-34/54/55/59 150 PT-76	2,300: 350 T-34 1,800 T-54/55 100 PT-76; 50 T-62
South Korea	2 Armored Brigades: M-48, M-4, M-24	860: 60 M-60 800 M-47/48
APC's		
North Korea	*	800
South Korea	*	520
Artillery/Missile Systems		
North Korea	200 SU-76 100 SP assault guns 6,000 other guns/mortars 300 SA missiles	3,500 guns/howitzers 9,000 mortars 9 FROG-5 SSMs 1,300 rocket launchers 250 SA missiles
South Korea	80 artillery battalions 2 sqd, Hawk SAMs 1 btn, Honest John SSMs	2,000 105 mm, 155 mm, 203, towed 1 btn, Honest John SSMs 102 self-propelled howitzers 1 btn, Nike-Hercules SAMs

Source: *The Military Balance*, 1970-1971 and 1979-1980
Note: * data not included in *The Military Balance*

The North Korean Navy also increased in size and capability, more than doubling its personnel from 13,000 in 1970 to 27,000 in 1979. Pyongyang acquired eleven more submarines bringing the total to fifteen. Along with the procurement of three frigates and other vessels, the DPRK Navy was now capable of "anti-shipping, amphibious raiding and mining operations in South Korean waters."[148] Though South Korea began work on countering this threat, the ROK relied heavily on U.S. naval and air support to confront DPRK naval assets should war break out.

North Korean air power, an area where the DPRK already held a large advantage, had the smallest increase. The number of combat aircraft remained essentially the same, however, Pyongyang replaced some older planes with the more modern MiG-21. The South Korean Air Force increased from 200 to 254 planes and made important strides in modernizing its force by acquiring more F-4s and F-5s and reducing the number of Korean War vintage F-86s. Though these qualitative improvements offset a share of the DPRK's numerical advantage, the ROK still needed U.S. air power.

Table 2.4

NORTH AND SOUTH KOREAN COMBAT AIRCRAFT, 1970 and 1979

		1970		1979
North Korea	580:	70 IL-28	565:	85 IL-28
		60 MiG-15		20 SU-7
		340 MiG-17		40 MiG-15/17
		20 MiG-19		300 MiG-15/17/19
		90 MiG-21		120 MiG-21
South Korea	200:	15 F-4	254:	37 F-4
		100 F-86F		135 F-5
		55 F-5		50 F-86F
		20 F-86D		12 RF-5A
		10 RF-86F		20 ASW S-2F

Source: *The Military Balance*, 1970-1971 and 1979-1980

The DPRK force buildup exacerbated other long-standing concerns. The location of Seoul, approximately twenty-five miles from the DMZ and vulnerable to a sudden strike from the North, constitutes a difficult problem for the defense of South Korea. Consequently, the North has a credible threat of punishment—North Korean artillery could shell the southern capital from positions close to the DMZ—since it could seriously damage Seoul even if it could not conquer the entire peninsula. The DPRK would also have the benefits of tactical surprise.[149] One analyst gave South Korean and U.S. forces only an estimated 12 hours warning of a North Korean invasion. Another analyst has indicated the warning could be even less since "the North Korean counterintelligence screen is so effective that a three-dimensional attack could be launched with no more than a few hours' warning."[150] During the 1970s, the North forward deployed an increasing share of its forces close to the DMZ, maintaining a high degree of readiness. U.S. officials regarded the deployments as threatening and clearly "not geared for defensive operations."[151]

Despite North Korean numerical advantages, Pyongyang also had several liabilities. North Korea maintained an advantage over the South in APCs (800 to 520), but this was only enough to motorize a small portion of North Korean infantry.[152] There were also questions whether North Korean tanks, many of which were produced indigenously, were equal to ROK and U.S. counterparts. In particular, the T-34 was outdated and the T-62, a Chinese version, was more appropriately classified as a light tank and was inferior to the M-48 and M-60. Also, the PT-76 was a light amphibious tank.[153]

The terrain these weapons needed to traverse for an invasion of the South further limited North Korean numerical advantages in armor, artillery, and APCs. The geography of the DMZ consists of numerous mountain ranges running in a north-south direction. Consequently, only a few invasion routes extend into South Korea. American and ROK military planners believed an invasion would most likely come through either the Kaesong-Munsan route, which is north of Seoul, or the Chorwon Valley to the northeast.[154] Other routes further east have been discounted because of even more mountainous terrain and the lack of any significant military objectives. However, while confining North Korean invasion routes, the north-south mountains also hinder the South's ability to rapidly shift reinforcements to counter a concentrated DPRK thrust at a particular point.

In 1950, North Korean forces used the Chorwon approach to invade the South, but the war altered the borders making this a more difficult passage. Before the Korean War, the border was the 38th parallel, which extended farther south in this area than the current border. This more southerly border meant North Korea had less of the Chorwon Valley to travel on the South Korean side. The current border, which angles north from the 38th parallel, would confine North Korean forces to the relatively narrow valley in hostile territory for a much longer period of time. U.S. and ROK military officials concluded that this route was too dangerous and that the likely invasion corridor was through the Kaesong-Munsan corridor that leads more directly to Seoul.[155]

Abandoning a plan that would trade Seoul for time, U.S.-ROK military planners devised a strategy of forward defense named, "the Hollingsworth Line," that seeks to halt a North Korean invasion before Seoul is overrun. Heavy fortifications along the likely invasion corridors would put North Korean forces through a "meat grinder," stopping the assault before reaching Seoul.[156] While being an effective strategy if deterrence failed, this factor also discouraged the North from attacking in the first place.

A North Korean attack through the Kaesong-Munsan route, or the Chorwon Valley as well, would run a gauntlet of heavily fortified positions, consisting of South Korean forces equipped with anti-armor precision guided munitions and U.S.-ROK air support; these would bring devastating fire down on the invasion force as it passed through the valley. Despite large advantages in armor and other weapons, the terrain and U.S.-ROK firepower would limit the number of tanks North Korea could bring to bear in these narrow invasion corridors.

In October 1979, the head of the Korean Central Intelligence Agency assassinated South Korean President Park. U.S. officials feared North Korea might try to capitalize on the event, prompting the State Department to warn, "The United States Government wishes to make clear that it will react strongly in accordance with its treaty obligations to the Republic of Korea to any external attempt to exploit the situation in the Republic of Korea."[157] Sensing a potential shift towards immediate deterrence conditions, U.S. forces increased surveillance of North Korea to detect significant troop movements and raised the alert status of American military personnel in Korea to DEFCON 3 or "Defense Readiness Condition Three."[158] DEFCON is a graduated numbering system used to designate the alert status of U.S. armed forces. The system ranges from DEFCON 5 (normal readiness during peacetime) to DEFCON 1 (a severe emergency with war imminent). Not all U.S. forces are on the same level of alert at any given time. U.S. forces in South Korea are always on DEFCON 4 alert. Later, the Carter administration took additional steps to reinforce the U.S. deterrence posture by sending a squadron of F-4s, some AWACS planes, longer-range artillery, improved helicopter gunships, and a squadron of A-10 aircraft.[159] Together, these measures helped to "bolster deterrence and redress deficiencies in ROK defenses."[160]

While the North Korean military buildup of the 1970s was troublesome to U.S. defense officials, they remained optimistic that combined U.S. and ROK forces were sufficient to dissuade the North from attacking and were capable of defeating the attack, should deterrence fail. A 1980 Defense Department report noted that, despite the increased force levels, "North Korea would not have an easy time of it in trying to reach Seoul. Its forces would have to break through or otherwise circumvent extensive fortifications, and defeat strong South Korean forces." With U.S. and ROK tactical air power and the U.S. ground presence, "the deterrent on the Korean peninsula continues to look reasonably firm."[161]

Intentions

Though the United States remained cautiously optimistic about the military balance, more troubling was the possibility that the North Korean buildup signaled a change of intent in Pyongyang. In a 1980 press release, Kim Il Sung maintained:

> We must do away with the colonial fascist rule of the U.S. imperialists and their stooges in South Korea and reunify the country, and thus end the distress and tragedy of our fellow countrymen and carve out a bright future for our nation. If reunification does not come quickly and division continues, our nation will remain bisected forever, and the South Korean people will be unable to cast off the yoke of colonial slavery.[162]

Was the DPRK again willing to risk the use of force? In 1980, the Defense Department mused, "the intentions of North Korea are unclear, but its military forces clearly are not geared for defensive operations. Such a force is hardly conducive to stability on the Korean Peninsula."[163]

A 1979 press report quoted a U.S. official as saying, "every political animal says North Korea isn't going to start anything, but every military animal asks, why are they building this force?"[164] The military buildup only made it more ambiguous whether the North would resort to force to unify Korea. The North had not given an indication of imminent attack, yet the buildup made hostilities appear more dangerous. General Vessey noted in a 1979 statement to a Congressional committee that

> the North seems to be relying on the "wait and see option" while refining its capabilities to exercise the attack option. No one can predict with assurance whether Kim will resort to war to achieve his long-standing goal. We can only point to the very costly preparations that he has made and make all reasonable efforts ourselves to make deterrence effective.[165]

Thus, North Korean intentions remained unclear and the military buildup exacerbated concerns in the region.

In addition to increased military capabilities, North Korea demonstrated its potential for aggression in other ways. Moving on information obtained from a North Korean defector, ROK officials discovered in 1974, the first of three tunnels dug under the DMZ leading from North to South Korea. The other tunnels were discovered in 1975 and 1978 with information pointing to the existence of possibly twelve additional tunnels. The third tunnel measured approximately six feet in diameter. A South Korean government publication noted that this tunnel was large enough for "moving a full division per hour, plus their weapons."[166] ROK authorities found a fourth tunnel in March 1990. According to United Nations Command information, this tunnel was discovered twenty-six kilometers northeast of Yanggu in Kangwon-do province and is the first tunnel found in the eastern sector of the DMZ.[167] While found in 1990, this tunnel may have been completed much earlier. U.S. military officials feared the possible use of these tunnels to place special forces behind ROK lines either prior to or during an invasion. The tunnels known to U.S. and ROK authorities were easily neutralized. However, those that remain undiscovered could be a serious military liability.[168] In 2004, the South Korean Ministry of National Defense reported that North Korea was constructing 80 new tunnels, not necessarily across the DMZ, a likely response to U.S. air strikes by Stealth fighters during the Iraq war.[169]

Other incidents during the 1970s provoked concern. In August 1974 an assassin, presumably North Korean, attempted to kill President Park while giving a speech. The President escaped injury, but his wife was shot and killed in the attempt. In August 1976, North Korean soldiers killed two American servicemen at Panmunjom in the DMZ, the site of ongoing talks to maintain the 1953 armistice. Were these events an indication that Kim Il Sung was contemplating an attack? As these events unfolded, the Carter administration signaled its firm support for the ROK, sending additional aircraft and other military equipment to ROK and U.S. forces in Korea. President Carter also suspended his plan to withdraw U.S. ground forces. Thus, the Carter administration took measures to prevent the situation from shifting from general deterrence to one of immediate deterrence.

One more aspect of the North Korean threat needs discussion here. While North Korean military preparations and actions appear aggressive and menacing, there is another possible interpretation of its motives. Rather than indicating offensive intent, the North Korean military buildup and forward deployment may have been part of a defensive strategy directed against U.S. and ROK forces that Pyongyang believed might one day decide to reunify the peninsula by force. In 1979, Representative Les Aspin, member of the Select Committee on Intelligence, testified before the House Armed Services Committee noting that one possibility for the DPRK buildup is:

> the North Koreans fear a South Korean attack, perhaps a farfetched idea to many Americans, but not an unreasonable interpretation considering (a) the intense insularity and paranoia of the Kim Il-sung regime and (b) a 1974 CIA study allegedly concluding that the ROK might provoke a war with the North if President Park Chung-hee felt that his government was in danger of being toppled by radical forces from within.[170]

In fact, U.S. and ROK forces are similarly forward deployed so that DPRK preparations also focus on defending the forward area between the DMZ and Pyongyang to deter and prevent any deep incursions into its territory. U.S. nuclear weapons deployments further complicated the North's calculus, providing important motivation to match U.S.-ROK capabilities. This is also one of the reasons North Korea began to pursue its own nuclear weapons program. Thus, U.S. efforts to enhance deterrence in Korea with nuclear weapons may have provoked the North into escalating the stakes by forward deploying massive conventional forces as well as developing a nuclear option.

In addition to deterring a possible invasion, DPRK forward deployment may be the result of an inadequate transportation system. According to North Korean military defectors, a majority of the North Korean army must supply their own food from farms and dairies operated by individual units. A poor transportation system made it difficult to transport food from one region to the next. Since the best agricultural regions are in the western areas of the North, these military units may have been deployed there to simplify distribution.[171]

The North was also aware that the South Korean economy had begun to outpace their own, allowing Seoul to devote sizeable resources to its military. While South Korea was spending approximately 6 percent of its GNP on defense and receiving considerable military aid, the North was spending close to 20 percent of its GNP on defense despite receiving aid from China and the Soviet Union.

Finally, North Korea was also feeling isolated as its defenders provided them with decreasing military and diplomatic support. Without a strong extended deterrence commitment and assurances from its defenders, North Korea very likely believed it needed to build up its own military capability and assume a self-reliant posture in political, economic, and security matters. *Juche*, or self-reliance, continued to be a cornerstone of North Korean policy.

In short, it is plausible that North Korea, threatened by U.S.-ROK deployments, fearful of ROK military and economic progress, and abandoned by its defenders, felt it necessary to build up its own independent military capability. Certainly, North Korea concluded it had security threats; most states do. However, it would have been difficult for U.S. policy makers to appreciate this conclusion. Thus, U.S. and DPRK leaders had different interpretations of the North's military buildup. Given the 1950 invasion and the provocations of the 1960s and 1970s, U.S. planners could not assume the North Korean military buildup was purely "defensive." With the tunnels, assassination attempts, and continuing incidents along the DMZ, U.S.-ROK authorities had little evidence to indicate that DPRK had abandoned its goal to unify the peninsula and might exploit an opportunity should the U.S. deterrence commitment wane. As noted by a State Department official, "in light of North Korea's past actions and its present capabilities, simple prudence requires that we and the Republic of Korea maintain a strong and credible military deterrent."[172]

1980-1991: To the End of the Cold War

North Korean military capabilities continued to grow in the next decade. By 1990, DPRK total military personal exceeded 1.1 million soldiers, creating one of the most militarized nations in the world. U.S. officials believed North Korea had not relinquished its goal of forceful reunification, and new acts of terrorism sustained U.S. assessments of DPRK hostile intent. In 1989 congressional testimony, Carl W. Ford Jr., Principle Deputy Assistant Secretary of Defense noted: "Even today, there are no indications that the Pyongyang regime has abandoned its goal of uniting the peninsula under communist rule, by force of arms, if necessary." [173]

U.S. policy makers also faced some new challenges. By the end of the 1980s, suspicion was growing that North Korea was vigorously pursuing a nuclear weapons program. In 1991, the dissolution of the Soviet Union altered the challenger configuration again. Finally, on 8 July 1994, the longtime ruler of North Korea, Kim Il Sung, died at the age of 82. For a time, the transition to power of Kim Jong Il, Kim Il Sung's son and hand-picked heir, and the overall future direction of North Korea after the death of the "Great Leader" remained in doubt.

Source

Though China and the Soviet Union remained supporters of the DPRK, U.S. leaders continued to view their threat to South Korea as minimal. Concerning the Chinese, one analyst noted, "although the Chinese are willing to go a long way to maintain friendly relations with the DPRK, they have no desire to support North Korean aggression against South Korea."[174] While Beijing publicly supported DPRK demands for a U.S. troop withdrawal from Korea, China did not demand immediate removal, viewing the U.S. presence as a stabilizing factor. A 1979 press report noted that Carter's plan to withdraw U.S. ground forces from Korea evoked concern from Chinese military leaders. According to the report, "the military leaders in Peking appreciate what one termed the stabilizing influence of an American military presence in South Korea and its role as a restraint on Soviet adventures."[175] Moreover, Chinese-South Korean trade ties grew from $18.8 million in 1979 to $1.5 billion in 1987.[176] A 1980 Defense Department report noted that "a strong, secure, and modernizing China is in the interest of the United States" and "we expect . . . that our relationship with the PRC will grow in scope and detail."[177] A 1986 Defense Department report noted: "Building a stable relationship and cooperating in China's modernization is an important element of U.S. strategy for the region" and that "U.S.-PRC military cooperation can enhance China's security and promote a stable regional environment."[178] Though China continued cordial relations with North Korea, Beijing did not wish to see its relations with the ROK and the United States disrupted by a war in Korea.

In December 1979, the Soviet invasion of Afghanistan rekindled U.S. fears of Soviet expansion. In 1982, the Pentagon reported "one of the most demanding challenges facing the United States in the 1980s will be to develop and demonstrate the capability to deter or defeat Soviet and other aggression against U.S. vital interests in the region [East Asia]."[179] Yet, while U.S.-Soviet relations remained tense during the early 1980s, U.S. threat assessments for Korea contained few references of a Soviet danger to the South. U.S. statements typically focused on the North as the "primary threat" in Korea.

In 1985, Mikhail Gorbachev became general secretary and, soon after, initiated several actions that improved Soviet-South Korean relations. For example, despite Pyongyang's intention to boycott the 1988 Summer Olympics in Seoul, Moscow announced the year before that it would attend the games. In 1988, the USSR and the ROK established trade offices in each other's country that helped encourage annual trade to increase from $85 million in 1985 to $1 billion by 1990. In 1990, Moscow and Seoul announced the establishment of full diplomatic relations, and a year later Gorbachev indicated that the Soviet Union would support South Korean membership in the United Nations.[180] According to one scholar, "under Gorbachev, Moscow's 'love-hate relationship' with North Korea reversed. Moscow increasingly alienated its traditional ally—North Korea—and cultivated friendship and cooperative relations with its former enemy—South Korea."[181] Further change was coming in 1992 with the dissolution of the Soviet Union and the end of the Cold War.

These events significantly altered the security environment in Korea. There was little indication Russia would support aggressive North Korean behavior. Moscow favored stability on the Korean Peninsula and sought closer economic ties with the South. Thus, the links between Russia and North Korea as defender and protégé became weaker.

For the United States and the ROK, North Korea remained the chief threat to peace in the region. In 1981, Secretary of Defense Harold Brown maintained, "North Korea has undertaken a sustained military buildup during the 1970s, which, relative to the population and economy, exceeds anything else in the region and poses the main military threat to stability in Northeast Asia."[182] In 1990, Defense Secretary Richard Cheney warned, "the threat to peace of the Peninsula has not changed. The significant military offensive capability of North Korea still provides them the ability to attack at a time and place of their choosing."[183]

Capabilities

The military strength of North Korea continued to grow at impressive rates during the 1980s. By 1990, the total armed forces of the DPRK had grown from 678,000 in 1980 to 1,111,000, a 68 percent increase. Most of this increase occurred in the army where force levels rose from 600,000 to one million. Army personnel included 80,000 soldiers in special operations forces. The DPRK also maintained a reserve force of 5 million. South Korean personnel grew during the 1980s though by more modest amounts that continued to lag behind those of the North. In 1980, the ROK had a total of 600,600 men under arms with 543,000 in army and marine units. By 1990, ROK total forces had increased to 750,000 with 675,000 in ground force units.

Table 2.5

NORTH AND SOUTH KOREAN MILITARY PERSONNEL, 1989-1990

	North	*South*
Total Armed Forces	1,111,000	750,000
Ground Forces	1,000,000	675,000

Source: *The Military Balance*, 1989-1990

North Korea also made significant improvements in its military equipment by acquiring more tanks, APCs, and artillery pieces. From 1980 to 1990 the number of tanks rose from 860 to 1,550, APCs from 1,000 to 4,000, and artillery pieces from 4,000 to 5,800. North Korean artillery had better range and more rapid firing rates than those of the South.[184] Also, North Korean tanks were "larger and more modern than those of the ROK."[185] The advantages in tanks were offset partially by an improving anti-armor capability, particularly ROK acquisition of TOW (Tube-launched, Optically-tracked, Wire-guided) missiles and AH-1 Cobra helicopters from the United States. In 1989, ROK armor was upgraded with the first delivery of a locally produced version of the M-1A1 Abrams tank. Moreover, the mountainous terrain limited the number of DPRK tanks that could be utilized at any given location. Finally, U.S. and ROK officials believed that North Korea had acquired a chemical weapons capability.[186] Since the North possessed the missiles to deliver chemical warheads at long ranges, this was a particularly dangerous weapon.

Table 2.6

NORTH AND SOUTH KOREAN MILITARY EQUIPMENT, 1989-1990

		North		*South*
Tanks	4,150	200 T-34	1,500	250 Type-88
		1,600 T-54/55		350 M-47
		1,500 T-62		95 M-48A5
		179 Type-59		
		650 light tanks		
Armored Personnel Carriers		4,000		1,550
Artillery		2,500 towed artillery		4,000 towed artillery
		3,300 self-propelled		
Multiple Rocket Launchers		2,300		140
SSMs		54 FROG 3/5/7		12 Honest Johns
		some SCUD Bs		
Naval Vessels		24 submarines		3 submarines
		3 frigates		9 destroyers
		364 patrol/coastal ships		25 frigates
				81 patrol/coastal ships
Combat Aircraft	716	*Ground Attack:*	469	*Ground Attack:*
		290 J-5/6 & Q-5		204 F-5
		20 Su-7; 20 Su-5		48 F-16
		Fighters:		*Fighters:*
		180 J-5/6/7		128 F-4
		120 MiG-21; 46 MiG-23		
		30 MiG-29		

Source: *The Military Balance*, 1989-1990

North Korean combat aircraft showed only a modest increase of 17 percent going from 615 planes in 1980 to 716 in 1990. Yet, Pyongyang's acquisition of MiG-29s in 1989, the most advanced fighter in the Soviet inventory, worried the Pentagon.[187] These fears were countered by ROK deployment of the F-16, "an aircraft believed to be technologically superior to similarly designed communist aircraft, including the Soviet-produced MiG-29, the most sophisticated aircraft employed by the North Korean air force," helped to even the equation.[188] The Soviets also supplied the North with modern air defense systems, providing the

DPRK with the best air defense outside the Soviet Union.[189] U.S. officials feared these acquisitions signaled a new level of Soviet-North Korean cooperation.

North Korean naval strength grew during the 1980s, though not nearly in the same proportion as ground forces. U.S. and ROK leaders were particularly concerned with the increased number of submarines. With these craft, the North could attack ROK shipping on which Seoul depended for economic and military supplies. The South developed an anti-submarine capability, but likely needed some U.S. help in this area should war break out.

The North Koreans also built a large indigenous arms industry that manufactures most of their own military equipment except for technically advanced items such as combat aircraft. The military also began production of ballistic missiles by reverse engineering Soviet-designed Scud missiles acquired from Egypt. The defense industries are controlled by the military and most of the profits remain in the military sector. North Korea produces its own artillery and tanks, as well as all of its small arms. Estimates indicate production from the North's weapons industry, along with the stockpiling of equipment, gave Pyongyang the capability to fight without outside support for approximately three months.[190] However, if a conflict lasted for any extended period of time, the North Koreans would have been hard-pressed to sustain their fighting capability.

To offset DPRK improvements, the South launched a major force modernization program aided by U.S. Foreign Military Sales credits. These modernization efforts included the acquisition of the F-16, more A-10 aircraft, TOW missiles, and the Type-88 tank, a ROK version of the M-1A1. Seoul also upgraded most of its M-48 tanks and more than doubled the number of artillery pieces from 2,000 to 4,200 while increasing the size of its guns for increased range.[191]

In the early 1980s, the United States believed that the DPRK buildup had shifted the military balance in favor of the North. The one exception was air power where DPRK aircraft were "generally older and inferior to the ROK/USAF assets."[192] Yet, when U.S. air and ground forces were factored in, Defense Department officials believed "a rough overall balance" existed in Korea.

By 1989, Pentagon assessments of the military balance were more favorable, but still cautious. According to one Pentagon report, "North Korea continues inexorably to modernize its large military forces" and "the current overall balance of military forces on the [Korean] peninsula continues to favor the North."[193] However, the report maintained, ROK modernization efforts, spurred by an economy that was four times the size of the North's, was offsetting "the North's considerable numerical superiority."[194] Continued U.S. support, particularly air power, was necessary but "ROK forces are becoming increasingly self-sufficient in their capability to defend against North Korea."[195] Concern remained that the North's forward deployment of its forces gave them the ability to initiate a sudden surge that could grab Seoul. However, in a conflict that lasted more than a few months, ROK economic strength and other U.S. assets that would be introduced into the region made North Korean success unlikely. In the final analysis, the Pentagon concluded, "U.S. and ROK forces are capable of blunting a North Korean attack and restoring the Republic of Korea's territorial integrity."[196]

Intentions

The U.S. assessment of North Korean intent changed little during the 1980s. According to a State Department official, Pyongyang gave "no credible evidence that the North has abandoned the goal of reunifying Korea on its own terms," and remains "generally isolated and is widely seen as an unpredictable, if not bizarre actor on the world stage whose behavior flouts international law and traditional norms."[197] Appropriate to conditions of general deterrence, in 1989, the Pentagon noted that "North Korean armed forces continue to prepare for a military reunification of the Korean peninsula should circumstances prove favorable."[198]

Two serious terrorist actions taken against South Korea reinforced U.S. concerns and helped land North Korea on the U.S. State Department list of countries that sponsor terrorism. In 1983, a bomb planted by North Korean agents exploded in Rangoon, Burma, an effort to assassinate South Korean President Chun Doo Hwan. The bomb detonated prematurely and did not injure President Chun. However, seventeen other Koreans that were part of the President's entourage, including four cabinet members, were killed by the blast. In 1987, Korean Airlines flight 858 was downed over the Gulf of Thailand by a bomb on board. Again, North Korea was believed to be responsible, another indication to U.S. and ROK officials of North Korea's hostile intent. ROK leaders surmised that the North was attempting to disrupt upcoming presidential elections on 16 December 1987 and the Olympic games scheduled for fall 1988.[199] Prior to the 1988 Summer Olympic games held in Seoul, there was great concern that North Korea might attempt further terrorist actions to disturb the proceedings. Though it's not clear why, North Korea did not interfere with the Olympics.

Conclusion

Though deterrence theory often assumes the challenger is a single entity, in Korea in these early years, this was not case. The challenger was composed of a more complex configuration of North Korea, China, and the Soviet Union. As the years passed, North Korea emerged as the chief concern, demonstrating an evolutionary nature to the configuration. Pyongyang's emergence as the chief threat was also accompanied by a significant increase in its conventional military capability.

Throughout these years, evaluating North Korean intentions remained problematic. U.S. threat assessments since the 1950s assumed that it was difficult to understand Kim Il Sung's motivation, and that he might behave irrationally. Typical was an assessment by the Defense Department in the 1970s that "our intelligence does not pretend to understand the convolutions of Kim Il Sung's mind."[200] Though at times U.S. and ROK officials fretted about the regional military balance and their ability to influence the strategic calculations of North Korean leadership, overall, they were relatively confident of that balance and their ability to deter North Korean aggression.

Beginning in the 1990s, an important shift began to occur in the nature and perceptions of the North Korean threat. In addition to continuing concerns for the conventional military balance, North Korea generated increasing worries over its production and export of ballistic missiles and its possible development of nuclear weapons. These were significant changes in the nature of the threat and had an important impact on U.S. security policy.

Notes

1. Dean Rusk, *As I Saw It* (New York: W.W. Norton, 1990), 161.

2. Douglas Jehl, "C.I.A. Opens Files On Cold War Era," *New York Times*, 1 October 1993, A7.

3. "Truman's Statement on the Korean War, June 27, 1950," in Henry Steele Commager, ed., *Documents in American History*, Volume II (New York: Appleton-Century-Crofts, 1962), 560-561.

4. As quoted in Walter LaFeber, *The American Age: U.S. Foreign Policy at Home and Abroad* (New York: W.W. Norton, 1994), 512.

5. "Intelligence Estimate Prepared by the Estimates Group, Office of Intelligence Research," 25 June 1950, *FRUS, 1950*, VII, 148-154.

6. Rusk, *As I Saw It*, 166.

7. "Memoranda of National Security Council Consultants' Meeting, 29 June 1950, 11:30 a.m. and 2:00 p.m.," *FRUS, 1950*, I, 324-330.

8. "Report by the National Security Council, NSC 73/4," 25 August 1950, *FRUS 1950*, I, 378.

9. "Report by the National Security Council, NSC 73/4," *FRUS 1950*, I, 380.

10. "Report by the National Security Council, NSC 73/4," *FRUS 1950*, I, 380.

11. "Memorandum of National Security Council Consultants' Meeting," 29 June 1950, *FRUS 1950*, I, 325 and 330.

12. "Memorandum of National Security Council Consultants' Meeting," 29 June 1950, *FRUS 1950*, I, 325 and 330. In response to this concern, Truman sent the 7th fleet to the Taiwan Strait.

13. "Statement of Policy Proposed by the National Security Council on United States Objectives and Courses of Action in Korea, NSC 118/2," 20 December 1951, *FRUS, 1951*, VII, 1384.

14. "Statement of Policy Proposed by the National Security Council on United States Objectives and Courses of Action in Korea, NSC 118/2," 20 December 1951, *FRUS, 1951*, VII, 1396-1397.

15. "Statement of Policy Proposed by the National Security Council on United States Objectives and Courses of Action in Korea, NSC 118/2," 20 December 1951, *FRUS, 1951*, VII, 1396-1397.

16. "Memorandum by John Foster Dulles to Dwight D. Eisenhower," 26 November 1952, *FRUS, 1952-1954*, XV, Korea, part 1, 692.

17. U.S. Senate, "Appendix IV: Declaration of the Sixteen Nations Relating to the Armistice," 27 July 1953, *Mutual Defense Treaty With Korea*, Hearings before the Committee on Foreign Relations, 83rd Congress, 2nd Session, January 13 and 14, 1954, 58. Hereafter cited as *Mutual Defense Treaty Hearings* (1954).

18. Dwight D. Eisenhower, *Public Papers of the President, 1957* (Washington, D.C.: Government Printing Office, 1958), 385-396. Hereafter, this series will be cited as *Public Papers*.

19. "Special National Intelligence Estimate," 5 March 1954, *FRUS, 1952-1954*, XV, 1759. Throughout the documents in this volume, as well as *FRUS, 1955-1957*, there is continual reference to "the Communists," a designation that included the North Koreans, the Chinese, and the Soviets.

20. John Foster Dulles, "The Evolution of Foreign Policy," *Department of State Bulletin*, XXX, no. 761, 25 January 1954, 107-110.

21. "Minutes of the Fourth Meeting of US-ROK Talks," 30 July 1954, *FRUS, 1952-1954*, XV, part 2, 1858.

22. "Memorandum of Discussion at the 318th Meeting of the National Security Council," 31 January 1957, *FRUS, 1955-1957*, XXIII, part 2, 394.

23. Dwight D. Eisenhower, "Radio and Television Report to the American People Regarding the Situation in the Formosa Straits," 11 September 1958, *Public Papers, 1958*, 261.

24. Dwight E. Eisenhower, "Special Message to Congress Concerning Increased Aid for the Republic of Korea," 27 July 1953, *Public Papers, 1953*, 523-524.

25. "Radio and Television Report to the American People on the Cost of Their Government," 14 May 1957, *Public Papers, 1957*, 341-352.

26. "Report on the Counter-Subversive Capacity of the Republic of Korea," 30 April 1955, *FRUS, 1955-1957*, XXIII, part 2, 74-80.

27. "Report on the Counter-Subversive Capacity of the Republic of Korea," 30 April 1955, *FRUS, 1955-1957*, XXIII, part 2, 74-80.

28. "Report on the Counter-Subversive Capacity of the Republic of Korea," 30 April 1955, *FRUS, 1955-1957*, XXIII, part 2, 74-80.

29. An intelligence estimate on probable developments in the Republic of Korea through mid-1957, title and date not declassified but is listed in February 1956, *FRUS, 1955-1957*, XXIII, part 2, 215-217.

30. A contemporary intelligence estimate on probable developments in North Korea over the next few years, title and date remain classified, listed in July 1956, *FRUS, 1955-1957*, XXIII, part 2, 286-289.

31. "Memorandum of a Conversation," 18 June 1955, *FRUS, 1955-1957*, XXIII, part 2, 114-116.

32. Later, Mao Zedong also "put forward the opinion that the USA would not intervene since the war would be an internal matter which the Korean people would decide for themselves." Nikita Khrushchev, *Khrushchev Remembers*, translated and edited by Strobe Talbott (Boston: Little, Brown, 1970), 368.

33. Gregory F.T. Winn, "Riding the Tiger: Military Confrontation on the Korean Peninsula," in *U.S.-Korean Relations, 1882-1982*, eds. Tae-Hwan Kwak, et al. (Seoul: Kyungnam University Press, 1982), 266.

34. "National Intelligence Estimate-80, Communist Capabilities and Probable Courses of Action in Korea," *FRUS, 1952-1954*, XV, part 2, 874-875.

35. Byung Chul Koh, "The Korean War as a Learning Experience for North Korea," *Korea and World Affairs* 3, no. 3 (Fall 1979): 377.

36. Winn, "Riding the Tiger," 266.

37. Koh, "The Korean War as a Learning Experience for North Korea," 377.

38. A contemporary intelligence estimate on probable developments in North Korea over the next few years, title and date remain classified, listed in July 1956, *FRUS, 1955-1957*, XXIII, part 2, 286-289.

39. "Memorandum by the Joint Chiefs of Staff to the Secretary of Defense (Wilson)," 31 March 1954, *FRUS, 1952-1954*, XV, part 2, 1784.

40. The following excerpts of the Armistice were taken from *Department of State Bulletin*, XXIX, No. 736, 3 August 1953, 132-139.

41. "Memorandum From the Officer in Charge of Korean Affairs to the Director of the Office of Northeast Asian Affairs," 1 October 1956, *FRUS, 1955-1957*, XXIII, part 2, 315-320.

42. The full text of this announcement can be found in Paul E. Zinner, ed., *Documents on American Foreign Relations, 1957* (New York: Council on Foreign Relations, 1958), 332-334.

43. This comment is part of a footnote to NSC 5702/2, a "Statement of U.S. Policy Toward Korea." See "National Security Council Report," 9 August 1957, *FRUS, 1955-1957*, XXIII, part 2, 489-498.

44. A contemporary intelligence estimate on probable developments in North Korea over the next few years, title and date remain classified, listed in June or July 1956, Ibid., 286-289.

45. "The Commander in Chief, Far East to the Chief of Staff, U.S. Army," 5 July 1954, *FRUS, 1952-1954*, XV, part 2, 1822-1825.

46. "The Commander in Chief, Far East to the Chief of Staff, U.S. Army," 5 July 1954, *FRUS, 1952-1954*, XV, part 2, 1822-1825.

47. Comments given by President Eisenhower in "Memorandum of Discussion at the 173d Meeting of the National Security Council," 3 December 1953, *FRUS, 1952-1954*, XV, part 2, 1636-1644.

48. "Memorandum of Discussion at the 173d Meeting of the National Security Council," 3 December 1953, *FRUS, 1952-1954*, XV, part 2, 1636-1644.

49. "Memorandum by the Joint Chiefs of Staff and the Department of State to the Executive Secretary of the National Security Council," 7 January 1954, *FRUS, 1952-1954*, XV, part 2, 1700-1703. Similar statements are also contained in NSC 5702/2, which was the current policy statement regarding Korea. See *FRUS, 1955-1957*, XXIII, part 2, 9 August 1957, 489-498.

50. A contemporary intelligence estimate on probable developments in North Korea over the next few years, title and date remain classified, listed in June or July 1956, *FRUS, 1955-1957*, XXIII, part 2, 286-289.

51. "United States Objectives and Courses of Action with Respect to Korea," 29 December 1954, *FRUS, 1952-1954*, XV, 1950.

52. "National Security Council Report - NSC 5514," 25 February 1955, *FRUS, 1955-1957*, XXIII, 43.

53. "National Security Council Report," 14 January 1957, *FRUS, 1955-1957*, XXIII, 374-384.

54. Kathryn Weathersby, "To Attack, or Not Attack? Stalin, Kim Il Sung, and the Prelude to War," *Cold War International History Project*, <wwics.si.edu/index.cfm?-topic_id=14-09&fuseaction=library.document&id=169> (August 2004).

55. A contemporary intelligence estimate on probable developments in North Korea over the next few years, title and date remain classified, listed in July 1956, *FRUS, 1955-1957*, XXIII, part 2, 286-289.

56. "Memorandum From the Officer in Charge of Korean Affairs to the Director of the Office of Northeast Asian Affairs," 1 October 1956, *FRUS, 1955-1957*, XXIII, 315-320.

57. "Memorandum of Discussion at the 179th Meeting of the National Security Council," 8 January 1954, *FRUS, 1952-1954*, XV, 1706.

58. "Special National Intelligence Estimate," 5 March 1954, *FRUS, 1952-1954*, XV, 1759.

59. "National Security Council Report," 9 August 1957, *FRUS, 1955-1957*, XXIII, part 2, 492.

60. "Letter From President Eisenhower to President Rhee," 31 January 1955, *FRUS, 1955-1957*, XXIII, 11-12.

61. John F. Kennedy, "Remarks at a Luncheon in Honor of a Japanese Trade Delegation," 3 December 1962, *Public Papers, 1962*, 850.

62. President Lyndon Johnson, "The State of the Union," *Department of State Bulletin* LIV, no. 1388, 31 January 1966, 153.

63. Lyndon B. Johnson, "Joint Statement of President Johnson and President Park on the Occasion of President Johnson's Visit to Korea," 2 November 1966, *Public Papers, 1966*, Book II, 1294.

64. Unless otherwise noted, the force numbers given here were obtained from: 1961-1963, *The Communist Bloc and Western Alliances*, and 1964-1969, *Military Balance*.

65. U.S. Senate, *United States Security Agreements and Commitments Abroad: Republic of Korea*, Hearings before the Subcommittee on United States Security Agreements and Commitments Abroad of the Committee on Foreign Relations, 91st Congress, 2nd Session, 24, 25, and 26 February 1970 (Washington, D.C.: GPO, 1970), 1620. Hereafter referred to as *Security Agreement Hearings* (1970).

66. Ralph N. Clough, *Deterrence and Defense in Korea: The Role of U.S. Forces* (Washington, D.C.: The Brookings Institution, 1976), 10.

67. Larry Niksch, "North Korea" in Richard A. Gabriel, ed., *Fighting Armies* (Westport: Greenwood Press, 1983), 111.

68. Niksch, "North Korea," 111.

69. *Security Agreements Hearings* (1970), 1603.

70. See Clough, *Deterrence and Defense in Korea*, 11-12, and *Security Agreements Hearings* (1970), 1603.

71. Rusk, *As I Saw It*, 394.

72. Clough, *Deterrence and Defense in Korea*, 12-13. Appendix II, "Statement furnished by General J.H. Michaelis, CINC/USFK," *Security Agreements Hearings* (1970), 1730.

73. Appendix II, "Statement furnished by General J.H. Michaelis, CINC/USFK," *Security Agreements Hearings* (1970), 1730.

74. Clough, *Deterrence and Defense in Korea*, 12.

75. Appendix II, "Statement furnished by General J.H. Michaelis, CINC/USFK," *Security Agreements Hearings* (1970), 1729.

76. *Security Agreements Hearings* (1970), 1759.

77. Department of State, "News Conference Remarks by Secretary of State Rusk," 12 October 1967, *American Foreign Policy Current Documents, 1967* (Washington, D.C.: Government Printing Office, 1968), 273-276. Hereafter cited as *AFP Current Documents*.

78. Appendix II, "Statement furnished by General J.H. Michaelis, CINC/USFK," *Security Agreements Hearings* (1970), 1759.

79. Arthur Goldberg, "U.N. General Assembly Again Rejects Move To Representation of China," *Department of State Bulletin* LIII, no. 1381, 13 December 1965, 944-945.

80. Dean Rusk, "Secretary Talks About Viet-Nam on 'Issues and Answers," *Department of State Bulletin* LIII, no. 1362, 2 August 1965, 189.

81. Department of State, "News Conference Remarks by Secretary of State Rusk," 12 October 1967, *AFP Current Documents, 1967*, 275.

82. "Joint Communique of the President and Prime Minister Eisaku Sato on Talks,"

12-13 January 1965, *AFP Current Documents, 1965,* 197.

83. "The White House-Joint Statement of President Johnson and President Park on the Occasion of President Johnson's State Visit to Korea," Appendix No. 7, *Security Agreements Hearings* (1970), 2 November 1966, 1721.

84. "Statement of Hon. William J. Porter, Ambassador to the Republic of Korea," Appendix I, *Security Agreements Hearings* (1970), 1709.

85. In 1961, North Korean per capita GNP was $123, while in South Korea the per capita GNP was $83. Sang Woo Rhee, *Security and Unification of Korea,* footnote #1, 200.

86. Han Sung-joo, *The Failure of Democracy in South Korea* (Berkeley: University of California Press, 1974), 28.

87. Carter J. Eckert, Ki-baik Lee, Young Ick Lew, Michael Robinson, Edward W. Wagner, *Korea Old and New: A History* (Cambridge: Harvard University Press, 1990), 354-355.

88. Eckert et al., *Korea Old and New: A History,* 356-358.

89. See *AFP Current Documents, 1961,* 973-974.

90. Byung Chul Koh, "The Pueblo Incident in Perspective," *Asian Survey* (April 1969): 270.

91. Based on a Chong-Sik Lee interview of Kim Sok-yong, a North Korean official in Seoul on 15 December 1968 in Robert A. Scalapino and Chong-Sik Lee, *Communism in Korea* (Berkeley: University of California Press, 1972), footnote #74, 983. Another scholar argues that Kim Il Sung missed the chance to exploit the unrest because of "the beginning of the Sino-Soviet dispute" and "shuttling back and forth from Moscow to Beijing." Dae-Sook Suh, *Kim Il Sung, The North Korean Leader* (New York: Columbia University Press, 1988), 224.

92. Byung Chul Koh, "Unification Policy and North-South Relations," in Robert A. Scalapino and Jun-Yop Kim, eds., *North Korea Today: Strategic and Domestic Issues* (Berkeley: Institute of East Asian Studies, University of California, 1983), 270-271, and William T. Tow, *Encountering the Dominant Player,* 182.

93. As quoted in Yong Soon Yim, "The Dynamics of North Korean Military Doctrine," in Tae-hwan Kwak, ed., *The Two Koreas in World Politics* (Seoul: Kyungnam University Press, 1983), 122.

94. Osgood Caruthers, "Khrushchev Signs Defense Treaty with Korea Reds," *New York Times,* 7 July 1961, A1, A2.

95. Caruthers, "Khrushchev Signs Defense Treaty with Korea Reds," A1, A2.

96. "U.S. Calls Treaty 'colonial',"*New York Times,* 7 July 1961, A2.

97. "China Says Pacts Show Reds' Unity," *New York Times,* 13 July 1961, A2.

98. "Communist China and Korean Reds Sign Defense Pact," *New York Times,* 12 July 1961, A1, A2.

99. Han, "North Korea's Security Policy and Military Strategy," *North Korea Today,* 150-153.

100. As quoted by Koh, "Unification Policy and North-South Relations," 274.

101. Koh, "Unification Policy and North-South Relations," 274-275.

102. Woo, *Security and Unification of Korea,* 144.

103. Koh, "Unification Policy and North-South Relations," 273.

104. Koh, "Unification Policy and North-South Relations," 273.

105. For discussions of this, see Larry Niksch, "North Korea," *Fighting Armies,* 106-107 and Koh, "The Pueblo Incident in Perspective," 271.

106. Niksch, "North Korea," *Fighting Armies,* 106-107; Koh, "The Pueblo Incident in Perspective," 271; Suh, *Kim Il Sung, The North Korean Leader,* 224-231.

107. "The White House-Joint Statement of President Johnson and President Park on the Occasion of President Johnson's State Visit to Korea," Appendix No. 7, *Security Agreements Hearings* (1970), 2 November 1966, 1721.

108. "Letter From the President of the United States to the President of the Republic of Korea," 13 August 1965, *AFP Current Documents, 1965*, 781.

109. See Mao Tse-tung, "On Protracted War," in Stuart Schram, ed., *Selected Works on Mao Tse-tung*, Volume II (Peking: Foreign Language Press, 1965) and Michael Elliott-Batem, *Defeat in the East: The Mark of Mao Tse-tung on War* (London: Oxford University Press, 1967), 109-110.

110. A similar argument is made in David C. Kang, "International Relations Theory and the Second Korean War," *International Studies Quarterly* 47, no. 3 (September 2003): 301-324.

111. See *Security Agreements Hearings* (1970), 1611.

112. Suh, *Kim Il Sung, The North Korean Leader*, 230-231.

113. *AFP Current Documents, 1967*, 788-790.

114. Koh, "Unification Policy and North-South Relations," 277.

115. Rusk, *As I Saw It*, 393-394.

116. Suh, *Kim Il Sung, The North Korean Leader*, 233-234.

117. *Security Agreements Hearings* (1970), 1761.

118. Rusk, *As I Saw It*, 392. For details of the composition of the task force, see *Security Agreements Hearings* (1970), 1748.

119. Appendix II, "Statement furnished by General J.H. Michaelis, CINC/ USFK," *Security Agreements Hearings* (1970), 1761.

120. *Security Agreements Hearings* (1970), 1749-1750.

121. *Security Agreements Hearings* (1970), 1611.

122. Suh, *Kim Il Sung, The North Korean Leader*, 238-242.

123. *Security Agreements Hearings* (1970), 1611.

124. Scalapino and Lee, *Communism in Korea*, part 2, 973.

125. Koh, "Unification Policy and North-South Relations," 276.

126. Koh, "The Pueblo Incident in Perspective," 278-279.

127. As quoted in Koh, "Unification Policy and North-South Relations," 281.

128. Don Oberdorfer, "North Korea's Army Now Ranked Fifth-Largest in the World by U.S.," *Washington Post*, 14 January 1979, A9.

129. Philip Taubman, "Washington Warns North Koreans It Will 'React Strongly' to Intrusion," *New York Times*, 27 October 1979, A1, A6.

130. U.S. Department of Defense, *Annual Report, FY 1981*, 29 January 1980, 52.

131. Ralph N. Clough, "The Soviet Union and the Two Koreas," in Donald S. Zagoria, ed., *Soviet Policy in East Asia* (New Haven: Yale University Press, 1982), 178, and Zagoria, "North Korea: Between Moscow and Beijing," *North Korea Today: Strategic and Domestic Issues*, 351.

132. *Khrushchev Remembers*, 1970, 370.

133. Clough, "The Soviet Union and the Two Koreas," 178-188, and Zagoria, "North Korea: Between Moscow and Beijing," 352.

134. Norman Levin, "Global Detente and North Korea's Strategic Relations," *The Korean Journal of Defense Analysis* II, no. 1 (Summer 1990): 38-40.

135. Koh, "Unification Policy and North-South Relations," 289-290.

136. Department of Defense, *Report of Secretary of Defense Harold Brown to the Congress on the FY 1980 Budget, FY 1981 Authorization Request and FY 1980-1984 Defense Programs* (Washington, D.C.: GPO, 25 January 1979), 50.

137. *Report of Secretary of Defense Harold Brown to the Congress on the FY 1980*

Budget, FY 1981 Authorization Request and FY 1980-1984 Defense Programs, 54.

138. Department of Defense, *Report of Secretary of Defense James R. Schlesinger to the Congress on the FY 1976 and Transition Budgets, FY 1977 Authorization Request and FY 1976-1980 Defense Programs* (Washington, D.C.: GPO, 5 February 1975), I-4.

139. U.S. House of Representatives, *Impact of Intelligence Reassessment on Withdrawal of U.S. Troops from Korea*, Hearings before the Investigations Subcommittee of the Committee on Armed Services, 96th Congress, 1st Session, 21 June and 17 July 1979 (Washington, D.C.: Government Printing Office, 1979), 64. Hereafter these hearings will be referred to as *Intelligence Reassessment Hearings* (1979).

140. Don Oberdorfer, "North Korea's Army Now Ranked Fifth-Largest in World by U.S.," *Washington Post*, 14 January 1979, A9.

141. Representative Les Aspin, "The Korean Troop-Withdrawal Plan: A Reassessment," *Intelligence Reassessment Hearings* (1979), 5.

142. *Report of the Secretary of Defense for FY 1977* (Washington, D.C.: Government Printing Office, 1976), III-30.

143. U.S. Department of Defense, *Report of Secretary of Defense Harold Brown to the Congress on the FY 1980 Budget, FY 1981 Authorization Request and FY 1980-1984 Defense Programs* (Washington, D.C.: Government Printing Office), 25 January 1979, 105.

144. U.S. Department of Defense, *Annual Report, Fiscal Year 1982* (Washington, D.C.: Government Printing Office, 1981), 89.

145. *The Military Balance, 1980-1981*, 70.

146. Joseph S. Bermudez, Jr., "North Korea's Light Infantry Brigades," *Jane's Defence Weekly* (15 November 1986), 1178.

147. "Korean People's Army," <www.globalsecurity.org/military/world/dprk/army.htm>.

148. Testimony of Nathaniel Thayer, Central Intelligence Agency, *Intelligence Reassessment Hearings* (1979), 25.

149. Testimony of Nathaniel Thayer, Central Intelligence Agency, *Intelligence Reassessment Hearings* (1979), 25.

150. Hakjoon Kim, "U.S.-South Korean Security Relations: A Challenging Partnership," *The Korean Journal of Defense Analysis* II, no. 1 (Summer, 1990): 152-153, and Detrio, 47.

151. U.S. Department of Defense, *Report of the Secretary of Defense Harold Brown to the Congress on the FY 1981 Budget* (Washington, D.C.: GPO, 1980), 50.

152. See Niksch, "North Korea," *Fighting Armies*, 111.

153. See Clough, *Deterrence and Defense in Korea*, 80; Niksch, "North Korea," *Fighting Armies*, 111; and Jong Youl Yoo, "Military Capabilities of North and South Korea: A Comparative Analysis," in *U.S.-Korean Security Relations: New Challenges and Opportunities*, third annual conference sponsored by the Council on U.S.-Korean Security Studies, 29 November-2 December 1987 in Seoul, South Korea, 73.

154. U.S. House of Representatives, Investigations Subcommittee and Committee on Armed Services Hearings, *Review of the Policy Decision to Withdraw United States Ground Forces from Korea*, 1978, 31. Hereafter cited as *Review of Ground Force Withdrawal Hearings* (1978). See also Russell Spurr, "The Hollingsworth Line," *Far Eastern Economic Review* (27 February 1976), 26-28 and Larry Niksch, "South Korea," in Richard A. Gabriel, ed., *Fighting Armies* (Westport: Greenwood Press, 1983), 136-139.

155. Spurr, 26-28.

156. Interview with Lieutenant-General James F. Hollingsworth, I Corps Commander in Korea, in Spurr, 26-28.

157. Philip Taubman, "Washington Warns North Koreans It Will 'React Strongly' to Intrusion," *New York Times*, 27 October 1979, A1, A6.

158. Taubman, "Washington Warns North Koreans It Will 'React Strongly' to Intrusion," A1, A6.

159. U.S. Department of Defense, *Annual Report, FY 1981*, 52.

160. U.S. Department of Defense, *Annual Report, FY 1981*, 110.

161. U.S. Department of Defense, *Annual Report, FY 1981*, 113.

162. *Korean Central News Agency*, 10 October 1980 as cited in Koh, "Unification Policy and North-South Relations," 265.

163. U.S. Department of Defense, *Annual Report, FY 1981*, 50.

164. Don Oberdorfer, "North Korea's Army Now Ranked Fifth-Largest in World by U.S.," *Washington Post*, 14 January 1979, A9.

165. Testimony of General John Vessey, *Intelligence Reassessment Hearings* (1979), 66.

166. Korean Overseas Information Service, *Tunnels of Aggression*, undated pamphlet obtained in July 1984 at tunnel #3.

167. Information furnished by Jim Coles III, Chief, Public Information, United Nations Command on 12 March 1992.

168. Testimony of Nathaniel Thayer, CIA and General Vessey, *Intelligence Reassessment Hearings* (1979), 43-44 and 91.

169. "North Korea Laying 80 New Tunnels," *Donga Ilbo*, 8 July 2004 as cited in NAPSNET, 8 July 2004 <www.nautilus.org>.

170. See *Intelligence Reassessment Hearings* (1979), 6.

171. Pyung-Gil Chay, "Current Characteristics of the North Korean Military," in *U.S.-Korean Security Relations: New Challenges and Opportunities*, third annual conference sponsored by the Council on U.S.-Korean Security Studies, 29 November-2 December 1987 in Seoul, South Korea, 84.

172. Address by the Assistant Secretary of State for East Asian and Pacific Affairs (Wolfowitz) Before the Asia Society, 31 January 1984, *AFP Current Documents, 1984*, 736.

173. U.S. House of Representatives, *Developments in United States-Republic of Korea Relations*, Hearing before the Subcommittee on Asian and Pacific Affairs of the Committee on Foreign Affairs, 26 July 1989, (Washington, D.C.: GPO, 1990), 18.

174. Detrio, *Strategic Partners: South Korea and the United States,* 27.

175. Drew Middleton, "Seoul Events May Reshape U.S. Military Stance in Asia," *New York Times*, 27 October 1979, A6.

176. Chong-Wook Chung, "Chinese Foreign Policy in East Asia: Trends and Implications," in William J. Taylor Jr., Young Koo Cha, John Q. Blodgett, and Michael Mazarr, eds., *The Future of South Korean-U.S. Security Relations* (Boulder: Westview Press, 1989), 71.

177. U.S. Department of Defense, *Report of Secretary of Defense Harold Brown to the Congress on the FY 1981 Budget*, 52.

178. United States Department of Defense, *Military Posture, 1987* (Washington, D.C.: GPO, 1986), 45. Hereafter noted as *Military Posture*.

179. *Military Posture, 1983*, 40.

180. Paul Marantz, "Moscow and East Asia: New Realities and New Policies," in Sheldon W. Simon, ed., *East Asian Security in the Post-Cold War Era* (Armonk, New York: M.E. Sharpe, 1993), 30-31.

181. Seung-ho Joo, "The New Friendship Treaty between Moscow and Pyongyang," *Comparative Strategy* 20, no. 5 (December 2001): 468.

182. Harold Brown, Secretary of Defense, U.S. Department of Defense, *Annual Report, Fiscal Year 1982* (Washington, D.C.: U.S. GPO, 1981), 84.

183. Press Conference by Secretary of Defense Cheney and Defense Minister Lee, *AFP Current Documents, 1990*, 16 February 1990, 715.

184. Detrio, *Strategic Partners: South Korea and the United States*, 65.

185. Prepared Statement by the Assistant Secretary of State for East Asian and Pacific Affairs (Paul Wolfowitz) Before a Subcommittee of the House Foreign Affairs Committee, 6 February 1984, *AFP Current Documents, 1984*, 740.

186. Joint Communiqué of the 20th Annual ROK-U.S. Security Consultative Meeting, 9 June 1988, *AFP Current Documents, 1988*, 559.

187. *The Military Balance, 1989-1990*, 165.

188. "Air Force - ROK," <www.globalsecurity.org/military/world/rok/airforce.htm>.

189. Detrio, *Strategic Partners: South Korea and the United States*, 67.

190. Detrio, *Strategic Partners: South Korea and the United States*, 69.

191. "Republic of Korea Army," <www.globalsecurity.org/military/world/rok/army.htm>.

192. U.S. Department of Defense, *Annual Report, FY 1982*, 87.

193. U.S. Department of Defense, *Soviet Military Power, 1989* (Washington, D.C.: GPO, 1989), 119.

194. *Soviet Military Power, 1989*, 119.

195. *Military Posture, 1989*, 26.

196. *Soviet Military Power, 1989*, 119.

197. "Address by the Deputy Assistant Secretary of State for East Asian and Pacific Affairs (Sherman) Before the Conference on Tensions in the Korean Peninsula," 18 November 1984, *AFP Current Documents, 1984*, 747, 749.

198. *Military Posture, 1989*, 24.

199. Clyde Haberman, "Seoul Suspects North in Jet Crash," *New York Times*, 3 December 1987, A5.

200. James R. Schlesinger, Secretary of Defense, U.S. Department of Defense, *Annual Report, FY 1977*, III-11.

Chapter 3

THE NORTH KOREAN THREAT:
Conventional and Nuclear Weapons, 1991 to the Present

The end of the Cold War brought profound change not only to the Korean peninsula but also to the entire world. The superpower rivalry that dominated post-World War II international relations ended with the collapse of Soviet control in Eastern Europe and the disintegration of the Soviet Union. From these events flowed significant changes in the security environment in Northeast Asia and the nature of the threat in the region. North Korea remained the chief security threat, and relationship between North Korea and its allies, China and now Russia, drifted apart. Moreover, the nature of the DPRK threat changed as it sought to acquire nuclear, chemical, and biological weapons along with the ballistic missiles capable of delivering them. The danger here included not only North Korea acquiring these weapons but also the possibility of selling them to others. Indeed, North Korea became one of the foremost proliferators of ballistic missiles and missile technology, behavior that could be repeated with Pyongyang's nuclear weapons. As a result, the threat now included not only the North's military capabilities and possible intention to use force, but also North Korea as a serious proliferation threat. Finally, on 8 July 1994, Kim Il Sung died at the age of 82, raising concerns about the succession of his son Kim Jong Il, forcing U.S. and ROK officials to reassess the North's leadership and its intentions. Using framework from the previous chapter—source, capabilities, and intentions—this chapter will assess this important period of change in the North Korean threat.

1991 to the Present

Source

The end of the Cold War brought significant changes to the threat configuration on the Korean peninsula and to the relationships among the regional players. North Korean relations with China and Russia were strained as the end of the Cold War prompted some shifting in regional interests. Beijing and Moscow continued to oppose any North Korean threat to peace and stability as both also sought to build a relationship with the South. Thus, it was clear to U.S. policy makers that the threat to peace and stability in the region was squarely focused on Pyongyang but now for reasons that went beyond the fear of invasion.

China attempted to maintain a balancing act, preserving ties with its historical and ideological ally in Pyongyang while also courting a new relationship with the growing economic power in Seoul. Abandoning its "one Korea" policy, Beijing attempted to develop a "two-Koreas" approach in an effort to foster strong ties with both. In 1992, Beijing and Seoul normalized relations, further increasing political and economic contacts between the former adversaries. According to one scholar, "The ROK's contribution to China's economic development goals is seen as far more important than the ideological ties binding Pyongyang and Beijing, even at a time when the Chinese leadership sees all socialist states as under siege from the corrosive Western strategy of 'peaceful evolution.'"[1] Despite Pyongyang's sense of betrayal and outrage at normalization, economic links with the South were far too important for Beijing.

While developing this new relationship, China also worked to maintain its ties with North Korea. On the 1994 death of Kim Il Sung, China went out of its way to demonstrate its grief and was quick to recognize the succession of Kim Jong Il in the interests of ensuring a smooth and stable transition. China also maintained significant levels of aid and trade, especially important after the loss of Soviet support.[2] Beijing continued security ties and the maintenance of the 1961 bilateral Treaty of Friendship, Cooperation, and Mutual Assistance. However, Beijing made it clear that all bets were off should Pyongyang instigate an attack on the South. As Kim and Lee note, "the treaty is kept partly as a convenient fiction and partly as a convenient fact. . . . Beijing projects a strategic posture of calculated ambiguity, letting it be known to all that its treaty commitment to Pyongyang can be interpreted as Chinese leaders wish."[3] Despite Beijing's efforts to continue its relationship with the DPRK, relations remained frosty throughout much of the 1990s.

Located on its border, Chinese leaders fear the dangers and uncertainty that could result from a collapse or change in the North Korean regime. Among these dangers are a flood of refugees, conflict on its border, and the likelihood a unified Korea would mean a government run by Seoul and allied to the United States. As a result, China goes to great lengths to maintain the North through trade, opposition to UN/U.S. sanctions, and diplomatic support. Economic punishment of the North would only lead to greater cost for China. The Chinese have also tried to urge Pyongyang to embark on a more pragmatic and less ideological path to economic development. North Korea has implemented some reform measures, but it has been far less than hoped for. In the end, Beijing is often exasperated with the North Korean leadership and the DPRK remains a serious problem for China.

While the United States and China see their common interests in maintaining peace in Korea, Sino-U.S. relations more broadly have been tenuous. In 1999, NATO planes accidentally bombed the Chinese embassy in Belgrade and in 2001 the confrontation between a U.S. spy plane and Chinese fighter pushed the relationship to its lowest point since China conducted missile tests near Taiwan in 1996. After September 11th, U.S.-China relations began to improve. Chinese cooperation in the war on terror was quick in coming, based on Beijing's own problems with separatists in Xinjiang province in western China. There has also been increasing U.S.-Chinese cooperation in settling the nuclear confrontation in North Korea, particularly as China has helped to push North Korea to the bargaining table. In 2003, White House Press Secretary Scott McClellan noted, "China has been helpful. China has made it clear that they don't want to see a nuclearized peninsula. I don't think anyone in the region wants to see a nuclearized peninsula, so this is something that we're in close discussions with our friends and allies on."[4]

Despite these common interests, there remains considerable debate in the United States concerning China's future as a "strategic partner" or "strategic competitor."[5] In the *Nuclear Posture Review*, submitted to the U.S. Congress on 31 December 2001 and subsequently leaked to the press, it notes: "Due to the combination of China's still developing strategic objectives and its ongoing modernization of its nuclear and non nuclear forces, China is a country that could be involved in an immediate or potential contingency."[6] Later, in the Bush administration's *National Security Strategy* document, it notes: "We welcome the emergence of a strong, peaceful, and prosperous China." However, "in pursuing advanced military capabilities that can threaten its neighbors in the Asia-Pacific region, China is following an outdated path that, in the end, will hamper its own pursuit of national greatness."[7] U.S.-China relations have also been strained over trade issues, including greater access to Chinese markets and Beijing's insistence on maintaining a fixed exchange rate for its currency. Thus, while the United States believes China can be a positive influence on resolving the problem of North Korea's nuclear weapons program, there exists considerable uncertainty over the future of Sino-U.S. relations.

After the collapse of the Soviet Union in 1991, Russia's North Korea policy under Boris Yeltsin shifted as it transitioned to a democracy and market economy. As one scholar maintained, "North Korea now has very little to offer Moscow. A democratic Russia . . . sees no ideological value in links with an unreformed Stalinist regime, which it regards as a lingering relic from its own tragic past."[8] In 1992, Russia and South Korea normalized relations, and Moscow halted military cooperation with the North while pressuring Pyongyang to drop its efforts to acquire nuclear weapons. To make matters worse, Yeltsin also declared that the long-standing 1961 Soviet-DPRK security treaty was of little value and his Information Minister encouraged Japan, Korea's former occupier, to refrain from paying war reparations lest this prop up a dying and anachronistic regime.[9] Military ties between Russia and South Korea also grew, including the transfer of $240 million in military equipment to cover a debt to Seoul and the exchange of military personnel.[10] North Korea's reaction was predictable; "Russia's arms export to South Korea at this time is a reckless act fanning the flame. It has sparked off great resentment of the entire Korean people."[11] Pyongyang maintained Russia "is all but in the camp of forces hostile to the Democratic People's Republic of Korea. If Russia continues . . . we will have to settle scores with it."[12] In 2003, South Korea wrote off $660 million from a Russian debt of $2.24 billion. The remaining $1.58 billion will be paid off over the next 23 years, including the delivery of more military equipment.[13]

When Kim Il Sung passed away in 1994, Yeltsin failed to send his personal condolences to North Korea, and the Russian press took the opportunity to bash the failing communist regime.[14] The decline in Russian-North Korean political ties accompanied a fading economic relationship. Trade between the two in 1990 stood at over $2.3 billion; by 2000, trade levels had shrunk to only $105 million.[15] Finally, in 1995, Russia indicated its desire to renegotiate the 1961 treaty of alliance with North Korea that was set to expire in 1996. Russian leaders hoped their intent to revise the treaty rather than scrap it altogether would indicate their wish to maintain a relationship with the DPRK without being tied to the mutual defense provisions of the agreement.[16]

In 1996, DPRK-Russian relations began to warm as Moscow sought to balance ties with both Koreas and to increase Moscow's influence in the region.[17] On 9 February 2000, Russia and North Korea signed the new Treaty of Friendship, Good Neighborliness, and Cooperation to replace the 1961 alliance.[18] The security clause in this agreement was far more vague than the 1961 agreement, stating, "in the event of the emergence of the danger of an aggression against one of the countries or a situation jeopardizing peace and security, and in the event there is a necessity for consultations and cooperation, the sides enter into contact with each other immediately."[19] The agreement contained no language that would commit Russia to the DPRK's defense, and earlier, Moscow had indicated that Russian assistance would be forthcoming only if Pyongyang were attacked. Despite these reservations, Seung-Ho Joo notes, the treaty marked "the beginning of a new era in their bilateral relations."[20] Later, in July 2000, the new Russian president, Vladimir Putin traveled to North Korea, the first Soviet or Russian president to do so. While there, he and Kim Jong Il signed a joint declaration that expressed "the willingness to get in touch with each other without delay if the danger of aggression to the DPRK or to Russia is created or when there is the need to have consultations and cooperate with each other under the circumstances where peace and security are threatened."[21] While Russian-DPRK relations improved, Moscow remained firmly committed to the status quo on the peninsula and the maintenance of peace and stability.

For U.S. policy makers, North Korea was the chief threat in the region. According to a 2000 U.S. Defense Department Report, "North Korea remains the major threat to stability and security in Northeast Asia and is the country most likely to involve the United States in a large-scale war."[22] In 2001, George W. Bush entered office with many misgivings about the Clinton administration's North Korea policy and a general distrust of the North Korean regime. Early in his administration, President Bush remarked that he was skeptical of Kim Jong Il's trustworthiness, that "we're not certain as to whether or not they're keeping all terms of all agreements," a comment that proved to be prophetic.[23] Initially, Secretary of State Colin Powell indicated the Bush administration would "pick up where President Clinton and his administration left off."[24] However, in March 2001, a reporter asked Powell whether the United States still viewed North Korea as a threat. Powell responded, "It is a threat; its got a huge army poised on the border within artillery and rocket distance of South Korea. . . . they still have weapons of mass destruction and missiles that can deliver those weapons of mass destruction. So we have to see them as a threat."[25] In reference to the June 2000 summit between North and South Korea where progress was made on North-South relations, Powell remarked, "we have to not be naïve about the nature of the threat, but at the same time, realize that changes are taking place."[26] In his now famous January 2002 State of the Union address, Bush noted, "States like these [Iran, Iraq, and North Korea] and their terrorist allies, constitute an axis of evil, arming to threaten the peace of the world."[27] Many critics challenged the wisdom and accuracy of including North Korea on this list. However, Undersecretary of State John Bolton defended the remark in a speech in South Korea arguing that "President Bush's use of the term 'axis of evil' to describe Iran, Iraq and North Korea was more than rhetorical flourish—it was factually correct."[28]

In the 1990s, U.S. concerns for the North Korean threat went beyond the usual worry of Pyongyang's conventional capabilities and the danger of an attack on the South. While this threat remained, concern shifted to North Korea's growing ballistic missile capability and its willingness to sell these weapons to others. Moreover, North Korea began efforts to acquire nuclear weapons, an equally saleable commodity. For a time it appeared that the North's nuclear ambitions were curtailed, but in October 2002, the world learned of Pyongyang's efforts to develop another nuclear weapons program. CIA Director George Tenet noted in a report to Congress, "The recent behavior of North Korea regarding its long-standing nuclear weapons program makes apparent to all the dangers Pyongyang poses to its region and to the world."[29] The wedding of ballistic missile technology with nuclear, chemical, and biological weapons created another aspect to this problem. It is estimated that North Korean missiles, equipped with a nuclear warhead, might be able to reach the continental United States by 2015.[30] In the past, threat assessments focused largely on the danger to South Korea and so was a problem of extended deterrence. However, as the North's ability to threaten the United States directly grew, the security concerns began to take on some of the characteristics of a primary deterrence problem. Indeed, this has been a significant part of the U.S. argument for developing missile defense systems. In any case, the threat to U.S. interests in the region changed. The source was still confined to North Korea but was now far different than a threat of conventional attack. Now, the danger included the proliferation of nuclear weapons and ballistic missiles, a threat that provided different challenges to U.S. policy makers.

Capabilities

Conventional Weapons

In the last fifteen years, North Korea has continued to maintain a strong, conventional military capability with an active duty force that is the fifth largest in the world.[31] In recent years, the DPRK has maintained a "military first" policy that ensures the armed forces receives top priority for national resources despite its dismal economy. A 2000 report by the Commander of U.S. forces in Korea warned that "in the last 12 months, North Korea has done more to arrest a decline in readiness and to improve its military capability than in the last five years combined." These efforts included a particularly "ambitious program to improve ground forces capabilities."[32] Moreover, since a large share of DPRK forces are forward deployed, warning time of an impending attack would be minimal, perhaps as little as 2 to 3 days. The total number of North Korean military personnel in 2003 dipped only slightly, remaining at approximately 1.1 million soldiers under arms. Ground forces decreased by 50,000 to a total of 950,000. The ground force total includes over 100,000 soldiers in special operations forces (SOF) units with missions that include: "reconnaissance, establishing a 'Second Front' within the ROK strategic rear, decapitation and disruption, . . . neutralisation of ROK and U.S. airbases, and neutralisation of ROK and U.S. missiles and weapons of mass destruction."[33] According to ROK estimates, over 20,000 of the SOF forces could be placed in South Korea by sea or air. These soldiers along with other light infantry units are also likely to use the tunnel system to infiltrate the South to conduct rear area actions.[34] General Thomas Schwartz, commander of U.S. forces in Korea in 2002 maintained:

> We consider them a tough, dedicated, and profoundly loyal force. They undergo year-round training to develop and maintain their skills. During wartime, these forces would attack from the ground, air and sea against both our forward and rear areas. The North will concentrate SOF against our critical war fighting nodes and seek to prevent rapid force and sortie generation by U.S. and ROK forces.[35]

North Korea also increased the strength of its reserve forces to 4.7 million men and women. ROK troop strength declined somewhat during the period, dropping from 750,000 to 683,000. A similar decrease in ground troops occurred moving from 675,000 in 1991 to 585,000 in 2003.

DPRK tank force numbers remained approximately the same with current numbers at 4,060. However, the size of the force is offset by its increasing age.

Most of the tanks are old Soviet design T-34, T-54/55, and T-59s. According to Michael O'Hanlon, "a traditional armored assault by North Korean forces would amount to putting metal into a metalgrinder, and be fairly straightforward for the allies to stop."[36] The number of APCs dipped substantially from 4,000 in 1992 to 2,500 in 2003. As a result, approximately 40-60 percent of the Korean People's Army (KPA) would be transported by trucks rather than with APCs or other infantry assault vehicles.[37] Transportation dilemmas are lessened since close to 70 percent of North Korean ground forces remain forward deployed within 100 miles of the DMZ.[38] Yet, North Korean efforts to mechanize its ground forces are complicated by numerous transportation problems. According to a 2000 U.S. Defense Department report, the DPRK transportation system including rail and road nets would function sufficiently during the initial phases of a military operation. However, "the infrastructure would experience difficulties supporting sustained operations. Rugged terrain; limited east-west routes; numerous bridges, tunnels, and other chokepoints; and inferior road surface types would be limiting factors during combat operations."[39] To oppose DPRK armor, the ROK has 2,330 main battle tanks, a force that will be further improved with the future acquisition of Russian equipment, including T-80 tanks, and BMP-3 armored vehicles.

Table 3.1

NORTH AND SOUTH KOREAN MILITARY PERSONNEL, 2003-2004

	North	*South*
Total Armed Forces	1,082,000	686,000
Ground Forces	950,000	588,000*

* includes 28,000 Marines
Source: *The Military Balance*, 2003-2004

A dramatic rise occurred in DPRK artillery pieces increasing from 5,800 in 1991 to 10,400 towed and self-propelled pieces. An additional 2,500 multiple rocket launcher systems were also added. Many of the artillery and rocket launchers are deployed in hardened, underground facilities, or tunnels burrowed into the sides of mountains providing protection and the ability to attack with little warning. According to testimony given in 1999, by General John H. Tilelli Jr., commander of U.S. forces in Korea, "the North continues a reorganization of artillery assets and the fielding of long-range systems near the Demilitarized Zone. . . . this large number of long-range artillery provides devastating indirect fire support."[40] His successor, General Thomas A. Schwartz, noted, "without moving any artillery pieces, the North could sustain up to 500,000 rounds an hour against Combined Forces Command defenses for several hours."[41] In June 2003, the United States announced it would move its forces off the DMZ to positions south of Seoul. The move was partly designed to pull U.S. forces out of

Table 3.2

NORTH AND SOUTH KOREAN MILITARY EQUIPMENT, 2003-2004

		North		*South*
Tanks	4,060	3,500 T-34, T-54/55, T-62, Type-59 560 light tanks	2,330	1,000 Type-88 80 T-80U 400 M-47; 850 M-48
Armored Personnel Carriers		2,500		2,480
Artillery		10,400		3,500 towed artillery
Multiple Rocket Launchers		2,500		185
SSMs		24 FROG 3/5/7 30 Scud B/C, 10 Nodong		12 NHK-I/-II
Naval Vessels		26 submarines 3 frigates 310 patrol/coastal ships		20 submarines 6 destroyers 9 frigates 84 patrol/coastal ships
Combat Aircraft	605	*Fighter/Ground Attack:* 396 J-5/6/7(MiG 17/19/21) 18 Su-7, 35 Su-25 46 MiG-23, 30 MiG-29 *Bombers:* 80 H-5 (Il-28)	468	*Fighter/Ground Attack:* 130 F-4D/E 185 F-5E/F 153 F-16C/D 0
Armed Helicopters		24		0

Source: *The Military Balance, 2003-2004*

DPRK artillery range. However, the North's multiple rocket launchers would still be able to reach these more southerly positions.[42]

While North Korea has a sizeable contingent of combat planes, their effectiveness is reduced considerably by age. In 2003, only 111 of the North's 605 combat aircraft were the more advanced MiG-23s, MiG-29s, and SU-25s. The majority were the older MiG-17, 19, and 21 of Soviet design that face U.S. and South Korean F-15s and F-16s. Most of the U.S. and ROK planes are outfitted with precision-guided munitions and further advantaged with better intelligence, targeting, and command and control systems than their counterparts in the North.[43] Due to chronic shortages in fuel, DPRK pilots spend limited hours training in their aircraft, possibly only seven to eight hours each year. The aircraft are also plagued by shortages of spare parts and the difficulties of keeping an aging fleet in the air.

The DPRK has made greater use of helicopters since the 1980s, increasing their numbers from 40 to 130. In 1985, North Korea purchased 87 U.S.-made, civilian version, MD-500 helicopters indirectly by circumventing U.S. export regulations. The United States stopped further sales, but North Korea is reported to have converted 60 of these helicopters into gunships. Since South Korea produces a licensed version of the MD-500 for its military, the U.S. helicopters provided North Korea with an aircraft useful for covert operations in the South.[44]

To protect its air assets, North Korea continues to rely on "one of the world's most dense air defense networks."[45] The DPRK utilizes over 8,800 anti-aircraft guns along with various types of surface-to-air missiles supplied largely from the old Soviet Union. The North's aircraft are protected in underground facilities or hardened shelters, and based at facilities that are widely dispersed. According to one source, "it thus seems highly improbable that the NKAF [North Korean Air Force] would be knocked out in one strike.[46]

DPRK naval forces continue to have two chief missions: coastal defense and assisting in the insertion of special operations units. Northern boats are small with only three frigates and no ships in the destroyer class or larger. Most of its surface vessels are patrol craft or coastal ships giving the DPRK Navy little blue-water capability. Pyongyang's submarines remain a concern given their ability to disrupt ROK shipping. Most of these submarines are Romeo-class, "outdated and slow, but they are sufficiently capable of blocking sea lanes."[47] The North has approximately 47 midget submarines that could be used for intelligence and special operations missions. As with the air force, a shortage of fuel and other resources has meant far fewer DPRK ships are seaworthy while irregular and limited training hampers readiness.[48]

According to Bermudez Jr., the North Korean Navy, despite many obstacles, "maintains the capability to conduct sustained offensive and defensive wartime operations." However, he also argues the effective use of its capabilities would be limited to the early stages of a conflict, likely the first 30 to 90 days. U.S. and ROK advantages in night and bad weather operations, early warning radar, intelligence, advanced weapons, joint operations capability, and air superiority "would quickly render the vast majority of [North Korea's] surface combatants ineffective."[49] Referring to a North-South naval engagement in 1999, the Pentagon noted, "ROK naval weapon systems and combat capability are superior to those of North Korea."[50] In the last five to ten years, South Korea has undertaken significant efforts to improve its naval capability and develop its force beyond earlier coastal defense missions to a blue-water navy. Seoul will acquire new, Aegis-class destroyers, and, after increasing its number of submarines from 3 to 20 over the last decade, has begun an effort with Germany to build advanced submarines.[51] Thus, despite some dangerous North Korean naval assets, combined U.S.-ROK naval capability would be no match for North Korea, especially in any conflict that would last longer than a few months.

Any accurate assessment of the military balance on the Korean peninsula must include U.S. forces, both those stationed in South Korea and other military assets in the region. After the Korean War, the United States maintained two infantry divisions in Korea positioned between Seoul and the DMZ. Nixon removed one of these divisions in 1971, but the remaining units aided ROK firepower and were an important signal of the U.S. deterrence commitment to fight if South Korea were attacked. Today, the United States has 36,000 troops, including a Marine division stationed in Japan along with 90 combat aircraft. Japan is also the homeport for the U.S. 7th Fleet. In the event of a North Korean attack, these forces could be deployed quickly to assist U.S.-ROK units in Korea. The United States also contributes to reconnaissance and surveillance capabilities to make detection of DPRK troop movements easier and aid in combat operations. Finally, the United States maintains 90 combat aircraft in Korea, most being advanced F-16s. Thus, so long as the U.S. commitment remains, North Korea faces a combined adversary with overwhelming military power, circumstances North Korea's leadership is well aware of.

Overall, U.S.-ROK forces have a considerable advantage over the North. According to Michael O'Hanlon, "large allied forces are highly ready, well armed with potent weaponry, served by sophisticated all-weather day-night reconnaissance assets, and aided by terrain that is naturally favorable to a defender as well as being thoroughly prepared with explosives and obstacles."[52] The balance of forces is in favor of the United States and South Korea, and according to the Defense Department in 2000, "the current force capability of the ROK Armed Forces is quantitatively inferior to that of North Korea. However, once the capacity of their equipment and ROK-US combined force capabilities are taken into account, they are qualitatively superior."[53]

Nuclear, Chemical, and Biological Weapons

Growing evidence of a possible North Korean nuclear weapons program, along with efforts to acquire chemical and biological weapons represented another serious concern for the United States and South Korea. After a tense crisis in the early 1990s, it appeared the North had given up its desire to acquire nuclear weapons.[54] However, since October 2002, there has been grave concern that the North may become a nuclear power after all.

North Korea's interest in nuclear weapons began shortly after the Korean War, a response to U.S. nuclear threats during the conflict and the South's inclusion under the U.S. nuclear umbrella. Pyongyang worked with the Soviets and Chinese on a nuclear research program and in 1967, began operations with a small research reactor supplied by the Soviet Union and installed at Yongbyon.[55] The North had asked Moscow for help in developing a parallel nuclear weapons program but the Soviets were not interested; the nuclear energy program was an effort to mollify Pyongyang.[56] Despite these signals, U.S. and ROK officials did not view North Korea as a serious proliferation threat. American satellite photos taken in 1982 indicated more construction at the site including additional reactors and a reprocessing facility, raising further concern. North Korea allayed U.S. and ROK fears somewhat by signing the Nuclear Nonproliferation Treaty (NPT) in 1985. Under the terms of this agreement North Korea was required to declare all nuclear material in its possession and allow international inspection of its nuclear facilities by the International Atomic Energy Agency (IAEA), an arm of the UN, to verify that no weapons production was taking place. However, the inspection process was delayed by close to three years due to an error by the IAEA. To implement the inspections, the IAEA sent paperwork to the North shortly after to finalize the safeguards agreement and arrange formal inspections. Pyongyang was given the standard 18-month deadline to return the papers. Close to the end of the 18 months, the IAEA realized it had given North Korea the wrong forms. New forms were sent that gave them another 18 months—until December 1988—to return.[57] When the deadline finally arrived in 1988, North Korea balked at fulfilling the inspection requirements.

As this confusion dragged on, a series of negotiations ensued during the latter months of 1991 between the two Koreas that held out hope for ensuring North Korean compliance with the NPT as well as greater peace and stability in the region. On 13 December 1991, Seoul and Pyongyang signed a historic treaty of reconciliation and nonaggression where both agreed to renounce the use of force against each other. Later that same month, they signed another agreement that banned nuclear weapons from the peninsula including the possession of "nuclear reprocessing and uranium enrichment facilities." However, the two sides could not agree on a formula to ensure compliance and North Korea's nuclear ambitions remained unclear.[58]

After numerous fits and starts, in which it appeared to U.S. and ROK authorities that the North was stalling, inspections did occur during the summer and fall of 1992. The IAEA requested further inspections, but again the North delayed. On 12 March 1993, North Korea shocked the world by announcing its intention to withdraw from the NPT, the first nation ever to do so. The withdrawal was to take affect on 12 June 1993, ninety days after the announcement. Shortly before the June 12th deadline, the North reversed its position and announced that it would remain a signatory of the NPT. However, Pyongyang continued to stall its compliance with IAEA demands. The Clinton administration responded by threatening the imposition of economic sanctions if the North did not fully comply with inspection requirements and began plans for air strikes to destroy the North's nuclear facilities.

Eventually, Pyongyang allowed some inspections but not complete access to its nuclear facilities, particularly two nuclear waste dumps. Inspection of these waste sites was necessary to determine whether spent fuel was diverted for weapons production during a previous reactor shutdown. Two months later, despite pressure from the United States, Russia, and China, North Korea unloaded its nuclear reactor producing 8,000 fuel rods that could be reprocessed for weapons production.

Once again, the Clinton administration broke off talks with the DPRK and threatened sanctions. U.S. and ROK troops were placed on heightened alert and the United States sent Patriot missile batteries to the ROK.[59] U.S. efforts also included inducements of increased diplomatic and economic contacts, suspension of Team Spirit military exercises, and economic aid packages, an early recognition that deterrence threats alone might not achieve U.S. goals. Finally, President Clinton sent a letter to South Korean President Kim Young Sam that a North Korean attack on the South would be considered an attack on the United States.[60] Issuing its own deterrence threats, Pyongyang countered that sanctions would be tantamount to war, and "Seoul will turn into a sea of fire."[61] The Clinton administration considered a military strike to take out the nuclear facilities along with significant deployments of U.S. forces that, according to Secretary of Defense William Perry, "were certain to be considered provocative by North Korea."[62] The United States and North Korea were on a collision course.

A crash was averted in June 1994 when former-President Jimmy Carter journeyed to Pyongyang and convinced Kim Il Sung to freeze the nuclear program in return for high-level talks with the United States. Subsequent negotiations produced the "Agreed Framework" signed on 21 October 1994 by U.S. and DPRK delegates in Geneva. In the "Agreed Framework," North Korea consented to freezing, and later dismantling, its nuclear program, storing and eventually shipping the 8,000 fuel rods to a third country, and full NPT compliance including IAEA inspections. In return, the North would receive two light water reactors (LWR) and annual deliveries of fuel oil during construction of the LWRs.[63] The United States organized a consortium (Korean Peninsula Energy Development Organization—KEDO) that consisted of South Korea, Japan, the European Union, and over thirty others. With South Korea providing 70 percent of the funding, KEDO supervised and financed the construction of the LWRs that were projected to cost over $4 billion dollars. U.S. negotiators made efforts to conclude the deal with conventional power reactors however the North insisted on LWRs. In the end, the United States relented given the LWRs produced far less weapons grade plutonium than the North's existing reactors, and the North lacked the technology to reprocess the spent fuel. The agreement was a complex arrangement with many overlapping and phased provisions that attempted to ensure compliance on both sides.[64]

For several years, the parties struggled to implement the Agreed Framework, a project that was plagued by numerous delays. Yet, the agreement seemed to put a cap on the North's nuclear weapons program with Pyongyang apparently in compliance. In fact, as late as March 2002, CIA Director George Tenet stated before the Senate Armed Services Committee: "North Korea continues to comply with the terms of the Agreed Framework that are directly related to the freeze on its reactor program," which was true despite the second clandestine program.[65] However, lingering doubts remained regarding the North's nuclear status. Since 1993, the CIA maintained that prior to the Agreed Framework, North Korea might have diverted sufficient plutonium for one or two nuclear weapons. Five to six more could be added if the 8,000 fuel rods were reprocessed. Yet, North Korea had conducted no definitive tests to demonstrate conclusively it had a nuclear capability. However, after several years of what the North may have believed were purposeful delays by the United States and KEDO, Pyongyang began to explore other options that became public in October 2002.

Sometime in the late 1990s, North Korea began to pursue a nuclear weapons program based on highly enriched uranium (HEU), a route different from the plutonium-based reactors sealed under the Agreed Framework. North Korea turned to Pakistan for help concluding a barter deal that sent ballistic missile plans to Islamabad in return for parts and technology to begin an HEU program. By summer 2002, evidence pointed to a program that had gone beyond purely research into one more fully developed. However, the full extent of the program remains unclear.[66]

At an October 2002 meeting with DPRK officials, U.S. representatives confronted their counterparts with the evidence of an HEU program. After initially denying the existence of the program, the next day, DPRK representatives confirmed the allegations and declared "they have more powerful things as well."[67] These were likely references to the one or two plutonium-based nuclear weapons they may possess and chemical and biological weapons. While described by U.S. representatives as "assertive, aggressive," and "belligerent," the North Korean representatives also indicated they would be willing to relinquish the program if the United States provided a guarantee not to attack the DPRK, concluded a peace treaty, and accepted North Korean sovereignty.[68]

The U.S. response was cautious and measured, insisting that North Korea must first comply with existing agreements regarding its nuclear weapons program and that the issue should be resolved through multilateral diplomacy. Shortly after the crisis, a White House spokesperson remarked "the president believes this is troubling, sobering news. We are seeking a peaceful resolution. This is best addressed through diplomatic channels at this point."[69] Preoccupied with matters in Iraq, the Bush administration was reluctant to take on another foreign policy emergency. As one official in the Bush administration later put it, "One rogue state crisis at a time!"[70] However, the administration did succeed in convincing the KEDO executive board to suspend the shipments of heavy fuel oil, an action that drew immediate condemnation from the North. The following year, in November 2003, KEDO also suspended construction of the LWRs.

While the United States continued to downplay the crisis, North Korea ratcheted up the pressure. In December 2002, Pyongyang disabled the seals and dismantled the surveillance equipment maintained by IAEA monitors and ordered them to leave the country. On 10 January 2003, the North announced its exit from the NPT, stating, "we can no longer remain bound to the NPT, allowing the country's security and dignity of our nation to be infringed upon."[71] However, the North reiterated its intent to not produce nuclear weapons and its willingness to hold a dialogue with the United States over these issues. In February, North Korea restarted one of the sealed reactors, a dangerous signal since the reactor is not connected to the power grid, indicating little purpose other than to produce spent plutonium. The North also stated on three separate occasions that it had completed reprocessing the 8,000 spent fuel rods and had begun manufacturing nuclear weapons. On 10 February 2005, North Korea announced that it had "manufactured nukes for self-defence to cope with the Bush administration's evermore undisguised policy to isolate and stifle the DPRK. Its nuclear weapons will remain [a] nuclear deterrent for self-defence under any circumstances."[72] Yet, barring any North Korean nuclear test or on-site inspections, the exact state of North Korea's nuclear weapons capabilities remains uncertain.

North Korea also possesses a chemical and biological weapons capability. It is estimated that Pyongyang has numerous chemical agents in its stockpile but has focused on mustard gas, phosgene, sarin, and V-agents (VM and VX).[73] The chemical agents are produced indigenously and deliverable through artillery, rocket systems, and ballistic missiles.

The North's biological weapons (BW) capability consists of several agents including anthrax, botulism, cholera, small pox, and typhoid. The extent of their BW stockpiles is not clear. The agents have been developed indigenously, and it appears that Pyongyang has devoted more effort to defending against these weapons than in preparing them for an offensive threat.[74] However, some U.S. reports indicate North Korea could deliver a BW warhead on a ballistic missile. In addition, there is also concern that the North may sell materials or technology from either its chemical or biological weapons programs. The DPRK has signed the Biological Weapons Convention but has not signed the Chemical Weapons Convention while South Korea has signed and ratified both agreements.

Ballistic Missile Development and Proliferation

Another serious North Korean proliferation threat concerns its production, testing, and export of ballistic missiles. North Korea began its acquisition of missile technology in the 1960s with the delivery of Soviet-made surface to air missiles. In 1965, Kim Il Sung began the Hamhung Military Academy to aid in the DPRK's development of advanced weaponry. At the time Kim stated, "If war breaks out, the United States and Japan will also be involved. In order to prevent their involvement, we have to be able to produce rockets that fly as far as Japan."[75] Later in the decade, Pyongyang acquired Soviet FROG (Free Rocket Over Ground) missiles and by the 1970s began producing their own versions through a process of reverse engineering. Moscow supplied conventional, high explosive warheads with the FROG missiles and Pyongyang used these to design their own chemical warheads.[76] In the early 1980s, the North acquired the Scud B missile from Egypt and developed its own model, again through reverse engineering. Other improvements later yielded an enhanced Scud C that had a range sufficient to hit any part of South Korea.

Beginning sometime in 1988, the North began work on another improved version of the Scud, the Nodong 1 missile. Flight-tested only once in 1993, the Nodong 1 is a one-stage, MRBM (medium range ballistic missile) with a range of between 1,350 to 1,500 km, depending on the size of the warhead.[77] It is likely that North Korea intends to configure the Nodong to carry a nuclear payload. The increased range of the Nodong 1 brought all of Japan and U.S. personnel located there, including bases in Okinawa, within its range, generating even more worry in Tokyo and Washington. It is likely that the Nodong was operational by 1993 or 1994, and according to the 1998 Rumsfeld Commission report on ballistic missile threats, "the Nodong was operationally deployed long before the U.S. Government recognized that fact. There is ample evidence that North Korea has created a sizable missile production infrastructure, and therefore it is highly likely that considerable numbers of Nodongs have been produced."[78] However, the accuracy of the Nodong and other long-range DPRK missile systems remains in doubt.

There is also some concern that the Nodong missile is the precursor to a DPRK submarine-launched ballistic missile (SLBM) capability. The Nodong has a design similar to the Soviet SS-N-4 and SS-N-5 SLBMs and there is evidence that Russian/Soviet scientists specializing in submarine ballistic missiles traveled to North Korea in the early 1990s for collaboration on the project. In 1992, 60 Russian missile scientists from the V.P. Makayev OKB, the submarine missile bureau, were stopped at the airport just prior to leaving for North Korea. According to the Federation of American Scientists, "it is difficult to assess the full extent of collaboration and technology transfer between the Makayev bureau and North Korea during this Gorbachev era, although such a large, senior delegation almost certainly meant that an earlier contact had already been substantially completed with certain critical documentation as a part of an agreement."[79] In August 2004, *Jane's Defence Weekly* reported that Pyongyang was preparing to deploy a submarine-launched ballistic missile or ship-mounted ballistic missile system based on an old Soviet model that may have been part of the 1992 collaboration with V.P Makayev Design Bureau. The report also noted the development of a road-mobile medium to intermediate range ballistic missile.[80] If Pyongyang chooses to deploy these SLBMs, old Soviet, Golf-class diesel submarines would be compatible and have already been used by China to test similar submarine launched missiles.[81] Even a limited submarine missile force would greatly enhance the survivability of the North's missile capability and significantly alter strategic calculations for the United States and others in the region.

Concerns for North Korea's missile program took a dramatic turn on 31 August 1998 when Pyongyang launched a new missile, the Taepo Dong, ostensibly to put a satellite in orbit. Though many were initially skeptical of the satellite explanation, later intelligence reports confirmed that it was indeed an effort to put a satellite in space but one that had failed.[82] At the time of the launch, Pyongyang claimed they had been successful:

> The satellite is now transmitting the melody of the immortal revolutionary hymns "Song of General Kim Il Sung" and "Song of General Kim Jong Il" and the Morse signals "*Juche* Korea" in 27 MHz. The rocket and satellite which our scientists and technicians correctly put into orbit at one launch are a fruition of our wisdom and technology 100 percent [sic]. The successful launch of the first

artificial satellite in the DPRK greatly encourages the Korean people in the efforts to build a powerful socialist state under the wise leadership of General Secretary Kim Jong Il.[83]

The rocket, normally a two-stage missile, was equipped with a third stage and had an estimated range of just over 2,500 km. Development of the Taepo Dong 1 began sometime in 1987 after Kim Jong Il reportedly said, "if we can develop this we have nothing to fear. Even the American Bastards won't be able to bother us."[84]

Japan was outraged as the launch sent part of the rocket over its airspace. In response, Tokyo immediately terminated all food aid and talks between the two countries. Despite the failure of the third stage, the launch demonstrated that Pyongyang was closer to developing an ICBM capable of reaching the United States than many had thought. In 2001, CIA Director Tenet noted, "This missile would be capable of delivering a small biological or chemical weapon to the United States, although with significant targeting inaccuracies. Moreover, North Korea has retained the ability to test its follow-on Taepo Dong-2 missile, which could deliver a nuclear-sized payload to the United States."[85]

In May 1999, U.S. intelligence detected North Korean preparations for another launch. These reports mobilized a concerted diplomatic effort by the United States, South Korea, Japan, China, and Russia to dissuade the North from conducting another test. On 24 September 1999, Pyongyang announced a one-year moratorium on missile tests, contingent upon continued U.S.-DPRK talks. The following year North Korea extended the moratorium for another three years. Kim Jong Il confirmed the pledge in 2001 during his visit to Russian President Putin.[86] The moratorium on flight-testing remains in effect but does not include research and development of missile components and engines, or the sale of missiles and missile technology.

In 2000, the United States and North Korea came close to concluding a comprehensive deal on Pyongyang's ballistic missile program.[87] According to U.S. officials involved in the proceedings, Kim Jong Il promised to refrain from producing, testing, and deploying missiles with ranges over 300 miles. The 300-mile range was problematic because this placed almost all of Japan within range, including U.S. troops stationed there. Kim Jong Il also agreed to end missile sales, including components, technology, and training arrangements. Any previous contracts with other countries would be terminated. Finally, Kim dropped the demand for $1 billion annually to compensate for lost missile revenue. Instead, he indicated that $1 billion total in nonmonetary compensation, including food aid, coal, and other items would suffice. Obstacles remained concerning verification procedures and the status of North Korea's existing missile force, which was not included in the North Korean proposal. U.S. negotiators hoped to include an intrusive verification plan, the destruction of existing DPRK missiles, and lowering the missile threshold to the requirements of the Missile Technology Control Regime (MTCR), namely the DPRK would possess no missiles that carry more than a 1,100 kg payload or have a range of over 180 miles. In November 2000,

Secretary of State Madeline Albright traveled to Pyongyang to conclude a deal but fell short; one more trip was necessary to nail down the agreement, possibly a summit between Kim Jong Il and President Clinton. However, Clinton was reluctant to make the trip. According to National Security Advisor Sandy Berger, the president was hesitant to leave the country with the disputed election of 2000 between George W. Bush and Al Gore undecided. Once the results were sorted out, Clinton advisors conferred with the Bush team who indicated only lukewarm support for a deal. With time running out, Clinton announced he would not make the trip to Pyongyang. According to President Clinton, "[president-elect Bush] did not discourage it at all. And it would not be fair to put that on him." Instead, Clinton maintained, "I concluded that I did not have sufficient time to put the trip together and to execute the trip in an appropriate manner in the days remaining."[88] Clinton believed the next administration would pick up where he left off and finish the deal.

Though the North placed a hold on testing, most intelligence analyses indicate the North is continuing its own development program of an improved Taepo Dong-2. Research and development has proceeded with static flight tests, but the precise extent of the program is difficult to determine.[89] According to the Rumsfeld Report, this missile could reach portions of Hawaii or Alaska and "lightweight variations of the TD-2 could fly as far as 10,000 km, placing at risk western U.S. territory in an arc extending northwest from Phoenix, Arizona to Madison, Wisconsin."[90] These missiles would be capable of carrying a chemical, biological, or nuclear warhead. However, there is a good deal of variance in the range estimates, and according to the Federation of American Scientists, "the performance attributed to the various missile systems appear to far exceed the performance that would be seen under real-world conditions while carrying a legitimate strategic lethal payload mass, which would not be sufficient to reach the continental United States."[91] There is also some question regarding the exact military purpose of the missiles. There is no evidence yet that the Taepo Dong-1 or 2 are deployed and it is possible these missiles are not intended for strategic military purposes. The Federation of American Scientists notes again,

> The configuration of the missiles suggests that they were designed for use not as weapons, but simply for space flight. Furthermore, the inability of the launch infrastructure to support anything other than limited operations under non-winter weather conditions indicates that North Korea has not seriously contemplated deploying the Taep'o-dong as an offensive weapon system. This brings into serious question whether more has been read into this program that can be legitimately justified.[92]

Significant technical problems remain for North Korea to develop an ICBM that can threaten the United States, including the development of reentry vehicles that can withstand the heat of passing through the earth's atmosphere and more sophisticated guidance systems. However, U.S. intelligence maintains, "by 2015 the U.S. most likely will face ICBM threats from North Korea."[93]

Finally, the DPRK has also been a serious threat because of its willingness to sell or share its missile technology. According to CIA Director George Tenet, "our main concern is P'yongyang's continued exports of ballistic missile-related equipment and missile components, materials, and technical expertise. North Korean customers include countries in the Middle East, South Asia, and North Africa."[94] Tenet continued: "As worrying as the ICBM threat will be, the threat to U.S. interests and forces from short- and medium-range ballistic missiles is here and now. The proliferation of MRBMs—driven largely though not exclusively by North Korean Nodong sales—is altering strategic balances in the Middle East and Asia."[95] According to Bermudez Jr., "Without the DPRK sales the ballistic missile capabilities and developments in these countries would be 5-10 years behind their current levels and South Asia would be more stable."[96] In 1996 U.S. officials began talks to bring the North into the MTCR, an arrangement that currently has 28 members who agree to implement national export controls on surface-to-surface missiles and related technology. To date, these efforts have been unsuccessful, and sales remain problematic as demonstrated by the 2002 sale of fifteen Scud missiles to Yemen.

For North Korea the development of ballistic missiles is not only a security issue. For a country that has few valuable exports, ballistic missiles are an important source of revenue for the cash strapped economy. Estimates indicate that in various years, North Korea has earned over $500 million annually on the sale of ballistic missiles and related technology.[97] During negotiations, the DPRK demanded $500 million in compensation and help in launching satellites in return for ending its ballistic missile program. Currently, North Korea has approximately 500 Scud missiles of various types in its arsenal along with at least 10 Nodong missiles.[98]

Food Crisis and Economic Meltdown

Despite its threatening military capabilities, North Korea's overall strength is tempered by a deteriorating economy and a serious food shortage.[99] North Korea remains a centrally planned economy where the state owns most of the country's economic assets. For years the government bureaucracy determined prices, production targets, and the allocation of resources. The economy continues to struggle with outdated technology, failing infrastructure, and a lack of investment capital. In the 1950s and 1960s, North Korea was a relative success story surpassing ROK economic performance. Slowly, the inefficiencies of a command economy, the *juche* ideology, and the meddling of Kim Il Sung in economic policy began to take its toll. In one example of mismanagement, farmers were urged to clear hillsides in an effort to increase land under cultivation. However, removing this vegetation increased soil erosion and made these areas more susceptible to flooding.

The 1990s were particularly serious for the North Korean economy. First, with the end of the Cold War, Soviet and Chinese aid came to an end along with extensive trade links to the former communist bloc. Second, beginning in 1994, a series of floods and droughts rocked North Korea, producing large-scale famine in a region that has historically had difficulty being self-sufficient in food. Using a study by the Johns Hopkins University of Public Health, Andrew Natsios estimates the death toll may have been as high as two to three million due to starvation.[100] A United Nations report in 1998 indicated that 63 percent of the children in North Korea were shorter in height than they should have been for their age due to persistent malnutrition.[101] In 2001, Catherine Bertini, executive director of the World Food Program, noted after a visit to North Korea: "There is no question that for the foreseeable future North Korea will be the recipient of international assistance. It is not possible for the country to be food self-sufficient in the next few years."[102]

From 1991 to 1996, North Korean economic output shriveled with industrial and mining production operating at only 30 percent capacity.[103] The economic infrastructure is poor with a lack of paved roads and an outdated telecommunications system. Industrial technology is over 20 years old and reform efforts have been minimal. Instead, the government has relied on campaigns that urge the populace to work harder.[104] Particularly serious is the shortage of energy, a condition North Koreans have been coping with for several years. In one telling example in 2002, Masood Hyder, chief UN representative in Pyongyang, lamented, "When you walk down the corridors in schools and hospitals in the winter, it is colder inside than outside. Even in the meetings with senior officials in these palatial settings, it is very, very cold. When we stay in government guest houses in the winter, the toilets are freezing over."[105] In another sign of the paucity of electricity, an evening satellite image taken in 2001 shows most of the country almost completely dark while much of the Northeast Asia region is aglow.[106]

In 2002, the North took some important though tentative steps towards economic reform including wage and price reforms on numerous items such as food, electricity, and housing to bring them closer to international levels. Food rationing ended along with subsidies for some of the DPRK's failing industries. Those industries are now expected to earn a profit. Pyongyang also announced the opening of an "autonomous capitalist investment zone" on its northwest border with China that will operate "free of central government interference for a period of 50 years."[107] However, these measures have brought little success. According to one press report,

> Wages increased by 20 times or more after the July [2002] reforms, but prices have gone up by even wider margins. The reforms were supposed to give enterprises greater responsibility for their balance sheets: bigger profits could, in theory, mean bigger wages. In practice, hardly any factory in the country can turn a profit. Energy and fuel shortages are crippling, the cost of inputs is soaring, and the economy has been reduced to little more than trade in absolute necessities.[108]

North Korea has undertaken several other major economic initiatives over the years including creation of the Ranjin-Sonbong special economic zone, the Mt. Kumgang tourism venture with Hyundai of South Korea, the opening of a road route through the DMZ to the resort area, and reestablishing rail and road links with the South. The Ranjin-Sonbong area, created in 1991, was an effort to attract foreign investment by creating a special zone that allowed investors complete ownership of their projects, the right to lease land for fifty years, tax breaks, protection against nationalization, and the right to channel profits out of the country. DPRK officials chose the site because it was isolated and could contain the influence of foreigners from the remainder of the country. According to one North Korean official, "We no longer have an iron curtain, but we still do have a mosquito net. It can let in breezes, and it can also defend against mosquitoes."[109] The effort has failed to achieve the desired results due largely to poor infrastructure, mandated wage rates that were higher than those in other parts of Asia, and an inability to sell goods made in the DPRK to the United States because of continuing economic sanctions and lack of normalized relations with Washington.[110]

It is unclear what effect these economic woes have had on DPRK military preparations. The regime has declared a "military first" policy that ensures scarce resources are channeled into the military's coffers. In addition, profits from the North's arms industry, especially the ballistic missile trade are utilized by the armed forces to maintain its capability. Despite these efforts, it is likely that the economic crisis in North Korea has significantly degraded Pyongyang's military capability. According to Joseph Bermudez Jr., military readiness declined significantly during the late 1980s and mid-1990s, particularly in the Air Force and Navy. However, the Army has stabilized its decline but at reduced levels of readiness and Pyongyang has significantly increased its deployment of long-range artillery systems and multiple rocket launchers.[111] Thus, Bermudez Jr. maintains,

> The KPA [Korean People's Army] is currently judged to be capable of defending the territory of the DPRK, conducting special operations against the ROK and Japan during peacetime, and maintaining internal security. It maintains the capability to initiate a war of reunification against the ROK on extremely short notice. However, it has a declining capability to prosecute such a war for more than six months.[112]

While the deteriorating economy may have eroded the North's military capabilities, there are some serious dangers should the economy move further towards collapse including refugees and the instability that could result from a DPRK implosion. Even the U.S. Defense Department recognizes the dangers of a collapsing economy. According to a 2000 report,

> If economic conditions worsen, we must consider that the North Korean economy could break down completely, precipitating social chaos and threatening the existence of the regime itself. We should anticipate a flood of refugees, humanitarian needs, and the potential for chaos, military coup, or the devastation of civil war. We continue to update our contingency plan to deal with these possibilities.[113]

Thus, while many hope for regime change through economic collapse, the uncertainties of how this might occur and the final results of the collapse make this a dangerous proposition.

Intent

Gauging North Korean intent remains as difficult an exercise as ever. Information on the inner workings of the DPRK regime is scarce. Yet some important questions remain. Is Kim Jong Il and his regime still determined to reunify the peninsula by force if the opportunity arose? Is the overriding goal regime survival in the face of daunting economic and security threats? Is North Korea determined to become a nuclear power? Some have suggested that North Korea is unpredictable and irrational, deserving of the title "rogue state" and its inclusion in the "axis of evil." Yet, Pyongyang's actions can also be viewed as highly rational as it struggles for survival with few allies, a decrepit economy, and few levers available to achieve its interests. North Korea has periodically increased pressure through crisis brinkmanship to bring attention to national interests it deems important. One scholar noted that North Korea's actions, though dangerous, have gained it a seat at the negotiating table, and "capturing international headlines has afforded a poor and strategically disadvantaged state great attention."[114] Former U.S. Ambassador to South Korea Donald Gregg remarked, "I don't think these guys are crazy. As poker players, they have always had an ability to play a very poor hand very well, and they are showing that again."[115] However, the vexing questions remain and there are several possible answers to these questions. Debate continues regarding which ones are correct but these answers are crucial to understanding the security threat posed by the North.

Would North Korea invade the South should an opportunity arise? For the U.S. military, North Korea remains a dangerous threat. According to General Thomas Schwartz, Commander of U.S. forces in Korea:

> Despite North Korea's continuing interests in foreign aid and economic reform, the Kim Regime continues to field far more conventional military force than any conceivable sense of self-defense would warrant. We and our allies in the Pacific must encourage tangible military confidence building measures that are verifiable and reciprocal. The measures taken so far [economic, diplomatic, and cultural] are first steps, but tangible military measures are key to reducing the risk of conflict.[116]

Yet, it seems highly unlikely that Pyongyang would conclude that another attack such as the one it undertook in 1950 had much chance to succeed. The North has significant military assets but much of the equipment is well past its prime. Conversely, the ROK military is prepared, modern, and buttressed by U.S. forces and a U.S.-ROK alliance that is determined to maintain peace and stability in the region. Any expectation by Pyongyang that the United States would abandon its commitment to the South after more than 50 years is foolhardy. Should the North initiate an attack, it is likely to receive international condemnation for its actions. Moscow and Beijing have already expressed their refusal to support any DPRK action of this sort. A North Korean attack that capitalized on surprise might be very destructive and have some success in the short run. However, the U.S.-ROK response would be disastrous and likely bring an end to the North Korean regime. DPRK leaders and military planners must realize that the use of force in a bid to reunify Korea would be a desperate act that is likely to fail. Thus, invasion remains an unlikely possibility. Instead, regime survivability remains the paramount goal of the regime.

Pyongyang's apparent determination in the early 1990s to develop nuclear weapons accompanied by its bellicose rhetoric and brinksmanship heightened tension on the peninsula. With the signing of the Agreed Framework in 1994, it appeared for several years that North Korea was indeed willing to forgo a nuclear option as all indications showed Pyongyang was in full compliance with the agreement. Hope reached even higher levels on 13 June 2000 when Kim Dae Jung and Kim Jong Il met in Pyongyang for a historic summit meeting, the first ever between leaders of the North and South. When arriving at the state guesthouse, Kim Jong Il remarked, "June 13 will be a day recorded in history," to which Kim Dae Jung replied, "Let's go on and make that history."[117] The summit concluded with an agreement where both pledged to improve North-South relations and work towards peaceful reunification. Kim Jong Il also received an invitation to visit Seoul. Though there were high expectations of a return visit in the months after the June summit, the trip did not occur.[118]

Other important visits followed the summit. North Korean General Jo Myong Rok, first vice chairman of the National Defense Commission, made a historic journey to Washington, D.C. where he spoke to President Clinton on a variety of issues. During the meeting, General Jo wore his uniform, widely interpreted as a sign of the military's support for this diplomatic undertaking. General Jo brought an invitation for President Clinton to visit Pyongyang and repeated the North's willingness to scrap its missile program in return for assistance in launching satellites. Secretary of State Madeline Albright followed in November with a visit to Pyongyang, hopeful of bringing the United States and DPRK closer to a missile agreement. Secretary Albright indicated progress was made, and there was speculation that President Clinton would travel to Pyongyang to conclude a deal. However, Clinton decided that he could not finish the deal in the waning days of his administration. North Korea had also embarked on a diplomatic blitz that saw it establish formal relations with over 140 countries including the Netherlands, Belgium, Italy, Australia, the United Kingdom, Canada, Spain, the Philippines, Kuwait, and Germany. In July 2000, North Korea began participation in the ASEAN Regional Forum with all of ASEAN's members—excluding Myanmar—agreeing to open diplomatic relations with Pyongyang. In May 2001, a delegation from the European Union visited Pyongyang and later announced its intention to open diplomatic relations with the DPRK. It appeared that a new era of peace and stability on the Korean peninsula might be at hand.

Others, however, cautioned that tough issues remained. As Victor Cha quipped, "let's not get summit slap happy."[119] A U.S. Defense Department report concluded that: "While the historic summit between the North and the South holds the promise of reconciliation and change, no evidence exists of the fundamental precursors for change. There is little or no evidence of economic reform or reform-minded leaders, reduction in military spending or a lessening of anti-US rhetoric."[120] U.S.-DPRK relations cooled considerably with the Bush administration, highlighted by North Korea's inclusion in the "axis of evil." Though many in the Bush Whitehouse had long questioned North Korea's intent, even more ominous danger signs appeared with the 2002 revelation of a parallel HEU nuclear weapons program and the rapid unraveling of the Agreed Framework that, since 1994, had frozen Pyongyang's plutonium program.

Is North Korea determined to develop a nuclear weapons capability or is it willing to forgo this option for the right incentives? According to Michael Mazarr, "states do not pursue the development of weapons without a reason. The associated costs, both financial and political, establish a presumption against acquiring nuclear arsenals. It is only when a state's perceived vulnerability or desire for attention or prestige overcomes that presumption that proliferation will take place."[121] Thus, possessing nuclear weapons may fulfill a number of North Korean objectives. First, nuclear weapons address some legitimate security concerns. North Korea faces a well-armed and modern ROK military, 32,500 U.S. troops in addition to other forces Washington could bring to bear in a conflict. The breakup of the Soviet Union and increasingly friendly relations between Pyongyang's defenders and South Korea has increased the North's sense of isolation. Nuclear weapons would act as a counterbalance to lost Soviet and Chinese support and the continued growth of ROK economic and military capability. Nuclear weapons are also a more cost effective option to continuing a conventional arms race with South Korea. According to the ROK Ministry of Defense, instead of continuing a stress on conventional weapons, "Pyongyang has placed emphasis on developing such resource-saving strategic weapons as nuclear weapons and long-range missiles and artillery."[122]

Thus, an important motivation for the North is deterring the United States and the South. When asked about DPRK motivations regarding long-range ballistic missiles, former Defense Secretary William Perry, who had just returned from a visit to North Korea in September 1999, responded, "I believe their primary reason is security, is deterrence. Whom would they be deterring? They would be deterring the United States. We do not think of ourselves as a threat to North Korea. But I truly believe that they consider us a threat to them."[123] According to Selig S. Harrison, who has made numerous visits to the North, "I have found unmistakable anxiety that the United States might stage a surprise attack designed to destroy the Kim Jong Il regime and pave the way for the absorption of North Korea by South Korea."[124]

Security concerns became an even greater issue following the events of September 11th and the Bush administration's response to terrorism. In his 2002 State of the Union address, President Bush maintained the United States is determined "to prevent regimes that sponsor terror from threatening America or our friends and allies with weapons of mass destruction. Some of these regimes have been pretty quiet since September the 11th. But we know their true nature." Citing Iraq, Iran, and North Korea, Bush declared, "States like these, and their terrorist allies, constitute an axis of evil, arming to threaten the peace of the world." Moreover, "By seeking weapons of mass destruction, these regimes pose a grave and growing danger. They could provide these arms to terrorists, giving them the means to match their hatred. They could attack our allies or attempt to blackmail the United States. In any of these cases, the price of indifference could be catastrophic."[125] Later, the Bush administration indicated its willingness to wage preemptive war against those who threaten the United States with weapons of mass of destruction.[126] With Saddam Hussein ousted, North Korean leaders feared they would be the next member of the "axis of evil" to come under fire. Nuclear weapons, combined with North Korea's ballistic missile capability, provide an important measure of deterrence for Pyongyang's fears of a U.S. preemptive strike.

North Korea's security concerns were also evident from one of its chief demands in the nuclear crisis: a nonaggression pact with the United States. According to the North's state-controlled media, "The purpose of the DPRK's proposal for a non-aggression treaty with the U.S. lies in checking a new war on the Korean peninsula, ensuring well-being and prosperity to all the Koreas and making a contribution to the regional peace and stability."[127] North Korean leaders thought they had a commitment of this sort in the October 2000 joint communiqué signed at the conclusion of General Jo's visit that declared "neither government would have hostile intent toward the other." However, the Bush administration appeared to reverse this position soon after taking office. In a November 2002 meeting with senior North Korean officials, former U.S. ambassador to South Korea, Donald Gregg, remarked, "I strongly felt in the last few days that the North truly fears a possible attack from the United States." Regarding the nonaggression treaty he noted, "I think that they would like the United States to give them some assurances that we don't want to blow them out of the water."[128] As a result, Pyongyang has maintained it is "quite just for the DPRK to have built up a deterrent force to protect itself from the U.S. moves to mount a preemptive nuclear attack."[129]

Second, nuclear weapons are a valuable commodity providing export earnings for the ailing North Korean economy. CIA Director George Tenet noted, "incentive to engage in such behavior [proliferation activities] increases as its economy continues to decline. Missiles and WMD [weapons of mass destruction] know-how are North Korean products for which there is a real market."[130] Moreover, North Korea could include ballistic missiles to make a very saleable package to would-be proliferators.

A third explanation relates to DPRK domestic politics. In addition to addressing security needs, nuclear weapons may serve the political interests of various actors within the state.[131] When Kim Jong Il came to power after his father's death in 1994, there were doubts that his succession would be accepted, especially by hardliners in the armed forces. Given the DPRK's horrendous economic circumstances since Kim Jong Il succeeded his father, from time to time, there have been questions regarding his leadership and complete control of the military. The acquisition of nuclear weapons helps to bolster Kim's position and, in North Koreans' eyes, elevates the DPRK's prestige and role as a "major player" in Northeast Asia. In both instances, Kim Jong Il is able to further cement his control over the military and bolster his legitimacy as the ruler of the country.

Finally, it is possible that Pyongyang has manipulated the nuclear issue as a bargaining chip to obtain other objectives. In fact, North Korean "brinkmanship" in the early 1990s obtained numerous concessions in the 1994 Agreed Framework on a variety of economic and political issues such as light-water reactors, increased diplomatic contacts, and a U.S. pledge not to use nuclear weapons against the North. Mazarr argues that it was the ambiguous nature of the North's nuclear weapons program that was most important. In a prophetic statement, Mazarr maintained that a public commitment by the DPRK to develop nuclear weapons would bring certain denunciation and sanctions on the North. However, professing no nuclear ambitions would mean little attention from the international community for its policy concerns. By maintaining a somewhat ambiguous nuclear program, the North has reaped many economic and political benefits while avoiding the wrath that it would incur as a declared nuclear state.[132] In the words of a senior U.S. military official prior to the agreement, "it comes down to this. If we know that the bomb project is a dud, we'll forget about the North and move on to the next crisis. They get nothing. And if we know it is a success, we go to sanctions. So they want to keep it in-between."[133] However, these benefits have come at a price; as one scholar notes, North Korea damaged its international image and "bolstered the impression that it is a rogue state par excellence."[134]

With the admission of an HEU program and its race to restart the plutonium reactors, the North again turned to crisis diplomacy in an effort to pull the United States back into negotiations. However, this time, there was less ambiguity regarding the North's intentions; if the United States refused to open a dialogue and extend a formal security guarantee, it would continue on its path to develop nuclear weapons, which it appears to have done.

Is North Korea willing to forgo nuclear weapons? Critics of the North Korean regime maintain the HEU program began sometime in 1998, even before the Bush administration; this is proof of its intention to keep a nuclear option open and demonstrates its willingness to break international agreements. According to Henry Sokolski, "This shows that both Iraq and North Korea are nuclear cheaters. We need to stop coddling the North Koreans on the expectation that they'll behave."[135] Yet why would North Korea have been willing to halt its plutonium program under the AF? Why have they stated on several occasions their willingness to put all U.S. security concerns, including the HEU program, on the table?

Certainly, one answer is to use the negotiations to further extort concessions from the United States and its allies. The speed at which North Korea restarted its plutonium facilities at Yongbyon may have been a demonstration of its determination to develop nuclear weapons. However, another answer is also plausible. North Korea is pursuing its familiar pattern of manufacturing a crisis to draw reluctant parties to the negotiating table. Unsealing the reactors and subsequent steps to restart the plutonium program were a response to the suspension of HFO shipments and a steady ratcheting up of the pressure and potential dangers when the United States failed to reopen a dialogue with Pyongyang. Announcements that it had finished reprocessing the fuel rods and would conduct a nuclear test further added to tension in the region. Pyongyang has already demonstrated its willingness to relinquish its nuclear ambitions in the 1994 Agreed Framework. It was only after this agreement appeared to be failing with U.S. compliance less than enthusiastic that the HEU program began. For months, Pyongyang insisted that negotiations to address the issue could only occur in a bilateral format with the United States. Washington was equally adamant that talks occur only in a multilateral forum. After tentative discussions in Beijing in spring 2003 between North Korea, the United States, and China, Six-Party talks convened that also included South Korea, Japan, and Russia. Two more rounds have occurred and thus far, these meetings have produced few results. All the parties agree that the meetings should continue but have been on hold until after the November 2004 U.S. presidential election. The North continues to insist that it would not relinquish its nuclear deterrent until the United States drops its hostile policy and gives Pyongyang a security guarantee, something the Bush administration has been unwilling to give.

One other question regarding Pyongyang's motivation remains: Why did North Korean officials, after initially denying the October 2002 accusations of an HEU program, choose to admit its existence rather than continue the denials? This is a difficult question to answer. If the North were intent on developing a clandestine nuclear program, why not continue to deny the HEU program? The most plausible answer is that Pyongyang was maintaining the HEU program as a hedge against what it viewed as U.S. foot dragging to implement the Agreed Framework during the Clinton administration, and overall U.S. hostility, especially when the Bush administration came to Washington. When confronted with the initial accusations, Pyongyang reacted as it often did—it denied them. However, after a chance to ponder the options, the DPRK representatives returned the next day with their usual fiery rhetoric but this time admitting the program and offering to place it on the table for negotiations. This approach was consistent with an earlier admission to Japan in September 2002. After years of denial, Kim Jong Il apologized for the kidnapping of thirteen Japanese citizens in the late 1970s and early 1980s, lamenting, "This is truly regretful, and I offer my candid apology. This will never happen again."[136] According to Japanese officials, Kim said that security personnel conducted the abductions in an effort to acquire native Japanese speakers for training in DPRK intelligence. Kim is believed to have commented, "After I came to know about this, the persons responsible have been punished."[137] Kim hoped he could move DPRK-Japan relations forward with his frank contrition. The HEU admission, in what some have called "confessional diplomacy,"[138] may have been a similar olive branch to begin a dialogue with the United States. When Washington remained adamant that there could be no negotiations without North Korea abandoning its nuclear program, the North has since turned to its familiar approach of "crisis diplomacy." In the past year, North Korea has returned to denying the admission of the HEU program. However, given the information available from Libya and Pakistan, this is a difficult position to maintain.

The specter of a nuclear-armed North Korea worries everyone in the region and is a serious threat to peace and stability. However, short of a military strike to take out North Korea's nuclear weapons facilities, an option fraught with many dangers, there are few alternatives to stopping a determined North Korea from developing a nuclear capability. Seoul is only 25 miles from the DMZ, well within DPRK artillery range. A number of South Korean nuclear energy reactors are also vulnerable to North Korean retaliation. A military strike might provoke the North to retaliate against these targets. It is also difficult to determine where all of the North's nuclear installations are located, particularly those that might be underground. Efforts to obtain a diplomatic settlement to the nuclear crisis continue, but the North is unlikely to give up its nuclear trump card without a security guarantee from the United States.

Conclusion

Throughout the U.S. defense commitment, Washington's assessments of the threat changed. In the 1950s, China and the Soviet Union were perceived to be directing a monolithic communist threat while Pyongyang was preoccupied with rebuilding after the devastation of the Korean War. Threat assessments shifted somewhat during the 1960s as North Korea completed its rebuilding efforts and began to establish a formidable military capability. China continued to be a menace, particularly because of its proximity to Korea and its support for "wars of national liberation." However, concern for the Soviet threat diminished; few in the United States believed the Soviets would start another conflict in Korea. By the 1970s and 1980s, U.S.-ROK attention focused more squarely on North Korea. Improving relations with the United States made it less likely that the Soviets or Chinese would provoke a war in Korea.

North Korean conventional capabilities increased steadily after the Korean War with a particularly big push in the late 1970s, and its rhetoric and behavior continued to demonstrate hostile intent. Concerns remained that the North might be willing to risk the use of force to achieve its goal of reunification. Table 3.3 opposite indicates that from 1960 to 1980, DPRK total armed forces increased

Table 3.3

NORTH AND SOUTH KOREAN MILITARY CAPABILITIES, 1960-2003

NORTH (South)

	Armed Forces	Ground Troops	Tanks	Combat Planes
1960	338,000	[1]	[1]	[1]
	(600,000)	(550,000)	[1]	(75)
1965	353,000	325,000	600	500
	(604,000)	(550,000)	[2]	[3]
1970	413,000	370,000	900	580
	(645,000)	(570,000)[4]	[5]	(200)
1975	467,000	410,000	1,130	588
	(625,000)	(580,000)	(1,000)	(216)
1980	678,000	600,000	2,650	615
	(600,600)	(543,000)	(860)	(362)
1985	838,000	750,000	3,425	800
	(598,000)	(542,000)	(1,200)	(451)
1990	1,111,000	1,000,000	4,100	716
	(750,000)	(675,000)	(1,550)	(469)
1995	1,128,000	1,000,000	4,200	770
	(633,000)	(520,000)	(1,900)	(447)[6]
2000	1,082,000	950,000	4,060	621
	(683,000)	(560,000)	(2,330)	(555)
2003	1,082,00	950,000	4,060	605
	(686,000)	(560,000)	(2,330)	(538)

Source: *The Military Balance*

1. Data not available in *The Military Balance*
2. 7 tank divisions—number not specified
3. 9 squadrons—number not specified
4. Includes 50,000 troops in Vietnam
5. 2 armored brigades
6. Includes 52 more in storage

approximately 229 percent with ground forces and tanks rising 208 percent and 583 percent respectively. Combat aircraft showed only a modest increase of 43 percent. By 1980, North Korean forces had surpassed those of the South and continued to grow. A large percentage of North Korean forces are forward deployed and on a high state of alert. The threat in Korea was largely consistent with general deterrence—the danger of an attack was not imminent but there was fear that the North might act should the opportunity arise. Given these realities, U.S. and ROK leaders could not discount the possibility that the North might be willing to use force. Prudent planning in the face of these conventional capabilities dictated that the United States and ROK continue to implement a robust deterrence posture.

An alarming shift in the threat configuration occurred with North Korea's efforts to acquire ballistic missiles and nuclear weapons. Now, U.S.-ROK security concerns involved more than a conventional conflict on the peninsula. North Korea had the capability to hit targets in Japan, and possibly the United States, with ballistic missiles tipped with conventional, nuclear, and chemical warheads. Proliferation concerns were even more dangerous, especially given North Korea's history as a dealer of ballistic missiles. Sales of nuclear technology or material would be a serious blow to U.S. nonproliferation efforts. Moreover, a DPRK nuclear program might prompt South Korea and Japan to acquire their own nuclear deterrent. These are significant changes in the threat configuration and raise questions regarding the adequacy of relying solely on a deterrence strategy, a subject that will be explored in chapter 6.

Reading the intent of the North Korean leadership has always been an immensely difficult task. As a result, there is much room for debate regarding the motivations of the DPRK regime. Is the North willing to use force to reunify? History would indicate that Pyongyang has answered this question in the negative for over 50 years. After the Korean War, the North was involved in a massive rebuilding effort that consumed its planning and resources. Once this was completed in the 1960s, even then, North Korea was sobered by the memories of a near brush with regime change in 1950. During the 1960s, while provocative actions including infiltrations and assassination attempts rose dramatically, these likely were signs that Pyongyang was fully aware of the costs of a direct confrontation with U.S.-ROK forces. Instead, the DPRK relied on less direct action that could be ratcheted up or down depending on the level of success and the response of Washington and Seoul. Indeed, despite efforts to destabilize South Korea in 1967 and 1968, Pyongyang's efforts failed and eventually the costs of these operations required that they be scaled back. In the late 1970s, North Korea began a huge buildup in conventional forces, but it was also clear that China and the Soviet Union were no longer interested in fomenting unrest on the Korean peninsula. If North Korea was going to act, it would have to do it alone, a course that pitted the DPRK against the combined forces of the United States and South Korea.

Sometime in the 1990s, North Korean intent began to shift. North Korean conventional capabilities begin to deteriorate to the point where its effectiveness as an offensive force was limited to a short-term operation. Instead, North Korean efforts began to focus on a posture based more on deterrence. The DPRK's efforts to acquire ballistic missiles, nuclear and chemical weapons had relatively little value to retake the South, but were of enormous value for deterrence and its fear of a possible U.S. attack.

Deterrence theory usually treats the challenger as a single, relatively static entity. Given the more than 50 years of the U.S. defense commitment to South Korea, this has not been the case. The challenger has changed significantly in its source, capabilities, and intent, requiring adjustments to U.S. deterrence policy over the years. The proliferation threat posed by the DPRK created a new challenge, one that deterrence had a difficult time addressing. As a result, U.S. policy makers had to utilize new measures, in addition to deterrence, to deal with the security problems present in Korea.

Notes

1. Paul H.B. Godwin, "China's Asian Policy in the 1990s: Adjusting to the Post-Cold War Environment," in Sheldon W. Simon, ed., *East Asian Security in the Post-Cold War Era* (Armonk, New York: M.E. Sharpe, 1993), 132.

2. Chae-Jin Lee, "China and North Korea: An Uncertain Relationship," in Dae Sook Suh and Chae-Jin Lee, *North Korea after Kim Il Sung* (Boulder: Lynne Rienner, 1998), 195-196.

3. Samuel S. Kim and Tai Hwan Lee, "Chinese-North Korean Relations: Managing Asymmetrical Interdependence," in Samuel S. Kim and Tai Hwan Lee, *North Korea and Northeast Asia* (Lanham: Rowman and Littlefield, 2002), 121.

4. Scott McClellan, "Press Briefing on North Korean Report of Fuel Rod Reprocessing Concerns," 15 July 2003, <www.usinfo.state.gov>.

5. For some of this debate, see David M. Lampton, *Same Bed, Different Dreams: Managing U.S.-China Relations, 1989-2000* (Berkeley: University of California Press, 2001); Robert L. Suettinger, *Beyond Tiananmen: The Politics of U.S.-China Relations, 1989-2000* (Washington, D.C.: Brookings Institution, 2003); Warren I. Cohen, *America's Response to China: A History of Sino-American Relations* (New York: Columbia University Press, 2000); and Ezra Vogel, ed., *Living with China: U.S.-China Relations in the Twenty-First Century* (New York: W.W. Norton, 1999).

6. *Nuclear Posture Review*, 31 December 2002, 16-17 at <www.globalsecurity.org>.

7. *The National Security Strategy of the United States of America*, 27 September 2002 <www.whitehouse.gov.> (July 2003).

8. Marantz, "Moscow and East Asia," 35.

9. See Eugene Bazhanov and Natasha Bazhanov, "The Evolution of Russian-Korean Relations," *Asian Survey* 34, no. 9 (September 1994): 789-799.

10. Joo, "The New Friendship Treaty between Moscow and Pyongyang," 478.

11. Korean Central News Agency (KCNA), 30 September 1996 as quoted in Joo, "The New Friendship Treaty between Moscow and Pyongyang," 478.

12. As quoted in Herbert J. Ellison, "Russia, Korea, and Northeast Asia," in Nicholas Eberstadt and Richard J. Ellings, eds., *Korea's Future and the Great Powers* (Seattle: National Bureau of Asian Research, 2001), 177.

13. "South Korea Forgives $660 million of Russia's Debt," *Korea Now* 32, no. 13 (28 June 2003): 18.

14. Bazhanov and Bazhanov, "The Evolution of Russian-Korean Relations," 794.

15. Elizabeth Wishnick, "Russian-North Korean Relations: A New Era?" in Samuel S. Kim and Tai Hwan Lee, eds., *North Korea and Northeast Asia* (Lanham: Rowman & Littlefield, 2002), 143.

16. Wishnick, "Russian-North Korean Relations," 142.

17. Wishnick, "Russian-North Korean Relations," 144.

18. For a good assessment of the agreement, Joo, "The New Friendship Treaty be-

tween Moscow and Pyongyang," 467-481.

19. Joo, "The New Friendship Treaty between Moscow and Pyongyang," 475.

20. Joo, "The New Friendship Treaty between Moscow and Pyongyang," 467.

21. "DPRK-Russia Joint Declaration," 19 July 2000, <www.globalsecurity.org>.

22. U.S. Department of Defense, *2000 Report to Congress: Military Situation on the Korean Peninsula*, 12 September 2000, 5 <http://www.dod.gov> (June 2002).

23. David E. Sanger, "Bush Tells Seoul Talks with North Won't Resume Now," *New York Times*, 8 March 2001, A1, A6.

24. Sanger, "Bush Tells Seoul Talks with North Won't Resume Now," A1, A6.

25. Colin Powell, "Remarks by Secretary of State Colin Powell," 7 March 2001, <www.whiteHouse.gov/news/releases/2001/03/20010307-3.html>.

26. "Remarks by Secretary of State Colin Powell," 7 March 2001.

27. President George W. Bush, *State of the Union Address*, 29 January 2002, <http://www.whiteHouse.gov/news/releases/2002/01/20020129-11.html>.

28. Martin Nesirky, "U.S. Official Calls N. Korea 'Peddler' of Missile Technology," *Reuters* as printed in *Washington Post*, 30 August 2002, A17.

29. George Tenet, *The Worldwide Threat in 2003: Evolving Dangers in a Complex World*, 11 February 2003, <www.cia.gov>. Hereafter these statements by George Tenet will be noted as *The Worldwide Threat*.

30. Tenet, *The Worldwide Threat in 2002*, 13.

31. The discussion of military capabilities that follows draws extensively from *The Military Balance*; Joseph S. Bermudez Jr., *The Armed Forces of North Korea* (New York: I.B. Tauris, 2001); and <www.globalsecurity.org>.

32. U.S. Senate, *Statement of General Thomas A. Schwartz, Commander in Chief United Nations Command/Combined Forces Command and Commander, United States Forces Korea*, testimony before the Senate Armed Services Committee, 106th Congress, 2nd Session, 7 March 2000, 7.

33. Bermudez, *The Armed Forces of North Korea*, 5.

34. *1996 South Korea Defense White Paper*, <www.mnd.go.kr.>.

35. U.S. Senate, *Statement of General Thomas A. Schwartz, Commander in Chief United Nations Command/Combined Forces Command and Commander, United States Forces Korea*, testimony before the Senate Armed Services Committee, 107th Congress, 2nd Session, 5 March 2002, 8.

36. Michael O'Hanlon, "Stopping a North Korean Invasion," *International Security* 22, no. 4 (Spring 1998): 136.

37. Bermudez, *The Armed Forces of North Korea*, 61.

38. U.S. Senate, *Statement of General Thomas A. Schwartz, Commander in Chief United Nations Command/Combined Forces Command and Commander, United States Forces Korea*, testimony before the Senate Armed Services Committee," 106th Congress, 2nd Session, 7 March 2000, 5.

39. *2000 Report to Congress: Military Situation on the Korean Peninsula*, 7.

40. U.S. Senate, *Statement of General John H. Tilelli Jr., Commander in Chief, United Nations Command/U.S. Forces Korea/Combined Forces Command Korea*, testimony before the Senate Armed Services Committee, 106th Congress, 1st Session, 4 March 1999, 7.

41. U.S. Senate, *Statement of General Thomas A. Schwartz, Commander in Chief United Nations Command/Combined Forces Command and Commander, United States*

Forces Korea, testimony before the Senate Armed Services Committee, 106th Congress, 2nd Session, 7 March 2000, 5.

42. James Brooke, "Along Korean DMZ, G.I.'s Ponder Order to Pull Back," *New York Times*, 8 June 2003, A3.

43. Harrison, "The Missiles of North Korea," 14.

44. "Air Force-North Korea," <www.globalsecurity.org/military/world/dprk/air-force.htm> (July 2003).

45. "Air Force-North Korea," <www.globalsecurity.org/military/world/dprk/air-force.htm>.

46. "Air Force-North Korea," <www.globalsecurity.org/military/world/dprk/air-force.htm>.

47. "DPRK Navy," <www.globalsecurity.org/military/world/dprk/navy.htm>.

48. Bermudez Jr., *The Armed Forces of North Korea*, 106-110.

49. Bermudez Jr., *The Armed Forces of North Korea*, 92.

50. *2000 Report to Congress: Military Situation on the Korean Peninsula*, 10.

51. *The Military Balance, 2002-2003*, 140, and "ROK Navy," <www.globalsecurity.org>.

52. O'Hanlon, "Stopping a North Korean Invasion," 136.

53. *2000 Report to Congress: Military Situation on the Korean Peninsula*, 10.

54. The events leading up to this period are a long and complicated story. For more detailed treatments see Michael J. Mazarr, *North Korea and the Bomb* (New York: St. Martin's Press, 1995); Leon Sigal, *Disarming Strangers: Nuclear Diplomacy with North Korea* (Princeton: Princeton University Press, 1998); Don Oberdorfer, *The Two Koreas* (New York: Basic Books, 1997); and Scott Snyder, *Negotiating on the Edge: North Korean Negotiating Behavior* (Washington, D.C.: United States Institute of Peace Press, 1999).

55. Mazarr, *North Korea and the Bomb*, 24-25.

56. Harrison, "The Missiles of North Korea," 15.

57. Oberdorfer, *The Two Koreas*, 254-255, and Mazarr, *North Korea and the Bomb*, 25.

58. "2 Koreas Agree on Nuclear Ban, But Not on Method of Inspections," *New York Times*, 1 January 1992, A2.

59. Michael R. Gordon, "U.S. Goes to U.N. to Increase The Pressure on North Korea," *New York Times*, 22 March 1994, A1, A20.

60. Gordon, "U.S. Goes to U.N. to Increase The Pressure on North Korea," A1, A20.

61. Michael R. Gordon, "U.S. Will Urge U.N. To Plan Sanctions For North Korea," *New York Times*, 20 March 1994, A1, A3.

62. Ashton R. Carter and William J. Perry, *Preventive Defense: A New Security Strategy for America* (Washington, D.C.: Brookings Institution Press, 1999), 131.

63. "U.S.-North Korean 'Agreed Framework' on Nuclear Issue," *Korea Focus* 2, no. 5, Appendix (September-October, 1994): 166-168, and U.S. Arms Control and Disarmament Agency, *Fact Sheet - U.S.-Democratic People's Republic of Korea Agreed Framework*, 21 October 1994.

64. For a more detailed discussion of the agreement, see Terence Roehrig, "One Rogue State Crisis at a Time!: The United States and North Korea's Nuclear Weapons Program," *World Affairs* 165, no. 4 (Spring 2003): 155-178.

65. U.S. Senate, *Worldwide Threat-Converging Dangers in a Post 9/11 World*, Tes-

timony of Director of Central Intelligence George J. Tenet Before the Senate Armed Services Committee, 107th Congress, 2nd Session, 19 March 2002, 14.

66. David Sanger, "In North Korea and Pakistan, Deep Roots of Nuclear Barter," *New York Times*, 24 November 2002, A1, A6.

67. David Sanger, "North Korea Says It Has a Program on Nuclear Arms," *New York Times*, 17 October 2002, A1.

68. Peter Slevin and Karen DeYoung, "N. Korea Admits Having Secret Nuclear Arms," *Washington Post*, 17 October 2002, A1, and Doug Struck, "Nuclear Program Not Negotiable, U.S. Told N. Korea," *Washington Post*, 20 October 2002, A18.

69. Peter Slevin and Glenn Kessler, "Bush Plans Diplomacy on N. Korea's Arms Effort," *Washington Post*, 18 October 2002, A1.

70. Howard French and David Sanger, "North Korea to Reactivate an Idled Nuclear Reactor," *New York Times*, 13 December 2002, A16.

71. Christopher Torchia, "N. Korea Leaves Nuclear Weapons Treaty," *Washington Times*, 10 January 2003, <www.washingtontimes.com>.

72. *Korean Central News Agency* (KCNA), "DPRK FM on Its Stand to Suspend Its Participation in Six-party Talks for Indefinite Period," 11 February 2005, <http://www.kcna.co.jp> (May 22, 2005).

73. Bermudez Jr., *The Armed Forces of North Korea*, 226.

74. Bermudez Jr., *The Armed Forces of North Korea*, 231-235.

75. As quoted in Joseph S. Bermudez Jr., *A History of Ballistic Missile Development*, Occasional Paper No. 2, Monterey: Monterey Institute of International Studies, 1999, 2.

76. Hyun-Kun Yoon, 74.

77. For a table of the capabilities and characteristics of North Korean ballistic missiles, see Bermudez Jr., *A History of Ballistic Missile Development*, 27.

78. *Executive Summary of the Report of the Commission to Assess the Ballistic Missile Threat to the United States*, 104th Congress, 1st Session, 15 July 1998, <http://www.fas.org/irp/threat/bm-threat.htm> (June 2003).

79. Federation of American Scientists, "Nodong," <http://www.fas.org/nuke/guide/dprk/missile/nd-1.htm> (January 2002).

80. *Jane's Defence Weekly*, 2 August 2004.

81. Lee Jang Wook, "North Korea's Nuclear and Missile Ambitions," *New Asia* (September-October 2001) as contained in *Korea Focus* 9, no. 5 (September-October 2001): 58-59.

82. According to the Federation of American Scientists, the launch failed when "the third stage solid motor ruptured, de-orbiting the satellite, almost immediately after achieving orbital velocity." Federation of American Scientists, "Nodong," <http://fas.org/nuke/guide/dprk/missile/nd-1.htm> (June 2002).

83. "Successful Launch of first satellite in DPRK, *Korean Central News Agency*, 4 September 1998, <http://www.kcna.co.jp/calendar/frame.htm> (July 2002).

84. Federation of American Scientists, "Taep'o-dong 2 (TD-2)," <http://fas.org/nuke/guide/dprk/missile/td-2.htm> (March 2002).

85. Tenet, *The Worldwide Threat in 2001*, 3.

86. Michael Wines, "North Korea, With Putin, Vows to Curb Missile Program," *New York Times*, 5 August 2001, A4.

87. The details that follow are contained in Michael R. Gordon, "How Politics Sank Accord on Missiles With North Korea," *New York Times*, 6 March 2001, A1, A8.

88. William J. Clinton, "Remarks on the Budget and an Exchange with Reporters," *Public Papers,* 28 December 2000, 2807.

89. *Washington Times,* 3 July 2001, A1.

90. Rumsfeld Commission Report, 7, <http://www.fas.org/irp/threat/bm-threat.htm> (June 2003). Bermudez Jr., cites a range of 4,000 to 8,000 km for a warhead of 1,000 to 1,500 kg. However, these ranges could be increased with a smaller payload. *A History of Ballistic Missile Development in the DPRK,* 26.

91. Joseph S. Bermudez Jr., *The Armed Forces of North Korea* <http://www.fas.org/nuke/guide/dprk/missile/overview.htm> (June 2002).

92. Joseph S. Bermudez Jr., *The Armed Forces of North Korea.*

93. Tenet, *The Worldwide Threat in 2002,* 13.

94. Tenet, *The Worldwide Threat in 2001,* 5.

95. Tenet, *The Worldwide Threat in 2001,* 3.

96. Bermudez Jr., *The Armed Forces of North Korea,* 236.

97. Chun Chae-sung, "Missile Technology Control Regime and North Korea," *Korea Focus* 8, no. 1 (January-February, 2000): 28.

98. Data produced by the Center for Nonproliferation Studies, Monterey Institute for International Studies for the Nuclear Threat Initiative, "North Korea Missile Capabilities Table," 2002, <www.nti.org/db/profiles/dprk/msl/cap/NKM_CcGO.html> (July 2003).

99. For a more detailed treatment of North Korea's economic plight see Nicholas Eberstadt, *The End of North Korea* (Washington, D.C.: AEI Press, 1999), Marcus Noland, *Avoiding the Apocalypse* (Washington, D.C.: Institute for International Economics, 2000), and Andrew S. Natsios, *The Great North Korean Famine* (Washington, D.C.: U.S. Institute of Peace Press, 2001).

100. Natsios, *The Great North Korean Famine,* 215.

101. Elisabeth Rosenthal, "Collapse of Health System Adds to North Korea's Crisis," *New York Times,* 20 February 2001, A1, A8.

102. Elisabeth Rosenthal, "North Korea Still in Need of Food Aid," *New York Times,* 22 August 2001, A7.

103. Kim Hak-joon, "Prospects for Change in Kim Jong-il Regime," *New Asia* (Autumn 1998) reprinted in *Korea Focus* 6, no. 5, 29.

104. Noland, *Avoiding the Apocalypse,* 84-85.

105. Howard French, "North Korea Says It Will Bar Atom Inspectors," *New York Times,* 23 November 2002, A11.

106. See <http://www.globalsecurity.org/military/world/dprk/dprk-dark.htm> (July 2003).

107. Howard W. French, "North Korea Adding a Pinch of Capitalism to Its Economy," *New York Times,* 9 August 2002, A1, A9, and "North Korea to Let Capitalism Loose in Investment Zone," *New York Times,* 25 September 2002, A3.

108. "Desperate straits," *Economist* 367, 3 May 2003, 26.

109. Selig S. Harrison, *Korean Endgame: A Strategy for Reunification and U.S. Disengagement* (Princeton: Princeton University Press, 2002), 32.

110. Harrison, *Korean Endgame,* 33.

111. Bermudez, *The Armed Forces of North Korea,* 17.

112. Bermudez, *The Armed Forces of North Korea,* 19.

113. *2000 Report to Congress: Military Situation on the Korean Peninsula,* 6.

114. Stephen Noerper, "Summit Success: Toward a New Stability on the Korean

Peninsula," *Northeast Asia Peace and Security Network Special Report*, 21 August 2000, <www.nautilus.org> (September 2000).

115. Howard French, "Nuclear Fear as a Wedge," *New York Times*, 24 December 2002, A1, A8.

116. U.S. Senate, *Statement of General Thomas A. Schwartz, Commander in Chief United Nations Command/Combined Forces Command and Commander, United States Forces Korea*, testimony before the Senate Armed Services Committee, 107th Congress, 1st Session, 27 March 2001, 9.

117. Howard French, "2 Korean Leaders Speak of Making 'A Day in History,'" *New York Times*, 14 June 2000, A1.

118. Terence Roehrig, "Assessing North Korean Behavior: The June 2000 Summit, the Bush Administration, and Beyond," in Uk Heo and Shale A. Horowitz, eds., *Conflict in Asia: Korea, China-Taiwan, and India-Pakistan* (Westport, CT: Praeger Pub., 2003), 67-88.

119. Victor Cha, "Let's Not Get Summit Slap-Happy in Korea," *Nautilus Policy Forum Online*, 27 June 2000, <www.nautilus.org/fora/security/0005B_Cha.html> (June 2000).

120. Steven Lee Myers, "Pentagon Says North Korea Is Still a Dangerous Military Threat," *New York Times*, 22 September 2000, A10.

121. Mazarr, *North Korea and the Bomb*, 16.

122. *1996 South Korea Defense White Paper*, <www.mnd.go.kr.> (July 2003).

123. Interview on "The News Hour," Public Broadcasting System, 17 September 1999, as quoted in Harrison, "The Missiles of North Korea," 13.

124. Harrison, "The Missiles of Korea," 14.

125. President George W. Bush, *State of the Union Address*, 29 January 2002, <http://www.whitehouse.gov/news/releases/2002/01/20020129-11.html> (June 2002).

126. *National Security Strategy of the United States*, September 2002, <http://www.whitehouse.gov/nsc/nssintro.html> (July 2003).

127. "KCNA on Main Way for Settlement of Nuclear Issue," *KCNA*, 20 August 2003.

128. Seo Hyun-jin, "Pyongyang ready to act in concert with Washington over nuke issue," *Korea Herald*, 8 November 2002.

129. "Denuclearization of Korean Peninsula depends on U.S. policy," *KCNA*, 12 May 2003.

130. U.S. Senate, *Statement of the Director of Central Intelligence George J. Tenet As Prepared for Delivery Before the Senate Armed Services Committee Hearing on Current and Projected National Security Threats*, 106th Congress, 1st Session, 2 February 1999, 2.

131. See Scott D. Sagan, "Why Do States Build Nuclear Weapons," *International Security* 21, no. 3 (Winter 1996/1997): 63-65.

132. Michael J. Mazarr, "Going Just a Little Nuclear," *International Security* 20, no. 2 (Fall 1995): 92-122.

133. David E. Sanger, "The Pyongyang Puzzle," *New York Times*, 1 June 1994, A1.

134. Byung Chul Koh, "Confrontation and Cooperation on the Korean Peninsula: The Politics of Nuclear Proliferation," *The Korean Journal of Defense Analysis* VI, no. 2 (Winter 1994): 77.

135. David S. Cloud and Jay Solomon, "North Korea Has Nuclear Program," *Wall*

Street Journal, 17 October 2002, A4.

136. Howard W. French, "North Koreans Sign Agreement With Japanese," *New York Times*, 18 September 2002, A1, A10.

137. French, "North Koreans Sign Agreement With Japanese,"A1, A10.

138. Steve LaMontagne, "North Korea's Nuclear Program: An Assessment of U.S. Options," *Nautilus Institute—Northeast Asia Peace and Security Network Special Report*, 30 October 2002, <http://nautilus.org/fora/security/0218A_LaMontagne.html> (November 2002).

Chapter 4

U.S. INTERESTS IN KOREA

The U.S. security guarantee to South Korea that began during the Cold War, represents a significant commitment. Why did the United States choose to extend this security guarantee, and why did the guarantee continue for such a long time, even after the Cold War had ended? The short answer to these questions is that American decision makers have consistently concluded that the maintenance of security ties with the ROK is in America's interest. This chapter examines the interests that U.S. policy makers believe have been and continue to be at stake in Korea.

Interests play an important role in an extended deterrence commitment. If a defender has few or no interests present in the protégé, there is little reason to make such a commitment. In this study, the term "interests" refers to the specific goals and objectives that a state has in a particular region or area of foreign policy. This conceptualization of interests should not be confused with the term, "national interest." National interests refer to the more general ambitions of all states such as political independence, territorial integrity, and economic prosperity. Use of the concept "national interest" poses numerous difficulties. Who determines the national interests of a state? What criteria determine these interests? What occurs if competing visions of the "national interest" are present within a state? This study will avoid these problems by focusing on the particular interests—specific goals and objectives—that U.S. leaders saw present in Korea.

Interests also help to determine the degree of effort the defender will exert on the protégé's behalf when constructing the security guarantee. The greater the interests, the more likely a defender will actually remain with the protégé in a crisis. However, as George and Smoke point out, state leaders can have a difficult time "attempting to judge and foresee the 'value' of a weaker country within the framework of the objectives and means of their overall foreign policy."[1] Thus, the Truman administration did not foresee South Korea's value until after the North attacked.

Yet, the defender's security guarantee depends on more than an inventory of interests. Interests are closely linked to assessments of stakes—the costs and benefits of pursuing those interests. Thus, national leaders evaluate their interests and assess the stakes for achieving their goals and objectives. States have many interests but the stakes for each may vary. For example, consider three states A, B, and C where all three are allies, and A and B share a border. State A has an interest in preventing the conquest of both B and C by an adversary. Yet, the stakes are much higher in relation to state B; the loss of B would put the adversary on A's own border. Thus, A may work much harder to prevent B's subjugation than C's. The higher the stakes, the more important it is to achieve the goal. Consequently, the defender's assessment of the interests and the stakes related to those interests affects the security commitment. The greater the stakes, the more likely a defender will risk implementing a deterrence guarantee and remain with the protégé in a crisis.

For the purposes of this book, U.S. interests are identified as those expressed by American policy makers. The objective here is not to evaluate whether they were correct in their assessment of interests. Rather, the goal is to identify the interests that U.S. policy makers concluded to be present and to determine the role these interests played in the U.S. security guarantee to South Korea.

To analyze U.S. interests in South Korea, this study utilizes three categories of interests: security; political; and economic. The first category includes U.S. global and regional security interests, including Korea's link to Japanese security. Until the Korean War, U.S. policy makers disagreed on the stakes present in Korea for U.S. security interests. The North Korean attack, assumed by Washington to have been instigated by the Soviet Union, demonstrated that communism was now resorting to a new level of aggression. The attack in Korea raised the stakes for U.S. security interests considerably; the spread of communism in Korea was an unacceptable alteration of the status quo. According to NSC 68, the document that laid out the rationale for U.S. strategy during the Cold War, the Soviet Union "requires the dynamic extension of their authority and the ultimate elimination of any effective opposition to their authority. . . . To that end Soviet efforts are now directed toward the domination of the Eurasian land mass."[2] Korea became an important part of U.S. global containment strategy to halt Soviet expansion. By the late 1960s U.S. perceptions of the global communist threat had changed, and Korea became more of a regional security concern.

However, throughout the 1990s, the North Korean security threat again became more ominous. The fear of a possible nuclear weapons program compounded by the North's testing, production, and sale of ballistic missiles generated new concerns for security in Northeast Asia, issues that had serious ramifications for all countries in the region. Moreover, the North Korean threat became more closely tied to U.S. nonproliferation goals and, after September 11th, fears that North Korea might supply weapons to terrorists. These concerns were complicated further by the North's deteriorating economy and widespread famine that generated intense speculation and debate over the future of North

Korea, including whether U.S. interests were better served by a collapse of this decrepit communist regime or through assistance to the DPRK to help their economy achieve a "soft landing."

The second category of interests focuses on Cold War politics, American support of the United Nations, and issues of U.S. prestige and credibility with its allies. Political interests were present for the United States before arriving in Korea in September 1945. U.S.-Soviet tension had already begun to grow over issues in Europe, and American leaders believed similar events might occur in Asia. Until the Korean War, U.S. leaders saw their interests in Korea primarily in political terms—opposition to the spread of communism. The war demonstrated Korea's importance to U.S. security and the security of others in the region, particularly Japan.

Finally, the United States also has significant economic interests in maintaining a security guarantee for the ROK. In contrast to the first two categories, U.S. economic interests developed primarily in the latter half of the U.S.-ROK alliance. South Korea's economic growth since the mid-1960s forged important economic ties with the U.S. and with other U.S. allies in the Asia-Pacific region, raising significantly the economic stakes in maintaining peace and stability in the region. War on the Korean Peninsula would do serious damage to the economic activity there and disrupt U.S. economic links to South Korea and others in East Asia.

U.S. extended deterrence in Korea protected a number of interests. The stakes have varied over the years as security conditions changed; while some stakes remained relatively consistent, others changed considerably. Yet, as South Korea grew economically, politically, and militarily, U.S. officials developed a greater appreciation of the ROK's value as an ally. The remainder of this chapter will explore U.S. interests in Korea from 1882 to the present, and argue that given the turbulent events that have affected the security relationship, particularly the Vietnam War, the changes in the global and regional environment, and the length of time the U.S. extended deterrence commitment to South Korea has lasted, U.S. interests in Korea have been relatively consistent and clear, fostering a robust security guarantee.

Early U.S. Interest in Korea: 1882-1910

In its early contacts, the United States saw little value in the Kingdom of Korea. The United States was increasingly drawn to the Pacific region in the late 1800s, yet Korea functioned primarily as a port of call on journeys to other areas of importance in Asia, particularly China.

In 1882, the United States and the Kingdom of Korea established official diplomatic relations with the signing of the Treaty of Amity and Commerce, also known as the Shufeldt Treaty for Commodore Robert Shufeldt, the commander of the expedition. The King of Korea at that time, King Kojong, was hopeful that political and economic ties with the United States, a nation apparently not interested in colonization, would protect Korea from the growing rivalry of China, Russia, and Japan.[3] In particular, Korea found encouragement from a section in the treaty known as the "Good Offices" clause. Here, it stated, "if other powers deal unjustly or oppressively with either Government, the other will exert their good offices, on being informed of the case, to bring about an amicable arrangement, thus showing their friendly feelings."[4] While the Koreans took this clause to be a serious commitment, for the United States, it was simply a statement of diplomatic support and friendship often included in treaties of this kind. Later events would demonstrate that the American government had little interest in implementing this pledge of support.

The Korean government was also encouraged by remarks they received from American diplomatic personnel in Seoul. Frequently, U.S. representatives overstated the degree of U.S. support for Korea and encouraged the king to make greater economic concessions in the hopes of further cementing a U.S. commitment to Korea. These actions were often self-serving since U.S. representatives usually profited themselves from their assurances of U.S. interest in Korea.[5] Yet for all of these hopes, the American government remained only minimally concerned about Korea.

American interest in concluding the Shufeldt Treaty was essentially twofold. First, the United States wanted to improve the lot of shipwrecked sailors on the peninsula. The "Hermit Kingdom," as Korea was known, did not treat these sailors with a great deal of hospitality. These concerns were addressed in Article III of the 1882 treaty whereby "people of the locality shall display their sympathy by rendering full assistance, and liberality by furnishing the necessities required."[6] Second, U.S. interests in the Far East at this time revolved primarily around commerce. In contrast to European colonial ambitions, the United States tried to promote an "Open Door" policy that allowed trade access to all areas. The Shufeldt Treaty helped to ensure this access, though the United States knew Korea was relatively poor with only limited commercial potential.[7]

The beginning of U.S.-Korean relations coincided with a period of intense rivalry among the regional powers in the Far East. For many years China had held suzerainty over Korea in a "big brother-little brother" relationship the Koreans called *sa dae ju ui*. In a very Confucian and hierarchical relationship, Korea, the little brother, offered tribute and loyalty to China, the big brother, in return for protection. In the 1800s, Chinese domination of Korea deteriorated due to the decay of Chinese power, and the rising strength of Japan and Russia. Control of Korea became a central issue in the rivalry of these three regional competitors. King Kojong hoped that the U.S. presence in the region would replace China as Korea's big brother, but this was not to be the case. The American government had little interest in assuming a prominent role in Northeast Asia, preferring instead to allow a dominant regional hegemon to emerge.[8] The result was a power struggle that led to the Sino-Japanese War (1894-1895) and the Russo-Japanese War (1904-1905) with Japan emerging the victor and dominant power in the region.

During both of these wars, the United States did very little to aid Korea in retaining its independence, despite Korean hopes in the Shufeldt. President Theodore Roosevelt was much more concerned with halting what he perceived to be the growing imperialist threat of Russia than with any worries over Korea's sovereignty. In fact, Roosevelt was quite admiring of the political, economic, and military accomplishments of the Japanese, hopeful that they could check Russian expansion in Asia. "I should like to see Japan have Korea. She will be a check upon Russia, and she deserves it for what she has done."[9] Furthermore, Roosevelt had a very low opinion of the Koreans, based partially on reports he received from U.S. ministers there.[10] In a handwritten note at the bottom of a letter to John Hay, the president's secretary of state, Roosevelt noted, "we cannot possibly interfere for the Koreans against Japan. They [the Koreans] couldn't strike one blow in their own defence."[11]

In the negotiations led by Theodore Roosevelt to end the Russo-Japanese War, Roosevelt is reported to have told a member of the Japanese delegation with whom he was friends, "sooner or later it will be better for Japan to takeover [sic] Korea. I rather think that Japan should takeover [sic] Korea for the sake of the Koreans and for Asia."[12] The United States gave further indication of its intent in the Taft-Katsura memorandum signed in 1905, an agreement negotiated with Japan to establish their respective spheres of interest in Asia. In a clear quid pro quo, the United States recognized Japanese interests in Korea and in turn, Japan agreed to respect U.S. interests in the Philippine Islands. When Japan forced Korea to sign the Treaty of Protection in November 1905 creating a Japanese protectorate over Korea, the United States was the first to pull out its legation from Seoul. Some U.S. business ventures continued to operate in Korea after 1905, but most were sold to the Japanese in the next few years.[13] American missionaries continued their activity on the peninsula but, in 1910, the Japanese formally annexed Korea, greatly reducing U.S. interest there until the end of the Second World War.

American Interest Rekindled: 1943-1950

The close of World War II brought Korea back to the attention of U.S. policy makers.[14] The sudden collapse of Japan in the fall of 1945 forced the United States to scramble for a hastily designed plan to deal with Korea. During the war, the only major policy declaration indicating any U.S. objectives in Korea came from the Cairo Conference held in November 1943. At this gathering, Roosevelt and Churchill met with Chinese leader Chiang Kai-shek to discuss the war in Asia. The resulting "Declaration of Cairo" announced that the United States, Great Britain, and China, "mindful of the enslavement of the people of Korea, are determined that in due course Korea shall become free and independent."[15] The leaders presumed Korea would need a period of trusteeship, directed by the United States, the Soviet Union, and China before gaining independence, and Roosevelt believed a period of twenty to thirty years would be appropriate.[16]

The United States had given little thought to eventualities in post-World War II Korea and virtually no preparations had been made for the military occupation that was to follow; Korea was simply a region of little significance for the United States. The lack of planning forced Washington to improvise some swift decisions. Most important was the proposition that the United States and the Soviets divide the peninsula to accept the Japanese surrender.

In hasty deliberations on the evening of 10 August 1945, Colonel C.H. Bonesteel III and Colonel Dean Rusk devised a proposal that would have U.S. forces receive the Japanese surrender in Korea as far north as possible.[17] Both men were mindful that Soviet forces were already present in Manchuria and U.S. troops would not arrive in Korea for some time. Given these circumstances, Rusk and Bonesteel chose the 38th parallel, a demarcation line that would include the capital, Seoul, in the U.S. zone. Washington stated consistently that it had no intention of making the division permanent. The Russians accepted the division at the 38th, much to Rusk's surprise who believed the military situation would have allowed Moscow to insist on a line further south. The official decision to have both the United States and Soviets accept the surrender of the Japanese in Korea was contained in General Order No. 1, issued by the Imperial General Headquarters of Japan under Order from the Supreme Commander for the Allied Powers, 7 September 1945.[18]

These early events indicate Korea was already being drawn into the rivalry of the Cold War. U.S.-Soviet conflict was increasing in Europe and these concerns were spilling over into Asia. Korea was rapidly becoming intertwined in the political objectives of U.S. Cold War policy.

For two years after World War II, Washington and Moscow tried to negotiate reunification of the two zones of occupation. Despite numerous attempts, the two sides were unable to reach an agreement and, in frustration, the United States turned to the United Nations. On 14 November 1947, the United Nations approved a plan that would unite the two Korean zones and hold elections throughout Korea to set up a government for the entire peninsula. However, Moscow and Pyongyang refused to allow elections in the North. Despite the refusal, separate elections occurred in the South and on 15 August 1948, the Republic of Korea was created under the auspices of the United Nations. Shortly after, the Soviet Union created a separate government in the North and installed Kim Il Sung as its leader.

Prior to the election in May 1948 that established a separate South Korean state, President Harry Truman approved NSC 8 outlining American policy goals in Korea.[19] NSC 8 linked U.S. objectives to growing Cold War tension with the Soviet Union and stated, "the predominant aim of Soviet policy in Korea is to achieve eventual Soviet domination of the entire country."[20] The United States must prevent this because "Soviet control over all of Korea would enhance the political and strategic position of the Soviet Union with respect to both China and Japan, and adversely affect the position of the United States in those areas and throughout the Far East."[21] In addition, NSC 8 noted that the United States could not abandon South Korea without leaving sufficient strength in the hands of the ROK armed forces to defend themselves from all but an "overt act of aggression."[22] A precipitous U.S. withdrawal "could be interpreted as a betrayal by the United States of its friends and allies in the Far East and might well lead to a fundamental realignment of forces in favor of the Soviet Union throughout that part of the world."[23] Not only would a sudden withdrawal provide a bad signal to U.S. allies, abandonment would also be "patently unacceptable from the point of view of U.S. prestige. It [any plan to leave South Korea] would violate the spirit of every international commitment undertaken by the U.S. during and since the war with respect to Korea."[24] Thus, the United States believed keeping Moscow out of South Korea and maintaining support for this beleaguered country were important objectives.

Finally, NSC 8 linked U.S. goals and objectives in Korea with the United Nations. Soviet domination of all of Korea would "constitute a severe blow to the prestige and influence of the UN; in this respect the interests of the United States are parallel to, if not identical with, those of the UN."[25] By this time, the United States had already expended considerable energy to make the UN a viable organization in the post-World War II world, including having the UN attempt to mediate a solution to the impasse in Korea. In particular, President Truman believed in the importance of the UN. In the 1948 State of the Union address, Truman declared, "we are giving, and will continue to give, our full support to the United Nations. While that organization has encountered unforeseen and unwelcome difficulties, I am confident of its ultimate success."[26] In another message to Congress on 20 February 1948, Truman stated, "our faith in the United Nations is ever-constant. We should seek to demonstrate that faith both by energetic support and by the spirit of our participation."[27] Thus, Truman championed a prominent role for the United Nations in the post-war order.

Moreover, for Truman, Soviet intransigence in Korea, and in other post-war trouble spots such as Greece and Iran, was not only a rebuff to the United States. Truman believed it was evidence of Soviet disregard for the will of the entire world as expressed through the United Nations. In a commencement address delivered shortly after the adoption of NSC 8, President Truman gave his response to why solutions in Korea had not been forthcoming. "The answer is not hard to find. It lies largely in the attitude of one nation—the Soviet Union."[28] Furthermore, it was not exclusively a problem between the United States and the Soviets according to Truman. "It is between the Soviet Union and the rest of the world."[29] The opinion of the world was manifested by decisions in the UN, and concerning actions in Korea and elsewhere, the Soviet Union "defied the clearly expressed will of an overwhelming majority in the United Nations."[30] Truman believed that if the Soviets could thwart the will of the UN, the reputation of this international body would be seriously compromised.

However, during the U.S. occupation of South Korea from September 1945 to June 1949, there was also pressure from other corners in the United States to end the American presence there. Congress and most Americans were anxious for a reduction in defense spending and the demobilization of large portions of the armed forces.[31] Military officials were particularly adamant, given the limited resources provided by Congress, in calling for disengagement from Korea. For the military, Korea was not only insignificant, but also a potential problem. In 1948, the Joint Chiefs of Staff noted that

> the U.S. has little strategic interest in maintaining its present troops and bases in Korea. Moreover, in the event of hostilities in the Far East, these troops would constitute a military liability. U.S. troops could not be maintained there without substantial reinforcement prior to the initiation of hostilities, but this would be militarily inadvisable since any land operations would, in all probability, bypass the Korean Peninsula.[32]

The Pentagon believed that a future war with the Soviet Union would likely occur in Europe. A U.S.-Soviet conflict would "bypass" a large contingent of troops in Korea and be of little value in the war effort. In George Kennan's memoirs, he recalls a high-ranking Air Force officer assuring him during a 1948 visit to Japan that "we had no need for any ground forces in Korea anyway, because the Air Force could control from Okinawa, through our strategic bombing capability, anything that went on in the way of military operations on the Korean peninsula."[33]

Later, the Department of the Army solicited General MacArthur to add his views to their argument for withdrawal from Korea. MacArthur maintained that it was better for the United States to withdraw soon while it could leave voluntarily. If the United States remained, according to MacArthur, American forces might be compelled to abandon Korea during armed conflict, a situation that would damage U.S. prestige.[34] For the American military, the stakes in Korea for U.S. security interests were not that high.

Besides pressure from the military, Truman also questioned the wisdom of maintaining U.S. troops in Korea for an extended period of time. Though he recognized U.S. interests, Truman favored troop withdrawals since "there is nothing that more easily creates antagonisms than the presence of unwanted soldiers, foreign or domestic."[35] He also worried about growing American involvement in the morass of Korean domestic problems; as Korean factions battled for political power, U.S. forces were often caught in the middle.[36] Despite these concerns, American troops remained in Korea until June 1949, but, according to Dean Rusk, "because of cuts in our defense budget and the paucity of American forces in general, President Truman finally sided with the Pentagon and ordered our last regimental combat team out of Korea."[37] That these troops stayed this long was an important signal of U.S. interest in the region.

As the United States prepared to withdraw its occupation forces from Korea, the Truman administration also sought to bolster the newly elected Syngman Rhee regime with military and economic aid, another sign of continued U.S. support. In addition to the aid already distributed through the Army occupation, NSC 8 contained a recommendation of $185 million for fiscal year 1949.[38] In June 1949, Truman asked Congress to approve the appropriation of $185 million as "the minimum aid essential during the coming year for progress toward economic recovery."[39] Truman's message to Congress also sheds light on the administration's thinking concerning Korea, and the political interests at stake there.

> Korea has become a testing ground in which the validity and practical value of the ideals and principles of democracy which the Republic is putting into practice are being matched against the practices of communism which have been imposed upon the people of north Korea. . . . [Progress in the South] will encourage the people of southern and southeastern Asia and the islands of the Pacific to resist and reject the Communist propaganda with which they are besieged.[40]

For U.S. officials, aid would help to establish an economically and politically stable regime in Korea, making the country an important example for others in Asia that resisted communism.

Yet, a formal security guarantee to protect South Korea once U.S. forces left was not part of the discussion. President Rhee lobbied hard for such a guarantee but did not receive one primarily for fear that he might attack the North knowing he had U.S. backing. For this reason, the United States furnished South Korea with only defensive military equipment and turned down a request for combat aircraft.[41]

Since the United States had decided to turn over the Korea problem to the UN in the fall of 1947, a number of disconcerting events had occurred: the crushing of the Czech uprising (March 1948), the Berlin crisis (June 1948), the Soviet explosion of an atomic weapon (August 1949) and the fall of China to Communism (October 1949). All of these events highlighted a growing communist threat that needed to be hemmed in through a policy of containment. Korea was rapidly becoming a part of Cold War hostility, and the United States could not allow the region to fall to Communism.

Events in China had a particularly important bearing on U.S. decision making. During World War II, the United States had planned that China, under the leadership of Chiang Kai-shek would be the chief U.S. ally in Asia. Chiang's fall in 1949 changed those plans. Indeed, two years earlier, Truman and Acheson already began to see that despite the large amounts of aid, Chiang was unlikely to defeat Mao Zedong. Slowly, the Truman administration pulled its support from Chiang, provoking criticism from congressional Republicans for "losing China."[42]

The fall of China prompted a reexamination of U.S. policy in East Asia. In Japan, U.S. occupation efforts shifted to a "reverse course" that focused less on reforming Japanese society—restructuring education, government, business, and labor—and more on rebuilding Japan as a valuable ally and base in the Pacific. Furthermore, U.S. leaders became increasingly aware of the connections between South Korean and Japanese security. With China "gone," South Korea became even more important to the security of Japan. As the saying went, "Korea was a dagger pointed at the heart of Japan."

Despite the ROK's links to Japanese security, the Truman administration chose not to provide a formal security commitment, deciding instead to promote a strong South Korean economy and democratic government as the best route for achieving American goals in Korea. U.S. officials saw how Chiang Kai-shek had squandered huge amounts of aid and lost the support of the Chinese populace by failing to implement much needed economic and political reforms. Korea afforded U.S. officials a second chance to promote economic development and political stability to help an ally stave off a communist threat without a large commitment of American forces.[43] U.S. officials believed that a line against Communist expansion could be drawn with economic prosperity and political stability without giving Rhee the military strength and unconditional security guarantee that might embolden him to attack the North. U.S. policy tried to steer a "middle course" between abandoning Korea and giving an unconditional guarantee.[44] Regarding the withdrawal of U.S. forces, NSC 8/2 concluded that "the U.S. should make it unmistakably clear that this step in no way constitutes a lessening of U.S. support of the Government of Korea."[45]

Critics of U.S. policy, who believed Washington abandoned Korea because U.S. officials did not recognize the important interests there, often point to the Acheson "defense perimeter" speech.[46] Given on 12 January 1950 to the National Press Club, Acheson outlined a defense perimeter that stretched from the Aleutian Islands in Alaska to Japan, the Ryukyu Islands off the coast of Japan and on to the Philippines, a line that excluded South Korea. Regarding criticism that his speech gave a "green light" to invade South Korea, Acheson maintained, "this was specious, for Australia and New Zealand were not included either, and the first of all our mutual defense agreements was made with Korea."[47] Later, Acheson defended his perimeter as the same drawn earlier by MacArthur and the Joint Chiefs of Staff remarking, "it did not occur to me that I should be charged with innovating policy or political heresy."[48]

While this defense perimeter excluded Korea, the speech also declared continued U.S. interest there. Acheson noted that nations outside the perimeter must first prepare to defend themselves and then appeal to "the commitments of the entire civilized world under the Charter of the United Nations which so far has not proved a weak reed to lean on by any people who are determined to protect their independence against outside aggression."[49] When speaking specifically about Korea, Acheson noted that the United States invested a great deal of aid and effort in Korea and the administration intended to continue its support. Acheson asserted, "the idea that we should scrap all of that, that we should stop half way through the achievement of the establishment of this country, seems to me to be the most utter defeatism and utter madness in our interests in Asia."[50]

Following the speech, others in the State Department feared Acheson might have sent a mixed message to North Korea, the Soviet Union, and China. Dean Rusk, who at the time was Deputy Undersecretary of State for Far Eastern Affairs, observed in his memoirs that several drafts of the speech were prepared, but Acheson disliked them all, deciding to make his own notes. "True to form, Acheson spoke extemporaneously; we had no chance to flyspeck the language and consider what implications others might draw from the text." According to Rusk, Acheson did not "intend to brush aside everything beyond our so-called defense perimeter, but his remarks were nevertheless subject to misinterpretation. We at the department decided that issuing clarifiers after the speech would simply make matters worse. I advised Acheson to sit tight and let the matter blow over. But it didn't."[51]

Acheson's speech also demonstrated the rationale of U.S. policy makers to focus on the economic and political development of Korea. For U.S. officials, the greatest threat in Asia was not outright invasion by Communist states, but rather subversion and infiltration. U.S. policy must focus on the economic and political obstacles so that an economically robust and democratic state would develop strong popular support, denying Communist agents the social and economic turmoil they exploited. According to Acheson, the United States needed to

> develop a soundness of administration of these new governments and to develop their resources and their technical skills so that they are not subject to penetration either through ignorance, or because they believe these false promises, or because there is real distress in their areas. If we can help that development, if we can go forward with it, then we have brought about the best way that anyone knows of stopping this spread of communism.[52]

Truman confirmed this rationale soon after the start of the Korean War. "The attack upon Korea makes it plain beyond all doubt that Communism has passed beyond the use of subversion to conquer independent nations and will now use armed invasion and war."[53] U.S. policy makers had believed that the major threat to South Korea was not outright invasion but rather infiltration and subversion. The North Korean invasion in June 1950 demonstrated to the United States that the Soviet Union and its proxy North Korea were far more determined to obtain total control of the Korean peninsula than previously believed.

The United States in Korea, 1943-1950: An Assessment

Public declarations of American interests in Korea during this period were ambiguous. U.S. policy makers did believe there were important American goals at stake in Korea, despite the military's narrow assessment that there was little at stake in terms of American security. However, the articulation of those interests was unclear and inconsistent. Acheson's perimeter speech, congressional delays and reductions of aid packages to Korea, and the failure to provide air and tank units reflected the limits of what was at stake. Yet the United States refrained from removing its forces until June 1949 for fear of a North Korean takeover. Also, as late as 19 June 1950, U.S. Ambassador John Foster Dulles proclaimed in a speech to the Korean National Assembly, "You are not alone. You will never be alone so long as you continue to play worthily your part in the great design of human freedom."[54]

Despite the importance of achieving the goals articulated in NSC 8, other considerations complicated American interest assessments and policy decisions. After World War II, the Congress and the American public were anxious to demobilize and reduce military spending. A security guarantee to the ROK would have made this more difficult. The JCS concluded that Korea offered little benefit to U.S. security interests and might actually be a liability in a general war. Also, many feared that a continued and substantial U.S. presence might entangle the United States in the "mess" that was developing in ROK domestic politics. If the guarantee led to a long occupation, Truman feared that South Koreans would grow resentful of the U.S. presence. Finally, U.S. leaders feared that a security commitment might embolden President Rhee to "march north." All of these considerations suggested that significant costs and risks accompanied the benefits of a security guarantee. Thus, the United States had a complicated cost-benefit calculus, leading to several differing assessments concerning the stakes for U.S. interests in Korea and a reluctance to give a deterrence commitment.

Threat assessments also affected U.S. decision making. The Truman administration had received warnings that the military balance on the peninsula favored the North and that, in 1949 and 1950, North Korea had been moving forces closer to the 38th parallel. Secretary Acheson was aware of an intelligence estimate, dated 4 May 1950, that "North Korean airpower and heavier artillery make North Korean armed forces superior and capable of successful operations against [the] South."[55] A CIA report based on data available before 15 May 1950 concluded that North Korea had "a superiority in armor, heavy artillery, and aircraft."[56] The report also noted that the North's military strength would allow it to attain "limited objectives in short-term military operations against southern Korea, including the capture of Seoul."[57]

Yet, these warnings of DPRK military capabilities were not the only reports that U.S. officials were receiving. The same CIA assessment drew the conclusion that "despite the apparent military superiority of northern over southern Korea, it is not certain that the northern regime, lacking the active participation of Soviet and Chinese Communist military units, would be able to gain effective control over all of southern Korea."[58] Assessments from Americans in Korea were also contradictory. For example, Brigadier General William L. Roberts, chief of the Korean Military Advisory Group (KMAG) believed that the South would have little difficulty repelling a northern invasion as long as the Russians or Chinese did not participate.[59] However, others in KMAG and the U.S. Ambassador in Korea did not share this assessment. In 1993, declassified CIA documents indicate that six days before the invasion, American intelligence reports dismissed the likelihood of war in Korea. According to the documents, Director of Central Intelligence, General Walter Bedell Smith approved an intelligence estimate arguing an invasion by the North had been postponed in favor of a continuing propaganda and subversion campaign.[60]

In his memoirs, Truman noted that he and his advisors recognized Korea as a place where the Soviets or their allies might choose to attack. However, he added that the same could be said of "every other point of contact" between the East and West. Intelligence estimates received in the spring of 1950 indicated a North Korean military buildup, infiltration of guerrilla groups into the South, and ongoing incidents along the 38th parallel. According to Truman, these assessments maintained that North Korea could at any time switch from "isolated raids to a full-scale attack." Yet Truman lamented that these assessments did not specify whether the attack was certain or when it would occur. Furthermore, these reports "did not apply alone to Korea. These same reports also told me repeatedly that there were any number of other spots in the world where the Russians 'possessed the capability' to attack."[61] A CIA report ranked Korea only as high as fifth as a potential trouble spot with the Soviet Union behind Indo-China, Berlin and West Germany, Iran and Yugoslavia.[62]

Finally, from interviews of U.S. officials, Glenn Paige concluded that all agreed the invasion came as a surprise. Paige later received a letter from one of those officials (unnamed) arguing that after the investigation of intelligence failures at Pearl Harbor intelligence agencies were warning about everything. The letter continued:

> During the week of the attack nothing was called to the attention of the policy makers pointing a finger toward Korea. It would be interesting to know where key intelligence officers were on the weekend of the attack, to ascertain whether they were sufficiently impressed by their own warnings to be on any special duty.[63]

Other evidence pointed to a lack of warning. In June 1950, prior to the North's invasion, Secretary of Defense Louis Johnson traveled to Asia visiting U.S. military installations. A year later in congressional hearings, Johnson was questioned whether he received any warning by intelligence officials during his trip of the impending attack. Johnson replied, "in the briefing of my intelligence covering all that part of the world, nothing was said about any immediacy of trouble in Korea, nor did anyone else on that trip give to me or to General Bradley . . . any indication of such."[64] Given this contradictory evidence, U.S. leaders found it difficult to see clearly an approaching crisis, and, Korea was not the only potential trouble spot.

Thus, U.S. officials believed important interests were present in Korea, but these were poorly articulated, largely because American leaders disagreed on the stakes—the costs and benefits of a vigorous security commitment to South Korea. In the words of a former Soviet diplomat, "You did everything you could to tell us you were not interested in Korea, and when the North Koreans went in there, you put your troops in."[65]

Thus, U.S. leaders concluded that the threat, particularly their judgment that an invasion was unlikely, did not warrant a security guarantee. George and Smoke note that the basic assumption of American policy was still that Soviet leaders were not immediately ready to risk a world war, and would not be at least until they had acquired an adequate operational A-bomb capability. In the meantime, the Soviets were expected to continue to press for their objectives indirectly, avoiding overt forms of aggression that might risk a general war.[66]

Since the threat of invasion did not appear great, the Truman administration concluded that its policy of military and economic aid with no security guarantee was sufficient to protect South Korea. Despite the uncertainty over interests and stakes, the Truman administration implemented a policy that they believed would achieve their goals while avoiding the potential costs and risks of a security guarantee. U.S. policy at this time was not a deterrence commitment; no clear or formal declaration of intent and willingness to respond was given. In fact, U.S. intent was unclear and ambiguous and the removal of U.S. ground troops in June 1949 removed an important barrier for the North's invasion. Kim Il Sung believed DPRK forces could overrun the peninsula before the U.S. would be able to respond, presenting American officials with a fait accompli.[67] Yet, leaders in Washington believed they established some sort of commitment to the ROK and were surprised and alarmed when the North tested that commitment.

The Korean War, 1950–1953

On 25 June 1950, North Korean forces rolled across the 38th parallel in a bid to reunify the peninsula under their control. Despite Pyongyang's hopes that the United States would concede the South, Washington intervened quickly and decisively with military force. In Truman's words to Secretary of State Dean Acheson, "Dean, we'v [sic] got to stop the sons of bitches no mater [sic] what."[68] Why did the United States intervene rather than allow the North to retain its conquests?

Korea was already connected to a number U.S. interests: containment of Soviet expansion, the reliability of U.S. commitments elsewhere, and a strong, credible United Nations. However, the Truman administration could not agree on what was specifically at stake in Korea. Before the invasion, Truman concluded that economic aid and limited amounts of military assistance were sufficient to support U.S. goals in Korea. The Soviet-instigated North Korean attack raised the stakes by directly challenging U.S. interests in Korea. The attack endangered America's reputation as a supporter of South Korea and the UN, a serious challenge to American determination. In turn, the invasion and the U.S. response had implications for American interests elsewhere; a vigorous U.S. response was necessary to demonstrate American resolve in the face of communist aggression. American leaders now had more to lose or gain with its policy decisions in Korea.

Furthermore, the attack raised the stakes by altering U.S. threat assessments. Limited U.S. support was appropriate when the primary threat to the South was infiltration and subversion, not invasion. However, now the Soviets had made their intentions overt and clear; through their proxy in the North, Moscow was willing to use armed force to secure its territorial objectives. Thus, the stakes increased because, in the estimates of the defender, the threat—the Soviet Union—had changed its intentions and demonstrated its willingness, through its protégé, to use force. Korea was now on the front line of American efforts to halt the spread of Communism.

The U.S. response was also driven by the fall of China to Communism in October 1949. This changed the regional balance of power focusing greater attention on Japan and Korea. Likewise, Truman had been roundly criticized for "losing China" to Communism. U.S. domestic pressure to be "tough" on Communism added further incentive for a strong response to the DPRK invasion. Thus, in light of the North Korean attack, the Truman administration reevaluated the stakes for U.S. interests in Korea.

First, President Truman and his advisors regarded the North Korean attack as a direct challenge to the power and prestige of the United Nations. The UN was involved in many important decisions concerning Korea and, eventually, sanctioned the creation of South Korea in 1948. To let the South fall would severely damage the prestige of the world body and its commitment to collective security. In a message to Congress in the first month of the war, Truman stated

> This attack was . . . a demonstration of contempt for the United Nations, since it was an attempt to settle, by military aggression, a question which the United Nations had been working to settle by peaceful means. The attack . . . therefore was a clear challenge to the basic principles of the United Nations Charter and to the specific actions taken by the United Nations in Korea. If this challenge had not been met squarely, the effectiveness of the United Nations would have been all but ended, and the hope of mankind that the United Nations would develop into an institution of world order would have been shattered.[69]

Washington believed that an important goal of the UN was to provide collective security guarantees whereby the nations of the world would come to the aid of others threatened with unprovoked aggression. In congressional hearings conducted in 1951, Secretary of State Dean Acheson argued for the United States to uphold collective security in Korea.

> The attack on Korea was a blow at the foundation of this whole program. It was a challenge to the whole system of collective security, not only in the Far East, but everywhere in the world. It was a threat to all nations newly arrived at independence. . . . If we stood with our arms folded while Korea was swallowed up, it would have meant abandoning our principles, and it would have meant the defeat of the collective security system on which our own safety ultimately depends.[70]

In his memoirs concerning the first meeting at Blair House following the invasion, Truman recalled, "there was no suggestion from anyone that either the United Nations or the United States could back away from it. This was the test of all the talk of the last five years of collective security."[71] The attack threatened the UN's reputation, and American support for that institution. Truman believed the UN would be an important institution in the post-World War II order, and the United States could not afford to see the UN's prestige damaged in Korea.

The challenge to the UN and to collective security intertwined with another interest. The attack by North Korea, unanimously perceived by Truman and his advisors as "encouraged" by the Soviet Union, put the crisis at the forefront of U.S. efforts to contain Soviet expansion in Asia. For Truman, the U.S. stood as a bastion against one of the world's most dreaded evils, Communism. He predicted: "As the strength and effectiveness of the system of freedom are made clear on the globe, as the peoples who now stand in doubt turn to democracy—the danger of Communist domination will dwindle and finally disappear."[72] An intelligence estimate prepared by the State Department noted that "the North Korean Government is completely under Kremlin control and there is no possibility that the North Koreans acted without prior instruction from Moscow."[73] In congressional hearings, Secretary Acheson stated, "I think the Soviet Union has complete domination over the Government of North Korea."[74]

U.S. concern for halting Soviet expansion joined with fears of communist encroachment. As the "inheritor of Russian imperialism,"[75] U.S. policy makers had long been concerned about the size, resources, and strategic location of the Soviet Union/Russia. However, communist ideology energized Moscow to pursue its territorial ambitions with greater determination. NSC 68 asserted that "the Soviet Union, unlike previous aspirants to hegemony, is animated by a new fanatic faith, antithetical to our own, and seeks to impose its absolute authority over the rest of the world. Conflict, has therefore, become endemic."[76] Moreover, the Kremlin is "inescapably militant because it possesses and is possessed by a world-wide revolutionary movement . . . and because it is a totalitarian dictatorship. Persistent crisis, conflict and expansion are the essence of the Kremlin's militancy."[77] The Truman administration saw little difference between halting Soviet hegemony and the spread of Communism. Since Moscow controlled the worldwide communist movement, Truman saw these two threats as largely the same. NSC 68, which represented the views of the Truman administration, made continual reference to the threat emanating from Moscow with little distinction between Soviet territorial ambitions and national communist movements.[78] "A true internationalist is defined as one who unhesitatingly upholds the position of the Soviet Union and in the satellite states true patriotism is love of the Soviet Union."[79] The USSR was the key concern; Communism made that threat more menacing as a motivation for Soviet expansion and as it united those within the Soviet sphere. Truman administration officials used the terms "the Soviets" and "the communists" almost interchangeably. Yet, halting Soviet hegemony was the primary interest of American policy makers.

Moscow's involvement in Korea demonstrated to American officials that events there were more than an isolated regional conflict. Truman believed that

> if South Korea was allowed to fall Communist leaders would be emboldened to override nations closer to our own shores. If the Communists were permitted to force their way into the Republic of Korea without opposition from the free world, no small nation would have the courage to resist threats and aggression by stronger Communist neighbors.[80]

Truman assumed the Soviets were testing U.S. resolve to find a soft spot. Though they were not sure, Truman and his advisors believed that the Soviets were not ready to start a general war over Korea, but further probing in areas such as Iran, Yugoslavia, and Formosa might follow.[81] In recollections a decade later, Acheson recalled,

> This was an occasion upon which a perfectly clear alternative was presented to the United States, an alternative between withdrawing, retreating in front of Russian pressure brought through a satellite, or standing up and fighting and taking the consequences. . . . But when the Russians, to their great surprise, found that they had started something which the United States met absolutely squarely and hit with the utmost vigor, I think they stopped, looked, and listened.[82]

Consequently, America had to demonstrate its determination to prevent Soviet expansion and "the line would have to be drawn" in Korea.[83]

The North Korean invasion also reminded the Truman administration of events that preceded World War II. In the 1930s, appeasement had only encouraged the appetites of aggressors in Germany, Italy, and Japan. Appeasement, especially the British and French version at Munich in 1938, made further aggression more likely. U.S. policy makers vowed not to make that mistake again. As Truman saw it:

> this was not the first occasion when the strong had attacked the weak. I recalled some earlier instances: Manchuria, Ethiopia, Austria. I remembered how each time that the democracies failed to act it had encouraged the aggressors to keep going ahead. Communism was acting in Korea just as Hitler, Mussolini, and the Japanese had acted. . . . If this was allowed to go unchallenged it would mean a third world war, just as similar incidents had brought on the second world war.[84]

In congressional hearings in 1951, members asked General Omar Bradley, Chairman of the Joint Chiefs of Staff, why U.S. forces were sent to Korea. General Bradley, who was present at the initial meetings at Blair House with Truman and his other advisors when the war began, answered,

> if we appeased in this case, something else would come along, and you either appeased again or took action in the next one, and I think it was fully realized by

everyone [in these initial meetings], and it seemed to meet the approval of the people at that time, that one appeasement leads to another, until you eventually make war inevitable.[85]

If the United States did not stop Soviet aggression in Korea, the United States would have to stop it elsewhere and possibly at greater cost. Much more was now at stake in Korea for American interests. The Soviets and their allies had demonstrated their willingness to use force, not simply infiltration and subversion, to achieve their goals. It was clear to Truman that U.S. resolve was being tested. To affirm U.S. determination and deter further aggression, Truman and his advisers believed the United States had to take a firm stand in Korea.

Finally, the United States believed that its role in creating the UN-sponsored South Korean government obligated the United States to come to its defense. For five years, Washington had made significant efforts at nation-building in South Korea. U.S. abandonment of the ROK after all of these endeavors would have sent an ominous message to its allies. Separate communications from the U.S. Ambassador in France and the Soviet Union each note that they believed the world was watching U.S. actions and especially those in the Far East where the absence of a strong U.S. response would "require a fundamental reconsideration of orientation in cold war."[86] In particular, U.S. political and security interests in Japan might be in serious jeopardy. The United States was concerned about Soviet meddling in post-war Japan and froze out Moscow and other allies from a significant role in the occupation. As Cold War tension grew, Japan was viewed increasingly as a stronghold against communist expansion in Asia. When China fell to Communism and the Korean War erupted, the importance of Japan became central in U.S. policy. A weak U.S. response in Korea might "strengthen existing widespread desire for neutrality" in Japan. [87] Furthermore, "a Communist success in Korea would put Red troops and planes within easy striking distance of Japan, and Okinawa and Formosa would be open to attack from two sides."[88] As early as 1946/47, Dean Acheson and others in the State Department were arguing that Korea was crucial to Japan's survival. Citing Japanese dependence on Korean foodstuffs and the need for a healthy South Korean economy to purchase Japanese manufactured goods, Acheson maintained Korea was the key to Japanese recovery.[89] In a 1949 telegram to a number of U.S. diplomatic offices in Asia, Acheson maintained that the

Jap [sic] islands occupy such strategic position off Eastern Asiatic seacoast that Kremlin control thereof wld [sic] extend Sov [sic] power into Western Pacific to alarming degree. Command of seas and air over the seas along Eastern Asia littoral wld [sic] pass to Russians, and chain of islands leading southward as far as East Indies and Singapore wld [sic] be definitely threatened. Govts [sic] throughout that area wld [sic] be placed in great jeopardy by impact of militant Communism based on Jap [sic] islands. Effects cld [sic] spread westward into Indian sub-continent areas.[90]

As George Kennan contemplated in his memoirs, "hostilities in Korea converted everyone who had not yet been converted to the view that the American military presence in Japan was wholly essential to any future security of the area."[91]

The reasoning applied to Japan was appropriate for other U.S. allies as well and helped shore up the confidence of allies both in Europe and the Far East. NSC 73, written a week after the invasion, maintained, "if any weakness or hesitation is encountered on our part, anywhere, it will be instantaneously exploited by the Communists to undermine confidence in us in Europe and elsewhere and to promote a turn of political sentiment against us."[92] For the Truman administration, the connectivity of American relationships was a crucial consideration, and their response to events in Korea had important ramifications for U.S. interests elsewhere.

Thus, despite the ambiguous display of American interest in Korea from 1945 to 1950, the beginning of the Korean War forced U.S. policy makers to reassess what was at stake in Korea. Before the war the Truman administration had concluded that it was important to prevent South Korea from falling to Communism; Soviet domination of Korea would have important implications for U.S. containment strategy. Yet the stakes were not perceived to be high enough, nor was the threat adequate to warrant a formal pre-war commitment that included U.S. forces and an explicit security guarantee. Economic and political support with moderate amounts of military aid were sufficient to counter the threat of subversion and infiltration, and protect U.S. interests in South Korea.

With the beginning of hostilities, Washington's assessment of Korea's worth increased. American officials concluded that the Soviets were no longer content to employ a strategy of subversion and infiltration to obtain control of states on their periphery. They believed that events in Korea demonstrated that Moscow would use armed attack, particularly by a proxy when possible, to achieve its goal of world domination. U.S. leaders assumed that the Soviets had chosen Korea to test America's containment strategy and concluded that the stakes in Korea had suddenly escalated requiring immediate intervention. Based on these assessments, by 1953, American policy makers decided that U.S. interests required a more formal and resolute defense commitment to South Korea.

U.S. Interests in Korea: 1953 to the Present

The interests that Americans fought to defend in the Korean War carried over into postwar policy. Some of these interests remained consistent, while others changed. New interests also developed over the more than fifty subsequent years of U.S.-ROK security relations. The pages that follow are organized chronologically according to the presidential administrations since 1953. However, a number of U.S. interests overlap administrations or do not fit neatly into a chronological framework.

Containment in Korea: The Eisenhower Years

Following the war, Korea's link to America's global containment strategy and that the Soviet Union and China were willing to resort to force to extend their influence were the foremost concerns. Shortly after the end of the Korean War, U.S. Secretary of State John Foster Dulles noted: "We do not make the mistake of treating Korea as an isolated affair. The Korean war forms one part of a worldwide effort of communism to conquer freedom."[93] For Dulles, Communist aggression could not continue because "if unchecked, [it] would have gone on to imperil the United States."[94] President Eisenhower, elected in 1952, believed "American freedom is threatened so long as the world Communist conspiracy exists in its present scope, power and hostility. More closely than ever before, American freedom is interlocked with the freedom of other people.[95]

In response to the Soviet and Chinese threat and their challenge to American credibility, the United States implemented a formal security guarantee—to be discussed at length in chapters 5 and 6—that included a mutual defense treaty and the maintenance of ground forces in Korea. In particular, U.S. leaders believed that American interests and actions before the Korean War did not adequately signal their resolve to defend the South. An early goal of U.S. policy after the Korean War was to make those interests and U.S. determination to protect South Korea explicit.

In his message to the Senate in 1954 that accompanied the U.S.-ROK security treaty, Eisenhower argued that the treaty was "evidence of our common determination to meet the common danger. It thus reaffirms our belief that the security of an individual nation in the free world depends upon the security of its partners, and constitutes another in the collective security of the free nations of the Pacific."[96] Though Eisenhower's remarks blurred the distinction between collective security (the United Nations) and a U.S.-ROK bilateral alliance, his statement indicates the "connectedness" he and others in the administration saw for Korea with U.S. containment strategy elsewhere. The line against Communism drawn in Korea during the war had to hold because it affected U.S. credibility, particularly in Western Europe and other parts of Asia.

Japan was the cornerstone of U.S. security policy in the region and was one of the countries included within the 1950 Acheson defense perimeter. As noted earlier, keeping Japan from communist expansion was crucial to U.S. security interests in the Pacific. According to a 1957 memorandum from the Joint Chiefs, "Japan continues to be important to U.S. security interests and . . . must be prevented from coming under Communist domination."[97] Japan's "strategic location" and "military and industrial potential" were so important to America that the United States would be required to "fight to prevent hostile forces from gaining control of any part of Japan by attack."[98] Accordingly, a credible commitment to the defense of South Korea would safeguard America's interests in Japan as well.

The extended deterrence commitment to South Korea began and remains closely linked to the defense of Japan, helping to bring stability to Japanese foreign and defense policy. The U.S. presence in Korea helped to reduce Japan's need to rearm in the face of threats within the region, a measure that reassured other Asian states that Japan would not fill any regional power vacuum. This aspect was particularly evident in U.S. attempts to form a collective security arrangement in East Asia. In a letter from MacArthur to the State Department, he lamented "none of Japan's free Asian neighbors . . . wish to enter into a collective security or regional economic organizational arrangements."[99] Today, the U.S. presence in East Asia continues to fill that potential vacuum in relation to Japan, China, and a resurgent Russia.

There is no doubt that in the years since World War II, U.S. interests in Japan and Korea became closely linked. Moreover, Japan's role as a regional power and its economic and military potential, both before and after World War II, made it much more important for U.S. concerns in Asia. Thus, an important motivation for U.S. policy in Korea, especially during the first two decades after World War II, was the protection of Japan.

Despite these links to Japan, the security guarantee to South Korea was not based solely on Korea's importance to Japanese security. Recall that U.S. policy was also motivated by Korea's connection to U.S. containment strategy and the American support for the UN. As the ROK developed into an economic and military power, South Korea became an important regional player. Indeed, since the late 1960s U.S.-ROK ties have depended less and less on the South's relationship to Japanese security and more on South Korea's rise as a force in Northeast Asia.

Korea and the Vietnam War

In the 1960s, another American interest in South Korea became apparent.[100] The Johnson administration sought support from allies, particularly those in Asia, to demonstrate that U.S. actions in Vietnam were part of an international effort to halt communist aggression. Also, the United States looked for any operational support it might receive to aid the war effort.[101] However, South Korea was not Washington's first choice. When seeking support from Asian allies in 1964, President Johnson initially turned to Australia, New Zealand, and the Philippines. Only later did Johnson include South Korea in the request. Han Sungjoo argues that South Korean participation brought less "political benefit" for the United States because South Korea was not a member of the UN or SEATO and because the ROK military was under operational control of and heavily subsidized by the United States. Thus, Han maintains that South Korean participation was useful primarily for military reasons.[102]

South Korea responded in 1964 by sending the Dove Unit, a group of medical and engineering personnel to Vietnam numbering 2,128. Later, in 1965, in response to a request by the South Vietnam government instigated by the United States, Seoul sent an infantry division, the Tiger Division, along with some special forces and a Marine brigade totaling 18,904. The following year, South Korea deployed a second division to Vietnam, the White Horse Division that numbered 23,865. Other small units followed to bring the total number of ROK troops serving in Vietnam to 47,872.[103]

For South Korea, the troop deployments brought a number of purchasing contracts from the United States and other economic "gratuities." Most importantly, ROK assistance in Vietnam strengthened U.S.-ROK relations and allayed Seoul's fears of a declining U.S. security commitment to the South.[104] While in Korea in February 1966, Vice President Hubert Humphrey declared that the United States has a "firm commitment to the defense of Korea" and "we are allies, we are friends, you should have no questions no doubts."[105] Later in 1966, Presidents Johnson and Park issued a joint statement that "expressed the admiration of the American people for Korea's major contribution to the struggle in Viet-Nam."[106] The statement continued with President Johnson reaffirming "the readiness and determination of the United States to render prompt and effective assistance to defeat an armed attack against the Republic of Korea."[107] Thus, American leaders saw the value of having a well-armed ally on the periphery of the communist powers in Asia.[108] Unlike Japan and the limits imposed by Article IX of its constitution, South Korea can deploy its forces with far fewer international repercussions and with less domestic turmoil. For that reason, the U.S.-ROK relationship provided important benefits that Japan could not.

South Korea's response in Vietnam was an interesting anomaly to the expected behavior of the protégé in a deterrence relationship. Deterrence theory focuses most of its attention on the efforts of the defender to protect the protégé. Yet, in Vietnam, the protégé was beginning to show signs that it could shoulder a greater share of its own defense and aid the defender in achieving its goals and objectives elsewhere. The successful tours of two ROK combat divisions helped Seoul demonstrate that its forces were well trained and combat ready, and that it could send these forces without risking its defense posture at home. On both accounts, South Korea had an opportunity to impress the North with some of its military prowess. Thus, the protégé enhanced deterrence—deterrence by defense—with a display of its own military force, without directly confronting its adversary. A demonstration by the protégé rather than the defender had the added benefit of indicating a shift towards primary deterrence and away from the credibility problems of extended deterrence. Though only a small sign, ROK involvement in Vietnam was an early indication of Seoul's ability to handle an increasing share of its own defense.

ROK participation in Vietnam also provided important benefits for the U.S.-ROK alliance. U.S. leaders saw that American aid to rebuild the South's economic and military capabilities was working. The South was able to deploy two full divisions without weakening substantially its defense preparedness at home. The protégé successfully utilized the defender's aid and built a military capability that could support the goals and objectives of the defender. In addition, ROK deployments strengthened alliance cohesion, providing reassurance to the South of the U.S. commitment and displaying a robust bilateral relationship to the North. ROK involvement in Vietnam illustrates the potential role of the protégé to strengthen deterrence. During the Vietnam War, South Korea, in a limited way, "flexed its muscle" to demonstrate its ability to defend itself and provide tangible evidence that U.S. aid was being put to good use. In both instances, the action of the protégé enhanced the deterrence relationship.

Korea and the Nixon Doctrine

By the late 1960s, according to President Richard Nixon, "the whole pattern of international politics was changing."[109] He noted that the growing friction between the Soviet Union and China that began in the late 1950s had altered the perception of a monolithic communist threat intent on conquering the world through military force.[110] Improved relations between the United States and China and between the United States and Soviet Union during the Nixon administration helped alter the focus of U.S. interests in Asia. Furthermore, a number of thriving economies in East Asia had emerged that were more stable, but also rather authoritarian.[111] These circumstances, along with the unsettling events of the Vietnam War, prompted U.S. policy makers to reexamine American interests in Asia.

Soon after Nixon's election in 1969, his administration began an intense reevaluation of U.S. foreign policy, a review that concluded U.S. military capabilities were insufficient to support U.S. policy objectives in the region. American commitments required scaling back to allow a better "fit" with the military capabilities necessary to support those objectives. In a policy known as the "Nixon Doctrine," the president proposed to keep all existing treaty commitments, to continue to provide a nuclear umbrella for allies, and to furnish military and economic assistance when necessary. However, the United States would henceforth expect allies to provide their own manpower for local defense needs.[112]

For South Korea, the application of the Nixon Doctrine resulted in the removal of one of the two U.S. infantry divisions stationed on the peninsula. The remaining division withdrew from its frontline position on the DMZ so that automatic contact with hostile forces was less likely. To compensate for the troop reductions, the United States began a five-year military modernization program for ROK forces. However, Congress delayed some of the funding out of concern for the increasingly authoritarian character of the South Korean government under Park Chung Hee, who remained president from 1961 to 1979 until his assassination.

South Koreans worried that this force reduction signaled a decrease in the U.S. commitment and feared further retrenchment would follow. Yet, Nixon continued to assert that the United States retained important interests in Asia and more specifically, South Korea. Nixon explained that he was not changing the objectives of U.S. policy in South Korea, only the means. From this perspective, the United States had no desire to become involved in another Vietnam-type conflict, yet it could not afford to see its credibility damaged further with the fall of another ally. In his 1970 foreign policy report, Nixon stated: "we remain involved in Asia. We are a Pacific power . . . . we will maintain our interests in Asia and the commitments that flow from them."[113] A few years later, he reiterated, "as a matter of principle, and as a matter of preserving the stability of Asia, we made it clear that the United States would never repudiate its pledged word nor betray an ally."[114]

The changes under the Nixon administration were not signals of a U.S. retreat from Asia, but rather recognition that "the changes taking place in that region enabled the U.S. to change the character of its involvement. The responsibilities once borne by the United States at such great cost could now be shared."[115] The economic growth of South Korea and others in Asia allowed allies to assume a greater share of their defense burden. The commitment remained firm, though the means had been altered. In his memoirs, Nixon argued,

> The Nixon Doctrine announced on Guam was misinterpreted by some as signaling a new policy that would lead to total American withdrawal from Asia and from other parts of the world as well. In one of our regular breakfast meetings . . . Senate Majority Leader Mike Mansfield articulated this misunderstanding. I emphasized to him, as I had to our friends in the Asian countries, that the Nixon Doctrine was not a formula for getting America *out* of Asia, but one that provided the only sound basis for America's staying *in* and continuing to play a responsible role in helping the non-Communist nations and neutrals as well as our Asian allies to defend their independence.[116]

In congressional testimony, William Porter, Ambassador to Korea in 1970, stated that the U.S. commitment to Korea involved "matters of confidence which extend far beyond the borders of Korea . . . . It is a commitment of the United States to the freedom and development of the Korean people which . . . has attracted the attention and even the admiration of a very great part of Asia and other parts of the world."[117]

The measures taken by the Nixon administration—withdrawal of the 7th Division, moving the 2nd Division off the DMZ, and increased military aid—had some important effects on deterrence in Korea. Nixon believed that South Korea could assume a greater share of the costs for its own defense. Consequently, the United States could reduce the risks of involvement in another Asian conflict as well as lessening the financial burden of the U.S. commitment. Ample evidence existed in the late 1960s of the risks present in Korea. DPRK provocations at the DMZ rose dramatically in 1967 and 1968, and in 1968, North Korean naval forces captured the USS *Pueblo*. In 1969, the North shot down an EC-121 Navy reconnaissance plane off the North Korean coast. By reducing the costs and risks, Nixon hoped that the United States could sustain the commitment more easily over time.

When South Korea assumed a greater share of its own defense, the nature of deterrence changed. An extended deterrence commitment has an inherent credibility problem. Will the defender really remain with the protégé in a crisis? However, there is little doubt that a nation will defend itself, the conditions of primary deterrence. As the ROK's forces assumed a larger share of its own defense, the deterrence relationship shifted to one that relied less on the deterrence guarantee of the defender to one based more on the protege's own deterrent capability.

The crucial element of Nixon's force restructuring was South Korean prosperity; ROK economic and military growth made these burden-sharing alterations possible. Again, these developments point to the role played by the protégé in a deterrence relationship. By developing its own economic and military strength, the protégé enhanced deterrence by shifting security relations from extended to primary deterrence and made the costs of the security commitment more bearable for the defender.

Changing Interests? The Carter Administration

South Korea's fears of further U.S. retrenchment materialized when President Carter announced his intention to withdraw all U.S. ground forces from the peninsula, a pledge he made in the 1976 campaign. Soon after his election, he signed Presidential Review Memorandum/NSC 13 to review U.S. policy in Korea. Carter made it clear that this review was not to decide whether troops would be removed, but rather how to implement such a plan.[118] Carter's motivation was based on the fear of being involved in another Asian war and, according to Carter in 1994, "contrary to the opinion of many U.S. leaders, then and now, it was not a goal of mine just to deploy as many of our forces around the globe as host countries would accommodate."[119]

Most in the administration and many U.S. allies opposed the move, hoping at least to delay or dilute Carter's efforts to have troops removed by 1981/1982. Eventually, Carter agreed to limit the withdrawals to ground forces alone with other U.S. military personnel remaining, including air force units, a small naval unit and army intelligence, logistics, and communications personnel.[120] Despite continued opposition, Carter remained determined to implement his plan.

Two other events seemed to indicate a possible change in the assessment of U.S. interests in Korea. In 1972, the Park regime turned more authoritarian and critics voiced strong concerns over the ROK's human rights record. Presidents Nixon and Ford were always able to downplay public criticism opting instead for more quiet diplomacy to soften the regime. When Carter came into office, he made it clear that human rights would hold a much more prominent place in determining U.S. foreign policy in Korea and elsewhere.

The second event was an investigation that, following on the heels of Nixon's travails, became known as "Koreagate." In 1976, a *Washington Post* story reported that Park Tong Sun, a South Korean agent, had given between $500,000 and $1 million in bribes to close to 90 members of Congress.[121] In the end, only one member of Congress, House member Richard Hanna from California, was convicted of bribery, but the revelations soured the mood in Congress towards South Korea. Paradoxically, "Koreagate" actually helped derail the troop withdrawal plan since it became unlikely Congress would pass any increased aid package to offset the withdrawal's impact on the military balance.[122]

Justifying the troop withdrawal, Carter argued that the United States remained committed to the security of South Korea, explaining "our security relationship is not a static one, and the specific ways in which we seek to accomplish our basic policy must be evaluated."[123] Secretary of Defense Harold Brown, who opposed the plan privately but supported the president publicly, maintained Carter's proposal signified "no change whatsoever in either the U.S. security commitment to the Republic of Korea or the basic defense strategy of the United States on the Korean peninsula."[124] Furthermore, Brown stated that the United States would "provide prompt and effective support" to the ROK if attacked, reminding that South Korea remained under the U.S. nuclear umbrella.[125] To ensure ROK military capabilities were sufficient to offset the U.S. withdrawal, Carter included a substantial military aid package worth $800 million.[126] According to Carter, the U.S. withdrawal of ground forces would not alter the military balance and would not endanger the security of South Korea. He believed that South Korea's economic growth allowed the ROK to assume a greater share of its own defense burden.

In 1978, evidence began to surface that, in fact, the military balance in Korea may have been far different than earlier intelligence estimates had indicated. In the past, intelligence analysts focused primarily on the location of DPRK forces through the use of aerial photographs and other signals intelligence. Analysts were looking primarily at whether North Korean units had moved farther south indicating they were massing for another surprise attack as had been the case in 1950. Few attempted to count the visible units to determine the DPRK's overall strength, namely, the number of tanks, armored personnel vehicles, and artillery pieces. In 1975, an intelligence analyst undertook this task and discovered that North Korean tank forces were approximately 80 percent larger than previously believed. This discovery prompted further studies over the next several years that indicated a significant increase in Pyongyang's military capabilities. When the results of these studies became public, pressure increased to shelve the troop withdrawal plan.[127] Finally, in February 1979, Carter announced there would be no further withdrawal of U.S. forces, a decision reaffirmed in July pending a complete policy review in 1981.[128]

The Carter withdrawal plan, had it been executed, would have altered the substance of the U.S.-ROK security relationship. Yet, the plan expressed a consistent intention to defend South Korea. While stating his case for the troop withdrawal, Carter asserted, "peace and stability in Northeast Asia are vital to our national interests, and stability on the Korean Peninsula is essential to that goal."[129] Despite efforts to the change the specifics of U.S. policy, deterring war in Korea remained a crucial interest.

Reaffirming U.S. Interests: The Reagan Years

After defeating Carter in the 1980 election, Ronald Reagan took office concerned about the dangers of global Communism in general and the prospect of Soviet military superiority in particular. In East Asia, Reagan believed that a revitalized commitment to South Korea was necessary to counter the ill effects of the Carter years, particularly the proposed troop withdrawal and the criticism on human rights. According to Secretary of State George Shultz, the second to hold that position in the administration, "to Ronald Reagan, South Korea was a stalwart ally and a valiant symbol of resistance to communism."[130] The first foreign leader to visit the Reagan White House in February 1981 was South Korean President Chun Doo Hwan. The decision to let Chun visit was controversial since he had seized power in a military coup only a year before. The administration also delayed submission to Congress of a human rights report prepared by Carter officials until after Chun's visit who, according to Reagan's first Secretary of State Alexander Haig, "had encouraged our hopes for a liberalization of his country's practices."[131] In a reference to Argentina, Haig noted, "the practice of publicly denouncing friends on questions of human rights while minimizing the abuse of those rights in the Soviet Union and other totalitarian countries was at an end."[132]

Despite Chun's actions, concerns for South Korea's security were paramount. In the joint communiqué that concluded the visit, Reagan "reaffirmed the critical importance of maintaining peace on the Korean peninsula and in Northeast Asia," noting "that the United States has no plans to withdraw U.S. ground combat forces from the Korean peninsula," and "pledged to seek to strengthen U.S.-Korean cooperation in deterring and defending aggression as an indispensable contribution to peace and stability in Northeast Asia."[133] In March 1981, Secretary of Defense Caspar Weinberger assured the Japanese foreign minister that the Reagan administration was committed to staying in Korea, an effort to distance itself from any plans to withdraw U.S. troops and a Carter defense official's "private" suggestion that Japan could assume the U.S. role in South Korea.[134]

Reagan's policy shift did much to improve U.S.-ROK relations, especially through its affirmation of the U.S. commitment to South Korean security and its legitimization of Chun's rule. The following year, the joint communiqué from the annual Security Consultative Meeting (SCM) noted the United States and South Korea reaffirm "that the security of the Republic of Korea is pivotal to the peace and stability of Northeast Asia and, in turn, vital to the security of the United States."[135] However, President Chun's visit in 1981 severely tarnished America's reputation in the eyes of many South Koreans. After seizing power in May 1980, Chun ordered a violent crackdown of demonstrators in the city of Kwangju. Many of the demonstrators were students calling for the South Korean government to relax its authoritarian grip and begin a transition to democracy. The demonstrators hoped that the United States, "the champion of democracy," would come to their aid. However, Washington did not respond though there may have been little it could have done to influence Chun's actions, even had it chosen to do so. More than 2,000 died in the "Kwangju Massacre," the ROK version of events in Tiananmen Square. Welcoming President Chun so soon after Kwangju only served to further infuriate many South Koreans.

Throughout the Reagan years, the United States tried to strike a balance between support for South Korean security and stability for the Chun regime while encouraging greater political reform and liberalization. In particular, Reagan tried to ensure that Chun follow through on his pledge to step down in 1988 when his term ended. There was certainly precedent in South Korean political history for leaders to remain in office despite the constitutional mandate to do otherwise. As a result, in 1983, when Reagan visited South Korea, he delivered what Secretary of State Shultz described as "our central message: the importance of President Chun's commitment to step aside as president at the end of his term in 1988 and to turn power over to an elected successor, a commitment that we well knew would be difficult to fulfill."[136] When Chun visited Washington again in 1985, Reagan and Shultz reaffirmed the importance of Chun stepping down. Finally, in spring 1987, when Chun's intentions seemed in doubt, Reagan wrote Chun a letter "as a friend":

> I believe that political stability based on sound democratic institutions is critical to insuring the long-term security of your country, and you have often expressed the same sentiments. . . . I applaud your commitment to a peaceful transfer of Presidential power next year as a crucial—and, as you say, unprecedented and historic—step in strengthening that institution of democratic government.[137]

In the end, Chun did allow the election process to proceed and was succeeded by Roh Tae Woo, a former military colleague. While this was the first peaceful democratic transition ever in South Korea politics, many South Koreans were disappointed with the election of another former military man.

The End of the Cold War: George H. W. Bush Administration

The Bush administration was no less effusive than Reagan in its support for Korea. A 1990 statement by Secretary of State James Baker maintained, "Our security commitment to the Republic of Korea remains essential to peace and stability on the Korean Peninsula."[138] In the Joint Communiqué on the occasion of the November 1990 Security Consultative Meeting, Secretary of Defense Dick Cheney along with his counterpart in South Korea reiterated with phrasing similar to earlier documents that "the security of the Republic of Korea remains pivotal to peace and stability in Northeast Asia, which in turn is vital to U.S. security."[139] When Bush visited South Korea in 1992, he "reaffirmed the commitment of the United States to the security of Korea. And let there be no misunderstanding: The United States will remain in Korea as long as there is a need and that we are welcome."[140]

Though U.S. interests remained consistent during the Bush administration, the context for the U.S.-ROK security relationship changed greatly during these years. The end of the Cold War, the dissolution of the Soviet Union, and the fall of Communism in Eastern Europe reconfigured the international system and relations in Northeast Asia. In 1991, both North and South Korea entered the United Nations and by the end of the year had signed a non-aggression pact and an agreement to denuclearize the Korean peninsula. China and Russia also began to pursue more balanced relations with both Koreas, a move that greatly angered leaders in Pyongyang since their former allies were making peace with the enemy. For Beijing and Moscow, relations with South Korea held out far greater economic opportunities. The North Korean economy, already showing signs of great distress, had far less to offer by way of trade and foreign investment. Furthermore, the many years of economic subsidies provided to Pyongyang were a drag on Russian and Chinese growth. Ideological and historical ties with the North were no longer as crucial as the trade and investment opportunities offered by a relationship with Seoul. As a result, in 1992, the Russians and Chinese established full diplomatic relations with South Korea, cut subsidies to the North, and required all economic purchases be paid for with hard currency, something the cash-strapped DPRK economy had difficulty doing.

During the Bush years, and those of the Reagan administration as well, U.S. policy makers realized further the extent of American interests in the economic vitality of South Korea. The Nixon and Carter administrations had already recognized the economic progress of South Korea during the 1960s and 1970s and called for the ROK to assume a greater share of its defense costs. The South Korean economic miracle, the economic growth of the entire East Asian region, and U.S. links to these Pacific economies raised the stakes again for U.S. policy. Deterring a war in Korea assumed important implications for U.S. economic interests because a great deal more could now be lost. South Korea's economic prosperity generated a growing demand for U.S. exports. In 1990, U.S. merchandise exports to South Korea totaled $14.4 billion, a 6.8 percent increase from the previous year, making South Korea the 6th largest export market for American products. More specifically, in 1990 U.S. agricultural exports to South Korea reached close to $3 billion.[141]

South Korean economic ties with other nations in the Pacific such as Japan and the nations of ASEAN (Association of Southeast Asian Nations) were also important. Japan, for example, was the second largest export market of South Korea, totaling $12.6 billion for 1990. In return, South Korea imported $18.5 billion of Japanese goods during the same year, a 6.4 percent increase over the previous year.[142]

The economic ties between the United States, South Korea, and others in the East Asian region were significant and growing. A disruption of these ties through war on the Korean peninsula would have disastrous effects not only for South Korea, but also for the United States and others who have important economic links with the South. Thus, a 1990 U.S. Defense Department study concluded: "With a total two-way transPacific trade exceeding 300 billion dollars annually, almost 50 percent more than our transAtlantic trade, it is in our own best interest to help preserve peace and stability."[143]

South Korean economic strength aided U.S. goals and objectives in one other way; the Republic of Korea was an important success story for U.S. policy. The government of South Korea began under UN and U.S. auspices in 1948, and American economic and military aid provided an important stimulus to jump-start the South Korean economy. The U.S. extended deterrence commitment ensured ROK security and stability allowing it to devote its resources to economic development. In an address by Vice President Bush in 1982 to the ROK National Assembly, he stated: "Your hard work and determination to bring about these economic successes have validated, in the eyes of the world community, the United States' decision to help you sustain your freedom."[144] Furthermore, ROK success came through the U.S.-sponsored open market system and post-World War II international trading regime.

Economic development, in turn, aided the South's progress towards democracy. The ROK's economic success created strong forces in Korean society, particularly within the middle class, that clamored for greater political participation.[145] In 1987, South Korea made the transition to democracy, holding a presidential election that led to the first democratic transition of power in its history. American leaders applauded ROK prosperity since it vindicated U.S. values of capitalism and democracy. In a speech during his 1992 visit to South Korea, President Bush remarked that "the Republic of Korea has stood strong for democracy" and "the Korean people will demonstrate that freedom's way is the way of the future in Asia. Nations which build their prosperity on the freedom of their people know that there is no alternative."[146]

In addition to these economic and political interests, the South was a consistent ally of the U.S. on several fronts. South Korea provided political support for U.S. positions in a variety of forums as a strong economic power, supportive of the current international trading regime, a developing democracy, and since 1991, a member of the United Nations. A 1984 speech by Assistant Secretary of State for East Asian and Pacific Affairs, Paul Wolfowitz notes,

> Korea has become an increasingly active participant in international diplomacy, and more often than not its positions on issues far removed from Korea are similar to our own, because its interests, in an open international economic system and a stable nonviolent political order, also coincide fundamentally with ours.[147]

The ROK provided economic aid to the former Soviet Union as well as contributing to cooperative security ventures such as the Persian Gulf War in 1990-91. According to a U.S. Defense Department report, ROK support of U.S. operations during the Persian Gulf crisis was "timely and commendable."[148] The South Korean government provided $500 million in assistance, sent a medical support group consisting of 154 people, and deployed five C-130 aircraft along with 156 ground support personnel.[149] In his 1992 trip to South Korea, President Bush described the U.S.-ROK relationship as follows: "More than a military alliance, our countries are moving toward a political, economic and security partnership."[150] Thus, U.S.-ROK relations during the Bush years began to move away from a relationship dominated by the United States to one that resembled more of a partnership.

Another security issue began to take on greater importance during the Bush administration, one that would later haunt succeeding presidents: North Korea's efforts to acquire nuclear weapons. Intelligence officials in the Reagan administration were the first to discover large-scale evidence of a North Korean nuclear program. When Pyongyang signed the Nuclear Nonproliferation Treaty in 1985, U.S. leaders breathed a sigh of relief, assuming that North Korea would promptly sign the accompanying safeguards agreement to provide for inspections of its facilities. The problem faded from view but remained unresolved. According to an official in both the Reagan and Bush administrations, "the real problem was the policymakers' reluctance to face the issue, an avoidance of reality that probably flowed from the realization of the scope and difficulty of the problem."[151] In 1992 when Bush addressed the South Korean National Assembly, it was clear that this was a serious concern for the United States. He remarked, "I call on North Korea to demonstrate its sincerity, to meet the obligations it undertook when it signed the Non-Proliferation Treaty 6 years ago. North Korea must implement in full all IAEA safeguards for its nuclear facilities without exception, and I might add, without delay." Referring to the newly signed North-South accords on reconciliation and denuclearizing, he noted, "North Korea, together with the Republic of Korea, should proceed to implement the inspection and verification portions of their unprecedented joint declaration on nonnuclearization, signed one week ago. Prompt action by the North will mark a new milestone on the path toward peace."[152] Despite Bush's urgings and efforts to organize diplomatic pressure on the North, the problem remained.

The Reagan-Bush years were an important transition for U.S. interests in South Korea for two reasons. First, these interests no longer focused primarily on security and political matters. American leaders began to realize the importance of South Korea to U.S. economic interests in the region, a new set of interests that raised the stakes for U.S. policy. Seoul's economic growth strengthened its ties with the U.S. and others, and gave the South the resources to be a strong U.S. ally. The South vindicated U.S. policy through economic prosperity and a transition to democracy so that Bush could say, "Korea stands with us: a steadfast friend, ally, and partner; proud, prosperous, and free."[153] In all of these aspects, the protégé utilized the defender's aid efficiently and effectively to increase its "value" to the defender.

A second change was the growing prominence of nuclear proliferation in U.S. interest assessments. Though U.S. leaders hoped the North would eventually comply with the inspections requirements and adhere to its nuclear-free pledge, toward the end of Bush's term, it appeared unlikely that Pyongyang would acquiesce. Proliferation issues would be a serious concern for the United States in the years ahead.

Proliferation Woes: The Clinton Administration

With the end of the Cold War and the loss of its long-time foe, the Soviet Union, the United States lost its focal point for determining foreign policy goals and strategies. Now, the United States struggled to define its foreign policy interests and role in the world. Further complicating the ability to determine the direction of U.S. foreign policy, Bill Clinton entered the White House with little interest and almost no experience in foreign policy. However, soon after taking the oath of office, North Korea threatened to withdraw from the NPT, forcing some early attention on Korean security issues.

Early in his first term in a speech before the South Korean National Assembly, President Clinton outlined several priorities for the "security of our new Pacific community." The first was "a continued American military commitment to this region" while the second priority called for "stronger efforts to combat the proliferation of weapons of mass destruction."[154] Expanding on the first priority, he maintained: "Our commitment to Korea's security remains undiminished. The Korean Peninsula remains a vital American interest. Our troops will stay here as long as the Korean people want and need us here."[155] Despite the relative disinterest Clinton had for foreign affairs at this early stage in his presidency, he reaffirmed the U.S. security commitment to South Korea, as had the many presidents before him.

The second priority, already present for earlier administrations became the chief concern of U.S.-ROK relations in the first term of the Clinton presidency. For most of the time since 1950, the security commitment was based on more than the interest of preserving the peace and deterring an attack on the South. Now that commitment was tied to a broader goal of preventing the proliferation of nuclear weapons. In fact, on numerous occasions, Clinton maintained that nuclear nonproliferation was his chief concern.[156] Clinton was more specific regarding North Korea and its nuclear weapons program. "We seek a nonnuclear Korean Peninsula and robust global rules against proliferation. That is why we urge North Korea to reaffirm its commitment to the Non-Proliferation Treaty, to fulfill its full-scope safeguards obligations to the International Atomic Energy Agency, including IAEA inspections of undeclared nuclear sites."[157] This goal became so important that he even considered military action against the North to address the problem.

The possibility of a nuclear-armed North Korea raised concern for a number of American security interests in the region. First, the DPRK already possessed a well-armed conventional force of over 1 million soldiers with much of its fire power deployed close the DMZ. The North also has a formidable arsenal of chemical and biological weapons. Adding nuclear weapons to this mix would increase tension in the region.

Second, a nuclear capability in the North could place greater pressure on South Korea and Japan to pursue this option, creating the possibility of a nuclear arms race in the region. This scenario could seriously jeopardize regional stability.

Third, the DPRK already has a well-developed ballistic missile program that could furnish a ready delivery vehicle for nuclear warheads. In 1998, Pyongyang shocked the world with a missile launch that traveled over Japan, indicating it had made significant improvement in the capabilities of earlier versions.

Finally, a North Korean nuclear weapons program would be a blow to U.S. nonproliferation efforts in general.[158] Pyongyang signed the NPT in 1985, and reneging on the agreement would set a dangerous precedent for other signatories. In turn, the North might sell some of its nuclear stockpile to other would-be proliferators, a trait it had already demonstrated in its sales of ballistic missiles and related technology. In an answer to a news conference question about the consequences of a North Korean nuclear weapon, President Clinton responded as follows:

> This is an issue which is very important to the long-term security of the United States. The question of a country that belongs to the nonproliferation regime deciding to become a nuclear power, the prospect that a nuclear capacity could be transferred, either by design or by accident to other countries or to rogue groups, this is a very serious thing for our long-term security.[159]

Despite some modest economic reform, North Korea's economy continues to struggle, providing great incentive to sell anything on the international market. Pyongyang has sold missiles to Iran, Syria, and Egypt, while swapping nuclear technology for missiles with Pakistan. Including nuclear warheads or technology would be an enticing package deal and an excellent source of hard currency for the North Korean economy.

The 1994 Agreed Framework appeared to settle the nuclear issue and begin a process that would lead to the denuclearization of North Korea. Following the conclusion of the agreement, Clinton said:

> This agreement will help to achieve a longstanding and vital American objective: an end to the threat of nuclear proliferation on the Korean Peninsula. This agreement is good for the United States, good for our allies, and good for the safety of the entire world. . . . It's a crucial step toward drawing North Korea into the global community. . . . Three administrations have tried to bring this nuclear program under international control. There is nothing more important to our security and to the world's stability than preventing the spread of nuclear weapons and ballistic missiles. And the United States has an unshakeable commitment to protect our ally and fellow democracy South Korea.[160]

However, implementation of the agreement was tedious and plagued by many delays. Despite hopes that this ended the nuclear crisis, the issue would return in earnest in 2002.

Towards the end of the Clinton years, several important breakthroughs appeared on the horizon in Korea that could affect U.S. interests there. The most crucial event was the June 2000 Summit meeting in Pyongyang between South Korean President Kim Dae Jung and North Korean leader Kim Jong Il. The meeting was a tremendous symbolic success but left many difficult issues to resolve. Yet, the meeting seemed to be the precursor to improved relations between North and South. In September, the defense ministers for the North and South met for the first time ever. U.S.-DPRK contacts also improved. In October, General Jo Myong Rok, first vice chairman of the National Defense Commission met with President Clinton in Washington where they discussed nuclear weapons and North Korea's willingness to halt its ballistic missile program. The following month, Secretary of State Madeline Albright traveled to Pyongyang for a meeting that came close to finishing a deal to address the concerns for ballistic missiles. Reports indicated that one more trip, possibly a visit by President Clinton, would seal the agreement. According to Wendy Sherman, policy coordinator on North Korea for the administration, "although there were still critical details to be worked out, it appeared that an agreement was within reach."[161] However, Clinton declined to make the trip noting that he had insufficient time left in his administration to make the journey. The incoming Bush administration had already indicated its ambivalence to such an agreement so the matter was put on hold.

Taking a Tougher Line: The George W. Bush Administration

During the 2000 campaign, George W. Bush did much to distance himself from Clinton administration policies including those related to North Korea. Upon entering the White House, Bush announced that U.S.-DPRK talks to end North Korea's ballistic missile program would be suspended pending a thorough review of U.S. policy. Bush expressed skepticism in North Korean leader Kim Jong Il and his regime, stating, "we're not certain as to whether or not they're keeping all terms of all agreements."[162] Later, Bush indicated that he "loathed" Kim Jong Il. Throughout the Clinton years, conservatives voiced their discontent with the Agreed Framework maintaining it was tantamount to paying blackmail, and the Bush administration was equally concerned about the wisdom of the agreement.

Despite concerns for the Clinton policy, the Bush administration saw U.S. interests in a similar manner. Maintaining peace and stability in the region and protecting an important and valuable ally remained core interests. In a joint statement concluding the March 2001 visit of South Korean President Kim Dae Jung, Bush and Kim

> reaffirmed the fundamental importance and strength of the U.S.-ROK security alliance, which has prevented war and promoted stability, prosperity, and democracy on the Korean Peninsula for over five decades. The two Presidents

pledged to deepen further the comprehensive partnership shared by the United States and the Republic of Korea through enhanced security, political, economic and cultural cooperation.[163]

These reassurances aside, the U.S.-ROK alliance underwent significant strain during this period, testing U.S. interests in the region. In 2002, a U.S. armored vehicle killed two South Korean girls in a training exercise. When a military tribunal acquitted the soldiers of any wrongdoing, anti-American sentiment in South Korea swelled. Many South Koreans have also objected to the hard line taken by the Bush administration on North Korea's nuclear weapons program and apparent inflexibility in dealing with Pyongyang. The U.S. war in Iraq has also been highly unpopular, further stoking anti-U.S. sentiment. In spring 2004, the Pentagon announced that it would be pulling 12,500 troops from South Korea including 3,600 to be sent to Iraq. The formal reason given by the United States was that this was part of an overall realignment of U.S. forces worldwide, and the forces were needed to stabilize Iraqi security. However, some speculated that the pull-out was retribution for the rising lack of appreciation for the U.S. presence in the region.

In spite of largely hostile public opinion in the South, the ROK government committed to sending 3,600 troops to Iraq to support the U.S. effort. An early contingent of 600 medical and engineering personnel were followed by 3,000 combat troops to patrol the northern areas of Iraq. This troop deployment makes South Korea the 3rd largest member of the U.S.-led coalition in Iraq, increasing worries that the ROK will increasingly become a target of terrorist attacks. In June 2004, militants linked to al-Qaeda captured a South Korean national working in Iraq and beheaded the man when Seoul did not meet the captors' demand to renounce its commitment to send troops to Iraq. For the Bush administration and the U.S. military, stretched thin by the on-going security needs in Iraq, South Korean assistance is highly valued and helped addressed some of Washington's frustration with the anti-Americanism in the South.

Bush also remained committed to U.S. nonproliferation goals, equally determined to keep North Korea from acquiring nuclear weapons, though skeptical of Pyongyang's intentions to do so and international nonproliferation treaties in general. In May 2001, administration officials completed their policy review and announced their willingness to restart talks with the North. However, this time the United States pushed for discussion on a more comprehensive set of security goals, including efforts to end the North's ballistic missile threat, early implementation of the inspections required under the Agreed Framework, and a reduction of Pyongyang's conventional military forces. In response to the ballistic missile threat posed by North Korea and others, the Bush administration accelerated work on a national missile defense system.

Following the tragedy of September 11th, the Bush administration saw U.S. interests and the North Korean threat in a different light. In the now famous State of the Union address in January 2002, after noting some of the transgressions of Iraq, Iran, and North Korea, President Bush continued:

states like these, and their terrorist allies, constitute an axis of evil, arming to threaten the peace of the world. By seeking weapons of mass destruction, these regimes pose a grave and growing danger. They could provide these arms to terrorists, giving them the means to match their hatred. They could attack our allies or attempt to blackmail the United States. . . . I will not wait on events, while dangers gather. I will not stand by, as peril draws closer and closer. The United States of America will not permit the world's most dangerous regimes to threaten us with the world's most destructive weapons.[164]

The North's nuclear weapons and ballistic missile programs were now more than simply a concern for regional peace and stability; the DPRK was viewed as a direct threat to the security of the United States. As a "rogue nation," North Korea might allow these weapons to fall into the hands of terrorists. With improvements in North Korea's ballistic missile capability, it could eventually strike directly at the continental United States with nuclear, chemical, or biological weapons. Thus, while America's interest in nonproliferation remained relatively consistent, in the minds of Bush administration officials, September 11th had significantly escalated the stakes. Failure to reach U.S. nonproliferation goals had more serious consequences with the possibility of a more immediate threat to the United States.

By summer of 2002, the Bush administration had sufficient intelligence to believe the North was cheating on the Agreed Framework by developing a covert, parallel nuclear program based on highly enriched uranium. In the next several months, the Agreed Framework unraveled as Pyongyang announced it was leaving the NPT, expelled international inspectors, and restarted its nuclear weapons program at Yongbyon.

As the Agreed Framework fell apart, the Bush administration remained determined to halt the North's nuclear ambitions. In November 2002, President Bush maintained, "North Korea's nuclear weapons program is a challenge to all responsible nations. We are united in our desire for a peaceful resolution of this situation. We are also united in this situation for North Korea to completely and visibly eliminate its nuclear weapons program."[165] In February 2003 before the U.S. Senate, Defense Secretary Rumsfeld noted, "I see North Korea as a threat as a proliferator more than I see them as a nuclear threat on the peninsula. Unless the world wakes up and says this is a dangerous thing and creates a set of regimes that will in fact get cooperation to stop those weapons, we're going to be facing a very serious situation in the next five years."[166] These goals have been encapsulated in an acronym, CVID—the complete, verifiable, and irreversible dismantlement of North Korea's nuclear weapons program. For some time, the United States insisted that North Korea must give concrete evidence of fulfilling these requirements before Pyongyang might receive any aid or other benefits. Secretary of State Colin Powell noted, "we stand firm in the knowledge that if they give up this nuclear ambition once and for all, in a way that the world can verify, a better future awaits the people of North Korea. . . . But it must begin with North Korea giving up its nuclear ambitions, and we cannot pay them to give up something they were supposed to have given up in 1994."[167] However, in June 2004, the United States began to show signs it might be willing to be more flexible regarding interim steps while ultimately insisting on CVID.

While much of the administration's rhetoric indicated nuclear proliferation by "rogue states" was a serious threat to U.S. security, officials downplayed the 2002 nuclear crisis almost as soon as it became public. Partly, this was due to the administration's focus on Iraq and Saddam Hussein. However, the Bush administration delayed any public admission of North Korea's cheating until two weeks after confronting it with the evidence. Statements from Secretary of State Colin Powell indicated these matters were "not a crisis," and despite the elevated concern regarding North Korea and its nuclear weapons program, the Bush administration did not view Pyongyang as a more dangerous threat than Iraq. Attempting to downplay the crisis, Powell maintained that demands and threats might worsen the situation. Since North Korea likely had one or two nuclear weapons already, Powell argued, "what are they going to do with another two or three more nuclear weapons when they're starving, when they have no energy, when they have no economy that's functioning?"[168] North Korea was a de facto nuclear state, according to Powell but while Iraq has used its nuclear, chemical, or biological weapons, North Korea has not. As a result, dealing with the North's nuclear threat was less urgent allowing for greater use of diplomacy and economic pressure as desirable strategies.[169] While the interests had not shifted, the stakes were apparently not as high as in the Middle East. As a result, the administration could put this problem on the back burner, or as one Bush official cracked, "one rogue state crisis at a time!"[170] The administration derided containment and deterrence in Iraq but evidently felt sufficiently secure that these were working in North Korea to pursue this matter more slowly.

Bush administration actions here point to some interesting dynamics regarding interests and stakes. As noted earlier, stakes are an assessment of the costs and benefits associated with various interests. The calculation of stakes is based on perception and can be manipulated. White House spokesman Ari Fleischer argued, "I think North Korea would like nothing more than to make this a crisis, because the more they can make this a crisis, the more they think they will get things in return."[171] North Korea is well aware that its nuclear weapons program raises the stakes for U.S. security policy in the region, part of the North's periodic efforts at brinksmanship. While recognizing that a non-nuclear North Korea is an important interest, Washington's "go slow" approach may also be an effort to reduce the perception of what is at stake and thereby reduce DPRK leverage in the negotiations to settle the issue. However, this approach can be dangerous in this situation because of the time factors present in a proliferation problem. The longer North Korea is allowed to continue its nuclear program, the more developed it will become, the greater the number of nuclear weapons it will possess, and the less likely Pyongyang may be to give it up.

Stability and Restraint

One final aspect of U.S. interests in Korea requires discussion that does not fit into a chronological framework. The crucial U.S. interest of the American defense commitment to South Korea is the maintenance of peace on the Korean peninsula and the Northeast region as a whole. The U.S. military presence in Korea achieved this goal not only by deterring a North Korean attack, but also by restraining the South from taking actions that would disrupt regional stability.

The American presence helped restrain the South in two ways. First, during the years since 1953, tension between the two Korean adversaries has been high on numerous occasions. Many North-South clashes have occurred along the DMZ, and Pyongyang has sponsored numerous acts of terrorism against the South. During his tenure as president, Syngman Rhee often made statements indicating his willingness to "march North" to reunify Korea and U.S. policy makers tried to discourage Rhee from acting on his rhetoric. Yet, in a 1953 meeting in Seoul with Vice President Nixon, Rhee presented an interesting argument that his rhetoric was useful for deterrence. According to Rhee:

> The moment the Communists are certain that the United States controls Rhee, you will have lost one of your most effective bargaining points, and we will have lost all our hope. The fear that I may start some action is a constant check on the Communists. . . . the Communists think that America wants peace so badly that you will do anything to get it. At times, I think that this is true as far as I'm concerned. [172]

Though Eisenhower's reaction to this argument is not clear, Nixon believed Rhee's argument had some merit. The U.S. ambassador in Korea also agreed that "it was unwise to pull all of Rhee's teeth."[173]

On other occasions, in response to DPRK provocations, the ROK contemplated retaliation but was convinced by the United States to refrain from responding with force. According to former U.S. Ambassador to Korea William Porter, one benefit of the U.S. presence in Korea is "preventing hasty action or excessive action" taken by the ROK. According to Porter, "we are afraid of where retaliation, if automatic and instantaneous and severe might take us in terms of escalation. We want time to talk it over and see where we are going and not be automatically drawn in."[174] A 1992 RAND report prepared for the U.S. Pacific Command confirmed this objective, stating "concerns about precipitous South Korean actions are alleviated by U.S. involvement in military planning and operations."[175]

In 1996, following the North Korean submarine incident, a South Korean newspaper reported that the ROK armed forces had chosen twelve targets in North Korea for retaliation if further provocations occurred. These plans, which U.S. Command officials had never seen, were a serious surprise since the command structure specified their operational control of ROK forces in wartime. Despite South Korean statements downplaying the plans, the United States did not receive assurances from Seoul that it would approach the United States for discussion or approval before retaliating against the North.[176]

Second, the continued U.S. presence in South Korea helps restrain Seoul from developing its own nuclear option. The U.S. extended deterrence commitment provides an important guarantee for South Korean security, lessening the need for South Korea to develop nuclear weapons. Moreover, the United States regularly provides a "commitment to the defense of the ROK and to the provision of a nuclear umbrella for the ROK."[177] U.S. fears of an ROK nuclear weapons program were well founded. In the early 1970s, facing a growing military threat from the North and believing the U.S. defense commitment in the wake of Vietnam was receding, South Korea began its own nuclear weapons program.[178] After India's "peaceful" nuclear explosion in 1974 surprised U.S. intelligence agencies, a search began for other potential proliferators. Intelligence experts examined embassy records of foreign government import requests for critical materials and equipment including "plutonium metal, bulk orders of beryllium and boron, and exotic explosive chemicals and shaped-charge technology needed to detonate fission."[179] According to one analyst, "when they got to Korea, everything snapped into place."[180] Intense pressure from the Ford administration— threats to withhold export licenses and block Export-Import Bank financing— pushed the ROK to ratify the NPT in 1975[181] and abandon its drive for nuclear weapons.[182] There is also evidence that Seoul continued its program clandestinely until 1978, a reaction to Carter's withdrawal plan, and retained the necessary facilities to produce nuclear weapons, but chose not to operate them.[183] The U.S. security guarantee helps to restrain the South from developing its own nuclear capability, which could ignite a potential nuclear arms race on the peninsula and pose a severe threat to regional stability.[184] Indeed, the current concern over the nuclear weapons program in the North has rekindled speculation that the South might again consider a nuclear option. In September 2004, South Korean scientists admitted to reprocessing a small amount of uranium in 2000 as an "academic test," raising suspicion that Seoul may still harbor nuclear weapons ambitions.[185] Thus, U.S. interests in preventing nuclear proliferation and its destabilizing effects in East Asia are well served by the U.S. presence in South Korea.

The U.S. security commitment to Western Europe, similarly constrained the actions and policies of the allies, in particular West Germany. Except for limiting some of the options of West Germany, the United States had little fear that any one in Western Europe would "march east." Yet, the stability of superpower relations depended in part on the assurance that both side's allies would behave in a predictable fashion. Thus, the adage arose with respect to the significance of NATO that the alliance "kept the Russians out, the Americans in, and the Germans down." The Korean case also demonstrates the defender's need to restrain its protégé and ensure predictable behavior. Consequently, restraining the protégé seems obvious in situations of extended general deterrence where the protégé can attempt to use the defender's support to its own local advantage. However, as the U.S.-ROK relationship has evolved, alliance dynamics have meant less U.S. ability to restrain the ROK and more South Korean influence on U.S. policy in the region.

Conclusion

Prior to 25 June 1950, U.S. policy makers did not carefully or clearly articulate American interests in Korea. Also, U.S. leaders disagreed over the stakes—the costs and benefits of U.S. policy in the region. On the one hand, NSC 8, approved in 1948, maintained South Korea must not fall to the Soviets and that a precipitous U.S. withdrawal from Korea would send a dangerous signal to American allies. Recall that U.S. troops did not leave South Korea until June 1949, a date that was much later than previous Pentagon recommendations. Yet, the Joint Chiefs contended that Korea had little strategic value and was likely to be bypassed in a future war. Moreover, Acheson's defense perimeter speech undercut further the U.S. position in Korea.

NSC 8 did identify important goals and objectives in Korea, but it did not appreciate the stakes for U.S. global interests in the absence of an actual attack. Other mitigating factors, such as budget constraints and the need to temper U.S. support lest South Korean President Rhee start a war also influenced U.S. policy makers. Finally, U.S. threat assessments concluded that an invasion was not the most likely threat to South Korea. Rather, U.S. officials surmised that infiltration and subversion were the most probable dangers. They believed that these threats could be countered most effectively by building up the economic and political strength of the ROK. Thus, because they failed to connect America's global interests with the stakes at issue in the event of an attack on Korea—because an invasion appeared unlikely—U.S. policy overlooked the basic requirements for an immediate deterrence situation: evidence of determination to resist an attack. However, on 25 June 1950, U.S. assessments of its interests and its policy in Korea changed.

Now it became clear to Washington that Korea was important to American regional and global security interests. A communist victory in Korea would threaten U.S. positions elsewhere, particularly Japan. If aggression were not stopped in Korea, the threat would only grow and be an ever-greater danger to U.S. interests beyond Asia, possibly in Europe. Thus, the North Korean invasion challenged U.S. credibility in Korea and its reputation in general.

Following the Korean War, U.S. security interests in Korea were explicitly linked to a global containment strategy fashioned by Secretary of State John Foster Dulles through a series of bilateral and multilateral alliances. The communist threat was monolithic, requiring containment at a variety of points by many means, including deterrence. Korea was a financial burden; in two separate NSC meetings in 1956, President Eisenhower noted, "South Korea was getting to be a pretty expensive plaything" and "commented with a sigh that we were surely spending an awful lot of money in Korea."[186] Nevertheless, there remained a strong consensus of the need to protect the area.

Since the end of the Korean War, the specific policies and means have changed, but U.S. interests have been relatively consistent in their determination to promote peace and stability in the region. Even the Nixon Doctrine and Carter's plan to withdraw U.S. ground troops did not alter the assessment of vital American interests present in the region. This assessment has continued on through all U.S. administrations that followed.

Throughout the years of the U.S. defense commitment, South Korea's economic growth made it an important economic, military, and political force in the region, and a valuable American ally. Bases in South Korea afford American forces access to the region and establish a presence on the East Asian continent that helps stabilize the entire area. With sizeable contributions from the South Korean government, U.S. forces are less costly to maintain than American troops elsewhere, including the continental U.S. In a statement to a congressional committee in 1989, General Louis Menetrey, CINCUNC/USFK noted: "The only way to save money by withdrawing forces from Korea is to disband them."[187] Despite these considerations, the U.S. intends to remove one-third of its troops and relocate the remainder to positions south of Seoul.

South Korea's growth economically, politically, and militarily has been a two-edged sword for the United States. In addition to generating a robust U.S. ally to buttress American interests, a stronger and more assertive South Korea has also been able to shape the security relationship in ways more to its liking. U.S. dominance of the alliance has long been a sore spot in Seoul, particularly as Washington has taken actions unilaterally, at best with ROK consultation, and at worst without any prior discussion. Increasingly, South Korea has a greater ability to influence U.S. policy in its favor, for example as it has softened the hard line position of the Bush administration in relation to North Korea. Thus, the U.S.-ROK relationship has evolved into more of a partnership providing important benefits for both sides but also requiring greater accommodation to the interests of South Korea.

The end of the Cold War brought important changes to U.S. interest perceptions. The North Korean threat changed to include concerns for nuclear weapons and ballistic missiles, and September 11th heightened fears that a nuclear, chemical, or biological weapon might fall into the hands of terrorists. These factors changed the regional and global context to push U.S. interests beyond merely preserving the peace in Korea to also including regional and national security concerns that could directly threaten the security of the United States.

Finally, how does this discussion of American interests contribute to the understanding of extended deterrence? As noted earlier, interests and the stakes associated with those interests are important aspects of extended deterrence commitments. The more interests and the greater the stakes, the more effort a defender exerts to provide a security guarantee for the protégé.

After World War II, U.S. leaders were concerned primarily with security and political interests. The crucial element here was Korea's link to other U.S. interests in the region and globally. By the 1970s, security and political concerns had lessened, only to be joined by a new set of interests, namely ROK economic growth and its trade links with the United States and others in the region. Again, these economic interests were tied to peace and stability in the region. A war in Korea would seriously damage American economic interests. Thus, while interests and stakes in Korea have varied between security, political, and economic interests, their linkage to broader regional and global U.S. interests have helped ensure a consistent U.S. security guarantee.

Deterrence theory focuses most of its attention on the actions of the defender. Yet, ROK economic growth also points to the role of the protégé in a deterrence relationship. Through economic development, aided by U.S. economic and military assistance, a subject that will be considered in greater detail in the next chapter, the ROK has enhanced its "value" to the United States. South Korea developed the ability to deploy its forces abroad as it did in Vietnam, the 1990-1991 Persian Gulf War, and the 2003-2004 Iraq War. Moreover, Seoul has become a strong regional player, and an important backer of U.S. interests. As noted above, economic development can increase protégé-defender ties and ensure a strong security relationship. As the protégé grows in economic, military, and political strength, security relations can change from dependence on the defender to more of a partnership.

One final aspect of U.S. interests deserves note here. Throughout U.S.-ROK security relations, there has been an important relationship between stakes and U.S. threat assessments. When the Soviets and Chinese were the main threat, the stakes were higher since U.S. security and political interests intertwined with America's global containment strategy. U.S. assessments of the stakes changed when the threat from Moscow and Beijing diminished. American security and political interests were now less connected to interests elsewhere and the stakes lessened. While decreasing for political and security concerns, the stakes rose for U.S. economic interests. However, the worry over the North's suspected nuclear weapons program and ballistic missile production has focused new attention on security interests. After September 11th, the stakes rose again as U.S. leaders viewed North Korea more in terms of a direct security threat. Thus, throughout the U.S.-ROK security guarantee, there has been a fluid interplay of interest/stakes assessments and threat perception. The interests and stakes in a particular region are not determined in isolation and may be connected to the defender's threat assessments.

This chapter has outlined the evolution of U.S. interests present in its security commitment to South Korea. Yet, as these interests and the context in which they existed changed, how did U.S. policy adapt? The U.S.-ROK relationship has been dominated by efforts to deter a North Korean conventional attack on the South. However, as the threat and U.S. interests evolved during the post-Cold War period, was deterrence the appropriate policy and most likely to succeed in addressing the new configuration of threats and interests? Increasingly, U.S. policy makers were pushed in other directions, namely compellence and engagement, to pursue U.S. goals in the region. The evolution of U.S. security policy is the subject of the next two chapters.

Notes

1. George and Smoke, *Deterrence in American Foreign Policy*, 149.

2. "A Report to the President Pursuant to the President's Directive of January 31, 1950," *FRUS, 1950*, I, 238. Hereafter, this document will be referred to as "NSC-68." President Truman formally accepted the document on 30 September 1950. See *FRUS, 1950*, I, 400.

3. Hilary Conroy and Wayne Patterson, "Duality and Dominance: A Century of Korean-American Relations," in Yur-Bok Lee and Wayne Patterson, eds., *Korean-American Relations, 1866-1997* (Albany, NY: State University of New York Press, 1999), 2-4.

4. U.S. Department of State, *Treaties and Other International Agreements of the United States of America, 1776-1949, Volume 9*, compiled by Charles I. Bevans (Washington, D.C.: Government Printing Office, 1972), 470-476.

5. Fred Harvey Harrington, "An American View of Korean-American Relations, 1882-1905," in Lee and Patterson, eds., *Korean-American Relations, 1866-1997*, 46-47.

6. *Treaties and Other International Agreements of the United States of America, 1776-1949, Volume 9*, 471.

7. John Chay, "The First Three Decades of American-Korean Relations, 1882-1910: Reassessments and Reflections," in Tae-hwan Kwak, ed., *U.S.-Korean Relations, 1882-1982* (Seoul: Kyungnam University Press, 1982), 20.

8. Conroy and Patterson, "Duality and Dominance," 3.

9. Theodore Roosevelt to Hermann Speck Von Sternberg, *The Letters of Theodore Roosevelt, Volume II*, Elting E. Morrison, John M. Blum, and John J. Buckley, eds. (Cambridge: Harvard University Press, 1951), 1394.

10. Yur-Bok Lee, "A Korean View of Korean-American Relations, 1866-1905," in Yur-Bok Lee and Wayne Patterson, eds., *One Hundred Years of Korean-American Relations, 1882-1982*, (University, AL: University of Alabama Press, 1986), 19-21.

11. Theodore Roosevelt to John Hay, 31 January 1905, *The Letters of Theodore Roosevelt, Volume IV*, 1112.

12. Roosevelt, as quoted in Andrew C. Nahm, "American-Korean Relations, 1866-1978, An Overview," in Andrew C. Nahm, ed., *The United States and Korea* (Kalamazoo: The Center For Korean Studies, Western Michigan University, 1979), 15.

13. Chay, "The First Three Decades of American-Korean Relations," 30.

14. For more detailed and competing views on this period, see Bruce Cumings' 2 volume work, *The Origins of the Korean War, Volume I: Liberation and the Emergence of Separate Regimes, 1947-1950* (Princeton: Princeton University Press, 1981), *Volume II: The Roaring of the Cataract, 1947-1950* (Princeton: Princeton University Press, 1992), Bruce Cumings, ed., *The Child of Conflict: The Korean-American Relationship, 1943-1953*, and James Matray, *The Reluctant Crusade* (Honolulu: The University of Hawaii Press, 1985).

15. "Final Text of the Communiqué," 26 November 1943, *FRUS, Conferences at Cairo and Teheran, 1943*, 449. In July 1945, the pledge was reaffirmed at the Potsdam Conference, including Soviet acquiescence to the statement.

16. "Bohlen Minutes for the February 8, 1945 meeting at Yalta between Roosevelt and Stalin," *FRUS, Conferences at Malta and Yalta, 1945*, 766-771.

17. Taken from a memorandum/recollection of Dean Rusk, dated 12 July 1950, to explain the decision to accept the Japanese surrender at the 38th parallel. *FRUS, 1945*,

VI, 1037-1039.

18. Kim Se-Jin, *Documents in Korean-American Relations* (Seoul: Research Center for Peace and Unification, 1976), 28.

19. The report was reviewed in NSC 8/2 a year later, but did not make substantial alterations to U.S. policy. For a concise discussion of the debates within the Truman administration regarding Korea policy, see Ronald L. McGlothen, *Controlling the Waves: Dean Acheson and U.S. Foreign Policy in Asia* (New York: W.W. Norton, 1993), 50-85.

20. "Report by the National Security Council on the Position of the United States With Respect to Korea, NSC 8," *FRUS, 1948*, VI, 1167.

21. *FRUS, 1948*, VI, 1167.

22. *FRUS, 1948*, VI, 1167.

23. *FRUS, 1948*, VI, 1167.

24. *FRUS, 1948*, VI, 1167-1168.

25. *FRUS, 1948*, VI, 1167.

26. Harry S. Truman, "Annual Message to the Congress on the State of the Union," 7 January 1948, *Public Papers, 1948*, 7.

27. Truman, "Special Message to the Congress Transmitting Annual Report on U.S. Participation in the United Nations," *Public Papers, 1948*, 153.

28. Truman, "Commencement Address at the University of California," 12 June 1948, *Public Papers, 1948*, 337.

29. Truman, *Public Papers, 1948*, 338.

30. Truman, *Public Papers, 1948*, 338.

31. Harry S. Truman, *Memoirs, Volume Two: Years of Trial and Hope* (Garden City, NJ: Doubleday, 1956), 325.

32. "Report by the National Security Council to the President: NSC 8/2," *FRUS, 1949*, VII, 976.

33. George F. Kennan, *Memoirs: 1925-1950* (Boston: Little, Brown, and Company, 1967), 484.

34. As noted in *FRUS, 1949*, VII, 946. The original document is Department of the Army telegram CX 67198, 19 January 1949, summarized in Robert K. Sawyer, *Military Advisors in Korea: KMAG in Peace and War*, in Walter G. Hermes, ed., a volume in the *United States Army Historical Series* (Washington, D.C.: Government Printing Office, 1962), 37.

35. Truman, *Memoirs, Volume Two*, 328.

36. Truman, *Memoirs, Volume Two*, 329-330.

37. Rusk, *As I Saw It*, 165.

38. *FRUS, 1948*, VI, 1167.

39. "Message from U.S. President Truman to the Congress of the United States, Regarding Economic Assistance to the Republic of Korea," June 7, 1949, in Kim Se-jin, ed., *Documents of U.S.-Korean Foreign Policy*, 75.

40. *Documents of U.S.-Korean Foreign Policy*, 75.

41. Matray, *The Reluctant Crusade*, 173.

42. Walter LaFeber, *The American Age: U.S. Foreign Policy at Home and Abroad—1750 to the Present*, 502-504, and Michael Schaller, *The United States and China in the Twentieth Century*, 2ed. (New York: Oxford University Press, 1990), 123-127.

43. Matray, *The Reluctant Crusade*, 176.

44. "Report by the National Security Council to the President-NSC 8/2," *FRUS,*

1949, VII, part 2, 975-976.

45. *FRUS, 1949*, VII, part 2, 978.

46 For example, Gregory Henderson argued that the U.S. created South Korea and abandoned it so that "without requisite aid or defense the Korean policy created by Americans was a legless monster from birth." See *Korea: The Politics of the Vortex* (Cambridge: Harvard University Press, 1968), 150.

47. Dean Acheson, *Present at the Creation: My Years in the State Department* (New York: W.W. Norton, 1969), 358.

48. Acheson, *Present at the Creation*, 357.

49. Dean Acheson, "Crisis in Asia—An Examination of U.S. Policy," *Department of State Bulletin*, XXII, no. 551, 23 January 1950, 116.

50. Acheson, "Crisis in Asia—An Examination of U.S. Policy," 117.

51. Rusk, *As I Saw It*, 164.

52. Rusk, *As I Saw It*, 114.

53. "Truman's Statement on the Korean War," 27 June 1950, in Commager, ed., *Documents of American History, Volume II*, 560-561.

54. John Foster Dulles, "The Korean Experiment in Representative Government," *Department of State Bulletin*, XXIII, no. 574, 3 July 1950, 13.

55. "The Secretary of State to the Embassy in Korea," 13 June 1950, *FRUS, 1950*, VII, 104.

56. "Memorandum by the Central Intelligence Agency," 19 June 1950, *FRUS, 1950*, VII, 109-121.

57. *FRUS, 1950*, VII, 109-121.

58. *FRUS, 1950*, VII, 109-121.

59. Glenn D. Paige, *The Korean Decision* (New York: The Free Press, 1968), 71.

60. Douglas Jehl, "CIA Opens Files on Cold War Era," *New York Times*, 1 October 1993, A7.

61. Truman, *Memoirs, Volume Two*, 331.

62. George A. Brownell, *The Origin and Development of the National Security Agency* (Laguna Hills, CA: Aegean Park Press, 1981), 41.

63. Paige, *The Korean Decision*, footnote #71, 98.

64. U.S. Senate, *Inquiry into the Military Situation in the Far East and the facts surrounding the relief of General of the Army Douglas MacArthur from his assignment in that area*, Part 4, Hearings before the Committee on Armed Services and Committee on Foreign Relations (Washington, D.C.: Government Printing Office, 1951), 2572. Hereafter cited as *Military Situation in the Far East* (1951).

65. A conversation between an American businessman and Soviet diplomat Andrei Vyshinsky sometime after the Korean War began as recounted in Dean Rusk's memoirs. Rusk, *As I Saw It*, 164-165.

66. George and Smoke, *Deterrence in American Foreign Policy*, 156.

67. Khrushchev, *Khrushchev Remembers* (1970), 368.

68. Merle Miller, *Plain Speaking: An Oral Biography of Harry S. Truman* (New York: Berkley Publishing, 1973), 266.

69. Harry Truman, "Special Message to the Congress Reporting on the Situation in Korea," *Public Papers, 1950*, 19 July 1950, 527-537.

70. *Military Situation in the Far East* (1951), 1715.

71. Truman, *Memoirs, Volume Two*, 334.

72. As quoted in Paige, *The Korean Decision*, 53.

73. "Intelligence Estimate Prepared by the Estimates Group, Office of Intelligence Research, Department of State," 25 June 1950, *FRUS, 1950*, VII, 148-154.

74. *Military Situation in the Far East* (1951), Part 3, 1936.

75. "NSC 68," *FRUS, 1950*, I, 246.

76. "NSC 68," *FRUS, 1950*, I, 237.

77. "NSC 68," *FRUS, 1950*, I, 246.

78. Schaller, *The U.S. and China in the Twentieth Century*, 135.

79. "NSC 68," *FRUS, 1950*, I, 240.

80. Truman, *Memoirs, Volume Two*, 333.

81. Paige, *The Korean Decision*, 133.

82. Miller, *Plain Speaking*, 284-285.

83. Truman, *Memoirs, Volume Two*, 335.

84. Truman, *Memoirs, Volume Two*, 332-333.

85. *Military Situation in the Far East* (1951), Part 2, 890.

86. *FRUS, 1950*, VII, 174 and 199.

87. "Intelligence Estimate Prepared by the Estimates Group, Office of Intelligence Research," *FRUS, 1950*, XII, 151.

88. Truman, *Memoirs, Volume Two*, 337.

89. McGlothen, *Controlling the Waves*, 55-59.

90. "The Secretary of State to Certain Diplomatic Offices," 27 December 1949, *FRUS, 1949*, VII, 932. The abbreviations [sic] contained in this document are as they occurred in the original text of the telegram.

91. Kennan, *Memoirs*, 396.

92. "Report to the National Security Council by the Executive Secretary: NSC 73," 1 July 1950, *FRUS, 1950*, I, 336.

93. John Foster Dulles, *Department of State Bulletin*, XXIX, no. 742, 14 September 1953, 341.

94. Dulles, *Department of State Bulletin*, XXIX, no. 742, 339.

95. Dwight D. Eisenhower, "Annual Message to the Congress on the State of the Union," *Public Papers, 1954*, 8.

96. Eisenhower, "Special Message to the Senate Transmitting the Mutual Defense Treaty between the United States and the Republic of Korea," 11 January 1954, *Public Papers, 1954*, 45.

97. "Memorandum From the Joint Chiefs of Staff to the Secretary of Defense," 13 June 1957, *FRUS, 1955-1957*, XXIII, part 1, 349-351.

98. "NSC 5516/1," April 1955. For the complete text, see *FRUS, 1955-1957*, XXIII, part 1, 52-62.

99. "Letter From the Ambassador in Japan (MacArthur) to the Secretary of State," 25 May 1957, *FRUS, 1955-1957*, XXIII, part 1, 325-330.

100. For specific analyses of South Korea's role in the Vietnam War, see Sung-joo Han, "South Korea's Participation in the Vietnam Conflict: An Analysis of the U.S.-Korean Alliance," *ORBIS* (Winter, 1978): 893-912, and Chin-Ha Suk and James L. Morrison, "South Korea's Participation in the Vietnam War: A Historiographical Essay," *Korea Observer* XVIII, no. 3 (Autumn, 1987): 270-316, Robert M. Blackburn, *Mercenaries and Lyndon Johnson's "More Flags": The Hiring of Korean, Filipino, and Thai Soldiers in the Vietnam War* (Jefferson NC: McFarland, 1994), and Nicolas Evan Saran-

takes, "In the Service of Pharaoh? The United States and the Deployment of Korean Troops in Vietnam, 1965-1968," *Pacific Historical Review* 68, no. 3 (August 1999): 425-449.

101. Buss, *The United States and the Republic of Korea*, 79.

102. Han Sung-joo, "South Korea's Participation in the Vietnam Conflict," 896-897.

103. These figures were obtained from *Security Agreements Hearings* (1970), 1554.

104. Han Sung-joo, "South Korea's Participation in the Vietnam Conflict," 901-902.

105. Vice President Hubert Humphrey, "Extemporaneous in Korea," 23 February 1966, *Security Agreements Hearings* (1970), Appendix No. 10, 1725.

106. "The White House-Joint Statement of President Johnson and President Park on the Occasion of President Johnson's State Visit to Korea," *Security Agreements Hearings* (1970), Appendix No. 7, 1721.

107. *Security Agreements Hearings* (1970), Appendix No. 7, 1721.

108. Harold C. Hinton, "The U.S.-Korean Relationship: An American Perspective," in *The U.S.-Korean Security Relationship: Prospects and Challenges for the 1990s*, ed. Harold C. Hinton et al. (Washington, D.C.: Pergamon-Brassey's, 1988), 2.

109. Richard Nixon, *U.S. Foreign Policy for the 1970's: A New Strategy for Peace*, 18 February 1970 (Washington, D.C.: Government Printing Office), 1.

110. Nixon, *U.S. Foreign Policy for the 1970's*, 2-3.

111. Richard Nixon, *U.S. Foreign Policy for the 1970's*, "A Report to Congress," 25 February 1971 (Washington, D.C.: Government Printing Office), 93.

112. Richard Nixon, "American Policy in the Pacific: Informal Remarks of President Nixon with Newsmen at Guam," 25 July 1969, *Public Papers, 1969*, 545-549.

113. Richard Nixon, *U.S. Foreign Policy for the 1970's: A New Strategy for Peace*, 54.

114. Richard Nixon, "Fourth Annual Report to the Congress on United States Foreign Policy," 3 May 1973, *Public Papers, 1973*, 429.

115. Richard Nixon, *U.S. Foreign Policy for the 1970's: A New Strategy for Peace*, 54.

116. (Emphasis included in Nixon's memoirs) Richard Nixon, *The Memoirs of Richard Nixon* (New York: Grosset & Dunlap, 1978), 395.

117. *Security Agreements Hearings* (1970), 1578.

118. William H. Gleysteen Jr., *Massive Entanglement, Marginal Influence: Carter and Korea in Crisis* (Washington, D.C.: Brookings Institution, 1999), 22-23.

119. Oberdorfer, *The Two Koreas*, 86-87.

120. Jimmy Carter, "Transfer of Defense Articles to the Republic of Korea: Letter to the Speaker of the House, the President of the Senate, and the Senate Majority Leader Transmitting Proposed Legislation," *Public Papers, 1977*, Book II, 1822.

121. *Washington Post*, 24 October 1976.

122. Oberdorfer, *The Two Koreas*, 92, and Gleysteen, *Massive Entanglement, Marginal Influence*, 19-20.

123. Oberdorfer, *The Two Koreas*, 92, and Gleysteen, *Massive Entanglement, Marginal Influence*, 19-20.

124. Harold Brown, "Joint Communiqué of the ROK-U.S. Security Consultative Meeting," 26 July 1978, in Chong-Shik Chung, ed., *Korean Unification: Source Materi-*

als with an Introduction, Vol. II (Seoul: Research Center for Peace and Unification, 1979), 318.

125. Harold Brown, "Joint Communiqué of the ROK-U.S. Security Consultative Meeting," 318.

126. Carter, "Transfer of Defense Articles to the Republic of Korea," *Public Papers, 1977*, Book II, 1822.

127. Oberdorfer, *The Two Koreas*, 101-103.

128. *Public Papers, 1979*, Book I, 247-248; Gleysteen, *Massive Entanglement, Marginal Influence*, 28-29.

129. Carter, "Transfer of Defense Articles to the Republic of Korea," *Public Papers, 1977*, Book II, 1822.

130. George P. Shultz, *Turmoil and Triumph: My Years as Secretary of State* (New York: Macmillian, 1993), 975.

131. Alexander M. Haig Jr., *Caveat: Realism, Reagan, and Foreign Policy* (New York: Macmillan, 1984), 90.

132. Haig Jr., *Caveat*, 90.

133. Ronald Reagan, "Joint Communiqué Following Discussions With President Chun Doo Hwan of the Republic of Korea," 2 February 1981, *Public Papers, 1981*, 68-70.

134. Caspar Weinberger, *Fighting for Peace: Seven Critical Years in the Pentagon* (New York: Warner Books, 1990), 224.

135. "Joint Communiqué of the Fourteenth Annual Republic of Korea-United States Security Consultative Meeting," 31 March 1982, *AFP Current Documents, 1982*, 1101-1102.

136. Shultz, *Turmoil and Triumph*, 977-978.

137. As quoted in Oberdorfer, *The Two Koreas*, 168.

138. James Baker, "U.S. Policy Toward Korea," 1 February 1990, *AFP Current Documents, 1990*, 715.

139. "Joint Communiqué of the 22d Annual ROK-U.S. Security Consultative Meeting," 15 November 1990, *AFP Current Documents, 1990*, 720.

140. George Bush, "The President's News Conference With President Roh Tae Woo," 6 January 1992, *Public Papers, 1992-1993*, Book I, 34.

141. *Pacific Almanac*, 139-140.

142. Chwee Huay Ow-Taylor, "Korea's Economic Performance in 1990," *Korea Economic Update* 2, no. 1 (Spring, 1991): 2.

143. *A Strategic Framework for the Asian Pacific Rim: Looking Toward the 21st Century*, April 1990, 5.

144. "Address by Vice President Bush Before the Republic of Korea National Assembly," 26 April 1982, *AFP Current Documents, 1982*, 1102-1105.

145. For a discussion of the role of ROK civil society in the process, see Sunhyuk Kim, *The Politics of Democratizaton in Korea: The Role of Civil Society* (Pittsburgh: University of Pittsburgh Press, 2000).

146. Bush, *Public Papers, 1992-1993*, Book I, 38.

147. Paul Wolfowitz, "U.S.-Korean Relations: Auspicious Prospects," *AFP Current Documents, 1984*, 739.

148. U.S. Department of Defense, "Report to Congress" on the progress of *A Strategic Framework for the Asian Pacific Rim: Looking Toward the 21st Century* (Washing-

ton, D.C.: Government Printing Office, 28 February 1991), 6.

149. *A Strategic Framework for the Asian Pacific Rim: Looking Toward the 21st Century*, 6.

150. Bush, "Text of Remarks at Camp Casey in Yongsan, South Korea," January 6, 1992, *Public Papers, 1992-1993*, Book I, 43.

151. As quoted in Oberdorfer, *The Two Koreas*, 255.

152. Bush, "Remarks to the Korean National Assembly in Seoul," January 6, 1992, *Public Papers, 1992-1993*, Book I, 41.

153. Bush, *Public Papers, 1992-1993*, Book I, 43.

154. William J. Clinton, "Remarks to the Korean National Assembly in Seoul, July 10, 1993," *Weekly Compilation of Presidential Documents*, Monday, 10 July 1993, 1311.

155. Clinton, *Weekly Compilation of Presidential Documents*, 10 July 1993, 1311.

156. Ryan J. Barilleaux and Andrew Ilsu Kim, "Clinton, Korea, and Presidential Diplomacy," *World Affairs* 162, no. 1 (Summer 1999): 30.

157. Barilleaux and Kim, "Clinton, Korea, and Presidential Diplomacy," 30.

158. U.S. House of Representatives, Joint Hearing before the Subcommittees on International Economic Policy and Trade and Asia and the Pacific of the Committee on International Relations, "Statement of Hon. Thomas Hubbard, Deputy Assistant Secretary of State for East Asian and Pacific Affairs," *North Korean Military and Nuclear Proliferation Threat: Evaluation of the U.S.-DPRK Agreed Framework*, 104th Congress, 1st Session, 23 February 1995 (Washington, D.C.: Government Printing Office, 1995), 13.

159. Clinton, "President's News Conference," *New York Times*, 4 August 1994.

160. William Clinton, "Remarks on the Nuclear Agreement with North Korea," *Public Papers 1994*, Book II, 1794-1795.

161. Michael R. Gordon, "How Politics Sank Accord on Missiles With North Korea," *New York Times*, 6 March 2001, A1, A8.

162. David E. Sanger, "Bush Tells Seoul Talks with North Won't Resume Now," *New York Times*, 8 March 2001, A1.

163. George W. Bush, "Joint Statement Between the United States of America and the Republic of Korea," *Public Papers, 2001*, Book I, 204.

164. President George W. Bush, *State of the Union Address*, January 29, 2002, <http://www.whitehouse.gov/news/releases/2002/01/20020129-11.html>. Accessed June 26 June 2004.

165. President George W. Bush, "Statement by the President: Bush Backs KEDO Suspension of Fuel Oil to North Korea," U.S. Department of State, *Washington File*, 15 November 2002, <http://usinfo.state.gov>. Accessed 24 January 2003.

166. James Dao, "U.S. Planning Sanctions Against North Korea," *New York Times*, 17 February 2003, A1, A12.

167. U.S. Department of State, "Secretary Colin L. Powell—Press Conference," 25 February 2003, <www.state.gov/secretary/rm/2003/17933pf.htm> (August 2004).

168. David Sanger, "U.S. Eases Threat on Nuclear Arms for North Korea," *New York Times*, 30 December 2002, A1, A7.

169. Sanger, "U.S. Eases Threat on Nuclear Arms for North Korea," A1, A7.

170. Howard French and David Sanger, "North Korea to Reactivate an Idled Nuclear Reactor," *New York Times*, 13 December 2002, A16.

171. James Dao, "Criticism of Bush's Policy on Korea Sharpens," *New York Times*, 6 March 2003, A16.

172. Richard Nixon, *The Memoirs of Richard Nixon*, 128-129, and "Memorandum of Discussion at the 175th Meeting of the National Security Council," 15 December 1953, *FRUS, 1952-1954*, XV, 1661.

173. Nixon, *FRUS, 1952-1954*, XV, 1661.

174. *Security Agreements Hearings* (1970), 1590.

175. John Y. Schrader and James A. Winnefeld, *Understanding the Evolving U.S. Role in Pacific Rim Security* (RAND Corporation, R-4065-PACOM, 1992), 33.

176. Oberdorfer, *The Two Koreas*, 390-391.

177. U.S. Department of Defense, *Korea-U.S. Security Consultative Meeting Joint Communiqué*, 5 December 2002, <www.defenselink.mil/releases/2002/b12052002_bt-61902.html> (June 2004).

178. Ernest W. Lefever, *Nuclear Arms in the Third World* (Washington, D.C.: Brookings, 1979), 85-86.

179. Robert Gillette, "U.S. Squelched Apparent S. Korea A-Bomb Drive," *Los Angeles Times*, 4 November 1978.

180. Gillette, "U.S. Squelched Apparent S. Korea A-Bomb Drive," *Los Angeles Times*.

181. South Korea had signed the NPT in 1968 but it did not take effect until Seoul ratified the agreement in 1975.

182. Leonard S. Spector, *Nuclear Ambitions* (Boulder: Westview, 1990), 122; Lefever, *Nuclear Arms in the Third World*, 130.

183. Leonard S. Spector, *The Undeclared Bomb* (Cambridge: Ballinger, 1988), 70-71 and T.V. Paul, *Power versus Prudence: Why Nations Forgo Nuclear Weapons* (Montreal: McGill-Queen's University Press, 2000), 120-124.

184. Robert J. Art, "A Defensible Defense: America's Grand Strategy after the Cold War," *International Security* 15, no. 4 (Spring, 1991): 29. Art notes, "American actions, including the stationing of troops overseas, have played a critical role in retarding nuclear weapons spread among key states."

185. James Brooke, "South Korea Explains Uranium Misstep," *New York Times*, 7 September 2004, A12.

186. *FRUS, 1955-1957*, XXIII, Part 2, "Memorandum of Discussion at the 276th Meeting of the National Security Council," 9 February 1956, 217; "Memorandum of Discussion at the 297th Meeting of the National Security Council," 20 September 1956, 309.

187. United States Senate, "Statement by General Louis C. Menetrey, Commander in Chief, United Nations Command/U.S. Forces Korea statement before the Subcommittee on Defense Appropriations," 23 February 1989, 16.

Chapter 5

U.S. SECURITY POLICY:
Deterrence

U.S. assessments of the threat, interests, and stakes have helped to drive a U.S.-ROK alliance that has lasted over fifty years. Deterrence has been the crucial component of that alliance in seeking to prevent an attack on South Korea while maintaining peace and stability in the region. Though it is impossible to prove definitely that deterrence was the deciding factor, it seems apparent that it has been successful in its goals—relative peace and stability have endured on the Korean peninsula. Yet, as demonstrated in earlier chapters, the threat in Korea expanded as the Cold War came to an end to include proliferation concerns regarding the DPRK's nuclear weapons and ballistic missile programs. As these threats grew, it became evident that deterrence alone would no longer address these concerns. As a result, the United States included efforts to engage North Korea and implement a compellence strategy that alternated between incentives and threats to cajole or pressure North Korea into giving up its weapons programs. Beginning first with deterrence, the next two chapters examine the complex mix of policy options and their evolution over the years of the U.S. defense commitment to South Korea.

U.S. Extended Deterrence in Korea

The basic task for the defender in an extended deterrence relationship is to construct a credible security guarantee. When deterring an attack on your homeland, a threat to respond is very credible; there is little doubt that a nation will retaliate when it is the target of attack. However, when deterrence is extended to a third party, a threat to respond is less certain, varying with the value of the ally to the guarantor and the consequences for the defender. At any moment, the defender may decide the potential costs of supporting a protégé outweigh the benefits. Thus, credibility is a more difficult problem under extended deterrence despite giving strong declarations of support. Relying on William Kaufmann's criteria—capability, cost, and resolve—the goal of this chapter is to examine and evaluate the degree to which the U.S. extended deterrence commitment has met the "credibility criteria" of deterrence theory.

Since 1953, the U.S. has used four general approaches to demonstrate its commitment to defend South Korea: a mutual defense treaty and declarations of support; massive amounts of economic and military aid; the stationing of U.S. forces in Korea; and the deployment of U.S. tactical nuclear weapons to South Korea. Each of these techniques will be examined as indicators of the credibility of American policy to defend South Korea. Despite changes in the specific form, this chapter shows that U.S. deterrence policy has been consistent with the credibility requirements of deterrence theory. While the U.S. guarantee did not always supply sufficient reassurance to satisfy South Korean officials, it was, apparently, sufficient to deter a North Korean attack.

Capability and Cost

Recall that in a situation of general deterrence, the defender may not need to issue specific counterthreats, but rather support deterrence through military preparedness and statements of intent. The defender must possess the necessary military assets to support these warnings and be able to issue credible counterthreats should relations escalate to a crisis of immediate deterrence. Furthermore, according to the rationality assumptions embedded in deterrence theory, these warnings and the military capabilities that support them must be sufficiently threatening to raise the costs of aggression so that they outweigh the benefits for the challenger.

In Korea, the "challenger" consisted of three states with different intentions and military capabilities that varied over time. A complicated threat configuration made assessments of the military balance more difficult. During the 1950s, the Soviet Union and China were the primary threat. The Eisenhower administration chose to counter the conventional strength of these two foes with nuclear threats of "massive retaliation," relying primarily on nuclear capability to address the military balance with the Soviets and Chinese. Faced with daunting reconstruction efforts after the Korean War, the North and South were not major factors in the military balance, though they did tend to offset each other, according to U.S. planners.

ROK and DPRK military capabilities grew significantly during the 1960s, and became more important factors in calculations of the military balance. Yet, U.S. assessments concluded North and South Korean capabilities were largely equivalent. Moreover, U.S. leaders believed Moscow was not interested in starting another war on the peninsula. Hence, the United States did not factor in Soviet forces when considering the military balance in Korea. China was another matter. Beijing's large army and its proximity to the Korean border worried U.S. leaders. ROK forces could defend themselves against the DPRK, but not against a joint Sino-DPRK assault. Thus, U.S. forces were deemed necessary to maintain a satisfactory military balance in the region.

By the 1970s, U.S. threat assessments and calculations of the military balance centered primarily on the DPRK. U.S. relations with the Soviets and Chinese had improved considerably and neither was judged to be intent on provoking a war. However, the 1970s were also the beginning of a dramatic increase in North Korean military capabilities. By 1990, the DPRK had over one million men in its armed forces and large numbers of tanks, artillery pieces, and combat aircraft. North Korean military strength has remained relatively consistent though the quality of its equipment has deteriorated over time. Pyongyang has increased its military prowess through the development of ballistic missiles, chemical and biological weapons, and a likely nuclear capability.

Despite significant North Korean military capabilities, there was little doubt that the United States, alone or combined with ROK forces, possessed overwhelming military superiority over North Korea, even if the United States chose to employ only a portion of its military capability.[1] However, the overall strength of U.S. forces was not the most crucial aspect of capability and cost in extended deterrence. The key to U.S. deterrence policy in Korea was the troops stationed on the peninsula, close to the border because they functioned as a trip wire to bring in other U.S. units. American forces in Korea have varied in size from approximately 63,000 in the 1950s and 1960s to 44,000 in the 1970s and 1980s. In 1991, the United States reduced its troop strength to 37,500 as part of a Pentagon plan to draw down American military presence in Asia. Further phased reductions in Korea were planned but later suspended due to concerns over the North's nuclear weapons program. In 2004, Washington proposed another withdrawal plan to reduce U.S. forces by one-third, bringing the total down to 25,000.

U.S. forces based in Korea are not the only forces that could be brought to bear in the eventuality of a conflict in Korea. At present, regional forces include two U.S. naval fleets—the Third Fleet in the eastern Pacific headquartered in San Diego, and the Seventh Fleet based in Japan for duty in the western Pacific. These two fleets contain aircraft carrier battle groups that in a crisis could be used to underline U.S. determination to defend South Korea or for combat missions should deterrence fail. Of particular significance are the aircraft carriers, whose planes could be used to blunt a North Korean assault or to hit rear echelon targets in North Korea. Each carrier has an air wing of 75-80 aircraft capable of conducting 150-200 sorties daily.[2] Naval forces could also be used to bombard coastal targets, although Pyongyang has made an effort, based on painful memories of the Korean War, to move some of its industrial centers further inland.[3]

Besides naval forces, a number of air and ground force units based in the Pacific region could be deployed to a conflict in Korea. The III Marine Expeditionary Force, consisting of the Third Marine division and First Marine Aircraft Wing, are based in Japan, and the First Marine brigade is stationed in Hawaii. In addition to the Army units stationed in Korea proper, two brigades of the Twenty-Fifth light infantry division are located in Hawaii. Finally, the Air Force has units stationed in Japan, Guam, and Hawaii that could be utilized to fly missions over Korea. A U.S. response to hostilities in Korea would likely utilize some combination of these forces in the early stages of any conflict. If further support were deemed necessary, other U.S. ground and air units based in the continental United States could be employed to repel a North Korean attack. However, moving these forces might take several months.

Lastly, prior to December 1991, the United States had a variety of tactical nuclear forces deployed within South Korea and on naval forces in the Pacific theater. Despite their removal from the peninsula, nuclear weapons are still deliverable on North Korean targets by other U.S. forces in the Pacific.

Throughout the fifty years of U.S. extended deterrence, the combined U.S.-ROK force in Korea has been sufficient to pose a strong and determined defense of South Korea. Add to this the likelihood that contact with American forces in Korea would trigger the introduction of further U.S. military assets, U.S.-ROK forces have always had sufficient capability to deny the North a swift military success. Instead, Pyongyang would have faced either a war of attrition or a nuclear war that would lead to the destruction of the North.

A litany of the full range of U.S. military capabilities is not necessary to determine that the United States possessed sufficient strength to carry out any deterrent threat against the North Koreans, and that these forces raised significantly for North Korea the costs of an invasion. When North Korean forces went head to head with American troops in the Korean War, it almost resulted in the extinction of Kim Il Sung's regime. Only Chinese intervention rescued North Korea. The DPRK is well aware of the force the United States can bring to bear in Korea. Furthermore, over time, North Korea has lost the support of its patrons—China and the Soviet Union—should the DPRK initiate another war with the South. The possibility of facing the United States alone is thus an ominous proposition for North Korea.

Therefore, though North Korea succeeded in building a formidable military machine, there is little doubt that throughout the past fifty years, the United States possessed sufficient military capability to impose unacceptable costs on North Korea should the United States choose to do so. However, the central question of extended deterrence remains: How convincing has American *resolve* been to defend South Korea?

Resolve

As indicated earlier, the United States has demonstrated its determination to defend South Korea primarily in four different ways: declarations of resolve such as the mutual security treaty and statements by American leaders; U.S. military and economic aid supported by growing U.S.-ROK economic ties; the deployment of U.S. conventional forces; and until December 1991, the positioning of U.S. tactical nuclear weapons in Korea along with consistent inclusions of South Korea under the U.S. nuclear umbrella. In a number of respects, attention to the military balance (capability and cost) is relatively easy. However, developing the evident military capability to impose unacceptable costs does not ensure that the defender will remain with the protégé in a crisis. More difficult is demonstrating resolve whereby the defender shows it is willing to protect the protégé if a deterrence situation lurches towards a crisis of immediate deterrence where an attack is more likely.

(1) Declarations of Resolve

The most important formal declaration of the United States to defend South Korea is the Mutual Security Treaty, signed in October 1953. The Senate approved the treaty on 26 January 1954 by a vote of 81-6, and it would enter into effect whenever the two signatories exchanged ratifications. However, in response to a letter from Rhee, dated 11 March 1954, where he notified the United States that he might take unilateral action to reunify the peninsula, the enforcement of the treaty was delayed "pending further assurance of continued ROK cooperation."[4] Eventually, South Korea provided such assurance and the treaty took effect in November 1954.

U.S. officials believed that in 1950, North Korea was uncertain of U.S. intentions regarding South Korea. When John Foster Dulles, U.S. Secretary of State, submitted the treaty for Senate ratification, he noted its "primary value consists in giving the Communists notice, beyond any possibility of misinterpretation, that the United States would not be indifferent to any new communist aggression in Korea."[5] In a speech soon after the end of the Korean War, Dulles reiterated,

> the Korean war began in a way in which wars often begin—a potential aggressor miscalculated. From that we learn a lesson which we expect to apply in the interests of future peace. The lesson is this: If events are likely which will in fact lead us to fight, let us make clear our intention in advance; then we shall probably not have to fight.[6]

The implication was, of course, that the previous Administration had failed to do so. The U.S.-ROK treaty now made the American commitment explicit.

Prior to the security treaty, the United States gave another formal declaration of resolve by enjoining the other fifteen nations that fought in Korea to issue a "Greater Sanctions" declaration to the effect that any further unprovoked Communist aggression in Korea would not be tolerated. The declaration maintained, "the consequences of such a breach of the armistice would be so grave that, in all probability, it would not be possible to confine hostilities within the frontiers of Korea."[7] The warning here was that renewed Communist aggression would be met with a U.S./UN response that might be directed at targets in China and the Soviet Union and not limited to actions in Korea. President Eisenhower also indicated that he was ready to use nuclear weapons in these strikes on "the communists" if necessary. Eisenhower did not identify publicly the potential target states, but it was clear that these were the Soviet Union and China.[8]

The Greater Sanctions agreement was an important statement of "deterrence by punishment." Eisenhower threatened to "punish" renewed aggression not only by denying the adversaries' objectives, but also by inflicting nuclear strikes on their homeland. Most interesting here is the relationship of the Greater Sanctions declaration to the threat perceptions. Recall that U.S. leaders recognized that the Soviets and Chinese were the primary threat at this time, not the North Koreans. Consequently, U.S. warnings focused on the Soviets and Chinese by placing at risk something they valued—their homeland. Thus, the configuration of the threat helped to determine the response.

Despite South Korean hopes, the defense treaty did not provide the ironclad guarantee they sought. The key portion of the treaty, Article III, states:

> Each party recognizes that an armed attack in the Pacific area on either of the parties in territories now under their respective administrative control, or hereafter recognized by one of the parties as lawfully brought under the administrative control of the other, would be dangerous to its own peace and safety and declares that it would act to meet the common danger in accordance with its constitutional processes.[9]

President Rhee was concerned that this wording signaled a weak U.S. commitment, and he proposed a draft treaty that included a provision similar to one contained in the NATO treaty where "an armed attack against one shall be considered an attack against the other."[10] Two weeks later, in a letter to Secretary of State Dulles, Rhee implored: "in proposed mutual security pact, may we count upon inclusion of a provision for immediate and automatic military support in case ROK should be attacked by an external enemy? As you know, a pact that is sufficient for a nation not in our position would not be adequate to our needs."[11] It is also interesting to note that in a meeting between Rhee and a U.S. delegation headed by Secretary Dulles, the ROK President expressed greater fear of Japan than the Soviet Union. In an earlier letter to Dulles, Rhee stated, "I trust that [the security guarantee] may be extended to include contingency of an attack upon Korea by Japan."[12]

Despite Rhee's consternation, both Dulles and Eisenhower believed the proposed language of the treaty was not weak. The "constitutional processes" wording was designed to avoid certain constitutional questions that had arisen previously during hearings to approve the NATO treaty. This wording was not designed to hedge a U.S. response should external aggression occur in Korea. These two aspects of the U.S.-ROK treaty, the underlying U.S. commitment, and the "constitutional processes" wording are important elements of the treaty and warrant further exploration.

Weak Commitment?

President Rhee feared that the lack of an ironclad guarantee in the security treaty indicated a U.S. reluctance to respond should South Korea be attacked. However, the Eisenhower administration made a number of efforts to demonstrate that it was fully committed to defending the South. The reluctance shown by U.S. officials was due, in part, to a fear that President Rhee might initiate an attack on the North to reunify the peninsula.

A memorandum of a telephone conversation between Eisenhower and Dulles noted the following in response to Rhee's letter for an automatic security guarantee.

> The President said [concerning the security guarantee] . . . the answer was yes as long as we ourselves know it was a clear case of aggression (by the other side). The Secretary said, in connection with this point that in the case of all treaties, for instance the North Atlantic Treaty, our action must be taken through constitutional processes. The President said, of course, he understood that we had to say that. The Secretary said that actually the provision in the so-called "Greater Sanctions Agreement" does not contain that qualification ["constitutional processes"].[13]

In his reply to Rhee, Dulles noted,

> If in violation of the armistice the Republic of Korea is subjected to unprovoked attack you may of course count upon our immediate and automatic military reaction. Such an attack would not only be an attack upon the Republic of Korea but an attack upon the United Nations Command and U.S. forces within that Command.[14]

Finally, in the State of the Union Address on 7 January 1954, Eisenhower stated, "in the Far East, we retain our vital interest in Korea. We have negotiated with the Republic of Korea a mutual security pact, which develops our security system for the Pacific. . . . We are prepared to meet any renewal of armed aggression in Korea."[15]

While these documents demonstrate the American commitment to defend South Korea, the first two responses also imply American anxiety that Rhee would make good on his promises to renew the war if a political settlement did not unite the peninsula under his control. A commitment that would bind the United States to this type of action was unlikely to pass the Senate.[16] Numerous U.S. documents indicate concern that "result from feeling in some quarters that President Rhee desires to commit U.S. to a reckless suicide pact."[17] Language that did not guarantee an automatic response allowed the United States to discourage Rhee from initiating military action and distance itself from any use of force initiated by the ROK. President Rhee had argued that the Korean War should not end until Korea was reunited and threatened to begin hostilities should a postwar conference not achieve that result. Rhee's intransigence and provocative rhetoric so disturbed U.S. officials that they prepared a contingency plan to oust him, code named "Operation Everready."[18] Eisenhower and Dulles made it clear that the United States would extend a strong security guarantee so long as the ROK was not the instigator in a future conflict.

When ratifying the treaty, the Senate attached a rider to the document that stated, "neither party is obligated . . . to come to the aid of the other party except in case of an external armed attack against territory which has been recognized by the United States as lawfully brought under the administrative control of the Republic of Korea."[19] The Senate wished to make it clear that U.S. support would not be forthcoming if Seoul initiated the attack. Similar to the difficulties encountered by U.S. policy prior to the Korean War, American leaders had to fashion a security guarantee that deterred an attack on the South while also restraining President Rhee's ambitions.

"Constitutional Processes"

If the use of the wording "in accordance with its constitutional processes" was not intended as an escape clause for a weak American commitment, what was its purpose? Members of Congress were already concerned about requirements in the North Atlantic Treaty. In the hearings that preceded Senate approval of the NATO agreement, members of the Senate Foreign Relations Committee expressed fears that the treaty would usurp congressional authority to declare war. The Senate had grounds for these fears; in 1950, President Truman did not consult Congress before committing U.S. troops to Korea. Thereafter, the Senate was much more sensitive to the implications of a security guarantee that did not refer to "constitutional processes."

With the phrasing "an attack on one was an attack on all," Senators believed it implied an attack on Western Europe would be treated as an attack on the continental United States. It was assumed that the President had the power to act promptly as Commander-in-Chief, even without congressional authorization, to repel a direct attack on the United States. Would the NATO treaty give the President similar authorization to act if war came in Europe? The final report recommending ratification of the NATO agreement by the Senate Foreign Relations Committee concluded, "nothing in the treaty . . . including the provisions that an attack against one shall be considered an attack against all, increases or decreases the constitutional powers of either the President or the Congress or changes the relationship between them."[20] Thus, the Committee concluded that the treaty did not bind the United States to an automatic response, but rather allowed flexible action based "upon a number of factors, including the location, nature, scale, and significance of the attack."[21]

To avoid any similar debate with the U.S.-ROK treaty, Secretary Dulles decided to omit the "attack on one" phrasing, using instead the "constitutional processes" wording. When questioned at the ratification hearings, Dulles explained that this wording was "adequate for our purpose" and would "avoid raising a fresh constitutional debate."[22] In fact, this wording had already been used since the NATO agreement in treaties signed with the Philippines (30 August 1951) and Australia/New Zealand (1 September 1951). Consequently, the "constitutional processes" wording was not a signal of weak American resolve, but rather addressed Senate concerns for the constitutional issue of shared war powers between the President and Congress. Since Rhee's pronouncements to initiate hostilities with North Korea already portended difficulties for ensuring ratification, there was no need to raise constitutional questions and complicate the process further.

From the vantage of the challengers—the Soviet Union, China, and North Korea—any doubts regarding the wording of the treaty and the nature of the U.S. commitment were offset by the existence of a security treaty, the "Greater Sanctions" declaration of the sixteen UN command nations to defend South Korea, and the obvious lengths that the United States had just displayed from 1950 to 1953 to defend the area. Kaufmann argued that an important indicator of resolve to a challenger was the defender's "record of performance in comparable contingencies during the recent past."[23] The prompt U.S./UN response demonstrated a formidable commitment of American resolve that would have been difficult for the Soviet Union, China, and North Korea to ignore.

As the years passed, U.S. leaders continued to give strong declaratory support to the South Korean regime. After the ROK had sent two infantry divisions to support U.S. efforts in Vietnam in the mid-1960s, Vice President Hubert Humphrey in an address in Korea declared the U.S. Government had "a firm commitment to the defense of Korea. As long as there is an American soldier on the line of the border, the demarcation line, the whole and the entire power of the United States of America is committed to the security and defense of Korea. . . . We are allies, we are friends, you should have no questions, no doubts."[24] U.S. declarations of support were particularly important in the late 1960s when it was getting bogged down in Vietnam. As noted in chapter 2, it is likely that Kim Il Sung believed he could "test" the U.S. commitment with a compellent strategy of his own—numerous commando raids, the 1968 *Pueblo* seizure—while U.S. attention was on Vietnam. By raising the potential cost to the United States of its defense guarantee, Pyongyang hoped to compel the United States to withdraw its support from the South. However, a vigorous U.S. response by the Johnson administration, including sending over 370 additional combat aircraft to Korea, mounting losses of highly trained DPRK commandos, and growing anti-communism in the South exacerbated by the DPRK raids, convinced Kim Il Sung that his efforts at subversion were becoming too costly.

Under President Nixon and the Nixon doctrine, the declaratory support for South Korea was less effusive than during the Johnson years. By that time South Korea was expected to shoulder a greater share of the defense burden, particularly the will and manpower to defend itself. Yet, despite these modifications, Nixon remained committed to the defense of South Korea and pledged to maintain the Mutual Security Treaty. In Nixon's first enunciation of the Nixon Doctrine in Guam on 25 July 1969, he reaffirmed that the United States would maintain all of its treaty commitments in Asia. The following month, South Korean President Park visited Washington and the joint statement of Presidents Park and Nixon agreed that U.S. and ROK forces "must remain strong and alert and the two Presidents reaffirmed the determination of their Governments to meet armed attack against the Republic of Korea in accordance with the Mutual Defense Treaty."[25]

Later in his administration, Nixon announced the withdrawal of one of two U.S. infantry divisions stationed in Korea. Nixon was forced to walk a fine line that given the Vietnam experience, U.S. policy "serves the domestic imperative of restraint in our international role, without sacrificing our interests in Asia or defaulting on our obligations."[26] Moreover, Nixon did not believe his policy abandoned Korea. Citing South Korean economic growth rates that averaged more than 10 percent annually, Nixon noted in 1971 that the United States and the ROK decided together "that the Republic of Korea was now better able to meet its own defense needs, provided measures were taken to modernize the equipment of its existing forces."[27] Thus, U.S. extended deterrence policy and its overt support for South Korea was modified somewhat during the Nixon years. Yet, the presence of American forces in Korea, the continued adherence to the Mutual Defense Treaty, as well as other statements of U.S. interest in Asia, made it very questionable that North Korea might assume that the United States would not uphold its security commitment to South Korea. However, ROK leaders were still fearful this was a precursor to more U.S. withdrawals from the region.

When Vietnam fell in 1975, the Ford administration worried that U.S. allies would question the credibility of its commitments. In a press interview, Secretary of Defense James Schlesinger declared that despite events in Vietnam, "U.S. commitments to Northeast Asia, to Korea as well as to Japan, will be perceived as something no one should challenge."[28] To bolster U.S.-ROK relations, President Ford sent Secretary Schlesinger to Seoul to reassure them of the U.S. commitment. In South Korea, Schlesinger stated, "I have come here to exemplify both the high regard of the American people for their Korean ally and the continuing commitment to a common cause. Our purpose is to avoid conflict by any possibility of miscalculation on the part of others."[29]

Schlesinger informed the ROK that there would be no further troop reductions and that Washington would provide South Korea with more F-4 and F-5 aircraft. He also assured South Korea that every attempt would be made to prod the Congress into providing aid that had been pledged under the Nixon administration but held up over concerns for human rights in South Korea.[30] In 1974, President Ford traveled to South Korea himself to reassure the ROK government of the U.S. commitment "to render prompt and effective assurance to repel armed attack" and pledge no further troop withdrawals.[31] Upon arriving in Seoul, Ford also proclaimed that "I am here . . . to reaffirm our friendship and to give it new life and meaning. Nothing binds nations together closer than to have fought side by side for the same cause. Two times we have stood together, here as well as in Vietnam, to preserve the peace, to preserve the stability of Asia and the world. We can never forget this."[32]

In 1977, President Jimmy Carter entered the White House determined to remove U.S. forces from Korea. If he had fully implemented his plan, the structure of U.S. extended deterrence policy would have been greatly modified. ROK troops would have assumed greater responsibility for ground defense while the United States furnished air and logistics support. Despite these changes, U.S. declaratory support changed much less than most assumed. President Carter made it clear that the U.S. commitment to the ROK had not changed, only the method of implementing that commitment. In a news conference in May 1977 Carter noted that despite the withdrawals, the United States was "leaving intact an adequate degree of strength in the Republic of Korea to withstand any fore-seeable attack and making it clear to the North Koreans, the Chinese, the Soviets, that our commitment to South Korea is undeviating and is staunch."[33] The following year, Defense Secretary Harold Brown reaffirmed that "neither North Korea nor any other country should have any doubt or misunderstanding of the continuing strength of this security commitment."[34] Remaining air, naval, and logistic units, cooperative training exercises such as Team Spirit, and a new military aid program would continue to demonstrate that the "withdrawal decision signals no weakening of our commitment. The North Korean Government should be in no doubt about our position."[35]

As noted in chapter 2, by the end of Carter's term, estimates of North Korean military strength were revised upward and further troop withdrawals postponed. U.S. officials were also concerned about potential ROK instability in the wake of the 1979 assassination of President Park. To deter the North from exploiting this situation, U.S. declaratory support became even stronger. Sensing a potential shift towards an immediate deterrence situation, the United States moved to reinforce its deterrence policy. On 26 October 1979, the day of Park's assassination, the State Department announced, "The United States Government wishes to make clear that it will react strongly in accordance with its treaty obligations to the Republic of Korea to any external attempt to exploit the situation in the Republic Korea."[36]

Despite Carter's policy reversal to remove U.S. ground forces from South Korea, the perception remained that the American commitment was wavering. Ronald Reagan took office determined to check what he believed to be declining U.S. military power in the face of a persistent Soviet threat. Concerning Korea, President Reagan moved quickly to bolster American support for the South welcoming the new President of South Korea, Chun Doo Hwan, as the first head of state to visit the Reagan White House. President Chun's military coup the previous year short-circuited what many in South Korea and the United States had hoped would be a transition to democracy. Many South Koreans criticized Reagan's warm welcome, but the visit was a powerful signal to the North of America's continued commitment to the ROK. The joint communiqué issued after President Chun's visit declared that both Presidents would work to "uphold the mutual obligations embodied in the United States-Korea Mutual Defense Treaty of 1954" and "seek to strengthen U.S.-Korean cooperation in deterring and defending against aggression as an indispensable contribution to peace and stability in Northeast Asia."[37]

In November 1983, President Reagan visited South Korea where he pledged "steadfast support" for the ROK, calling Northeast Asia a "region of critical stra-

tegic significance" for the United States.[38] Though there was pressure from defense critics in Congress to reduce U.S. troop levels in Korea, Washington removed no American soldiers. The Reagan administration also modernized U.S.
forces in Korea by sending new artillery, antitank weapons, A-10 and F-16 aircraft.[39] In 1987, the United States deployed Lance surface-to-surface missiles
that could carry nuclear or conventional warheads.[40] All of these efforts were
intended by Reagan administration officials to shore up the U.S. commitment to
defend South Korea after, in their view, President Carter had been weakened it.

Strong declaratory support for South Korea continued during the first Bush
administration. When visiting Seoul in February 1989, President Bush stated in a
speech to the Korean National Assembly that "as President, I am committed to
maintaining American forces in Korea, and I'm committed to support our Mutual
Defense Treaty."[41] The following year, Secretary of State James Baker noted
"our security commitment to the Republic of Korea remains essential to peace
and stability on the Korean Peninsula."[42]

In April 1990, as the Cold War waned, the Bush administration announced a
plan to reduce U.S. troop levels in Korea and transition the United States to
more of a support role.[43] The following year, Bush also removed all U.S. tactical
nuclear weapons from the peninsula. However, then Secretary of Defense Richard Cheney made it clear that "these plans do not indicate any change in the
close and longstanding security relationship between the two countries, and the
United States remains fully committed to the defense of the Republic of Korea."[44] Soon after, attention shifted to the North's potential nuclear weapons program and the withdrawal plan was suspended.[45]

The Clinton administration faced difficult choices regarding U.S. policy in
Korea, particularly in regard to the North's zig-zag pattern of compliance with
inspection requirements of its nuclear facilities. In part, President Clinton pursued a compellent strategy, deploying a battery of Patriot missiles to the ROK,
and threatening economic sanctions and increased U.S. troop levels in the South.
These measures were also coupled with incentives: economic aid, and diplomatic
and trade relations. Throughout the nuclear crisis that dominated the early Clinton administration, the United States maintained strong declaratory support for
South Korea. In his 1993 visit to South Korea, President Clinton reaffirmed "a
dedicated partnership between our two peoples" and "our resolute commitment
to Korea's security."[46] In March 1994, President Clinton sent a letter to South
Korean President Kim Young Sam reassuring him that the United States would
consider a North Korean attack on the South as an attack on the United States.[47]
A few days later, another administration official stated: "We're trying to strike a
balance here where we make it very clear that we'll do anything that's necessary
for the defense of the South Koreans and our own forces and so on, but we still
prefer to solve this diplomatically."[48]

The second Bush administration continued the requisite declaratory support,
despite some disagreement with the ROK over the benefits of continuing a dialogue with the North. After President Bush met with South Korean President
Kim Dae Jung early in his administration, their joint statement

reaffirmed the fundamental importance and strength of the U.S.-ROK security alliance, which has prevented war and promoted stability, prosperity, and democracy on the Korean Peninsula for over five decades. . . . [and] pledged to deepen further the comprehensive partnership shared by the United States and the Republic of Korea through enhanced security, political, economic and cultural cooperation.[49]

Thus, as other administrations have done, the Bush administration maintained the declaratory support necessary to articulate the U.S. security guarantee to South Korea.

(2) U.S. Economic and Military Aid

Bruce Russett argued that economic and military ties are virtually essential for successful deterrence though their presence does not guarantee it.[50] This is particularly so in a situation of general deterrence where aid may be an integral part of military preparations and an important additional display of resolve. In the minutes from an NSC meeting in July 1953 that discussed economic aid to Korea, Eisenhower lamented, "all the world would be watching Korea after the armistice so we should set a purposeful objective for ourselves, quit dallying, and go forward rapidly."[51]

For years the United States poured massive amounts of military and economic aid into South Korea to rebuild the nation, and in the process, developed the kind of ties Russett believed were important to the credibility of deterrence. American leaders also used specific aid packages to demonstrate U.S. resolve and improve ROK capabilities preceding an action that might be misinterpreted as a lessening of the American commitment to South Korea.[52] The table opposite indicates that over the period from 1955 to 1967, the United States provided more than $5.8 billion in economic and military aid to the ROK.

Specifically, the United States provided over $3.2 billion in economic aid to the Republic of Korea during this period along with more than $2.5 billion in military aid. The military aid helped to complete major arms transfers from the United States including combat aircraft (F-5 and F-86), howitzers, and advanced missiles.[53] This aid represented 27 percent of all aid given to East Asia and the Pacific for that period.[54]

When Nixon announced the withdrawal of the 7th Division in 1971, he accompanied it with a military modernization program of $1.25 billion that included F-4 aircraft, M-48 tanks, APCs, artillery, and Honest John surface-to-surface missiles. Total military assistance to South Korea from 1971 to 1975 amounted to approximately $1.5 billion in Military Assistance Program (MAP) funds, $14.9 million in training assistance and $172.2 million in Foreign Military Sales (FMS) credits. By this time, the South Korean economy was making major strides so that aid was coming increasingly in the form of loans, as opposed to outright grants of military assistance.

Table 5.1

U.S. ECONOMIC AID AND MILITARY ASSISTANCE TO KOREA, 1955-1967
(in constant and million U.S. dollars)

	Economic Aid			Military Aid		
	Total	*Grants*	*Loans*	*Total*	*Grants*	*Loans*
1955	315	315	--	33	33	--
1956	387	387	--	226	226	--
1957	349	349	--	262	262	--
1958	292	284	8	331	331	--
1959	274	262	12	189	189	--
1960	216	215	1	184	184	--
1961	247	240	7	200	200	--
1962	190	165	25	137	137	--
1963	181	155	26	183	183	--
1964	218	190	28	124	124	--
1965	182	134	48	173	173	--
1966	262	181	81	210	210	--
1967	178	114	64	272	272	--
TOTALS	3,292	2,992	300	2,524	2,524	--

Source: U.S. AID, *Overseas Loans and Grants and Assistance from International Organizations* (Washington, D.C.: Government Printing Service, 1969). Taken from Yong Soon Yim, "U.S. Strategic Doctrine, Arms Transfer Policy, and South Korea"[55]

President Carter also offered a large aid package to offset his proposed withdrawal of U.S. troops containing $275 million in FMS credits for 1979 and each subsequent year over the course of the withdrawal. As American forces departed, their equipment, valued at $800 million, would have been left behind at no cost to South Korea. Also, an additional $2.5 million would have been provided for training the ROK armed forces with the new weapons systems. However, these assistance proposals ran into a good deal of opposition in Congress over the ROK's human rights record and the "Koreagate" scandal.[56]

In addition to U.S. assistance programs, the ROK also made numerous direct arms purchases during the Carter administration including TOW (tube-launched, optically tracked, wire-guided), Sidewinder and Sparrow missiles, F-4, F-5, and F-16 aircraft, C-130 transport planes, APCs, and advanced radar systems. The arms transfers during the Carter administration exceeded those of any other administration for a comparable period in both quantity and quality.[57]

The Reagan administration further strengthened the ROK military with sales of sophisticated equipment through continuing FMS credits. However, increasingly, the ROK acquired arms through direct purchases and less from U.S. assistance. From 1980 to 1988, South Korea purchased $4.31 billion in military equipment, which represented two-thirds of all ROK military purchases from the United States since 1950.[58]

From 1970 to 1986, the United States provided a total of $2.4 billion in direct credit or loan guarantees for the purchase of military equipment. The FMS credit program was terminated in 1986 and the only meaningful security assistance program that remains between the United States and South Korea is the International Military Education and Training program that provides education in political ideology and military doctrine for the military personnel of U.S. allies.[59]

The proposed troop withdrawal under the second Bush administration does not have an accompanying aid package for the ROK military as with previous administrations. However, the United States does intend to spend $11 million to improve and update U.S. forces in Korea. While different from previous administrations, it acts, nonetheless, as an indicator of the U.S. commitment.

The use of military and economic assistance has been primarily to build up the defense capabilities of South Korea, but it is also an important signaling device for U.S. extended deterrence policy. American military and economic assistance has helped to construct a powerful ally in the Pacific region while also developing the economic, political, and military ties Russett believed essential to successful extended deterrence.[60] Indeed, this sort of "investment" in an ally increases the stakes of the commitment. Once a large amount of aid is poured into a protégé, it becomes more difficult to abdicate from the commitment. Moreover, effective use of the defender's aid by the protégé can increase its "value" to the defender, vindicate the defender's decision to maintain the commitment in the first place, and enhance the deterrence relationship. As well, a strong protégé can help to shift the relationship from extended deterrence that depends on the defender, to primary deterrence where the protégé provides a large share of its own defense, avoiding the credibility problems of extended deterrence.

American presidents have also used declarations of increased aid packages to redress fluctuations in the military balance and to signal continued U.S. commitment to South Korea. Particularly during the Nixon and Carter years, military and economic assistance was designed to build up ROK capabilities, but also to discourage the conclusion that the U.S. commitment to South Korea was in decline. Military aid, along with a continued presence in the region, signaled that the United States remained committed to the defense of the South Korea.

(3) Deployment of U.S. Conventional Forces

A pledge to extend a security guarantee can be easily broken. Even with a formal alliance in place, a defender may hedge its response depending on the situation. As Thomas Schelling noted about promises to defend an ally, "saying so, unfortunately, does not make it true; and if it is true, saying so does not always make it believed. We evidently do not want war and would only fight if we had to. The problem is to demonstrate that we would have to."[61] According to Schelling, the resolve of "demonstrating we had to" needs to be fashioned with "The Art of Commitment."[62]

The best demonstration of resolve, in a situation of general or immediate deterrence, is one that guarantees a response from the defender. One of the ways the United States has attempted to fashion this automatic response is through the stationing of its forces in Korea along the likely invasion routes from the North.

At the end of the Korean War, the United States had eight combat divisions present in South Korea. By May 1955, U.S. troop strength was reduced to two divisions, despite a resolution opposing the move by the ROK National Assembly. President Rhee, in particular, was upset with the withdrawal because it removed the offensive potential of U.S. units to reunify the peninsula. The two remaining American infantry divisions were deployed along the invasion corridors leading from the DMZ to Seoul. The U.S. Second Infantry Division, the most forward deployed unit, defended an 18-mile long sector of the west-central portion of the DMZ. The Seventh Division defended an area south of the Second Division as a reserve force, but still along the main invasion routes leading to Seoul. Other elements of U.S. ground forces consisted of the 38th Artillery Brigade that included air defense units, the 4th Army Missile Command, the 2nd Engineering Group, and other support units.[63] Air Force and Navy units further complimented American ground forces. The average U.S. military presence in Korea from 1954 to 1971 was approximately 63,000.

In 1971, the size and location of American forces changed with President Nixon's reevaluation of U.S. deployments in Asia. The United States reduced its forces in Korea by approximately 20,000 soldiers with the removal of the 7th Division. Nixon planned to withdraw all but one brigade of the remaining 2nd Division by FY 1974, however this was never implemented.[64]

The United States also pulled the Second Division off its forward positions on the DMZ to be replaced by ROK units.[65] Located between the two major invasion routes to Seoul, the Second Division could move to either approach to blunt a North Korean assault.[66] Until recently, one company of the 2nd Division remained in the DMZ at the Joint Security Area surrounding Panmunjom where the Military Armistice Commission meets to monitor the armistice.

U.S. force levels changed again under President Carter though the change was much less than he had originally intended. Carter's first proposal called for the removal of all U.S. ground force units. Later, he scaled this back to the withdrawal of 6,000 soldiers, one brigade of the 2nd Division by 1978 with more to follow by 1980.[67] In the end, Carter succeeded in removing only 800 combat soldiers along with 2,600 support personnel mainly from the air defense battalions of the 38th Artillery Brigade and the 4th Missile Command. These units were deactivated and the equipment, outdated in the case of the 4th Missile Command, was turned over to South Korean forces.[68]

Reagan increased U.S. troop strength to 43,000, more than deployments during the Carter years. In addition, the Reagan administration modernized U.S. forces in Korea sending new artillery pieces, antitank weapons, and aircraft. In

1987, the United States deployed Lance surface-to-surface missiles capable of carrying nuclear or conventional warheads.

With the end of the Cold War approaching, plans for adjustments in troop levels in Korea were released in an April 1990 Defense Department report titled *A Strategic Framework for the Asian Pacific Rim: Looking Toward the 21st Century*. According to this document, the United States will "begin to draw down ground presence and modify command structures so as to transition from a leading to a supporting role for U.S. forces."[69] American troops would be withdrawn gradually in a three-phase process that would reduce troops to some lower, but yet to be determined, final number. Phase I envisioned the removal of 5,000 troops from the Army's 2nd Infantry Division, 1,987 support personnel primarily from air force units, and the closing of 3 of the 5 American air bases in South Korea at Kwangju, Taegu, and Suwon. The air bases at Osan and Kunsan would remain operational. The pace of these and any subsequent withdrawals as well as the final troop level was contingent on North Korean reaction to the cuts. However, in the fall of 1991, Secretary of Defense Dick Cheney announced a moratorium on further withdrawals due to concern for the North's suspected nuclear weapons program, and Pyongyang's refusal to allow International Atomic Energy Agency (IAEA) inspections.[70] Later, President Clinton reaffirmed the moratorium for the foreseeable future, and U.S. troop levels remained at approximately 37,500 for the next decade.

In the early days of the second Bush administration, the Pentagon began a review regarding how to better position U.S. forces abroad. The "Global Defense Posture Review" examined, among other things, where the United States positions its forces around the world and how it can better work with its allies in addressing regional security concerns.[71] For South Korea, the review generated a proposal to remove 12,500 American soldiers, one-third of the current force, by December 2005. This total includes a reduction of 3,600 transferred for duty in Iraq in August 2004. The United States also announced its intention to relocate its forces from positions between Seoul and the DMZ that sit astride the expected invasion routes to locations south of the capitol. This would take U.S. forces out of range of the thousands of North Korean artillery pieces and multiple rocket launchers forward deployed along the DMZ. The proposal addressed other forces in the region including a redeployment of 14,000 Marines from Okinawa to Hokkaido, upgrading U.S. air and naval facilities in Guam to support the Proliferation Security Initiative for interdiction of weapons shipments, and exploring joint training centers in Singapore and Australia. The plan also calls for pulling two divisions from Germany.[72]

Conservatives in South Korea have criticized the move as a response to growing anti-Americanism both within ROK society and elements within the Roh Moo Hyun government. Many fear this is only the beginning of a weakened U.S.-ROK alliance. However, others in South Korea welcome the move as recognition of South Korean sovereignty and a belief that U.S. troops are no long necessary to deter the North. In any case, the ROK government succeeded in convincing U.S. authorities to delay completion of the redeployments until 2008.

Despite the criticism, U.S. officials have argued the changes will not weaken deterrence and endanger ROK security. They maintain the troop realignment is not a retreat but rather an effort to use U.S. forces more effectively and utilize new technologies and strategies to defend South Korea. According to Secretary of Defense Donald Rumsfeld, "it is not numbers of things. It is the capability to impose lethal power, where needed, when needed, with the greatest flexibility and with the greatest agility."[73] Moreover, rather than have U.S. troops close to the DMZ to invite a first strike should the North attack, positions farther back allow these forces to absorb a first strike and counterattack more effectively any place on the peninsula.[74]

Regarding the troop withdrawals, these measures are also a recognition of growing ROK strength. According to Admiral Thomas Fargo, Commander of U.S. Forces in the Pacific,

> our friends and partners have vastly improved [their military capabilities] over the last 15 years. . . . Certainly no place is this more true than in South Korea, where you have a very professional army that numbers some 20 divisions of active forces and they fly a very modern capable aircraft. They've got a very solid and improving maritime capability. Their capability is vastly improved to take over a larger share of their own defense.[75]

To compensate for the withdrawals, the United States will spend $11 billion over five years on force upgrades including the deployment of new weapons systems such as Patriot missile batteries.[76] As a short-term measure, in June 2004, the U.S. sent ten F-117 Stealth fighters to South Korea to train for several months in an effort to bolster deterrence in the wake of the proposed troops reductions. The United States will also increase its air and naval presence in Asia allowing for greater flexibility in responding to regional crises.

To bolster arguments that these moves would not weaken deterrence, U.S. officials pointed to Pyongyang's reaction. DPRK officials noted that despite the planned reductions, the United States

> is massively shipping latest weapons and war means into south Korea under the "arms buildup plan" that calls for spending 11 billion dollars. . . . This clearly proves that the "arms reduction measure" does not mean any switchover in the U.S. Korea policy but is aimed at retaining a "qualitative edge" to stifle the DPRK by force. . . . If the U.S. truly hopes for peace and détente on the Korean peninsula, it should completely withdraw its troops from south Korea, far from deceiving the world public opinion with talk about so-called "arms reduction."[77]

Deputy Undersecretary of Defense for Asian and Pacific Affairs Richard Lawless noted, "they [North Korea] were the first to complain about the plan to relocate our forces and realign our forces south of the Han River. They suggested that we would be adding to our combat power by doing that. I think we have the advantage here of a regime that pays very close attention to how we are postured and where we are postured."[78] For North Korea, and some in the South, the moving of U.S. forces south raised fears that the United States could now strike the North while lessening the vulnerability of its troops to DPRK retaliation.

Finally, the Bush administration has also taken other measures to bolster deterrence with conventional force deployments in the region. In 2003, while the U.S. was involved in Iraq and the nuclear crisis dragged on, Washington feared the North might be tempted to exploit the situation. As a result, Secretary of Defense Rumsfeld ordered additional Air Force units to South Korea and Guam. In February, Rumsfeld sent a dozen each of B-52s and B-1s to Andersen Air Force Base in Guam and 24 F-15s and 6 F-117s to South Korea. Rumsfeld maintained that North Korea should not interpret the move as "aggressive or threatening or hostile . . . as the situation with respect to Iraq becomes somewhat tense, it seems to me that it's appropriate for the United States to look around the globe and say, 'Where might someone think of taking advantage of that situation with respect to Iraq?'"[79] All of these planes were capable of delivering precision-guided munitions on North Korean targets. By June 2003, almost all of these aircraft had returned to their U.S. bases.[80] The United States also ordered increased surveillance flights in international airspace in the region.[81]

Tripwire and Deterrence

American forces in Korea have fulfilled several roles: a tripwire to initiate a larger U.S. involvement in a conflict (deterrence by punishment); a contributor to the active defense of South Korea should deterrence fail (deterrence by denial); and though not a requirement of deterrence, the presence of U.S. forces also helps to reassure the ROK of the U.S. commitment. A 1977 Defense Department report notes that the "presence of U.S. conventional forces thus plays an important role as the source of psychological and political reassurance necessary to avert intimidation."[82] These roles have been important to U.S. extended deterrence policy, though the contribution of U.S. forces to the defense of South Korea has been quite small compared to ROK forces.

The presence of U.S. forces in Korea since 1953 have always played the role of a tripwire that would trigger a larger U.S. commitment of force. Whether as 63,000 troops with positions along the DMZ or 37,000 soldiers pulled off the line but not far behind, engaging these American troops held out a strong possibility that U.S. involvement would follow.

However, U.S. forces are more than a tripwire to trigger a U.S. response. In a North Korean assault, American troops would be engaged early in the battle and incur casualties. The deaths of U.S. personnel would raise the stakes for the United States and guarantee that Washington would not abandon Korea since this would mean abandoning Americans.

The logic at work here is similar to that of "existential deterrence"[83]; so long as U.S. troops are present, Pyongyang could never be certain that a massive U.S. response would not follow a North Korean invasion. Though arguing in the context of U.S.-Soviet strategic nuclear weapons, McGeorge Bundy's discussion of this concept is appropriate here. As almost occurred in 1950, U.S. intervention in

Korea came close to ending the North Korean regime, the political equivalent of nuclear destruction. If the DPRK attacked again, it might not be able to avoid annihilation as it had in 1950. Thus, U.S. deterrence policy "rests on uncertainty about what could happen"[84] and this uncertainty is not affected by marginal force changes. The presence of even a force of 5,000 to 10,000 that occupy the approaches to Seoul might be a sufficient tripwire for what "could be" and this uncertainty would evoke the necessary caution to deter a North Korean attack. So long as the United States possesses the essential military capability to eliminate the North Korean regime, and there exists the possibility that the United States might act, as it did in 1950, North Korea cannot assume the United States would not act.

The growth of ROK military capabilities has also enhanced "deterrence by punishment" on the peninsula. If the North initiated hostilities and lost, Seoul might not be content to simply repel the invasion by stopping at the 38th parallel. Instead, this might be an opportunity too good to pass up, giving the South the chance to reunify and destroy the North Korean regime. This is a serious threat of punishment for the North, and one that would likely enter into North Korean calculations.

During congressional hearings in 1977 and shortly after his "reassignment" for publicly criticizing President Carter's troop withdrawal plan, Major General John K. Singlaub raised another important aspect of the tripwire function played by U.S. forces in Korea. Singlaub argued that the Chinese and Russians wished to avoid a direct engagement with American soldiers, a danger if Kim Il Sung initiated hostilities. U.S. deployments in Korea furnish a crucial motivation for the Soviets and Chinese to restrain their protégé. Accordingly to Singlaub, without the presence of U.S. troops, "Kim could launch his attack without fear of running into U.S. ground forces. And if he got in trouble, . . . there would be far less reluctance on the part of Communist China or the Soviet Union to help him 'pull his chestnuts out of the fire.'"[85] Thus, the concept of a "confluence of interests" also works from the Soviet and Chinese side. As the United States wished to maintain peace to avoid drawing in the regional powers, so also did they—in this case, North Korea's defenders—have a similar wish.

An interesting dynamic is present here. While the United States worked to deter North Korea directly, U.S. policy makers also attempted to deter the North "indirectly" through its two defenders. After the improvements in U.S.-Soviet and Sino-U.S. relations in the 1970s, neither Moscow nor Beijing wanted to endanger their improved relations with the United States or disrupt the stability of East Asia, despite their continued support of the DPRK. In his memoirs, President Carter noted that

> both we and South Korean President Park wanted the Chinese to help prevent any military moves by North Korea and to help reduce existing tensions in that peninsula. One of the more interesting potential benefits of having China as a friend would be its ability to quietly sway some third-world countries with whom it was very difficult for us to communicate.[86]

Carter raised this issue in meetings with the Chinese in 1979. He recalled Chinese leader Deng Xiaoping's comment: "there was absolutely no danger of a North Korean attack." However, Deng cautioned that China could not push too hard, as the Soviets had done, to influence North Korean policy. "If China tried to pressure North Korea, it too would lose its influence."[87] The presence of U.S. troops in Korea meant that if the North attacked, Soviet and/or Chinese troops risked being engaged with U.S. forces, a scenario they wished to avoid. Consequently, U.S. leaders hoped to strengthen deterrence by influencing two of the challengers to restrain the third.

Equally crucial in signaling American resolve is the actual location of U.S. forces in South Korea. Until 1971, U.S. forces held frontline positions along the DMZ, making early contact a likely possibility in the event of invasion. In 1971, ROK forces assumed all frontline positions along the DMZ, an important recognition of South Korea's increased military capabilities and ROK sovereignty, and an effort to reduce the risk of automatic U.S. involvement in a conflict. Did this withdrawal from the frontline signal a reduced commitment and hurt the credibility of U.S. deterrence policy?

It is unlikely that this change had much affect on American credibility. The bulk of U.S. forces have always been stationed between the DMZ and Seoul along the major invasion routes to the capital. Given that North Korea could ill afford a lengthy war, a rapid conquest of Seoul would have to come through the routes protected by U.S. forces, making it virtually impossible to avoid incurring American casualties. A congressional report written in 1978 noted that

> the stationing of U.S. ground combat troops in the DMZ and in the nexus of the major invasion corridors means that a North Korean attack would almost certainly involve U.S. forces. . . . Any President faced with such an attack on U.S. forces would have little choice but to commit additional U.S. forces to that part of the world.[88]

So long as even a much smaller force of U.S. troops remained on the invasion routes with the possibility that a U.S. response would follow, the United States maintained a credible tripwire and demonstration of the U.S. commitment to defend South Korea that was difficult for North Korea to underestimate.

The current plan to reduce and relocate U.S. troops may have a political and economic impact signaling that the alliance needs attention and raising concerns that may spook foreign investors. Others have also criticized the moves on the grounds that no parallel concessions were sought from the North. However, concerning the military situation on the peninsula, these changes will have little effect for two reasons.

First, the remaining 25,000 U.S. soldiers are a significant presence and indication of the U.S. defense commitment to South Korea. Given the many other signs of U.S. involvement, the troop withdrawal will not have a major impact on U.S. credibility, especially in the minds of North Korean leaders. As with earlier troop withdrawals, so long as a sizeable contingent remained, a North Korean invasion would still incur U.S. casualties, making a U.S. response likely. The reduction does lessen America's ability to respond immediately with troops on the ground. However, given the well-trained and well-equipped ROK military and other U.S. forces in East Asia available for rapid deployment, the relocation may have little impact on Pyongyang's calculations. The overall balance of forces still points to a devastating defeat.

Second, the shift of troops south of Seoul will also have only a minimal effect on deterrence. The relocation does alter the tripwire function U.S. troops stationed close the DMZ have played for years. However, the tripwire is still there; it simply has a bit more "slack" in it. In case of a North Korean attack, these forces would be brought forward, incur casualties, and have the same tripwire effect as before. Moreover, it is not clear that the tripwire need be constructed as it was in earlier years. Given the other elements of the U.S. commitment, a North Korean invasion would still "trip the wire" making it unlikely Washington would back away from its commitment. Furthermore, with ROK troops manning the front lines, the deterrence situation becomes even more one of primary deterrence. There is no credibility problem here; the ROK would respond and given its military capabilities and U.S. support, the North would be in deep trouble.

Perhaps in an earlier time of the alliance, moving troops south of Seoul would have been a far more dangerous move. However, circumstances today are different. North Korea is struggling and its ability to conduct a successful military operation to unify the peninsula wanes. Pyongyang has few allies and none that would support a strike south. Finally, the U.S.-ROK alliance, while undergoing some growing pains and readjustments, would come together should the North attack. For the North, the likelihood of defeat and the end of its regime should it attack changes little by shifting U.S. troops south of Seoul.

U.S. Forces and the Defense of South Korea

While acting as a tripwire and symbol of U.S. determination to deter a North Korean attack, U.S. forces also help to contribute to the active defense of South Korea should deterrence fail. In a 1994 interview, 2nd Infantry Division commander Major General John Abrams "bristled" at the idea that his forces are only a tripwire. "Ours is one of the most powerful divisions in the Army. Our assets are tremendous and unique. We have heavy firepower, the ability to work this restricted terrain and the ability to conduct maneuver warfare in both offense and defense. We are tailored to the threat and the terrain."[89] The United States presence is small compared to ROK forces, but ground troops, air and naval units, tactical nuclear weapons in place prior to the Cold War, and other forces available in the Pacific have augmented the American contribution to South Korea's defense. U.S. forces in the Pacific region also demonstrate their military preparations to deploy to Korea in a crisis through the joint exercises such as Team Sprit, conducted from 1976 to 1993, and the current joint exercises of Foal Eagle and Ulchi Focus Lens.

U.S.-ROK plans to defend South Korea if attacked are contained in Operations Plan (OPLAN) 5027, the basic war plan of the joint force. Since the 1950s, OPLAN 5027 was largely defensive, focusing on containing a North Korean assault and restoring the current border. Beginning in the 1970s, defense planners made some important adjustments.[90] Fearing that North Korea might misinterpret the U.S. retreat from Vietnam as reluctance to defend the South, U.S. Commander James F. Hollingsworth shifted OPLAN 5027 to a more offensive-minded strategy that required more forward positioning of U.S. forces. Prior to this change, U.S.-ROK planning called for a "fighting retreat" that would trade land for time, holding positions south of the Han River until U.S. reinforcements arrived for the expected counterattack to reverse any North Korean gains. Hollingsworth moved U.S. forces forward and indicated that after blunting the North Korean invasion, the U.S. would move north, seize the North Korean city of Kaesong, bomb North Korean targets, and the eventually capture of Pyongyang.[91] The repositioning of U.S. troops also prompted North Korea to move its forces forward, a circumstance that is often cited as a threatening offensive posture on North Korea's part.

In 1994, in the wake of the nuclear crisis, the OPLAN was revised to include a counteroffensive to eliminate Kim Jong Il and the North Korean regime. In a 1993 interview, South Korean President Kim Young Sam confirmed, "once a major military confrontation occurs, North Korea will definitely be annihilated."[92] In 1999, another planning document stated, "all forces will continue combat operations to unseat current North Korean leadership to reinforce the message that US/South Korea Military forces are prepared to continue decisive combat operations until victory is achieved."[93] If North Korea decided to initiate a war in Korea, defeat would now mean the end of the Kim Jong Il regime. Further revisions in 1998 included preemptive strikes on North Korea should intelligence provide solid evidence of an impending attack. OPLAN 5029, acknowledged in 1999 by General John Tilelli, commander-in-chief of U.S. Forces Korea, outlines preparations following the collapse of the DPRK, particularly, plans to deal with the influx of North Korean refugees.[94] Earlier, Clinton administration officials drew up another plan, OPLAN 5026 that was designed specifically for precision air strikes to take out critical North Korean targets, presumably, the North's nuclear facilities at Yongbyon.[95]

The North Korean reaction to the 1998 OPLAN revisions was outrage, arguing the new plans were the precursor of an invasion of the North. Pyongyang viewed the plan as a sign of an impending U.S. attack raising the tension level with Washington. It is interesting to note that these events coincide with the beginning of North Korea's efforts to develop a parallel nuclear program based on highly-enriched uranium. Pyongyang may have viewed the OPLAN, along with difficulties in implementing the Agreed Framework, as another indicator of U.S. reluctance to improve relations with the DPRK. As a result, U.S. efforts to enhance deterrence through the OPLAN revisions may have aggravated the efforts to maintain a nuclear-free North Korea.

In 2003, Secretary of Defense Rumsfeld ordered U.S. military commanders to develop a new plan, OPLAN 5030. The draft gave regional commanders authority to conduct operations before war began to disrupt and reduce North Korea's ability to conduct a military operation. Specific measures included sending surveillance flights closer to North Korean airspace in an effort to force DPRK aircraft to respond and waste fuel, and conducting extensive, surprise military exercises to put North Korea on an elevated war-footing further consuming valuable resources such as pre-positioned food, water, and other supplies. Critics of the plan, including some within the Bush administration, fear that these measures are overly provocative and may start a war based on decisions made by regional commanders.[96] A final decision to approve the plan has not yet been made public.

The Command Structure

The U.S. deterrence posture is enhanced even further by dominance of the command structure and U.S. integration with ROK forces. Involvement in the preparation to defend the ROK reinforces the U.S. pledge that an attack on South Korea would initiate a vigorous American response. For the United States to be so involved at command levels, yet not fulfill its defense obligations to South Korea is difficult to imagine.

The command structure that links U.S. and ROK forces in Korea has taken two forms. In June 1950, the United Nations Security Council created the first structure when it formed the United Nations Command (UNC) to coordinate the war effort of the participating UN members. The Council further specified that the commander of the UNC be an American officer. In July 1950, the requirements of conducting the war compelled South Korean President Syngman Rhee to give operational control of ROK forces to the American commander of the UNC. During peacetime, ROK forces remained under South Korean control, but during war, the U.S. commander (Commander-in-Chief—CINC), who actually wore three hats—CINCUNC, CINCUSFK (U.S. Forces Korea), and commander of U.S. 8th Army—directed ROK and U.S. forces.

This arrangement lasted until 1978 when the United States and South Korea altered the structure to give Seoul greater participation in command decisions, though many South Koreans remain unhappy that the United States retained a dominant position in this new structure. For the fourteen sections in Combined Forces Command (CFC) headquarters, the structure mandates the positions of "Chief" and "Deputy." The United States retained the head position of "Chief" for the following sections: Commander-in-Chief, Chief of Staff, Planning, Operations, Logistics, Judge Advocate, Public Affairs, and Secretary Combined Staff. For each of these positions, a South Korean officer holds the second ranking position of "Deputy." In turn, ROK officers hold the "Chief" position for: Personnel, Intelligence, Communications, Engineer, Operational Analysis Group, and Headquarters Commandant with American officers holding the "Deputy" position in these areas.[97] The head of CFC, currently General Leon J. LaPorte, is a four-star general and serves as the Commander of the UNC and

U.S. Forces Korea. The table below provides a list of previous CINCs of the U.S.-ROK Combined Forces Command.

Table 5.2

CINC, U.S.-ROK COMBINED FORCES COMMAND

CINC	Dates of Service
General John W.Vessey	November 1978-July 1979
General John A. Wickham Jr.	July 1979-June 1982
General Robert W. Sennewald	June 1982-June 1984
General William J. Livsey	June 1984-June 1987
General Louis C. Menetrey Jr.	June 1987-June 1990
General Robert W. RisCassi	June 1990-June 1993
General Gary E. Luck	June 1993-July 1996
General John H. Tilelli Jr.	July 1996-December 1999
General Thomas A. Schwartz	December 1999-May 2002
General Leon J. LaPorte	May 2002-present

Source: *U.S. Forces Korea*, "Combined Forces Command," <www.korea.army.mil/cfc.htm>.

Despite appearances of partnership in the command structure, South Koreans are cognizant of continued U.S. control of the key positions such as Commander-in-Chief. Plans call for further relinquishing of U.S. command authority to ROK officers, placing the United States in more of a supporting role. As the nuclear crisis unfolded, the first Bush administration cancelled the second part of a planned troop withdrawal and pressured South Korea to assume a greater share of the defense burden. South Korea did so and on 1 December 1994, the United States returned peacetime operational control, absent since the Korean War, to the Chair of ROK Joint Chiefs of Staff, but the Combined Forces Command structure remains.[98]

For deterrence, the American dominance of the command structure helps to reinforce the credibility of the U.S. commitment to defend South Korea and demonstrates the preparations necessary in a situation of general deterrence. Because Americans are so deeply imbedded in CFC headquarters, it makes it much more difficult for the United States to "walk away" from a commitment to South Korea in the face of a crisis. Solitary U.S. Air Force units, or ground forces that were not integrated into defense operations, could be withdrawn or pulled back at any sign of impending conflict. Under current arrangements, it would be difficult for the United States to extricate itself without a severe loss of prestige. It would be an even worse disgrace for U.S. forces, after dominating operations and planning for the entire time of the alliance to pull out just prior to or during a conflict.

Despite the role that U.S. command of ROK-American forces has played in enhancing extended deterrence, the issue of turning over greater operational control to ROK officers remains an important one. Many South Koreans, both military officials and civilians, find the current arrangement an affront to their sovereignty. While they have been willing to tolerate the CFC structure, there is growing pressure for change that the United States will be hard-pressed to resist. While the command structure makes an important contribution to the credibility of extended deterrence, domestic political sensitivities will require that it be changed. Besides, the credibility of the U.S. commitment is secure enough at this point for this change to occur without undermining deterrence.

(4) U.S. Nuclear Weapons

The final element to U.S. extended deterrence policy in Korea was the deployment of U.S. tactical nuclear weapons with American forces on the peninsula. The withdrawal of these weapons, completed in December 1991, was undertaken to coax North Korea into international inspections of its nuclear weapons facilities, and was part of a larger effort by the first Bush administration to encourage the Soviets to reign in their tactical nuclear weapons.[99] However, for much of the period of the U.S.-ROK alliance, nuclear weapons based in Korea were an important part of the U.S. defense commitment. U.S. nuclear weapons also played a role by including South Korea under the U.S. nuclear umbrella, an effort that not only deterred North Korea but also provided reassurance to the South in an effort to restrain its nuclear ambitions. The deployment of nuclear weapons was likely unnecessary for deterring the North and overly provocative in the long run.

The U.S. Decision to Send Nuclear Weapons

Discussions to send tactical nuclear weapons to Korea appear to have begun sometime in late 1955 or early 1956. The issue arose as part of a larger concern regarding armistice violations by the Communist side. The Korean War armistice contained a subparagraph (13-d) prohibiting the introduction of military equipment that was not present at the end of the war. Any weapons that became obsolete could be replaced "on the basis of piece-for-piece of the same effectiveness and the same type."[100] While U.S.\UN forces were "faithfully and conscientiously" observing this portion of the armistice, "the Soviets constantly violated this provision by avoiding ports of entry where they could be supervised."[101] American officials believed that the military balance in Korea was slowly being skewed by weapons shipments from Moscow and Beijing.[102]

To address these inequities, Washington had to modernize its forces. American officials debated whether 13-d of the armistice should be scrapped altogether or if modernization should occur simply by using a more liberal interpretation of this subparagraph.[103] The Defense Department further complicated matters when it indicated modernization would include the deployment of nuclear-capable weapons systems such as Honest John missiles and 280 mm artillery.[104]

After vigorous deliberations that lasted over a year, the Eisenhower administration decided to suspend subparagraph 13-d. UNC officials announced to the North Koreans on 21 June 1957 that "the United Nations Command considers that it is entitled to be relieved of corresponding obligations under the provisions of this paragraph until such time as the relative military balance has been restored and your side, by its actions, has demonstrated its willingness to comply."[105]

The decision to include nuclear weapons in these modernization efforts was deferred to a later date. The State Department was particularly reluctant to include nuclear weapons in the modernization program. Referring to 280 mm cannons, Secretary Dulles believed these would be "very conspicuous weapons," "resented throughout Asia," and not worth the political costs.[106] Moreover, the communists could exploit in their propaganda, not only the suspension of 13-d, but also the deployment of these weapons. Dulles agreed that modernization needed to occur but it did not have to include nuclear weapons.[107] It was also hoped that the presence of these weapons would allow a reduction of ROK troop strength from twenty divisions to sixteen in an effort to reduce U.S. expenses. Dulles believed it was a mistake to send the nuclear weapons before Rhee had actually implemented the reduction.[108] The arguments to address the military balance were also countered by 1956 intelligence estimates indicating South Korean troop strength stood at 650,000 with the North's at 350,000 accompanied by an assessment that "the ROK army is superior in both offensive and defensive capabilities to the North Korean army alone."[109]

The Defense Department and Joint Chiefs of Staff were equally vehement in their counterarguments. They viewed modernization as a package deal to include "dual-capable" weapons as a critical component and part of a reorganization of Army units into "Pentomic" divisions, where Honest John Missiles (two launchers per division) were a major component of divisional firepower.[110] If denied the "nuclear upgrade," the two divisions in Korea would be the only two in the U.S. Army excluded from this reorganization.[111] As the Korean War had demonstrated, military planners thought it likely that any attack from the North would be a sudden, massive assault. Defense planners believed that U.S.-ROK conventional defenses could eventually stop a communist invasion, but not before 60,000 U.S. troops were overrun. Thus, according to the Pentagon, "Our Number One reason" for introducing nuclear weapons was to prevent U.S. forces from being overwhelmed in the initial stages of an invasion.[112]

Similarly, they reasoned that the proximity of Seoul to the border necessitated the use of tactical nuclear weapons to halt an attack before it reached the city. In particular, the 280 mm cannon would be crucial in covering the approaches to Seoul. The cannon provided a "pinpoint means of delivering atomic munitions under all conditions of weather, and it is also an excellent conventional artillery piece."[113] The Pentagon maintained that nuclear weapons would help to reassure the ROK of the U.S. commitment that, in turn, would persuade Rhee to reduce the level of ROK forces and generate cost savings for the United States.[114] Finally, the JCS argued that separating nuclear weapons from other

modernization measures only served to highlight their introduction. If modernization remained a "package deal," the introduction of nuclear weapons would be
less conspicuous.[115]

The decision to include nuclear weapons as part of the modernization program came with the adoption of policy document NSC 5702\2. The modernization program would continue, but deployment of dual capable weapons such as
the Honest John and 280 mm cannon "will be as and when determined by the
President after conference with the Secretaries of State and Defense."[116] President Eisenhower was very concerned about the cost of subsidizing ROK ground
forces. In a September 1956 NSC meeting, Eisenhower noted "we were surely
spending an awful lot of money in Korea" and that "Rhee was insisting on too
large forces."[117] President Eisenhower later determined that nuclear weapons
were needed by U.S. forces in Korea and was conditioned on ROK troop reductions. However, Rhee did not cooperate with the planned reductions but nuclear
weapons were deployed regardless. It is possible that Eisenhower, realizing
ROK reductions would not be forthcoming, decided to deploy the nuclear weapons anyway. On Christmas Eve, 1957, the Defense Department authorized the
Army to deploy the Honest John missile and 280-mm cannon, the first U.S. nuclear weapons in Korea,[118] which arrived in January 1958.[119]

The deployment of tactical nuclear weapons to Korea was part of a larger
effort by the Eisenhower administration called the "New Look." After the Korean War, Eisenhower was determined to balance the federal budget. Yet, the
United States also faced a mounting Soviet conventional threat that required a
large and costly U.S. military to contain. To counter the Soviet threat with a "fis-
cally responsible" alternative, Eisenhower relied on tactical and strategic nuclear
weapons. U.S. deterrence policy became "massive retaliation" where the United
States would respond to a challenge through its "great capacity to retaliate instantly and by means and at places of our own choosing."[120]

Soon after "massive retaliation" was enunciated, critics began to argue that
it was simply not credible to threaten full-scale nuclear war, especially for lesser
conflicts. By 1956, the Soviets possessed their own nuclear arsenal, making it
likely that a U.S. nuclear response would bring Soviet retaliation. Consequently,
the "New New Look" relied on "massive retaliation" only to deter an attack on
the U.S. homeland.[121] To deter attacks on other areas, the United States would
rely even more on tactical nuclear weapons. Consequently, the Army proceeded
to establish Pentomic Divisions in Europe and Korea.

Critics maintain that the Army had other motivations. Peter Hayes argues
that the introduction of nuclear weapons to Korea was not based on requirements
in Korea but rather "a move made to enhance the army's ability to attract congressional funds." He believes that an atomic mission in Korea helped the Army
compete with the Navy and Air Force for nuclear missions and funding.[122]

U.S. Nuclear Weapons and Extended General Deterrence

According to the Pentagon, the presence of tactical nuclear weapons accomplished a number of goals.

The U.S. theater nuclear forces have a symbolic importance that transcends their direct military value. They are the visible evidence of the broader U.S. commitment and of the linkage between our deployed posture and the strategic nuclear forces. . . . It continues to be U.S. policy that we will resist attacks on the United States and its allies by whatever necessary means, including nuclear weapons. . . . They [nuclear weapons] also dramatize to a potential attacker that any conventional attack could set off a chain of nuclear escalation, the consequences of which would be incalculable.[123]

Though U.S. policy had been to "neither confirm nor deny" the presence of nuclear weapons in South Korea, it was accepted knowledge that U.S. tactical nuclear weapons were in Korea. In June 1975, Defense Secretary Schlesinger confirmed that presence when he stated publicly: "We have deployed in Korea tactical nuclear weapons, as is, I believe, well known."[124]

U.S. nuclear weapons in Korea included nuclear tipped missiles (Honest John, Sergeant, and Nike-Hercules), atomic demolition mines (ADMs), nuclear artillery shells, and gravity bombs.[125] Nuclear artillery was the main component of American nuclear forces in Korea, intended to offset a numerically superior enemy. A 1981 Pentagon report stated that "because [nuclear shells] are controllable and usable, their presence provides a real threat to enemy forces, reducing their effectiveness in massing to conduct a conventional battle."[126]

The exact number of nuclear weapons deployed to South Korea is not public information, but just prior to 1977, one source estimated that over 600 nuclear weapons were present.[127] By 1979, the number had dwindled as President Carter prepared to withdraw all ground troops, presumably removing nuclear weapons as well. By the late 1980s, the number of nuclear weapons appeared to have been approximately 250.[128]

Until the mid-1970s, U.S. nuclear forces in Korea were deployed in positions close to the DMZ, so that in wartime, the weapons could be brought up rapidly to more forward positions. Artillery shells for nuclear capable 155-mm and 203-mm howitzers and ADMs were to be brought forward using trucks and helicopters. Nike-Hercules missiles were also forward deployed with the capability to hit targets in North Korea. These missiles were so far forward that a U.S. security official visiting a missile site by helicopter was aghast, noting "they [Nikes] were on hilltops within artillery range of the North Koreans. We were all just appalled. They were like tiny little outposts within spitting distance of the North Koreans, like little castles on hilltops."[129] After realizing the danger of close-proximity deployment, Pentagon officials ordered the missiles dismantled, incredulous that no one had previously raised any concern.[130]

Regarding ADMs, the United States maintained twenty-one of these devices, to be detonated with a timer or remote control, for use between Seoul and the DMZ to halt or disrupt a North Korean assault. A press report noted that the Army's intent with ADMs was to block avenues of approach by cratering defiles [narrow valleys] or creating rubble; sever routes of communication by destroying tunnels, bridges, roads, and canal locks; create areas of tree blowdown and forest fires; crater areas including frozen bodies of water subject to landings by hostile airmobile units, [and] create water barriers by the destruction of dams and reservoirs.[131]

In the 1970s, it was recognized that ADMs could not be used in close proximity to Seoul because the damage and fallout would be too severe. In addition, the adoption of a forward defense strategy by U.S. and ROK forces that would not trade territory for time made ADMs most useful only on or near the DMZ. Consequently, ADMs were designated for use close to the border, but were stored, most likely, at Kunsan Air Force base, 140 to 150 miles south of the DMZ. Once they were moved forward, the location of ADMs at the border meant that in the event of an attack, these weapons either had to be used early in the conflict, or be overrun by advancing North Korean forces. In 1987, the U.S. commander in Korea, General Louis Menetrey noted that it was "pretty dumb" to deploy them on the DMZ; most ADMs were dismantled and removed from South Korea in the late 1980s.[132]

Should deterrence fail, the Army wanted to use nuclear weapons as part of a war-fighting strategy that called for early use to blunt a North Korean assault. However, to use nuclear weapons early in a conflict meant that these weapons must be forward deployed. Yet that made them a likely target for a preemptive strike and risked the possibility of being overrun by North Korean forces. The United States would have to "use or lose" these weapons, creating an unintended need for escalation to a nuclear conflict. Moreover, the use of nuclear weapons in a Korean conflict would cause severe damage and fallout, endangering U.S. and ROK military personnel and the South Korean people. According to a senior U.S. military commander,

> In Korea, nuclear weapons are not surgical instruments regardless of how small they are. Where do you suckers think you are going to shoot those things? The Koreans are not dumb. They have to say: you look at the terrain, unless you preempt, which we're reluctant to do, and you target troops, they're all going to be in South Korea. You are blowing up what you are trying to save.[133]

Thus, dependence on nuclear weapons had its liabilities. The fallout from nuclear use would endanger Seoul and the Korean people as well as possibly drift over the Soviet Union, China, or Japan, contaminating battle areas for U.S. and ROK forces, and heightening tension between the United States and others in the region. It is not clear how the Soviet Union and China would have responded to Washington's use of nuclear weapons in Korea, raising the specter of further escalation.

The United States enhanced deterrence not only by the deployments of nuclear weapons but also by indications of its willingness to use them. In response to the killing of two U.S. soldiers in the Joint Security Area in 1976, B-52 bombers, which the North Koreans knew were capable of carrying nuclear weapons, flew from Guam up the Korean peninsula, turning away from North Korea at the last second. U.S. intelligence sources noted that the North Koreans were very fearful these aircraft were on a nuclear mission. Pentagon officials announced after the crisis that these flights would continue at a rate of once or twice a month.[134] In 1983, the U.S. employed the Airland battle doctrine in Team Spirit exercises for the first time.[135] Team Spirit simulated an invasion of the North to help defend the South and the use of nuclear weapons for strikes deep behind enemy lines to destroy follow-on echelons, disrupt support and logistic units, and alter terrain.[136]

In reference to Team Spirit 1982, North Korea noted, "nobody can guarantee that this unprecedentedly large-scale war exercise staged with many nuclear weapons will not escalate into a full-scale nuclear war against our republic."[137] A few years later, North Korean statements expressed similar worries, announcing that its forces were going to be placed on full alert during Team Spirit "in face of the grave situation under which the danger of a new war, a nuclear war, has been created in our country owing to the reckless military provocations of the U.S. imperialist and the South Korean puppet clique."[138] There seems to be little doubt, understandably so, that the North was very concerned about U.S. nuclear weapons.

North Korea's isolation further compounded the deterrence impact of U.S. nuclear weapons. Over the years, North Korea became less and less certain of the support it might receive from the Soviet Union and China in the face of U.S. nuclear threats. Soviet acquiescence in the Cuban missile crisis, the Sino-Soviet dispute, Soviet-U.S. detente, and Sino-U.S. rapprochement respectively, indicated to North Korean leaders that its allies were unreliable. While U.S. resolve to risk nuclear war on its homeland for the protection of Europe has often been questioned, the same had likely occurred to the North Koreans concerning any nuclear deterrence they were receiving from their defenders. Would Moscow or Beijing really threaten the United States with nuclear war to defend their protégé? It seems unlikely that North Korea felt confident of any nuclear extended deterrence guarantees it received from its allies. Since Chinese or Soviet retaliation on the U.S. homeland was unlikely, the United States could issue nuclear warnings to deter North Korean actions. Combined with U.S. demonstrations of intent to use nuclear weapons, the DPRK's lack of confidence in its allies made it likely that U.S. nuclear threats were taken seriously.

By the late 1980s, as the Cold War waned, the consensus surrounding the presence of U.S. nuclear weapons in Korea began to erode. In 1987, the U.S. commander in Korea, General Louis Menetrey stated, "I do not envision any circumstance which . . . would require the use of nuclear weapons."[139] Later, in 1988, Lt. General John Cushman, former commander of I Corps that guarded the vital western approaches to Seoul stated, "nuclear weapons are no longer necessary for the defense of Korea." In fact, he argued that the presence of nuclear weapons made the North more reckless and that "actual use would be an appalling catastrophe even to the victor."[140] Similar assessments followed arguing that

the dangers of nuclear use and growing opposition within South Korea did not
make them worth the trouble. One scholar argued that:

> the use of nuclear weapons against attack from the North is unnecessary and at
> the same time poses a great danger to the Korean nation. War-fighting capabili-
> ties on the Korean peninsula could be adequately maintained with ROK armed
> forces supported by the U.S. Air Force stationed in Korea. If nuclear deterrence
> failed, and tactical weapons were to be used on Korean soil, the fallout effect of
> nuclear weapons would be devastating both to the Korean people and its
> neighbors.[141]

In October 1991, President Bush announced that a process had begun to remove all U.S. nuclear weapons from the Korean peninsula. Bush hoped that this
would coax North Korea into giving up its nuclear ambitions and comply with
the now delayed IAEA safeguards agreement. In a news conference, the President noted, "I think it's evidence of our good faith. I am convinced that the next
move should be up to North Korea to meet the international standards to comply
with the IAEA and other rules. But the main thing is they've got to dispel the
mistrust that exists regarding North Korea and the way to do that is to be open,
openness in terms of inspections."[142] National Security Advisor Brent Scowcroft,
indicated concern about withdrawing these weapons only from Korea; "We did
not wish to make such a move solely in Korea, concerned that the North might
take our actions as the beginning of a US withdrawal."[143] As a result, the removal of tactical nuclear weapons from South Korea became part of a larger
effort to reign in tactical nuclear weapons during the breakup of the Soviet Union. By pulling in U.S. weapons, President Bush hoped that Gorbachev would
follow suit, making it more difficult for "stray" weapons to be picked up by
would-be proliferaters. By December 1991, South Korean President Roh Tae
Woo could announce that no nuclear weapons were present in South Korea.[144]

Though nuclear weapons are no longer located in Korea proper, the United
States maintains a significant number of battlefield nuclear weapons in the Pacific region and in the United States. These weapons could be used in Korea
whether stationed there or not. In any case, the United States has consistently
declared that South Korea remains under the U.S. nuclear umbrella. As part of
the 1994 Agreed Framework the United States was to provide "formal assurances to the DPRK against the threat or use of nuclear weapons by the U.S."[145]
However, the pledge was never formally given and in 2002, Secretary of Defense Rumsfeld reaffirmed "the provision of a nuclear umbrella for the ROK."[146]

The significance of these nuclear threats does not appear to be lost on the
North Korean government. When the North Korean parliament ratified an
agreement to allow international inspections of its suspected nuclear weapons
facilities, the parliament attached a condition to the agreement. Inspections
would be allowed only if North Korea were under no threat of nuclear attack
from some other country.[147] An implicit reference to U.S. nuclear forces in the
Pacific and the American nuclear umbrella, some viewed this condition as a stall
tactic by the DPRK to avoid inspections. However, it may also be an expression

of legitimate DPRK security concerns, and in fact, both analyses are probably correct.

Conclusion

The U.S. extended deterrence commitment to South Korea has existed for more than fifty years, a relatively long period of time for the maintenance of a bilateral alliance. Throughout this period, the United States implemented a number of approaches to construct the preparations necessary for deterrence under conditions consistent with the concept of general deterrence. Critics have argued that U.S. policy has "vacillated" and had a "quality of ambivalence" that has fluctuated "between the extremes of intervention and withdrawal, leaving in its wake a sense of ambiguity regarding the fundamental U.S. commitment to the defense of Korea."[148] But, the analysis presented here shows that the U.S. commitment, while changing in form, has been consistent in intent, given the length of time and events the commitment has had to weather. Most importantly, it has made an important contribution to maintaining peace and stability in the region. Any commitment of over fifty years will have periods when the defender questions the worth of the protégé or is distracted by other matters.

Throughout the U.S.-ROK alliance, even during the proposed Carter withdrawal, no one ever proposed that the Mutual Defense Treaty be terminated. Though different presidential administrations and Congresses have been exasperated at times with the ROK's authoritarian government and human rights record, Washington has always supported the treaty.

Some critics argued that the treaty lacked the guarantees of the NATO agreement. However, the evidence presented here indicates the Eisenhower administration, who negotiated the treaty, and succeeding administrations did not believe the treaty was constructed with loopholes, were concerned the treaty be compatible with U.S. constitutional provisions, and were reluctant to give Rhee an automatic guarantee that might tempt him to restart hostilities. Moreover, Senate ratification was not a foregone conclusion; Senators were already concerned that the automatic guarantee in the NATO treaty usurped their constitutional powers to declare war. Even if the treaty provided a less than automatic response as some analysts have maintained, North Korea certainly could not assume the United States would not disregard another invasion. The treaty may not have provided the degree of reassurance that South Korea desired, but it was sufficient to deter North Korea.

Whenever the United States proposed or implemented adjustments in the defense relationship, Washington buttressed the commitment with promises of additional military and economic aid. These programs supplied important financial support for the ROK to build up its own capabilities while providing important evidence of continued U.S. protection. At times, the effect of these programs was diminished somewhat by the reluctance of Congress to grant all of the funding. However, when combined with the other measures of U.S. extended deterrence, the aid packages were important signals of support, and helped South Korea develop its own military capability.

The deployment of U.S. troops to South Korea has been the most significant indicator of the American defense commitment. For many years, North Korea insisted on the removal of U.S. forces from South Korea. U.S. troops, located between Seoul and the DMZ on the major invasion routes into the South, made it virtually impossible for the North to invade without colliding with American forces, possibly triggering a larger response. Over the years, the United States has reduced the number of troops deployed to the Korean peninsula, but this did not diminish the deterrent effect of the remaining U.S. forces and the ROK's own defense capabilities. Even during the Carter administration's troop withdrawal efforts, it was clear the U.S. was not abandoning South Korea. It is unlikely that Carter would have pushed the plan if he believed it would have caused deterrence to fail and provoke a war on the peninsula. The planned withdrawal would have occurred gradually, left the defense treaty and U.S. air and logistics support in place, and continued joint U.S.-ROK exercises to demonstrate America's ability to redeploy in an emergency. The current plans of the Bush administration to remove one-third of U.S. forces will also have only a minimal effect on deterrence.

Tactical nuclear weapons represent a final element of U.S. deterrence policy. Although it is difficult to determine for certain the degree to which North Korea feared U.S. nuclear weapons, evidence indicates that it may have been a significant worry. Throughout much of the U.S.-ROK alliance, the North faced nuclear weapons in the South without a comparable nuclear arsenal and with serious doubts about the willingness of its own defenders, the Soviet Union and China, to provide a nuclear umbrella. U.S.-ROK conventional forces provided a significant and credible deterrent; nuclear threats were probably unnecessary for deterrence and were "overkill" that further heightened DPRK concerns for its security.

Through the use of declarations of support, the Mutual Defense Treaty, large infusions of military and economic aid, the deployment of U.S. combat troops and the positioning of tactical nuclear weapons, the United States has displayed a clear and credible extended deterrence commitment to South Korea. While this commitment may not have contained all of the reassurances that South Korea wished, U.S. actions have always displayed to North Korea a resolve to defend the South that the DPRK could not ignore and that posed very high costs should it misjudge American resolve.

Notes

1. For recent assessments see David C. Kang, "International Relations Theory and the Second Korean War," *International Studies Quarterly* 47, no. 3 (September 2003): 301-324, and O'Hanlon, "Stopping a North Korean Invasion," 135-170.

2. United States Navy <www.c3f.navy.mil> (November 2004).

3. Koh, "The Korean War as a Learning Experience for North Korea," 377.

4. "Progress Report on NSC 170/1, 'U.S. Objectives and Courses of Action in Korea'," *FRUS, 1952-1954*, XV, part 2, 1767-1770.

5. *Mutual Defense Treaty Hearings* (1954), 5.

6. John Foster Dulles, "Korean Problems," *Department of State Bulletin*, 14 September 1953, 339.

7. Dulles, "Korean Problems," 58.

8. "Memorandum of Discussion at the 168th Meeting of the National Security Council," 29 October 1953, *FRUS, 1952-1954*, XV, part 2, 1570-1576.

9. *Mutual Defense Treaty Hearings* (1954), 51-52.

10. "Republic of Korea Draft of Mutual Defense Treaty Between the United States and the Republic of Korea," 9 July 1953, *FRUS, 1952-1954*, XV, part 2, 1359-1361.

11. Mutual Defense Treaty, *FRUS, 1952-1954*, XV, part 2, 1428.

12. Mutual Defense Treaty, *FRUS, 1952-1954*, XV, part 2, 1440 and 1472.

13. Mutual Defense Treaty, *FRUS, 1952-1954*, XV, part 2, 1429.

14. Mutual Defense Treaty, *FRUS, 1952-1954*, XV, part 2, 1430-1431.

15. Eisenhower, "Annual Message to the Congress on the State of the Union," *Public Papers, 1954*, 8.

16. "Memorandum of Conversation, by the Director of the Office of Northeast Asian Affairs," 5 August 1953, *FRUS, 1952-1954*, XV, part 2, 1466-1473.

17. *FRUS, 1952-1954*, XV, part 2, 1340.

18. See "Memorandum by the Director of the Executive Secretariat to the Secretary of State," 28 October 1953, *FRUS, 1952-1954*, XV, part 2, 1569-1570.

19. Attachment to the Mutual Defense Treaty by the U.S. Senate on 26 January 1954 as reprinted in *Security Agreements Hearings* (1970), 1717-1718.

20. U.S. Senate, *The Vandenberg Resolution and The North Atlantic Treaty*, Hearings before the Committee on Foreign Relations, 81st Congress, 2nd session, 11, 12, 19 May, 3 June 1948; 18 February, 8 March, 5, 12, 19, 21 April, 2, 6 June 1949, (Washington, D.C.: Government Printing Office), 373.

21. *The Vandenberg Resolution and The North Atlantic Treaty*, 373.

22. *Mutual Defense Treaty Hearings* (1954), 24.

23. Kaufmann, "The Requirements of Deterrence," 19.

24. "Vice President Humphrey in Korea," 23 February 1966, *Security Agreements Hearings* (1970), Appendix No. 10, 1725.

25. Richard P. Stebbins and Elaine P. Adams, eds., *Documents on American Foreign Relations, 1968-69* (New York: Council on Foreign Relations, 1972), 334-336.

26. Nixon, *U.S. Foreign Policy For the 1970's: Building for Peace*, 94.

27. Nixon, *U.S. Foreign Policy For the 1970's: Building for Peace*, 96.

28. "Now—A Tougher U.S.," *U.S. News and World Report*, 26 May 1975, 25.

29. *Korea Times*, 27-30 August 1975, as quoted in Claude A. Buss, *The United States and the Republic of Korea*, 145.

30. *Korea Times*, 27-30 August 1975, 145.

31. Gerald Ford, "Joint Communiqué Following Discussions With President Park of the Republic of Korea," 22 November 1974, *Public Papers, 1974*, 654.

32. Ford, "Remarks on Arrival at Seoul," 22 November 1974; Ibid., 650.

33. *AFP Current Documents, 1977-1980*, 1062.

34. Harold Brown, "Joint Communiqué of the ROK-U.S. Security Consultative Meeting," July 26, 1978, in Chong-Shik Chung, ed., *Korean Unification: Source Materials with an Introduction*, II, 318.

35. Jimmy Carter, "Transfer of Defense Articles to the Republic of Korea," *Public Papers, 1977*, II, 1823.

36. Philip Taubman, "Washington Warns North Koreans It Will 'React Strongly' to Intrusion," *New York Times*, 27 October 1979, A1, A6.

37. *Department of State Bulletin* 81, no. 2048 (March 1981), 14.

38. Clyde Haberman, "Reagan Gives Vow of Solid Support to South Koreans," *New York Times*, 14 November 1983, A1, A13.

39. "Prepared Statement by the CINC, UNC/CFC and USFK (Sennewald) Before the House Armed Services Committee," 8 March 1983, *AFP Current Documents, 1983*, 1058.

40. William T. Tow, "Reassessing Deterrence on the Korean Peninsula," *The Korean Journal of Defense Analysis* III, no. 1 (Summer 1991): 189.

41. "Address by President Bush Before the Republic of Korea National Assembly," 27 February 1989, *AFP Current Documents, 1989*, 552.

42. "Statement by Secretary of State Baker," 1 February 1990, *AFP Current Documents, 1990*, 715.

43. *A Strategic Framework for the Asian Pacific* (1990). As the title indicates, the report also examined other U.S. commitments in Asia.

44. "Joint Communiqué of the 22nd Annual ROK-U.S. Security Consultative Meeting," 15 November 1990, *AFP Current Documents, 1990*, 719.

45. "Citing North Korean Atom Threat, U.S. to Delay Troop Cuts in South," *New York Times*, 21 November 1991, A6.

46. William Clinton, "Remarks at a State Dinner in Seoul," 10 July 1993, *Weekly Compilation of Presidential Documents* 29, no. 28, 19 July 1993, 1314.

47. Michael R. Gordon, "U.S. Goes to U.N. to Increase The Pressure on North Korea," *New York Times*, 22 March 1994, A1, A6.

48. Michael R. Gordon, "U.S. to Bolster Forces If U.N. Votes Korea Curbs," *New York Times*, 25 March 1994, A13.

49. George W. Bush, "Joint Statement Between the United States of America and the Republic of Korea," *Public Papers*, Book I, 7 March 2001, 204.

50. Bruce Russett, "The calculus of deterrence," 103-109. In this study, Russett analyzed cases of immediate deterrence.

51. "Memorandum of Discussion at the 156th Meeting of the National Security Council," 23 July 1953, *FRUS, 1952-1954*, XV, part 2, 1426.

52. For a detailed discussion of U.S. military assistance, see Dong Joon Hwang, "An Evaluation of US Security Assistance to the ROK and Some ROK-US Defense Cooperation Issues," *The Korean Journal of Defense Analysis* II, no. 2 (Winter 1990): 195-217.

53. For a complete list of U.S. arms transfers to South Korea for the period 1950-1968, see Norman D. Levin and Richard L. Sneider, "Korea in Postwar U.S. Security Policy," in Gerald L. Curtis and Han Sung-joo, eds., *The U.S.-South Korean Alliance* (Lexington: D.C. Heath and Company, 1983), 40-41.

54. Levin and Sneider, "Korea in Postwar U.S. Security Policy," 39.

55. Yong Soon Yim, "U.S. Strategic Doctrine, Arms Transfer Policy, and South Korea," in Tae-Hwan Kwak et. al., eds., *U.S.-Korean Relations, 1882-1982*, 307.

56. Levin and Sneider, "Korea in Postwar U.S. Security Policy," 51-52.

57. Levin and Sneider, "Korea in Postwar U.S. Security Policy," 51-52.

58. Dong, "An Evaluation of US Security Assistance to the ROK and Some ROK-US Defense Cooperation Issues," 209.

59. Dong, "An Evaluation of US Security Assistance to the ROK and Some ROK-US Defense Cooperation Issues," 200-205.

60. Russett, "The calculus of deterrence," 97-109.

61. Schelling, *Arms and Influence*, 35.

62. Schelling, *Arms and Influence*, 35-91.

63. *Security Agreements Hearings* (1970), 1733-1741.

64. U.S. House of Representatives, "Statement of General Bernard W. Rogers, Chief of Staff of the U.S. Army," *Review Of The Policy Decision To Withdraw United States Ground Forces From Korea*, Hearings before the Investigations Subcommittee and Committee on Armed Services, 95th Congress, 1st and 2nd Sessions, 25 May, 13, 14 July, 1 August, 3 September 1977; 4, 5, 6, 9, 10, 11, 12, 13, 14 January 1978 (Washington, D.C.: Government Printing Office, 1978), 89. Hereafter referred to as *Review of Ground Force Withdrawal Hearings* (1978).

65. Department of State, *United States Foreign Policy, 1971: A Report of the Secretary of State* (Washington, D.C.: Government Printing Office, 1972), 67.

66. "Testimony of Major General John K. Singlaub," *Review of Ground Force Withdrawal Hearings* (1978), 30-31.

67. Oberdorfer, *The Two Koreas*, 90.

68. Hayes, *Pacific Powderkeg*, 85.

69. *A Strategic Framework for the Asian Pacific Rim: Looking Toward the 21st Century* (1990), 7.

70. "Citing North Korean Atom Threat, U.S. to Delay Troop Cuts in South," *New York Times*, 21 November 1991.

71. Douglas F. Feith, "Transforming the U.S. Global Defense Posture," 3 December 2003, <www.dod.gov/speeches/2003/sp20031203-0722.html> (June 2004).

72. James Brooke and Thom Shanker, "U.S. May Cut Third of Troops in South Korea," *New York Times*, 8 June 2004, A1, A10.

73. Brooke and Shanker, "U.S. May Cut Third of Troops in South Korea," A1, A10.

74. Thom Shanker and David E. Sanger, "U.S. Defends Plan to Reduce Forces in South Korea," *New York Times*, 9 June 2004, A12.

75. "US Says Troop PullOut From South Korea a Part of Global Changes," *Agence France-Presse*, 22 June 2004 as quoted in NAPSnet <www.nautilus.org> (July 2004).

76. Thom Shanker and David E. Sanger, "U.S. Defends Plan to Reduce Forces in South Korea," *New York Times*, 9 June 2004, A12.

77. "Foreign Ministry Spokesman on U.S. 'Arms Reduction,'" KCNA, 24 June 2004, <www.kcna.co.jp> (July 2004).

78. Thom Shanker and David E. Sanger, "U.S. Defends Plan to Reduce Forces in South Korea," *New York Times*, 9 June 2004, A12.

79. James Dao, "Criticism of Bush's Policy on Korea Sharpens," *New York Times*, 6 March 2003, A16.

80. "OPLAN 5026—Air Strikes," <www.globalsecurity.org/military/ops/oplan50-26.htm> (July 2003).

81. James Brooke and Thom Shanker, "U.S. May Cut Third of Troops in South Ko-

rea," *New York Times*, 8 June 2004, A1, A10.

82. U.S. Department of Defense, *Report of Secretary of Defense Donald B. Rums-feld to the Congress on the FY 1978 Budget, FY 1979 Authorization Request and FY 1978-1982 Defense Programs*, 17 January 1977 (Washington, D.C.: Government Printing Office, 1977), 38.

83. McGeorge Bundy, "The Bishops and the Bomb," *The New York Review of Books*, 16 June 1983, 62-66.

84. Bundy, "The Bishops and the Bomb," 62-66.

85. "Testimony of Major General John K. Singlaub," *Review Ground Force Withdrawal Hearings* (1978), 31-32.

86. Jimmy Carter, *Keeping the Faith: Memoirs of a President* (New York: Bantam Books, 1982), 195.

87. Carter, *Keeping the Faith*, 206.

88. U.S. Senate, *U.S. Troop Withdrawal From The Republic of Korea*, A Report to the Committee on Foreign Relations by Senators Hubert H. Humphrey and John Glenn, 95th Cong., 2nd Sess., 9 January 1978 (Washington, D.C.: Government Printing Office), 40.

89. Joseph L. Galloway and Bruce B. Auster, "The Most Dangerous Place on Earth," *U.S. News and World Report*, 20 June 1994, 16.

90. Oberdorfer, *The Two Koreas*, 312.

91. "OPLAN 5027 Major Theater War—West," <globalsecurity.org/military/ops/oplan5027.htm> (July 2003).

92. Ranan R. Lurie, "In a Confrontation, 'North Korea Will Definitely be Annihilated,'" *Los Angeles Times*, 24 March 1994, 11.

93. "CFC (KOREA) OPLAN 9518," 29 December 1999, <www.globalsecurity.org/military/library/policy/dod/oplan9518/CFCIIOPLN.DOC> (July 2004).

94. "OPLAN 5029—Collapse of North Korea," <www.globalsecurity.org/military/ops/oplan-5029.htm> (July 2004).

95. "OPLAN 5026—Air Strikes," <www.globalsecurity.org/military/ops/oplan-5026.htm> (July 2003).

96. Bruce B. Auster and Kevin Whitelaw, "Upping the ante for Kim Jong Il: Pentagon Plan 5030, a new blueprint for facing down North Korea," *U.S. News and World Report*, 21 July 2003, 21.

97. Taek-hyung Rhee, *U.S.-ROK Combined Operations: a Korean Perspective* (Washington, D.C.: National Defense University, 1986), 43-47.

98. Barilleaux and Kim, "Clinton, Korea, and Presidential Diplomacy," 34.

99. Andrew Rosenthal, "U.S. To Give Up Short-Range Nuclear Arms: Bush Seeks Soviet Cuts and Further Talks," *New York Times*, 28 September 1991, A1, A5.

100. *Department of State Bulletin* 29, no. 736 (3 August 1953): 132-139.

101. "Memorandum of Discussion at the 245th Meeting of the National Security Council," 21 April 1955, *FRUS, 1955-1957*, XXIII, part 2, 69.

102. "Memorandum on the Substance of Discussion at the Department of State-Joint Chiefs of Staff Meeting," 13 April 1956, *FRUS, 1955-1957*, XXIII, part 2, 243-244.

103. See "Memorandum for the Record of a Meeting," 11 September 1956, *FRUS, 1955-1957*, XXIII, part 2, 305-309.

104. For a list of the equipment to be included in the modernization efforts, see "Memorandum to the President's Special Assistant for National Security Affairs," 29

March 1957, *FRUS, 1955-1957*, XXIII, part 2, 415-416.

105. *Department of State Bulletin* 37, no. 941 (8 July 1957): 58-59.

106. "Memorandum of Discussion at the 326th Meeting of the National Security Council," 13 June 1957, *FRUS, 1955-1957*, XXIII, part 2, 445.

107. "Memorandum of Discussion at the 318th Meeting of the National Security Council," 4 April 1957, 420-427; "Memorandum of Discussion at the 326th Meeting of the National Security Council," 13 June 1957, *FRUS, 1955-1957*, XXIII, part 2, 443-454.

108. "Memorandum of Discussion at the 334th Meeting of the National Security Council," 8 August 1957, *FRUS, 1955-1957*, XXIII, part 2, 480-489.

109. Two intelligence estimates, title and date remain classified but listed in *FRUS, 1955-1957*, XXIII, part 2, February 1956, 215-217, and July 1956, 286-289.

110. The following arguments are contained in three documents in *FRUS, 1955-1957*, XXIII, part 2, "Memorandum of Discussion at the 326th Meeting of the National Security Council," 13 June 1957, 443-454; "Memorandum From the Secretary of the Army to the Secretary of Defense," 27 June 1957, 464-465; "Memorandum From the Joint Chiefs of Staff to the Secretary of Defense," 17 July 1957, 467-468.

111. "Memorandum From the Secretary of the Army to the Secretary of Defense," 27 June 1957, *FRUS, 1955-1957*, XXIII, part 2, 464-465.

112. "Memorandum of Discussion at the 326th Meeting of the National Security Council," 13 June 1957, *FRUS, 1955-1957*, XXIII, part 2, 443-454.

113. "Memorandum From the Secretary of the Army to the Secretary of Defense," 27 June 1957, *FRUS, 1955-1957*, XXIII, part 2, 464-465.

114. *FRUS, 1955-1957*, XXIII, part 2, 464-465.

115. "Memorandum From the Joint Chiefs of Staff to the Secretary of Defense," 17 July 1957, *FRUS, 1955-1957*, XXIII, part 2, 467-468.

116. "National Security Council Report: NSC 5702/2," 9 August 1957, *FRUS, 1955-1957*, XXIII, part 2, 489-498.

117. *FRUS, 1955-1957*, XXIII, part 2, 309-310.

118. "Memorandum From the Deputy Secretary of Defense to the Secretary of the Army," 24 December 1957, *FRUS, 1955-1957*, XXIII, part 2, 532-533.

119. *FRUS, 1955-1957*, XXIII, part 2, 533. Footnote #3 on p. 533 cites a telegram from CINCUNC to the Department of the Army that nuclear units were ordered to move to Korea in January 1958.

120. John Foster Dulles, "The Evolution of Foreign Policy," *Department of State Bulletin*, Vol. XXX, No. 761, 25 January 1954, 107-110.

121. Amos A. Jordan, William J. Taylor Jr., and Lawrence J. Korb, *American National Security*, 4th ed. (Baltimore: Johns Hopkins University Press, 1993), 70-74.

122. Hayes, *Pacific Powderkeg*, 34.

123. Harold Brown, *Department of Defense: Annual Report, Fiscal Year 1979* (Washington, D.C.: GPO, 1979), 68.

124. Murrey Marder, "Schlesinger Sees Buildup in Soviet Arms," *Washington Post*, 21 June 1975.

125. Bruce Cumings, "The Conflict on the Korean Peninsula," in Yoshikazu Sakamoto, ed., *Asia: Militarization and Regional Conflict* (London: Zed Books, 1988), 105; Clough, *Deterrence and Defense*, 6.

126. U.S. Department of Defense, "FY 1981 RDTE Congressional Descriptive

Summary, Nuclear Munitions," Program Element 6.46.03.A, released under U.S. Freedom of Information Act request to William Arkin, quoted by Peter Hayes, *Pacific Powderkeg*, 95.

127. Hayes, *Pacific Powderkeg*, 102.

128. Cumings, "The Conflict on the Korean Peninsula," 105.

129. Hayes, *Pacific Powderkeg*, 49.

130. Hayes, *Pacific Powderkeg*, 49.

131. Jack Anderson, "Little Weapons with a Big Bang," *Washington Post*, 3 June 1984, B7.

132. Fred Hiatt, "U.S.: No Use of A-Arms Envisioned in S. Korea," *Washington Post*, 3 December 1987, A54.

133. Interview conducted by Peter Hayes of a senior U.S. military official, Washington, D.C., June 1987 as quoted in *Pacific Powderkeg*, 162-163.

134. Hayes, *Pacific Powderkeg*, 60.

135. Hayes, *Pacific Powderkeg*, 89-103.

136. "Pentagon Draws Up First Strategy for Fighting a Long Nuclear War," *New York Times*, 30 May 1982, A1, A12.

137. In Byung Chul Koh, *The Foreign Policy Systems of North and South Korea* (Berkeley: University of California Press, 1984), 90.

138. *The Pyongyang Times*, 3 March 1990 as quoted by Tae-hwan Kwak, "The Reduction of U.S. Forces in Korea in the Inter-Korean Peace Process," *The Korean Journal of Defense Analysis* 2, no. 2 (Winter 1990): 192.

139. Fred Hiatt, "U.S.: No Use of A-Arms Envisioned in S. Korea," *Washington Post*, 3 December 1987, A54.

140. J. McBeth, "Withdrawal Symptoms: Americans Ponder the Removal of Nuclear Weapons," *Far Eastern Economic Review*, 29 September 1988, 35.

141. Tae-hwan Kwak, "The Reduction of U.S. Forces in Korea in the Inter-Korean Peace Process," 192. Similar sentiments are expressed in William J. Crowe and Alan D. Romberg, "Rethinking Pacific Security," *Foreign Affairs* 70, no. 2 (Spring 1991): 134, and Bruce Cumings, "Conflict on the Korean Peninsula," 110.

142. George H. W. Bush, "The President's News Conference with Foreign Journalists," 2 July 1992, *Public Papers, 1992-93*, Book I, 1065.

143. George Bush and Brent Scowcroft, *A World Transformed* (New York: Alfred Knopf, 1998), 545.

144. J. Sterngold, "Seoul Says It Now Has No Nuclear Arms," *New York Times*, 19 December 1991, A3.

145. "U.S.-North Korean *Agreed Framework* on Nuclear Issues," *Korea Focus*, 168.

146. U.S. Department of Defense, "Korea-U.S. Security Consultative Meeting Joint Communiqué," No. 619-02, 5 December 2002, <http://www.defenselink.mil/releases/20-02/b12052002_bt619-02.html> (July 2004).

147. David E. Sanger, "North Korea Assembly Backs Atom Pact," *New York Times*, 10 April 1992, A3.

148. Levin and Sneider, 31. See also Joo-Hong Nam, *America's Commitment to South Korea: The First Decade of the Nixon Doctrine*, 80-82; Claude A. Buss, *The United States and the Republic of Korea*, xi-xii; and Edward A. Olsen, *U.S. Policy and the Two Koreas*, 10.

Chapter 6

U.S. SECURITY POLICY:
Engagement and Compellence

Since the end of the Korean War, the dominant focus of U.S. policy in Korea has been deterring a conventional attack on South Korea. While this threat to ROK security remained, the 1980s raised the specter of another danger to peace and security in the region: North Korean nuclear weapons and ballistic missiles. Deterrence remained the bedrock of U.S. policy but it became clear towards the end of this decade that deterrence alone would not address these additional threats. As a result, U.S. leaders had to include strategies of engagement and compellence to address this new danger. Recall from chapter 1 that a compellent strategy seeks to induce a challenger to halt an action already begun and can utilize sticks and carrots to compel the challenger to end the undesirable behavior. Throughout the past 10 to 15 years, the United States has moved, not always in a consistent and coordinated fashion, between the carrots and sticks of compellence along with attempts to engage the North. These efforts have been complicated by the need to retain a robust deterrence posture that sometimes worked at cross-purposes with the efforts to engage.

After inheriting the nuclear crisis from the Bush administration, President Clinton moved slowly in the direction of engagement while offering incentives for a deal and threatening to impose sanctions. Engagement won out, at least for a time, with the conclusion of a nuclear weapons deal and almost finalizing an agreement on ballistic missiles. However, his efforts were often inconsistent and lacked a clear direction for addressing U.S. proliferation concerns.

The second Bush administration has often been divided over its approach to North Korea but by and large has been dubious of engaging Pyongyang, convinced it will fail. In 2002, U.S. officials confronted the North with evidence that it had cheated on the Agreed Framework in developing a secret, parallel nuclear weapons program based on highly enriched uranium. As a result, Bush moved towards a policy of compellence threats. More recently, the administration has shown some flexibility and willingness to engage and offer incentives

201

but the issue remains unresolved. Through all of these efforts, a firm deterrence strategy remained the foundation of U.S. policy in the region. This chapter now turns to U.S. efforts to dissuade North Korea from acquiring a nuclear weapons capability and ending its ballistic missile program.

Reagan and the First Bush Administrations

In 1982, U.S. intelligence detected evidence of a growing North Korean nuclear weapons program, far more extensive than earlier reports. In addition to a small research reactor in operation since the 1960s, U.S. satellites discovered construction sites for new reactor facilities and a reprocessing plant. Particularly worrisome was that none of these facilities appeared connected to the country's power grid, making it likely Pyongyang intended to develop nuclear weapons rather than produce energy. In response, the United States pushed the Soviet Union to pressure Pyongyang to sign the NPT, which it did in 1985.[1] U.S. and ROK officials were relieved and hoped this settled matters, but the problem dragged on when North Korea balked at signing the inspections agreement required of NPT signatories.

In 1988, a South Korean official approached the United States with a proposal to change its North Korea policy in an effort "to help us draw [North Korea] out to the international community."[2] Washington was elated; up to this point, Seoul had always opposed any attempts to open a dialogue with the North. After discussions among U.S. planners, Gaston Sigur, Assistant Secretary of State remembered, "we came to the conclusion that if you're really going to achieve some sort of a semblance of peace on the Korean peninsula, the only way to do that is to take some steps to try to open the place."[3] With this hope, they developed a four-point plan:

(1) A new policy of encouraging unofficial, nongovernmental visits by North Koreans to the United States.
(2) Easing of stringent financial regulations that impeded travel to North Korea by American citizens.
(3) Permission for limited commercial export of American humanitarian goods, such as food, clothing, and medicine, to North Korea.
(4) Renewed permission for substantive discussions with North Koreans in neutral settings, with the expectation that this time serious communications might take place.[4]

North Korea was not required to reciprocate in any manner but in the words of one source, Reagan officials hoped "it might be possible both to persuade the North to join the community of nations and refrain from building nuclear weapons."[5] In response, Pyongyang requested to meet with U.S. officials, a gathering that took place in December 1988, the first American effort to engage North Korea for quite some time.

During these years following the signing of the NPT and the failure to solidify the inspections, an important shift occurred in the "situation" here, though

U.S. officials did not seem fully aware of it. During these years, North Korea began construction of a five-megawatt reactor, two larger reactors and a reprocessing facility, all evidence of a determined effort to develop nuclear weapons. According to one source, "the North Korean program metastasized during this period of indifference into a full-scale plutonium production effort that would require radical surgery to dismantle."[6] In theoretical terms, the situation had shifted from one of deterrence to that of compellence. Given the progress of the North Korean program, it was now a matter of reversing an action already underway rather than stopping an action already begun. Succeeding at compellence is a much more difficult task, as U.S. leaders would soon find out.

The first Bush administration continued these efforts to engage North Korea and soon after, the nuclear weapons issue began to stir again. North Korea had yet to sign the safeguards agreement providing for inspections and in 1989, new intelligence surfaced indicating Pyongyang was continuing its work. The Bush administration sought a diplomatic solution by briefing Soviet and Chinese officials in 1989 in hopes they would exert influence over the North and persuade it to stop. According to Secretary of State James Baker, "our diplomatic strategy was designed to build international pressure against North Korea to force them to live up to their agreement to sign a safeguards agreement permitting inspections."[7] Following these efforts, the Bush administration convened an interagency group to review its North Korea policy. The result was National Security Review 28, "United States Policy Toward North Korean Nuclear Weapons Program," dated 6 February 1991, a combination of carrots and sticks that one official noted was like "putting the North in a vise—smiling all the while—and offering it a way to get out."[8] The proposal had five components: maintain a strong deterrence posture; encourage North-South dialogue; convince North Korea to fulfill its obligations under the NPT; convince Pyongyang to refrain from terrorist acts; and constrain the sale of any nuclear/chemical weapons and ballistic missiles.[9] The withdrawal of U.S. nuclear weapons was not included as one of the carrots but it soon became part of the discussion. In return for these measures, the United States would move towards normalizing relations with the North.

When U.S. intelligence reports became public in 1989, North Korea immediately denied any efforts to develop nuclear weapons. Moreover, Pyongyang insisted there would be no inspections while it was threatened by U.S. nuclear weapons. To turn the pressure for inspections back on North Korea, the Bush administration removed U.S. tactical nuclear weapons from the peninsula in hopes of eliminating this obstacle. The measure provided a reward/incentive for North Korea to comply though it seems doubtful that the Bush administration intended it as such. Rather, it was an effort to force Pyongyang's hand by meeting their concerns and testing their sincerity.

After extensive debate within the administration—a familiar story of the State Department favoring engagement and incentives and the Pentagon pushing a tougher approach—the United States began implementing their plan to coax better behavior from Pyongyang and to encourage them to sign the safeguards agreement for nuclear inspections. First, as noted earlier, President Bush went forward with the plan to withdraw tactical nuclear weapons from the peninsula. Second, the United States reiterated its defense commitment, as President Bush noted in a visit to South Korea in 1992, "let this be clear: The United States has and will support the security aspirations of its ally in the South in the cause of peace. . . . Let there be no doubt: The people of this republic should know that the United States commitment to Korea's security remains steady and strong."[10] Secretary of Defense Cheney also postponed the planned withdrawal of 6,000 U.S. troops. Third, in December 1991, U.S. and ROK officials indicated they would be willing to cancel the 1992 Team Spirit exercises if North Korea signed the safeguards agreement. Washington and Seoul had already been considering this move given the $150 million price tag of the exercises, its disruption of South Korean society and commerce, and that the maneuvers were no longer necessary. Finally, the United States announced its willingness to hold a high level meeting with North Korean delegates, a goal of Pyongyang's for the past 20 years. On 22 December 1991, North Korea announced it would sign the safeguards agreement and did so on 30 January 1992. On December 31st, North and South Korea concluded the agreement that banned all nuclear weapons activity from the peninsula. Soon after, Seoul confirmed that Team Spirit had indeed been suspended.

In spring 1992, North Korea complied with the inspections requirements allowing six different visits to DPRK nuclear facilities. According to Michael Mazarr, "the gradual, nuanced strategy of pressure and incentives employed by Washington and Seoul had persuaded the North to take the step the world had awaited since 1985—allowing actual IAEA inspections of its nuclear facilities."[11] Despite these initial successes in bringing North Korea into compliance, debate within in the administration continued over whether to continue an engagement policy or whether North Korea would perceive these measures as a sign of weakness and push for more. As a result, U.S. representative Arnold Kanter entered the promised meeting with North Korea, the first high-level talks between the United States and North Korea in years, with little to offer Pyongyang besides general notions of "the bright future" should it continue to cooperate. Kanter did not even raise the possibility of normalizing U.S.-DPRK relations sometime in the future, an important goal for the North. Instead, he maintained that the future of U.S.-DPRK relations was now up to them. According to one source, "not surprisingly, Pyongyang declined to accept that burden; the U.S. promise of greater communication and commerce was so vague and intangible that it held little to attract North Korean cooperation."[12] After allowing several inspections, in the spring and summer of 1992, North Korea received little in return. Furthermore, political contacts with the U.S. and the anticipated aid and investment for North Korea were not forthcoming.[13]

To make matters worse, IAEA officials demanded challenge inspections to investigate other sites. It is important to note here that the request for special inspections was linked to IAEA worries following the Persian Gulf War. Despite Iraq's compliance with inspections, evidence indicated it had successfully maintained a secret nuclear program. After the war, the United States began providing the IAEA with intelligence information and, according to Don Oberdorfer, the IAEA was "determined not to be hoodwinked or embarrassed again. North Korea became the first test case of their new capabilities and attitudes."[14] In negotiations to implement the 1991 Joint Denuclearization agreement, South Korea also demanded the right to hold challenge inspections. In both cases, North Korea refused to comply. Finally, U.S. and ROK officials began to talk of reinstating Team Spirit exercises the following year. Slowly in the summer and fall of 1992, the progress achieved during the previous months unraveled. According to Mazarr, the "bland promises proved insufficient to persuade the North Koreans that they had something to gain by allowing full inspections. And even after the North did respond to U.S. overtures in 1992, Washington and Seoul failed to follow up their success with evidence that nuclear cooperation carried benefits."[15]

Clinton Administration

Upon entering the White House, Bill Clinton, who had little interest in foreign affairs, inherited the growing crisis in Korea. After many months of what appeared to be a cycle of apparent breakthroughs followed by renewed crises, the start of a final solution seemed to be in place with the conclusion of the October 1994 Agreed Framework. The details of the events leading up to this agreement are discussed at great length in other works and will not be addressed here.[16] However, important elements of these deliberations shed light on the difficulty of maintaining a credible extended deterrence commitment while also pursuing engagement to achieve nonproliferation goals.

In 1998 Clinton faced another dilemma when North Korea tested a ballistic missile that crossed over Japanese airspace. After addressing the immediate problem of deterring North Korea from conducting additional tests, the administration embarked on another engagement effort to conclude a comprehensive agreement on North Korea's missile program. Aided by the June 2000 Korea summit that greatly improved relations in the region, the Clinton administration came close to finishing a deal. The administration either ran out of time or courage, depending on one's view, to conclude the agreement before leaving office in January 2001.

The most immediate crisis for the incoming Clinton administration was North Korea's announcement on 12 March 1993 to withdraw from the NPT, a decision that would take effect after 90 days. The North's action, a complete surprise to U.S. officials who assumed this matter would blow over after Team Spirit, was based largely on anger for the resumption of these exercises in March and the IAEA's continued insistence on special inspections. While many sources were calling for a tough response, including economic sanctions and possibly a military strike, to Pyongyang's announcement, Clinton was inclined to pursue a more conciliatory approach while gradually building pressure on North Korea. It was clear early on that for any coercion to be successful, China had to be supportive of the measure. Initially, Secretary of State Warren Christopher expressed hope that North Korea would "withdraw their withdrawal" but turning the matter over to the Security Council would be the lead option "if they continue on the path that they are on."[17] North Korea responded that if sanctions were forthcoming, "we will be compelled to take a powerful self-defensive measure."[18] In the end, despite the conduct of Team Spirit, the North took no unusual military moves that indicated action of some sort. Later, the United States responded that it would be willing to meet with the North Koreans to discuss the matter, as one press report noted growing "wary of leaving North Korea feeling cornered," and prodded by Chinese officials who could veto any sanctions measure brought before the Security Council.[19] Another U.S. official noted, "we don't yet fully understand what their objectives are; in principle, we are prepared to talk."[20] Finally, prior to the scheduled talks on June 2nd to address the issue, chief negotiator Robert Gallucci said, "what we're prepared to do is to address concerns that we regard as legitimate concerns that they have raised to date," listing Team Spirit exercises, inspections demands, and the U.S. nuclear threat to North Korea as key concerns.[21]

On June 12, the deadline for North Korea to leave the NPT, Pyongyang announced it would suspend the decision pending future progress on settling outstanding issues. Though a short-term victory, this did little to settle the larger concerns of Seoul and Washington along with those of Pyongyang. In the months ahead, the Clinton administration continued efforts to engage North Korea holding subsequent rounds of talks while suspending Team Spirit exercises in 1994 and the years thereafter. When North Korea continued to hesitate, Washington raised again the possibility of turning the issue over to the UN Security Council for a sanctions resolution. Yet that never happened as, according to Mazarr, "North Korea would agree to a small portion of the IAEA and U.S. demands, thus putting off sanctions and prolonging the nuclear dispute, while leaving the most important issues on the table."[22] The next year brought a continuation of this pattern of events with no final resolution until Carter's trip to Pyongyang broke the deadlock.

Clinton administration policy throughout the crisis maintained the firm deterrent posture of previous years. Troop levels remained consistent, on a few occasions U.S. forces were placed on a heightened state of alert, and Washington sent Patriot missile batteries to the South.[23] President Clinton also sent a letter to South Korean President Kim Young Sam indicating that an attack by the North on South Korea would be considered an attack on the United States,[24] a statement that went beyond the "constitutional processes" clause of the security treaty. In March 1993, Secretary of Defense Perry noted that while there were no indications of an imminent attack by the North, the United States would ensure its ground troops could blunt an invasion and the Air Force "can quickly get overwhelming air power" within a day for "massive airstrikes on North Korean ground forces" before U.S. reinforcements arrive.[25]

While buttressing deterrence, Clinton also made specific threats to compel North Korea to give up its nuclear ambitions. Foremost was the reoccurring threat to take the matter to the UN Security Council for a resolution imposing sanctions. On all occasions, North Korea reacted angrily, fuming at one point that sanctions were tantamount to war whereby "Seoul will turn into a sea of fire."[26] In March 1994, Secretary of Defense William Perry warned that while the United States has no intention of taking preemptive action against the North, it would enforce the sanctions, even at the risk of war.[27] In July 1993, President Clinton visited the DMZ and while talking to the press remarked, "it is pointless for [North Koreans] to try to develop nuclear weapons because if they ever use them it would be the end of their country."[28] Clinton also made an ominous remark during an interview on NBC's *Meet the Press* in November 1993 when he said, "North Korea cannot be allowed to develop a nuclear bomb."[29] Should no diplomatic solution occur, the United States appeared willing to use force to end the DPRK's nuclear program. Later, White House officials retreated from this statement.

As tension escalated in 1994, Clinton also considered a "compellence by denial" strategy when he contemplated air strikes to take out the nuclear facilities at Yongbyon. Secretary of Defense Perry instructed the Air Force to develop a plan to destroy the nuclear facilities there but decided not to act fearing an air strike "was highly likely to start a general war."[30] Moreover, the costs of such an action were too dangerous and it was uncertain if intelligence could identify all relevant targets. If a substantial portion of the North's nuclear capability remained intact, a military strike might only accelerate Pyongyang's determination to pursue a weapons program. Moreover, any retaliation by Pyongyang put Seoul, only 25 miles from the border and well within DPRK artillery range, in grave danger. As Perry recalled, "the North Koreans were in a corner and might lash out in desperation."[31] As the crisis escalated in June 1994, Perry called on Pentagon planners to prepare for a possible conflict by updating OPLAN 5027 and outlining the necessary deployments should hostilities breakout. In addition to the North's possible use of nuclear weapons, planners also anticipated the use of chemical or biological weapons. In a meeting with President Clinton on 14 June 1994, Perry outlined three options "to defeat a North Korean attack, if that became the only way we could block the North Koreans from getting a nuclear arsenal." None of the options involved the United States striking first, "but they all involved increasing our military forces in South Korea, one of them by a very considerable increment," which the North Koreans were surely to view as provocative.[32] Extensive reinforcing of U.S. troops in Korea was a dangerous move. With the Persian Gulf War only a few years prior, DPRK officials might have assumed a U.S. attack was on the way, prompting them to consider a preemptive strike before the build-up was complete.[33] Clinton was considering these dangerous choices when Jimmy Carter called from North Korea informing him a deal with Kim Il Sung was possible.

Despite considering military options, the first inclination of Clinton officials was to solve the dilemma through an engagement strategy that offered, at various times, incentives including several rounds of direct, bilateral talks with the DPRK, a highly sought after prize by Pyongyang, canceling Team Spirit exercises, normalizing U.S.-DPRK relations, providing assurances the United States would not use nuclear weapons, and allowing DPRK officials to inspect U.S. and ROK military bases in Korea as a reciprocal measure for fulfilling IAEA inspections. The administration also offered direct reassurances of U.S. intentions to solve the matter diplomatically. In October 1993, Representative Gary Ackermann (D-NY) traveled to Pyongyang as part of a congressional delegation where he conveyed a message from the administration indicating its desire to solve the nuclear imbroglio through dialogue and negotiation.[34] As Mazarr noted, "with the end of the Cold War, U.S. officials saw an opportunity to conduct the first truly international diplomatic campaign to promote nonproliferation."[35]

In the end, Clinton's negotiators offered North Korea a package of rewards and incentives as contained in the Agreed Framework. North Korea agreed to freeze and eventually dismantle its nuclear facilities while coming under full compliance with the NPT and the required international inspections. In return, the North received shipments of heavy fuel oil and two modern light water reactors that were far more proliferation resistant than its older ones. The agreement also provided for eventual normalization of relations and the lifting of economic sanctions.

Critics of the Agreed Framework and Clinton's engagement strategy characterized the deal as "appeasement" and "blackmail." Leading up to the crisis, Charles Krauthammer argued U.S. policy

> has been all carrot and no stick. As inducement to be nice, we have already given the North Koreans their first direct high-level talks with the United States. We have dangled diplomatic recognition. We are now dangling an offer to cancel joint U.S. military exercises with South Korea. These are gestures of weakness. They have done nothing about North Korea's nuclear program. . . . Enough talk. The time has come for action. . . . The President's task is clear. Lead. Stop talking to the North Koreans—it is time for an economic blockade.[36]

After the Agreed Framework was concluded Senator Frank Murkowski (R-AK) lamented, "I think it is a bad agreement because it carries the scent of appeasement" while Senator John McCain (R-AZ) believed the Clinton administration "has extended carrot after carrot, concession after concession, and pursued a policy of appeasement based, in my view, on the ill-founded belief that North Koreans really just want to be part of the community of nations and want diplomatic relations, et cetera."[37] McCain also called for a massive increase of U.S. forces in Korea and specific threats of air strikes to take out the nuclear facilities; only under these circumstances did he believe North Korea would acquiesce. In 1994, Senator Charles Robb (D-VA) introduced a measure calling for the reintroduction of tactical nuclear weapons, an effort that passed in the Senate but failed in the House. Throughout the six remaining years of Clinton's stay in the White House, he battled the Congress to keep the funding and overall support for the Agreed Framework.[38]

Despite Clinton's inclination to pursue a negotiated settlement, the heavy criticism he received in the months leading to the Agreed Framework caused him to hesitate in proceeding further. According to Mazarr, the administration had "a general defensiveness caused by months of sustained and bitter criticism of the administration's overall foreign policy." Even those who supported engagement "believed the administration was on the right track, but simply wasn't going far enough." The result of being bombarded from both sides was to "deprive the administration of the confidence to take bold steps rather than providing. it with such confidence."[39] Another study maintained "the administration had waffled, wavered, and backtracked, squandering the essential element of coercive diplomacy, credibility. The new president and his administration inspired little fear or respect during the period."[40] Clinton was also criticized for being indecisive, overly flexible, lacking principle, and wedded to polling data.[41] In the end, as Mazarr notes, "U.S. policy . . . remained wedded to its own form of incrementalism and staunchly refusing to take decisive action of any sort, whether by offering the North a 'package deal' or attempting to impose sanctions."[42] Another source noted, "Clinton's policy had been confusing at best, vacillating between offers of economic assistance and threats of economic and military reprisal."[43]

The Clinton administration also faced the dilemma of defining whether the North Korean nuclear issue was a problem of deterrence or compellence. A deterrence situation requires stopping an action yet taken, an easier proposition than reversing a nuclear program that may have already completed the construction of a weapon. Available intelligence was sparse; the North's nuclear facilities were clearly in satellite photographs but the precise progress of construction of a nuclear weapon was uncertain. In 1993, the CIA estimated the North might have diverted sufficient plutonium to manufacture one to two nuclear weapons, however, this estimate was not verified. If indeed, this was a compellence problem, the ability to reverse a North Korean program already brought to fruition was a far more difficult task requiring more incentives or greater threats to dissuade the North from giving up what might have been its advanced nuclear program. As a result, the Clinton policy of steering a cautious, incremental course failed until it was willing to offer the large package deal that provided sufficient benefits to offset the costs of North Korea giving up its nuclear program.

Despite this apparent resolution, implementation of the accord was tentative, due to delays caused both by the United States and North Korea. An important dimension of any compellence situation is that the target state must be confident the imposing state will be willing and able to provide the incentives that are part of the deal. In North Korea's case, it entered the Agreed Framework with much skepticism regarding America's willingness to follow through on providing the rewards. Washington's credibility, already low in Pyongyang's estimation, was hurt further when the heavy fuel oil promised in the Agreed Framework was often late due to delays in congressional funding. Furthermore, the United States was slow to remove trade sanctions, failed to declare it would not threaten the North with nuclear weapons, and made little progress in normalizing relations. Finally, Pyongyang believed the delays in constructing the light water reactors were intentional foot-dragging. As a result of America's inability to deliver fully on its offer of rewards, North Korea may have felt it necessary to pursue an alternate nuclear weapons program based on highly enriched uranium, though these efforts remained secret for several years.

To be sure, North Korea's credibility was highly questionable as well. Throughout the process, it had been a difficult negotiating partner, utilizing provocative rhetoric and a strategy of brinksmanship that often frustrated talks. Moreover, Pyongyang was also responsible for some of the delayed implementation of the Agreed Framework through the submarine incidents of 1996 and 1998, disagreements over wages paid to workers at the LWR site, and the 1998 ballistic missile test. Yet, North Korea believed the delays were largely the responsibility of others. On several occasions, North Korea threatened to restart its Yongbyon facility over delays in the LWR project and the resulting lost electricity. The following are excerpts from a June 2001 Korean Central News Agency report.

> The construction of the LWRs . . . is too much delayed and thus the implementation of the agreement has reached a serious pass [sic]. Though 7 years have passed since the adoption of the agreement, the site preparation has not yet been completed, to say nothing of the start of the ground work. . . . As the DPRK repeatedly clarified, the demand for compensation for the loss of electricity is not a tactic but a crucial issue related to the right to existence. If this issue is not solved, the Democratic People's Republic of Korea will be left with no option but to restart the construction of graphite-moderated reactors for its existence. . . . If the U.S. fails to meet the demand for the compensation for the loss of electricity, it will be hard to save the AF from its collapse and the DPRK will find no option but to go its own way.[44]

Engagement continued throughout the Clinton administration, particularly to implement the various measures of the Agreed Framework. However, in 1998, North Korea made another effort at crisis diplomacy to gain Washington's attention by conducting a missile test that sent the final stage of a three-stage rocket traveling over Japanese airspace. The launch was another indication that U.S. engagement did not consistently follow through on its commitments.

One of the provisions of the Agreed Framework called for both sides to move towards normalization of relations and the lifting of economic sanctions present since the Korean War. These elements were extremely important to Pyongyang; lack of progress pointed to the continued state of war between the two sides and barred its desperate economy from access to badly needed capital and markets. However, in the face of strong criticism from Republicans in Congress, Clinton was reluctant to push for the end of sanctions. Indeed, many in the administration believed North Korea might be on the verge of collapse making these measures unnecessary. In North Korea, many leaders, particularly hardliners became exceedingly frustrated at the delays, and the military pushed for missile testing as a way of regaining U.S. attention. For several years, Kim Jong Il held back the military's demands, including the cancellation of a planned missile test in 1996. However, by 1997, the United States became increasingly late with the deliveries of heavy fuel oil promised in the Agreed Framework and pressure in Pyongyang was building to do something. On 9 May 1998, Kim Yong Nam, DPRK Foreign Minister fumed, "your government takes us for granted because you think we are weak. We are losing patience. Our generals and atomic industry leaders insist that we must resume our nuclear program and develop appropriate military capabilities. If you do not act in good faith, there will be consequences." To improve matters, Kim maintained the United States must show "us that you are serious about normalization. To us, it is clear that the sanctions are intended to pressure us because you hope we will collapse. If you were serious about normalization, you would end the Korean War. How can we have normal relations if we are still at war?"[45] Pyongyang gave Washington another verbal warning on 16 June 1998 but, again, the United States did nothing.

On 16 August 1998, North Korea tested the Taepo Dong I, creating a firestorm in the region, not only because it violated Japanese air space but also because it indicated an unexpected level of DPRK missile development, demonstrating significant progress towards manufacturing a longer range missile. The following year, North Korea began preparations for another missile test, starting a flurry of diplomatic pressure from Washington, Seoul, Tokyo, and Beijing to dissuade the North from such a test.

Soon after the 1998 missile test and in the face of congressional calls to scrap the Agreed Framework, Clinton announced the formation of an interagency group to review U.S. policy towards North Korea. Under the leadership of former Secretary of Defense William Perry, the group conducted countless interviews of government officials from the United States, South Korea, Japan, Russia, China, and Europe along with a trip to North Korea in May 1999 to solicit the views of leaders in Pyongyang. While this review was underway, the State Department conducted a series of negotiations with the North to halt further testing of its ballistic missiles, a matter that became more urgent in 1999 when Pyongyang prepared for another test. The Berlin talks laid the groundwork for a more comprehensive effort to address the testing, development, and export of DPRK missiles.

On 18 September 1999, Washington pronounced its willingness to lift some of the economic and trade sanctions in response to the North Korean moratorium on testing announced four days earlier. According to the deal, North Korea could buy consumer goods with hard currency, transport goods and passengers to and from the United States, and allow individuals in the United States to send funds back to North Korea.[46] However, other sanctions remained in place. In return, Pyongyang agreed to a one-year moratorium on missile tests while negotiations continued on a long-term missile agreement. It is important to note that U.S. concessions here were not new; these had been a part of the Agreed Framework but not delivered. In many respects, the United States was using the same incentive twice to obtain a different concession. Many critics argued the United States should not "buy off" North Korea yet this was not the first attempt to compensate North Korea for giving up its missile program. During the first Bush administration, Israel attempted to buy off North Korean missile sales to Iran but was discouraged by Washington from concluding a deal.[47] Despite the agreement, critics remained; "we are once again entering a cycle of extortion with North Korea," according to Benjamin A. Gilman (R-NY), chair of the House International Relations committee.[48]

Soon after the announcement of the missile test moratorium, Perry released the results of his study team. The report concluded, "the urgent focus of U.S. policy toward the DPRK must be to end its nuclear weapons and long-range missile-related activities." To achieve this goal, the report recommended a "Two-Path Strategy" to end the North's nuclear ambitions. The first path called for "complete and verifiable cessation" of the North's nuclear weapons program and the testing, development, and deployment of ballistic missiles beyond the ranges set by the Missile Technology Control Regime. The North would also terminate the export of missiles and technology. In return, the United States and its allies would "in a step-by-step and reciprocal fashion, move to reduce pressures on the DPRK that it perceives as threatening. The reduction of perceived threat would in turn give the DPRK regime the confidence that it could coexist peacefully with us and its neighbors." Washington would also "normalize relations with the DPRK, relax sanctions that have long constrained trade with the DPRK and take other positive steps." Movement along "the first path depends on the willingness of the DPRK to traverse it with us." Should Pyongyang reject the first path, "it will not be possible for the United States to pursue a new relationship with the DPRK." Moreover, the United States and its allies "would need to act to contain the threat that we have been unable to eliminate through negotiation."[49] The report also called for cooperation between the United States and its allies, Washington, Seoul, and Tokyo to form the Trilateral Coordination and Oversight Group (TCOG) that holds regular meetings to synchronize policy in the region.

Despite the Perry Review, efforts to engage North Korea were similar to past incremental proposals of "carrots and sticks" that did little to test North Korea's willingness to settle the issue with a "grand bargain." Furthermore, though talks continued between the United States and North Korea, Clinton was again slow to implement the recommendations of the Perry Review. Eventually, the United States lifted some sanctions but several important ones, including bans on North Korean access to World Bank and IMF funding based on its inclusion on the State Department list of states that sponsor terrorism, remained in place.

The Clinton administration's efforts to engage the North later received a push from political events in the South. In December 1997, Kim Dae Jung, long-time political dissident and a presidential candidate in 1971, 1987, and 1992, won the presidential election defeating the ruling party candidate Lee Hoi Chang by less than two percent of the vote. A cornerstone of Kim's foreign policy was engaging North Korea in a strategy that became known as the "sunshine policy."[50] Kim worked tirelessly to bring the two Koreas together, resulting in the Mt. Kumgang tourism project, foreign investment, family reunions, and the planned reopening of road and railroad links between North and South that were severed since the Korean War. The crowning achievement was the history-making June 2000 summit where Kim Dae Jung traveled to Pyongyang for several days of meetings. Though the progress generated by the summit was largely symbolic—few of the difficult political and security issues were solved—the meeting produced tremendous momentum for improving relations between the two Koreas. The 2000 summit also gave Clinton sufficient "political cover" to relax sanctions in the face of conservative criticism that was sure to follow.[51]

In an effort to follow-up on the progress made during the summit, in October, DPRK General Jo Myong Rok visited Washington in October where he indicated North Korea would be willing to end its ballistic missile program in return for help launching satellites. Secretary of State Albright responded with a visit to Pyongyang in November 2000 to conduct preliminary talks for concluding a comprehensive missile deal. Though the full agreement was not finalized during her visit, North Korea indicated that all the problems could be worked out if President Clinton came to the DPRK. Pyongyang believed a Clinton visit was important not only for the missile deal but also to generate further impetus for normalizing relations between the United States and North Korea.[52] Clinton declined to go citing a lack of time, a serious blow to engagement efforts that reversed much of the progress secured in U.S.-North Korean relations. In the years ahead, relations would sour even further and the possibilities held out by engagement in the fall of 2000 would be distant indeed.

Assessing Clinton's Security Policy in Korea

Throughout the Clinton years, deterrence remained robust and effective. Policy makers had little worry that North Korea would act on its long-stated goal of national reunification. Instead, most of the concern focused on fears, particularly during the years leading up to the Agreed Framework, that North Korea might lash out in response to the imposition of sanctions or a U.S.-ROK military strike to take out its nuclear facilities. While Pyongyang's rhetoric—"turn Seoul into a sea of flames"—was nothing new, Clinton officials were truly concerned the North might act on these threats if they felt sufficiently threatened. As a result, when tension mounted, policy makers began to perceive a possible shift in the deterrence situation from one of general deterrence to something more like immediate deterrence where the threat of attack appeared more plausible. What Pyongyang would have done in the face of sanctions or air strikes is a matter of conjecture. However, the Clinton administration saw danger and took some specific measures to reinforce deterrence in the face of a more menacing and cornered North Korea that might consider the use of force.

While these actions may have reinforced deterrence, they were also counterproductive to implementing the engagement policy that held the key to solving the nuclear weapons problem. For some time, Pyongyang stated that normalization of relations, concluding a formal peace treaty, and ending hostile relations with the United States were top priorities. When the Clinton administration balked at providing these items, even after concluding the Agreed Framework, and continued to reinforce deterrence, North Korean leaders viewed their security to still be in jeopardy. As a result, U.S. efforts to deter were provocative; North Korea was attempting to protect its security interests by deterring the United States with a nuclear weapons program. Upon returning from a visit with North Korean leaders in May 1999, William Perry argued, "I believe their primary reason . . . is deterrence. Who would they be deterring? They would be deterring the United States. We do not think of ourselves as a threat to North Korea, but I truly believe that they consider us a threat to them."[53] Thus, deterrence did not address the proliferation problem and may have made it worse.

To address the proliferation concerns, the Clinton administration vacillated between two compellence strategies, taking a hard-line stance that issued threats and engaging North Korea with incentives, with the result that neither measure was implemented fully and effectively. Instead, the administration seldom drew precise lines for North Korea not to cross, dates by which it must comply, and what would happen if it continued on its current course.

Despite these issues, there is a more fundamental question here. Compellence calls for issuing threats to prevent an adversary from taking a specific action by sufficiently raising the costs to outweigh the benefits. If North Korean motivation for acquiring nuclear weapons and developing and exporting ballistic missiles was rooted in fundamental security and economic concerns tied to regime survival, what more could the United States have threatened that would have altered their cost-benefit calculations? In addition, threatening military strikes might have posed the necessary costs, but these actions also entailed great risks for South Korea and the United States. With Seoul only 25 miles from the border, it was extremely vulnerable to North Korean retaliation. Moreover, a military strike might have precipitated a general war on the peninsula, a cost the United States and South Korea were unwilling to tolerate. Sanctions that increased economic and political isolation were less costly to impose but it was also unclear whether these had sufficient cost for North Korea. The DPRK already had minimal foreign trade and China and Japan, two countries that could make sanctions hurt, indicated they did not support them. Given North Korea's security concerns, these were costs it seemed willing to bear. Even if these efforts were successful in further degrading the economy, it would likely be the people of the DPRK who would suffer most, not the leadership and the military, and would further motivate North Korea to sell nuclear weapons and ballistic missiles to sustain its economy. It seems unlikely that a compellence strategy based on threats, even if implemented more vigorously, would have succeeded in altering North Korean cost-benefit calculations.

The Clinton administration was similarly uncertain regarding the policy of engagement it pursued though it tended to utilize this approach more. Despite recommendations to do so, the administration was reluctant to offer North Korea a comprehensive package deal that addressed a range of security, political, and economic concerns important to the DPRK until pushed by Carter's visit with Kim Il Sung. The incentives here were crucial. As noted earlier, there was significant cost for North Korea to give up its weapons programs, both in terms of security and domestic politics. Offering incentives piecemeal, with uncertain time lines, and in terms that were relatively vague, made it difficult to convince North Korea that it could give up the chief leverage it had.

In the end, the Clinton administration utilized engagement and incentives to conclude the Agreed Framework, a route that found a peaceful solution and avoided the other more dangerous options. The AF successfully froze North Korea's plutonium program and put U.S-ROK-DPRK relations on a path towards normalization. The United States and South Korea did not receive all that they wished in the agreement, which should not be a surprise; North Korea also had significant leverage to bring to the table.

Once the Agreed Framework was in place, the administration failed to implement several key aspects of the accord, at times slowed by a Congress that found the agreement appalling. Indeed, some in the administration thought the agreement might never have to be fully implemented based on the many predictions of an impending North Korean collapse. The fact that the United States engaged North Korea is only a starting point; the success of engagement based on a strategy of compellence through rewards requires that the incentives be sufficiently valuable and that the target knows it will receive them when it stops its objectionable behavior. As a result, U.S. credibility regarding its ability to deliver the benefits was damaged, making North Korean cooperation difficult and acquiescence to any future agreements more problematic.

To be sure, U.S. policy makers faced a challenging situation including provocative North Korean behavior such as the submarine incidents of 1996 and 1998, among others, the usual North Korean negotiating tactics, a U.S. Congress reluctant to fully implement the Agreed Framework, and the changing nature of South Korean positions under Kim Young Sam. Yet, the Clinton administration was slow to offer the package of incentives that might have convinced North Korea to give up its weapons programs and then balked at fully implementing the deal.

The Second Bush Administration

When George W. Bush entered the White House in January 2001, there was great speculation regarding his intentions to continue the engagement process and drive for better relations with North Korea begun by the Clinton administration.[54] A month after taking office, State Department spokesman Richard Boucher noted the United States was "very mindful of the work that had been done and looked forward to moving forward from there."[55] A few weeks later, Secretary of State Colin Powell indicated the Bush administration would pick up where the Clinton administration had left off. When U.S. special envoy for Korean affairs Charles Kartman visited South Korea on 21 February 2001, he said, "South Korea and the United States are not showing any differences in connection with their North Korea policies,"[56] a reference to South Korea's engagement efforts.

Yet President Bush indicated he had serious concerns about Clinton administration policy towards North Korea. Bush officials expressed particular concern about the Agreed Framework in that the light water reactors were ill-suited to North Korea's decrepit power grid, inspections had yet to occur to confirm

North Korea's previous nuclear activity, and the heavy fuel oil supplied by the United States had nearly tripled in price since the deliveries began in 1995. Efforts soon grew in Congress and the White House to possibly renegotiate the Agreed Framework, particularly replacing the light water reactors with conventional coal-fired power plants. In February 2001, despite indications by the State Department that U.S. policy would not change, President Bush suspended U.S.-DPRK dialogue and ordered a complete review of U.S. Korea policy. On 7 March 2001, in meetings between Bush and Kim Dae Jung in Washington, both declared the discussion as "honest" and "frank," but it was clear the administration was less than enthusiastic about Kim's "sunshine policy." While Bush indicated support for continued North-South dialogue, he reaffirmed his "skepticism about the North Korean leader" and whether an agreement with North Korea can truly be verified. Bush also made it clear that the United States would not resume a dialogue with the DPRK in the near future.[57] After the meetings, Secretary of State Powell emphasized the administration's view of the North Korean threat.

> It is a threat; it's got a huge army poised on the border within artillery and rocket distance of South Korea. And the President forcefully made this point to President Kim Dae-Jung, and they still have weapons of mass destruction and missiles that can deliver those weapons of mass destruction. . . . So we'll be formulating our policies and, in due course, decide at what pace and when we engage. But there's no hurry.[58]

In June, after completing the policy review, President Bush announced that talks with North Korea could resume but with a broader agenda that would include "verifiable constraints on North Korea's missile programs and a ban on its missile exports, and a less threatening conventional military posture." Talks would allow North Korea to "demonstrate the seriousness of its desire for improved relations" but the United States was not going to reward "bad behavior." However, the United States would respond with increased aid and the lifting of sanctions if North Korea responded favorably and took "appropriate action."[59]

Despite the U.S. offer to restart talks, the more comprehensive nature and increased demands for verification were unacceptable to North Korean officials, in addition to the earlier statements where Bush expressed his doubt and loathing of the regime. Regarding the inclusion of North Korean conventional forces in the agenda, a DPRK spokesman noted, "we cannot construe this otherwise than an attempt of the U.S. to disarm [North Korea] through negotiations."[60] As a result, these efforts to restart the dialogue languished. Later in October 2001, when a South Korean reporter asked President Bush if his administration was to blame for the lack of dialogue, Bush bristled:

> I want to remind your readers that we offered to meet with Kim Chong-il. In June of this year we said, "At a time of your choosing, we'll be glad to send a representative to meet with you to discuss a variety of issues." And yet, he chooses not to meet with us, either. He won't meet with you [South Korea]; he won't meet with us, which kind of leads me to believe that perhaps he doesn't

want to meet. So he can blame it on who he wants, but it's up to him to make that decision.[61]

High-level talks between the United States and North Korea did not resume until October 2002.

The Second Nuclear Crisis

In October 2002, the United States confronted North Korea with evidence it had begun a second, clandestine nuclear program. This undertaking was a violation of three important agreements: the 1994 Agreed Framework; the 1992 Joint Denuclearization agreement between the North and South; and the Nuclear Nonproliferation Treaty. After initially denying the secret program, North Korea admitted to the violation but offered to put all issues on the table, including terminating the program if the U.S. would guarantee not to attack it, conclude a peace treaty with the DPRK, and accept North Korean sovereignty.[62]

Soon after the October announcement, a White House spokesman commented: "The president believes this is troubling, sobering news. We are seeking a peaceful resolution. This is best addressed through diplomatic channels at this point."[63] With attention focused on Iraq, U.S. officials wanted to avoid another crisis that might distract from their efforts to oust Saddam Hussein. Later, one Bush administration official quipped, "one rogue state crisis at a time."[64] The early Bush administration position was simple and straightforward; North Korea was in violation of agreements it had signed and there would be no dialogue or negotiations until it was back in compliance. In November 2002, the United States implemented its first compellent action by convincing KEDO members to suspend the delivery of heavy fuel oil that was specified under the Agreed Framework. According to the KEDO statement, "future shipments will depend on North Korea's concrete and credible actions to dismantle completely its highly enriched uranium program. In this light, other KEDO activities with North Korea will be reviewed."[65] The last sentence was a reference to the ongoing construction of the light water reactors, another lever the United States and its allies held over North Korea. Construction continued for another year but in November 2003, KEDO, under pressure from Washington, suspended this project as well.

In December, North Korea responded by announcing that it would restart operations at Yongbyon by disabling the seals and the surveillance equipment maintained by the IAEA on the five-megawatt reactor, the storage area for the 8,000 fuel rods, and the reprocessing plant. Access to the 8,000 fuel rods and restarting the reprocessing facility were most serious because this gave Pyongyang quick access to sufficient material for five to six nuclear weapons. North Korea ordered IAEA inspectors to leave the country and reloaded the five-megawatt reactor with new fuel rods. The two remaining inspectors, one Chinese and the other Lebanese, left North Korea on December 31st. According to an IAEA spokeswoman, "Now we virtually have no possibility to monitor North

Korea's nuclear activities nor to provide any assurances to the international community that they are not producing a nuclear weapon." [66] On 10 January 2003, North Korea made good on an earlier threat to leave the NPT and in February, restarted the five-megawatt reactor, with the apparent intent of restarting its nuclear weapons program.

In early January 2003, Bush policy shifted slightly in the direction of engagement by approving an unofficial set of talks between North Korean representatives and New Mexico Governor and former American representative to the UN Bill Richardson. President Bush approved the talks despite the objections of hardliners in the administration who pushed for further pressure and isolation to force North Korean compliance.[67] Bush also announced a proposition to end the crisis: "We expect this issue to be resolved peacefully, and we expect them to disarm. We expect them not to develop nuclear weapons. And if they so choose to do so—their choice—then I will reconsider whether or not we will start the bold initiative that I talked to Secretary Powell about."[68] The "bold initiative," a plan proposed by Secretary Powell the previous year, called for increased food aid, energy assistance, and a security guarantee after Pyongyang relinquished its nuclear weapons program.

From North Korea's vantage, the U.S. proposal required giving up all of its leverage before President Bush would "reconsider" the package. These were a serious set of "ifs" and a day later, Pyongyang rejected the proposal. In a statement by the DPRK Foreign Ministry,

> in essence, there is no change in the U.S. conditional stand that it would have dialogue with the D.P.R.K. only after it scraps its "nuclear program." It is clear that the U.S. talk about dialogue is nothing but a deceptive drama to mislead the world public opinion. It is the consistent stand of the D.P.R.K. to settle the issue on an equal footing through fair negotiations that may clear both sides of their concerns.[69]

Despite the effort to soften the U.S. position, the end goal remained the same. According to White House spokesman, Ari Fleischer, North Korea must dismantle its nuclear programs in a "verifiable" and "irreversible" manner. Moreover, "North Korea wants to take the world through its blackmail playbook, and we won't play. It's up to North Korea to come back into international compliance with their obligations."[70]

While some in the administration favored even greater engagement, many in the Defense Department along with Vice President Cheney favored a much tougher policy on North Korea. In their view, North Korea was an unsavory regime and the sooner it was gone, the better and the implications of this view were not lost on North Korea. Following September 11th, the official policy of the Bush administration was to remove regimes that threatened the U.S. with weapons of mass destruction before they become an imminent threat. The "axis of evil" speech had already outlined a target list; with Iraq gone in 2003, North Korea believed they might be next. Many in the administration eventually recognized there were no good military options in Korea. Seoul's proximity to the border made a military strike dangerous and given the uncertain location of all

of the DPRK's nuclear facilities, an air strike was unlikely to sufficiently eliminate the North's nuclear potential. Despite this awareness, Rumsfeld and Powell
remarked on several occasions that "all options remain on the table," a clear
threat to North Korea that military action might still be considered. As the
United States became increasingly bogged down in Iraq, the possibility of any
military action against North Korea appeared exceedingly unlikely, even to Pyongyang.

In lieu of a military strike, many in the Bush White House favored greater
economic and political isolation, another possible compellent threat. However,
moving in this direction was complicated by the larger political context.
Throughout the crisis, the Bush administration insisted this was a regional problem and should be addressed in a multilateral setting, either at the United Nations or through a dialogue with all the affected parties including South Korea,
China, Japan, and Russia. In contrast, the DPRK maintained this was largely an
issue between Pyongyang and Washington and should be settled in bilateral negotiations. Eventually, North Korea gave in and participated in the multilateral
format.

Yet, U.S. policy making became more difficult due to the multilateral nature of the problem. South Korean president Kim Dae Jung remained adamant in
continuing engagement with his "sunshine policy" and in December 2002, South
Koreans elected Roh Moo Hyun, a former human rights lawyer and political
newcomer who had campaigned vigorously on the need for dialogue in addressing the North Korea problem. President-elect Roh maintained, "It is our judgment that we cannot face or embrace war with North Korea. It is such a catastrophic result that I cannot even imagine. We have to handle the North-South
relations in such a way that we do not have to face such a situation."[71]

The Chinese also opposed a tough approach towards North Korea. Despite
its frustration with Pyongyang's lack of cooperation, Beijing feared sanctions
could provoke a North Korean backlash or cause the regime to collapse. The
implosion of the DPRK raised a host of disturbing possibilities including a flood
of refugees and the danger of civil unrest on their doorstep. While China was
adamant in its desire for North Korea to give up its nuclear weapons programs,
it would not coerce Pyongyang to achieve this goal. In the end, pressure from
South Korea and China had a moderating influence on Washington and at various times helped to soften U.S. policy.

U.S. policy remained essentially unchanged throughout the first half of
2003, despite Pyongyang's efforts to raise the stakes. In April 2003, the United
States agreed to meet with North Korea in separate rooms with China as a me-
diator. This arrangement accommodated Washington's refusal to hold bilateral
talks with Pyongyang's demand for direct contact with the United States. The
talks accomplished little but started a modest process of dialogue.

China continued to push for dialogue and in August 2003, hosted the first
round of truly multilateral meetings dubbed the Six-Party talks. In addition to
North Korea, the talks included South Korea, the United States, China, Japan,
and Russia. As most expected, these meetings produced little substantive change
in the negotiating positions of the players. Washington remained adamant that

Pyongyang must first end both nuclear weapons programs before any discussion of benefits would commence. Most alarming, at one session Pyongyang threatened to test a bomb and after presenting its demands for a nonaggression pact, maintained, "if our reasonable proposal is turned aside, we will judge that the U.S. does not intend to give up its attempt to stifle the D.P.R.K. by force. In this case the D.P.R.K. cannot dismantle its nuclear deterrent force but will have no option but to increase it."[72] However, North Korea heard clearly from all parties at the talks that it must relinquish its nuclear weapons program, an important statement of solidarity viewed as a small victory by the Bush administration. In the end, North Korea agreed to return for further talks.

In October while attending a meeting of the Asia-Pacific Economic Cooperation forum in Thailand, Bush added one relatively small carrot to the U.S. position. In response to Pyongyang's desire for a security treaty, he offered a five-nation security guarantee if North Korea agreed to U.S. demands for complete dismantling of its nuclear weapons programs. Bush declared that a formal treaty, submitted to the Senate for ratification and more legally binding, was "off the table," but that a more informal guarantee was possible. American allies and the State Department supported this offer but hardliners in the administration remained opposed to any effort to negotiate with the North.[73] The following month, Washington pressured KEDO members to halt construction of the light water reactor project. While the official announcement indicated this move was a suspension, according to one administration official, "our view is that we want an end to the program."[74]

A second round of Six-Party talks were held in February 2004 producing only slight progress. First, the tone of the negotiations improved with far less invective both during and after the talks, particularly by North Korea. Second, Pyongyang stated it would dismantle its nuclear program. To reach this goal, North Korea indicated it would be willing to freeze its nuclear program in a first phase in return for aid while subsequent steps towards dismantling were addressed. Seoul, Beijing, and Moscow agreed to provide energy aid while the freeze was in place. The United States and Japan stated they would provide no aid during the freeze but did support others doing so before North Korea ended its weapons programs, an important softening of the U.S. stance. Laying out these positions was the extent of the progress, and unfortunately, two other serious problems remained.

First, in the months following the U.S. allegations of a uranium-based program, North Korea had reversed its position, denying the existence of any such endeavor. At the meeting, North Korea continued to deny it possessed the uranium program, a claim increasingly difficult to deny given the information available from investigations into the nuclear activities of Pakistan and Libya. Second, North Korea asserted its desire to maintain a civilian nuclear energy program.[75] This request is particularly problematic since Washington has been insistent that North Korea no longer be able to restart a nuclear weapons program. A civilian nuclear program would retain the infrastructure for the DPRK to breakout of any agreement. Again, the meetings ended with little substantive progress but all participants agreed to meet for a third round of talks and to convene smaller working groups to address the various issues. Some in the administration expressed doubt regarding the smaller working group venue noting, "if the North Koreans are not willing to show flexibility at a high level, they're not going to let their munchkins do the job."[76]

In June 2004, a third round of Six-Party talks commenced, this time, accompanied by a new proposal from the Bush administration. The new plan, initially crafted by South Korea and modified by Washington, laid out a more detailed set of provisions with a timeline. First, North Korea must give a commitment to dismantle both of its nuclear programs. From this point, Pyongyang has three months to: provide full disclosure of its nuclear facilities and material; shut down its facilities; seal the buildings and equipment; and submit to international inspections. When the North commits to the plan, South Korea, China, Japan, and Russia will resume shipments of heavy fuel oil that were suspended in November 2002. Allowing North Korea to receive aid with only a freeze in place was an important shift in U.S. policy; in the past, it had insisted that no aid be given prior to the start of concrete steps to dismantling the nuclear program. The plan also called on the United States to provide a provisional security guarantee pledging no invasion or efforts to oust the Kim Jong Il regime, along with direct talks to lift many economic sanctions and provide long-term energy aid with programs to retrain the DPRK's nuclear scientists. Continued oil shipments and U.S.-DPRK talks are contingent upon North Korea meeting the three-month deadline and other subsequent deadlines for dismantling and shipping its nuclear equipment out of the country, similar to the process that occurred in Libya.[77] In justifying the new offer, James Kelly, chief U.S. negotiator said, "it was time to start getting specific," and another U.S. official argued complete, verifiable, irreversible dismantlement (CVID) remained the end goal though "C.V.I.D. is a way of describing the end of the process but not the only way of describing the process."[78]

Why did the Bush administration change its negotiating position and offer this proposal? The most important motivation was pressure from China, South Korea, and Japan. On several occasions, Beijing expressed publicly its doubts regarding the U.S. accusations of a uranium-based weapons program and stated that the lack of progress in negotiations was due largely to Washington's inflexibility.[79] South Korea and more recently, Japan have also maintained that North Korea was ready to deal if a sufficiently tempting bargain was put on the table. Moreover, South Korea, Japan, and China were working on their own diplomatic initiatives, raising the possibility that Washington would be left behind while they concluded separate deals to settle the issue.[80] While the State Department and some in the National Security Council long supported a more conciliatory approach, hardliners from the Pentagon and Vice President Cheney's office believed this was a chance to test North Korea intentions. In their view, North Korea is intent on keeping a nuclear weapons program, and would never give them up. Once North Korea rejected this proposal, as hardliners were convinced it would, Washington could motivate others in the region to take a tougher stance on North Korea. According to a senior Bush official, "our allies have been telling us that they think Kim Jong Il is ready for a test of his intentions so we are prepared to offer them a strategic choice. They may say no—and in that case they will have failed the test."[81]

The new proposal also addressed some of the problem areas the Bush administration saw in the Agreed Framework. First, the time line is much tighter for North Korean compliance. In the AF, North Korea had until the completion of "a significant portion of the LWR project" to accept full inspections. Given the delay of the LWR project, this would have postponed inspections for almost ten years. Second, the dismantling and removal of nuclear components and material will occur much earlier, eliminating the possibility of North Korea restarting its program as it did with the 8,000 fuel rods that were reprocessed. Many sources note that the AF was flawed because it did not require the removal of these rods. This is false; the AF did require the rods be disposed of "in a safe manner that does not involve reprocessing in the DPRK" and full inspections once the LWRs were finished. Prior to October 2002, the fuel rods were canned and monitored by inspectors, awaiting shipment to a third country. However, the construction of the LWRs did not proceed sufficiently far to trigger this portion of the Agreed Framework before the agreement disintegrated. Finally, should North Korea begin to renege on its commitments, the proposal calls for simultaneous termination of the benefits.[82]

Once again, the talks showed little progress though North Korea indicated it would consider the proposal. A month later, North Korean officials gave a tentative rejection. In July, the North Korean ambassador to the United Nations, Pak Gil Yon, visited Washington to participate in a seminar. Pak's visit required permission from the Bush administration, an indication of Washington's interest in maintaining some level of dialogue. At the seminar, Pak argued the chief cause of the stalemate was the Bush administration's "hostile policy" and that North Korea "will give up its nuclear program if conditions are met through ending the USA's hostile policy against it. Mistrust and misunderstandings are the biggest obstacles" between the United States and North Korea.[83] Regarding the U.S. proposal, Pak noted it showed some positive improvements, "however, we also found a lot of regrettable elements in it. We concluded it was a roadmap to disarm [North Korea] step by step."[84] North Korea balked at attending another round of talks and appeared to be waiting until after the November 2004 election in hopes it could deal with a possibly more flexible Kerry administration. On this score, Pyongyang was disappointed as Bush defeated Kerry in the election.

Assessing the Second Bush Administration

As with previous administrations, President Bush maintained a strong deterrence policy along with firm declaratory support for South Korea. Though the planned withdrawal and relocation of U.S. forces has stirred debate regarding the U.S. defense commitment, the impact on deterrence is likely to be minimal. North Korea gave no signs it was contemplating an attack, but at a few points, the United States sent planes to South Korea and Guam to ensure North Korea might not be tempted to take advantage of U.S. distractions in Iraq. Given North

Korea's intent, these measures were unnecessary for deterrence but may have been intended more as a demonstration of compellence. The Bush administration has moved slowly in the direction of engagement, but only on a limited agenda—how Pyongyang can fulfill its commitments. Little progress occurred and most estimates indicate that North Korea has reprocessed all of the 8,000 fuel rods for another 5-6 bombs. While several rounds of talks occurred, it became clear that engagement per se was not the key to resolving the impasse. Throughout, the United States insisted that North Korea must first take verifiable steps to demonstrate that it was moving irreversibly towards nuclear disarmament, a demand Pyongyang has so far resisted.

Unlike the Clinton administration, George W. Bush did not enter the White House with a crisis in the works in Korea. The U.S. deterrence policy was stable and Bush felt no pressing reason to attempt to engage or compel North Korea into any particular action. The Agreed Framework was in place though implementation was slow. Conservatives had long held contempt for the agreement, yet few offered any alternatives. The administration indicated it would continue the deliveries of heavy fuel oil but would work to see if the light water reactor project could be converted to conventional coal-fired power plants. It was also clear that other benefits promised in the Agreed Framework and not delivered by the Clinton administration—lifting of sanctions and moving towards normalizing relations—would not be delivered by this administration either. Bush officials also talked about speeding up the inspections provisions that had yet to kick in given the lengthy time North Korea had avoided a full accounting of its past nuclear activity. A pact on ballistic missiles was a possibility, but the administration was lukewarm on such a deal and reluctant to engage North Korea in general.

After conducting the early policy review, the United States indicated it was ready to resume talks but would be a much tougher negotiating partner than the previous administration. With a broader, more demanding agenda, North Korea could expect any new deal to require more concessions on their part, including some revisions to the Agreed Framework and more rigorous, immediate verification requirements. However, whatever goals may have been in mind, Washington did little to articulate them formally to North Korea or pursue any formal strategy—engage, offer incentives, pressure—to reach those goals. All North Korea received was a vague offer to dialogue at any time, any place. Yet, for Pyongyang, it seemed clear they would need to give up more and it was unclear what they would receive in return. In fact, they had yet to receive concessions they believed had already been agreed to in the unfulfilled provisions of the Agreed Framework. As a result, there was little progress on any front.

September 11th changed the landscape in Washington. The United States began its war on terrorism, first eliminating the Taliban regime in Afghanistan and then turning is attention to Iraq. In January 2002, Bush put Iraq and Saddam Hussein in the crosshairs of a U.S. policy that maintained the right to preempt "rogue states" who threatened the United States with nuclear, chemical, or biological weapons. Curious to many Korea experts, North Korea was included in the "axis of evil" list along with Iraq and Iran. North Korea had almost no involvement in terrorism since the 1980s and had no involvement with the terrorist groups from the Middle East. The North's inclusion was an effort to show that the administration was not singling out only Middle East, Muslim countries.[85]

For North Korea, inclusion in the "axis of evil" coupled with the Bush Doctrine—the right to preempt—was a serious threat to North Korean security. Yet, if the United States intended the threat to obtain some corresponding action from North Korea, it was poorly articulated. What was North Korea expected to do to comply? Was it to cease being a "rogue state"? If so, what exactly did that mean? Was North Korea expected to disarm? North Korea had no links to terrorist organizations, and as far as Washington knew, was complying with its part of the Agreed Framework. Was Pyongyang expected to give up its ballistic missile program based on this threat? Would the North receive no concessions for abandoning one of the few exports that earned the country hard currency? When the United States toppled the Hussein regime, the threat of preemption became even more ominous. In many respects, U.S. policy makers threatened North Korea with the ultimate punishment—the end of its regime—without providing a clear description of the behavior it found objectionable, what North Korea must do to comply or remove the threat, and a timeline by which compliance was expected. Given the lack of precise goals articulated by the administration, it was unclear whether it approached North Korea as a problem of deterrence or compellence. However, in either case, the administration did not clearly articulate its goals and what North Korea must do to comply. As a result, U.S. policy was all coercive threat and no incentives but without an end goal for the DPRK that would allow it to avoid the threatened punishment. From North Korea's vantage, if the United States was willing to carry out its threat of regime change, there appeared little it could do to avoid that fate. This atmosphere was hardly conducive to addressing the proliferation concerns long present in Korea. As North Korea expressed on numerous occasions, without a change in America's hostile policy, Pyongyang would need to maintain its nuclear and ballistic missile capability to deter the United States from following through on its threat to preempt "rogue states" before they become dangerous to U.S. security.

In October 2002, U.S. officials dropped the bombshell that North Korea was developing a clandestine, parallel nuclear program based on highly enriched uranium. The North Korean problem was now clearly one of compellence, stopping the uranium program that was already up and running, and after the Agreed Framework unraveled, stopping a second nuclear program. The White House was adamant that there would be no dialogue to bring North Korea back into compliance. Pyongyang must honor the three agreements it violated and only after, could talks begin.

In contrast to the first years, the Bush administration clearly articulated its goals to North Korea: complete, verifiable, irreversible dismantlement. However, as noted earlier, this goal had significant cost for North Korea in terms of its security and domestic political factors. While the goal was clear, the precise timeline that is helpful in a compellent situation was lacking. President Bush and others in the administration repeatedly said there was no crisis here and the matter would be handled through diplomacy. The administration was preoccupied with Iraq but conveyed no sense of urgency to generate support in Washington or to push North Korean compliance. In the meantime, North Korea continued to move its nuclear weapons and ballistic missile programs further forward.

Offering incentives to obtain North Korean compliance was out of the question. This would have been difficult for any administration. North Korean actions violated three agreements—the NPT, the Agreed Framework, and the North-South Joint Denuclearization Agreement—and offering incentives, at least soon after the intelligence became public would have been an odd response. However, as the matter dragged on and it might have been possible politically to show some flexibility by offering incentives to return to the agreements, the Bush administration remained convinced that to offer any incentives before North Korea abandoned its nuclear programs would be rewarding bad behavior. At times Washington indicated incentives would follow North Korean compliance, yet these offers were unclear, with little indication of what the incentives might actually be. U.S. credibility to deliver on any incentives was already low, making it difficult for Pyongyang to find these offers convincing. In June 2004 the United States and other members of the Six Party talks offered North Korea a more tangible package of incentives. Yet, the time line for compliance was tight, three months, and North Korea again must give up most of its leverage up front with great potential cost and little assurance it will receive the promised benefits.

The most immediate response to the October 2002 revelations was an effort to compel North Korea through punishment by convincing KEDO members to suspend the heavy fuel oil deliveries. The suspension announcement indicated the deliveries would resume when North Korea complied and threatened further actions—perhaps halting construction of the light water reactors—should the DPRK continue to be uncooperative. For a time, U.S. actions in Iraq also conveyed an implied threat; as part of the "axis of evil," North Korea may be next if it refused to give up its nuclear ambitions. Yet, U.S. statements were also contradictory. President Bush stated on several occasions that it had no intention to invade North Korea and wished to settle the dispute diplomatically. There was some speculation that the word "invade" was chosen purposefully to exclude an air strike to take out the North's nuclear facilities. However, on several occasions, Secretaries of Defense and State Rumsfeld and Powell remarked that "all options remain on the table," another veiled threat that military force was still under consideration. In the end, officials realized there were no good military options. Moreover, as the United States became increasingly occupied in Iraq, the likelihood of an attack became remote and the coercive impact of these implicit threats became less and less. Finally, the Bush administration mentioned taking the problem to the UN in an effort to mobilize international pressure and impose economic sanctions. Yet, there was little support from others in the region for placing this type of pressure on the North. Should the latest proposal fail to generate results, hardliners in Washington hope there will be greater support for taking this tougher approach.

In the end, the Bush administration faced the same difficult compellence problem Clinton did: reversing an action already begun that entailed significant cost for North Korea to give up. Yet, they were unwilling, for a time to offer any incentives, or later to offer sufficient incentives to affect the DPRK's cost-benefit calculations. Moreover, Bush was unwilling and unable to coerce North Korea through the use of threats, an approach that may be particularly counter-productive when dealing with a proliferation problem. A final resolution to the problem may be some time in coming.

Conclusion

For over fifteen years, U.S.-ROK efforts to compel North Korea to give up its nuclear weapons and ballistic missile programs have failed. Compellence theory provides some answers. Several items are necessary for successful compellence. First, the initiator must clearly articulate the action it wishes the target to cease and provide a timeline for compliance. Second, the initiator issues threats or offers benefits to convince the target state that compliance with the demands offers lesser costs and greater rewards than holding to its current course of action. Finally, the threats or benefits must be credible; the target must know that its compliance will end the threats or punishment and provide the incentives, especially if compliance is part of a long-term arrangement that might take several years to implement. A compellence success requires the target to take an action that stops or reverses something already done. This can be a very difficult task that may require a public submission to the demands of the initiator. Compliance may have serious security, economic, and political costs both at home and abroad that will require great effort to offset.

Throughout the nuclear crisis, U.S.-ROK demands were relatively clear: North Korea must fulfill its obligations as a signatory of the NPT to allow full, international inspections and to foreswear efforts to acquire nuclear weapons. During the Clinton years, there was some question of whether it would be sufficient to bring a halt to the plutonium program while having a certain amount of ambiguity regarding past activities and assuming North Korea might have one or two nuclear weapons. The second Bush administration has been consistent in articulating its goal of CVID: complete, verifiable, and irreversible dismantlement. There should be little doubt currently about Washington's goals.

North Korean compliance to U.S.-ROK demands required a significant reversal in DPRK policy, a change that would be very public and potentially very costly. Full compliance meant signing the safeguards agreement and allowing inspections, including intrusive, challenge inspections of nuclear facilities and military bases. In terms of domestic politics, the costs would also be high as conservatives, especially those in the military would oppose strenuously such an obvious retreat in the face of U.S.-ROK pressure and ready access to DPRK military facilities. Most importantly, Pyongyang would have still faced daunting security problems—a well-armed ROK army, a U.S.-ROK alliance, and the loss of its Cold War allies—a circumstance, particularly vexing in light of the Bush administration preemption doctrine, that posed the tremendous cost of ending the North Korean regime.

For all of these very heavy costs, U.S. policy did not provide sufficient incentives to offset these costs or provide a precise timeline linking compliance with benefits. At several points, North Korea faced the prospect of submitting and accepting all of the costs with little assurance of the benefits that would follow. Despite the criticism of the Clinton administration Agreed Framework, this agreement came closest to laying out such a precise plan but failed to deliver all of the provisions during the follow-on phases. These are important aspects of the credibility of compellence when using rewards. The target must know that the imposer will follow through with the promised benefits. To be certain, there were questions with DPRK sincerity beginning with discrepancies in the initial report to the IAEA and continuing with its work on a clandestine nuclear program that violated the Agreed Framework. Why give North Korea further incentives for fulfilling agreements it had already signed? Why submit to North Korean blackmail and appease this nasty regime? The problem here is that the anticipated benefits for Pyongyang never materialized and a lack of follow-through hurt U.S. credibility, pushing North Korea to seek other alternatives.

Moreover, threats, either to compel North Korea to relinquish its nuclear weapons or to buttress U.S. deterrence, were counterproductive. Given that much of North Korea's nuclear motivation was grounded in security concerns, threats only exacerbated its worries. Indeed, since North Korea feared the demise of the regime should it give up its deterrent, it is difficult to imagine what threats would have raised the costs to the level that would have compelled them to relinquish its nuclear ambitions. Moreover, as North Korea's economic decline reduced its military capability, the United States might have needed less threat to deter. As a result, a robust deterrence and compellence policy may appear increasingly threatening over time to the adversary. Only incentives, particularly those that addressed Pyongyang's security concerns, held out the possibility of offsetting the costs of their acquiescence to U.S.-ROK demands. This does not mean U.S. negotiators should come loaded with a multitude of incentives to give away. Negotiations should concede only what is necessary to achieve the U.S. goal of a nuclear-free North Korea. Yet, at many points, the United States seemed to have a poor understanding of the costs to the North Korean regime, both to its domestic political interests and security concerns, and did not adjust its policy accordingly.

Notes

1. Mazarr, *North Korea and the Bomb*, 39-41.

2. Oberdorfer, *The Two Koreas*, 193.

3. Oberdorfer, *The Two Koreas*, 194.

4. Oberdorfer, *The Two Koreas*, 194-195.

5. Joel S. Wit, Daniel B. Poneman, and Robert L. Gallucci, *Going Critical* (Washington, D.C.: Brookings Institution, 2004), 7.

6. Wit et al., *Going Critical*, 4.

7. Oberdorfer, *The Two Koreas*, 256.

8. Mazarr, *North Korea and the Bomb*, 51.

9. Wit et al., *Going Critical*, 7.

10. George H.W. Bush, "Remarks to the Korean National Assembly in Seoul," *Public Papers, 1992-1993*, Book I, 41.

11. Mazarr, *North Korea and the Bomb*, 77.

12. Wit, et al., *Going Critical*, 12.

13. Mazarr, *North Korea and the Bomb*, 98.

14. Oberdorfer, *The Two Koreas*, 268.

15. Mazarr, *North Korea and the Bomb*, 53.

16. See Wit et.al., *Going Critical*; Mazarr, *North Korea and the Bomb*, Victor Gilinsky, *Nuclear Blackmail: The 1994 U.S.-Democratic People's Republic of Korea Agreed Framework on North Korea's Nuclear Program* (Stanford: Stanford University Press); and Selig S. Harrison, *Korean Endgame* (Princeton: Princeton University Press, 2002).

17. Douglas Jehl, "U.S. Pressing Plan on Arms Pact To Force North Korea to Comply," *New York Times*, 12 March 1993, A13.

18. David E. Sanger, "Neighbors Differ on How to Chasten North Korea," *New York Times*, 31 March 1993, A9.

19. Douglas Jehl, "U.S. Offers to Meet With North Koreans on A-Arms Impasse," *New York Times*, 23 April 1993, A10.

20. Peter Grier, "World Tries Diplomacy to Slow North Korean Nuclear Program," *Christian Science Monitor*, 3 May 1993, A7.

21. Douglas Jehl, "U.S. Eases Stand on North Korea," *New York Times*, 27 May 1993, A6.

22. Mazarr, *North Korea and the Bomb*, 121.

23. Michael R. Gordon, "U.S. Goes to U.N. to Increase the Pressure on North Korea," *New York Times*, 22 March 1994, A1.

24. Michael R. Gordon, "U.S. Goes to U.N. to Increase the Pressure on North Korea," *New York Times*, 22 March 1994, A1.

25. R. Jeffrey Smith, "Perry Sharply Warns North Korea," *Washington Post*, 31 March 1994, A1.

26. Michael R. Gordon, "U.S. Will Urge U.N. to Plan Sanctions for North Korea," *New York Times*, 20 March 1994, A1.

27. R. Jeffrey Smith, "Perry Sharply Warns North Korea," *Washington Post*, 31 March 1994, A1.

28. Oberdorfer, *The Two Koreas*, 288.

29. Oberdorfer, *The Two Koreas*, 295.

30. Harrison, *Korean Endgame*, 122-123.

31. Ashton B. Carter and William J. Perry, *Preventive Defense* (Washington, D.C.: Brookings Institution, 1999), 129.

32. Carter and Perry, *Preventive Defense*, 129-131.

33. Drennan, "Nuclear Weapons and North Korea," 190.

34. Oberdorfer, *The Two Koreas*, 293.

35. Mazarr, *North Korea and the Bomb*, 115.

36. Charles Krauthammer, "North Korea's Coming Bomb: It's Clinton's Crisis, and He's Not Ready to Lead," *Washington Post*, 5 November 1993, A27.

37. Pat Towell, "Senators Grudgingly Accept Nuclear Agreement," *Congressional Quarterly*, 28 January 1995, 294; Nancy Mathis, "U.S.-N. Korea Must Comply before Aid Is Considered," *Houston Chronicle*, 13 June 1994, A9.

38. Barilleaux and Kim, "Clinton, Korea, and Presidential Diplomacy," 35-38.

39. Mazarr, *North Korea and the Bomb*, 138-139.

40. Drennan, "Nuclear Weapons and North Korea," 193.

41. Barilleaux and Kim, "Clinton, Korea, and Presidential Diplomacy," 33.

42. Mazarr, *North Korea and the Bomb*, 121-122.

43. Barilleaux and Kim, "Clinton, Korea, and Presidential Diplomacy," 33.

44. "U.S. urged to compensate for DPRK's loss of electricity," *KCNA*, 6 June 2001. See also, Leon V. Sigal, "North Korea is No Iraq: Pyongyang's Negotiating Strategy," *Nautilus Institute-Northeast Asia Peace and Security Network, Special Report*, 23 December 2002, <nautilus.org/for a/security/0227A_Siga.html>.

45. Harrison, *Korean Endgame*, 227.

46. David E. Sanger, "Trade Sanctions On North Korea Are Eased By U.S.," *New York Times*, 18 September 1999, A1.

47. O'Hanlon and Mochizuki, *Crisis on the Korean Peninsula*, 13.

48. David E. Sanger, "Trade Sanctions on North Korea Are Eased By U.S.," *New York Times*, 18 September 1999, A1.

49. William J. Perry, "Review of United States Policy Toward North Korea: Findings and Recommendations," U.S. Department of State, 12 October 1999, <www.state.gov> (June 2001).

50. Uk Heo and Chong-Min Hyun, "The 'Sunshine' Policy Revisited: An Analysis of South Korea's Policy toward North Korea," in Uk Heo and Shale A. Horowitz, eds., *Conflict in Asia* (Westport, CT: Praeger, 2003), 89-103.

51. Harrison, *Korean Endgame*, 228.

52. Harrison, *Korean Endgame*, 228-229.

53. Selig S. Harrison, "Time to Leave Korea?" *Foreign Affairs* 80, no. 2 (March/April 2001): 64.

54. See Terence Roehrig, "Assessing North Korean Behavior: The June 2000 Summit, the Bush Administration, and Beyond," in *Conflict in Asia: Korea, China-Taiwan, and India-Pakistan*, eds. Uk Heo and Shale Horowitz (Westport, CT: Praeger Press, 2003), 73-74.

55. Howard W. French, "Signs of Uneasiness in Seoul Over Change at White House," *New York Times*, 19 February 2001, A7.

56. Shin Yong-bae, "Korea, U.S. Reaffirm N.K. Reactor Project," *Korea Herald*, 21 February 2001.

57. George W. Bush, "Remarks Prior to Discussions With President Kim Dae Jung of South Korea and an Exchange with Reporters, *Public Papers, 2001*, Book I, 201-204; David E. Sanger, "Bush Tells Seoul Talks With North Won't Resume Now," *New York Times*, 8 March 2001, A1, A6.

58. Colin Powell, "Remarks by Secretary of State Colin Powell," 7 March 2001, <www.whitehouse.gov/news/releases/2001/03/20010307-3.html>.

59. Jane Perlez, "U.S. Will Restart Wide Negotiations With North Korea," *New York Times*, 7 June 2001, A1, A9.

60. Howard W. French, "North Korea Rebuffs U.S. on Troop Talks," *New York Times*, 19 June 2001, A3, and Michael R. Gordon, "U.S. Toughens Terms for North Korea Talks," *New York Times*, 3 July 2001, A7.

61. George W. Bush, "Interview with Asian Editors," *Public Papers*, Book II, 16 October 2001, 1250.

62. Doug Struck, "Nuclear Program Not Negotiable, U.S. Told N. Korea," *Washington Post*, 20 October 2002, A18.

63. Peter Slevin and Glenn Kessler, "Bush Plans Diplomacy on N. Korea's Arms Effort," *Washington Post*, 18 October 2002, A1.

64. Howard French and David Sanger, "North Korea to Reactivate an Idled Nuclear Reactor," *New York Times*, 13 December 2002, A16.

65. "KEDO Executive Board Meeting Concludes," 14 November 2003, <www.kedo.org> (August 2004).

66. James Brooke, "South Opposes Pressuring North Korea, Which Hints It Will Scrap Nuclear Pact," *New York Times*, 1 January 1993, A9.

67. Steven W. Weisman, "Solving North Korean Puzzle: U.S. Tries Carrot Again, Saving Stick for Iraq," *New York Times*, 15 January 2003, A11.

68. David E. Sanger, "Bush Says Shift by North Korea Could Bring Aid," *New York Times*, 15 January 2003, A1, A11.

69. Howard W. French, "2 Koreas Agree to Resume Talks on Nuclear Crisis," *New York Times*, 16 January 2003, A12.

70. Howard W. French, "Aides Declare U.S. 'Willing to Talk' in Korea Dispute," *New York Times*, 14 January 2003, A1, A12.

71. Howard W. French, "South Korea's President-Elect Rejects Use of Force Against North Korea," *New York Times*, 17 January 2003, A11.

72. Joseph Kahn, "Korea Arms Talks Close With Plans For a New Round," *New York Times*, 30 August 2003, A1, A3.

73. David E. Sanger, "Bush Proposes a Security Accord for North Korea," *New York Times*, 20 October 2003, A1, A7.

74. David E. Sanger, "U.S. Persuades Allies to Halt North Korean Atom Project," *New York Times*, 5 November 2003, A12.

75. Joseph Kahn, "U.S. and North Korea Agree to More Talks," *New York Times*, 29 February 2004, A6.

76. Steven R. Weisman, "Lasting Discord Clouds Talks on North Korean Nuclear Arms," *New York Times*, 14 March 2004, A10.

77. David E. Sanger, "U.S. to Offer Incentives to Sway North Korea in Nuclear Talks," *New York Times*, 23 June 2004, A3.

78. Joseph Kahn, "North Korea is Studying Softer Stance From the U.S.," *New York Times*, 24 June 2004, A13.

79. See Joseph Kahn, "Chinese Aide Says U.S. Is Obstacle in Korean Talks," *New York Times*, 2 September 2003, A3, and Joseph Kahn and Susan Chira, "Chinese Official Challenges U.S. Stance on North Korea," *New York Times*, 9 June 2004, A12.

80. David E. Sanger, "About-Face on North Korea: Allies Helped," *New York Times*, 24 June 2004, A13.

81. David E. Sanger, "U.S. to Offer Incentives to Sway North Korea in Nuclear Talks," *New York Times*, 23 June 2004, A3.

82. Sanger, "U.S. to Offer Incentives to Sway North Korea in Nuclear Talks," A3.

83. Glenn Kessler, "North Korean U.N. Envoy Visits Capitol Hill," *Washington Post*, 21 July 2004, A15.

84. Kessler, "North Korean U.N. Envoy Visits Capitol Hill," A15.

85. For a discussion of this, see Bruce Cumings, Ervand Abrahamian, and Moshe Ma'oz, *Inventing the Axis of Evil: The Truth about North Korea, Iran, and Syria* (New York: New Press, 2004).

CONCLUSION

For more than fifty years, the United States has provided a security commitment for South Korea to deter an attack by the North alone or in earlier years, at the instigation and support of either China or the Soviet Union. The U.S.-ROK relationship is one of extended deterrence where a defender attempts to deter an attack on a protégé instead of primary deterrence where a state deters an attack against itself. The U.S. security guarantee has been given in response to a situation in deterrence theory known as general deterrence where a defender perceives a threat from a challenger who possesses the military capability and intent to initiate hostilities should the situation arise.[1] The two adversaries are antagonistic and suspicious, but neither side is actively contemplating an attack, the conditions for immediate deterrence. Integrating the concept of extended deterrence with general deterrence produces a specific type of deterrence situation Paul Huth labeled extended general deterrence.[2] Here, a defender provides a security guarantee for an ally under circumstances in which there is no imminent threat of attack by the challenger.

A security guarantee under conditions of extended general deterrence has two components. First, the defender and protégé undertake the necessary military preparations and are attentive to the military balance in the region. Second, the defender issues general warnings of determination to respond should the challenger consider attacking. These warnings should be credible; the adversary must believe that the defender will remain committed to the protégé in a crisis. The United States has utilized a variety of techniques to demonstrate the credibility of its commitment to South Korea including a security treaty and regular declarations of support, economic and military aid, the presence of U.S. conventional forces, and, prior to 1991, the deployment of nuclear weapons. These military and policy preparations are designed to deter the challenger from escalating the adversarial relationship into a crisis that might lead to war and to provide for the South's defense if deterrence fails.

Most of the U.S.-ROK security relationship has been a situation of extended general deterrence though on a few occasions, officials in Seoul and Washington believed the situation might be shifting to a crisis of immediate deterrence. Two occasions occurred, the first in 1968 when North Korea seized the USS *Pueblo*

231

and the second in 1979 when the Carter administration feared Pyongyang might exploit the confusion following the assassination of South Korean President Park Chung Hee.

Since the late 1980s, the U.S.-ROK alliance confronted another manifestation of the North Korean threat: nuclear weapons, ballistic missiles, and the dangers of weapons proliferation. The fear was not so much that North Korea would use the weapons offensively but that it would sell them to undesirable regimes or terrorists and possibly prompt others in the region to acquire a nuclear capability. As a result, policy makers attempted to engage and utilize the strategy of compellence to persuade North Korea to halt its nuclear weapons and ballistic missile programs. Under various administrations, compellence has utilized threats and incentives along with efforts to engage in hopes of convincing Pyongyang to give up its nuclear aspirations. While deterrence has been successful in keeping the peace in the region, U.S.-ROK efforts to compel the dismantling of North Korean weapons programs to date has not.

What are the lessons to be learned from this case study of the U.S. security commitment to South Korea? The following pages turn to the conclusions that can be drawn regarding deterrence theory, using compellence to obtain nonproliferation goals, and Korean security more broadly.

Threat Assessment: "Three versus One"

Source of the Threat

Deterrence theory often assumes the threat is largely a single entity. In Korea, the threat has been much more diverse, at various times consisting of three challenger states—North Korea, the Soviet Union, and China. Three challenger states made the assessment of intent and military capability, the two criteria used here to assess the threat in Korea, more difficult. The presence of three challenger states creates three sets of intent to monitor. Similarly, calculations of the challenger's military capability and the regional military balance become more complicated when the challenger consists of multiple states.

The presence of three challengers also raises questions about their relationship to each other. Does an extended deterrence relationship exist among them? If so, who is a defender and who is a protégé, and how might these roles affect their objectives and relations with each other? In Korea prior to the end of the Cold War, two of the three states—the Soviet Union and China—were defenders of their protégé, North Korea. However, other relationships are possible such as only one defender and two protégés where both compete for protection or one of the protégés might have a different value to the defender creating the possibility that the defender would sacrifice the one of lesser value depending on the circumstances. Another possibility is having no big power defender with three challengers linked together in some way, perhaps through an alliance of some type.

Though the Korean case does not include these scenarios, it does indicate how the "challenger" can be a more complex and varied entity for the defender's deterrence policy.

Change over time further complicates the challenger configuration in Korea. Throughout the 1950s, U.S. policy makers viewed the "monolithic communist threat" directed by Moscow and Beijing as the primary danger in Korea. North Korea was not the major concern; the DPRK was preoccupied with rebuilding its war-torn economy and with internal political struggles. During most of the 1960s, the Chinese threat was paramount but complemented by a resurgent North Korea, which had completed much of its rebuilding process. By the late 1960s, and continuing to the present, U.S. policy makers perceived the North, no longer a surrogate for Chinese and Soviet policy, to be most likely to threaten the status quo in Korea. The Soviet Union and China had developed better relations with the United States, and the objectives of all three major powers had become similar; no one wished to disturb the peace and stability of the region. At the end of the Cold War, China retained its security treaty with Pyongyang, but made clear it would not support any offensive action on the part of the North. Moscow went one step farther renegotiating the old treaty and removing any provision that committed it to the defense of North Korea.

The changing threat configuration also affected American assessments of the military balance in the region. First, as the Soviet and Chinese threat in Korea receded, U.S. troops were less likely to clash with their forces, reducing the danger of a nuclear conflict. The U.S. security guarantee no longer put the United States homeland at risk, a factor that made it easier to issue credible deterrence threats. When North Korea began to pursue nuclear weapons and improve its ballistic missile capability, this issue came back in play.

Second, by the 1960s, U.S leaders believed that it was unlikely either the Soviets or Chinese would join the North in an assault against the South. Perhaps later in a conflict begun by the DPRK, the Soviets and/or Chinese might be drawn in but, hopefully, the prospects of that occurring were also low. With the likelihood of facing only DPRK forces, U.S. and ROK planners were more confident that forces in place could defeat an attack. Thus, the United States felt less pressure to maintain a rapid deployment capability; U.S. and ROK forces in Korea could hold their own against a DPRK attack. However, North Korean planners always knew the United States could bring substantial reinforcements to the region. As ROK military capabilities increased, U.S. assistance in the actual defense of South Korea became less important, allowing various administrations to withdraw troops from Korea. Consequently, U.S. forces, though still formidable, became less crucial for the defense of South Korea and more of a signal of American support and a tripwire for U.S. involvement. The North's conventional military buildup evoked caution, but the United States and South Korea were optimistic about their ability to defeat a North Korean attack.

Finally, a complex challenger configuration also affects the challengers' goals and the degree to which those goals conflict with those of the defender and protégé. In an extended general deterrence situation, it is likely that the challenger wishes to alter the status quo should favorable circumstances arise. Yet, if the challenger consists of three states, the willingness to risk a confrontation may vary. In particular, if the challenger consists of states with their own deterrence relationship, there may be differences in their goals related to their roles as defender and protégé.

In Korea, all three challengers, at some point, desired a united Korea under Pyongyang's control. However, there was a fundamental difference in their willingness to achieve that goal and over time, support for this objective waned. For the Soviets and Chinese, a united communist Korea would have expanded their ideological influence and provided greater security for their borders. Yet, while Moscow and Beijing would have welcomed achieving these goals, they were unwilling to take significant risks to do so. As time passed, both became more in favor of the status quo. North Korea saw unification differently. For Pyongyang, unification was a drive for national unity, exacerbated by an intense desire for statehood following the Japanese occupation from 1910 to 1945. The North was much less willing to maintain the status quo and demonstrated so on 25 June 1950. Stalin supported the invasion but only if it was done quickly, preempting any U.S. involvement. In the years since, North Korea showed many times it was willing to take substantially more risks than Moscow and Beijing.

Maintenance of the status quo may affect one of the challengers more than the others. Indeed, a challenger more inclined to alter the status quo is demonstrating a willingness to implement a compellent strategy. While the challengers may have a *deterrence* relationship, as challengers, only some may be willing to implement a compellent strategy that challenges the existing order. North Korea was willing to risk compellent actions, particularly in 1967 and 1968 because its goals included a strong desire to alter the status quo. Despite the diminished Soviet and Chinese threat, the remaining challenger state, North Korea, was willing to risk a great deal to achieve its goals, while Moscow and Beijing were more risk averse in their support of Pyongyang. Thus, multiple challengers may have different goals and levels of risk acceptance to achieve those goals, a factor that further complicates threat assessment.

Threat assessment is a crucial starting point for the implementation of extended deterrence. Multiple challengers complicated this process in Korea. In Europe, the other major Cold War deterrence commitment, there was really only one target state for U.S. policy to influence while in Korea there were three target states. While this complicated the security guarantee, U.S. policy makers also had opportunities to utilize the differing goals and objectives of the challengers, as well as relations among the challengers, to enhance deterrence. As a result, the challenger configuration had an important impact on the U.S. policy response in Korea.

Influencing the Challenger

Deterrence theory and its assumption of rationality instructs policy makers to influence the cost-benefit calculations of the challenger so that the costs of an attack increase sufficiently to outweigh the benefits. In Europe, this task entailed modifying the cost-benefit calculations of one nation, the Soviet Union, while in Korea there were three sets of calculations to influence. What if each of the three target states has a different cost-benefit calculus? Are three distinct security policies necessary to deter each of the challenging states? Deterrence theory does not provide much insight here, generally assuming the challenger to be a single entity. Yet the Korean case demonstrates that more complicated threat arrangements are possible. What should policy makers do in these more complex situations?

Two approaches seem most feasible. First, the defender can attempt to fashion one deterrence policy that "fits all." The defender may assume that each challenger has a similar cost-benefit calculus or that despite different cost-benefit calculations, the policy contains sufficient measures to dissuade all three. It is also possible that multiple challenging states may divide into two or any number of groups with similar cost-benefit calculations. Thus, with three challenger states (A, B, and C), two of these (A and B) may have a similar cost-benefit calculus but differ from C. In this case, the defender may only need to plan for two, (A and B) and (C). For example, the defender may believe nuclear threats are necessary to deter two of the challengers, while a mutual defense treaty would be sufficient and less provocative to deter the third, but have little effect on the other two. In this approach, the defender may conclude the security treaty and issue nuclear threats to all three challengers to ensure a consistent policy that influences the calculations of all, despite the possible "overkill" for the third challenger.

A second and more complicated approach would be a deterrence policy that addresses the cost-benefit calculations of each target state. For example, nuclear threats might be communicated to challengers A and B while the defender might threaten challenger C with economic sanctions. While this approach allows the defender to put at risk what each challenger values most, there is also a potential for the defender to send mixed signals about its resolve to defend its ally.

Which of these approaches should a defender use to construct a deterrence policy for multiple challengers that may have different cost-benefit calculations? U.S. policy in Korea provides some tentative answers to this question.

In the 1950s, U.S. policy reflected its assessment that the Soviet Union and China were the chief threats in Korea and focused a larger share of its deterrence efforts on these two challengers. The Greater Sanctions agreement put the Soviets and Chinese on notice that they were likely targets, possibly with nuclear weapons, should another war begin in Korea. This declaration was later supported by the policy of massive retaliation that declared the United States would respond to communist provocations at a time and place of its choosing. Though Washington did not disregard the North, American deterrence efforts aimed more heavily at the Soviet Union and China. After the late 1960s, U.S. deterrence policy focused more directly on the DPRK and though the Soviets and Chinese remained in U.S. deterrence calculations, they were not the primary target states of U.S. policy.

While the threat configuration has changed since 1953, U.S. deterrence policy did not change significantly. There were some adjustments as the threat shifted such as an end to specific nuclear threats against the Soviet Union and China concerning Korea, and a decrease of U.S. ground troops. Yet, in large measure, U.S. policy remained relatively consistent. American declarations of support continued, the mutual defense treaty remained in force, and a significant contingent of U.S. air and ground forces stayed in Korea along with nuclear weapons. Thus, while the threat configuration evolved, U.S. deterrence policy changed only marginally from its original form when the Soviets and Chinese were believed the major threat in Korea.

The consistency of U.S. policy is due, in part, to two factors. First, though the threat configuration changed, U.S. leaders always perceived at least one of these challenging states to be willing to risk the costs of an assault on South Korea. Despite the diminished Soviet and Chinese threat, the North remained a potent adversary that required the maintenance of a vigorous U.S. defense commitment. Even though President Carter proposed a major alteration to that commitment, in the end, even he opted for a more cautious approach to U.S. policy because the North remained a serious threat to peace and stability.

Second, U.S. policy was consistent and cautious because most American officials believed it was a successful policy that had maintained the peace for a number of years. As time passed, U.S. officials believed American involvement was essential in preventing another war. So long as the United States remained committed to the ROK's security and maintained its defense commitment, particularly the presence of ground troops, American leaders believed the communist challengers would not test the U.S. security guarantee. In effect, U.S. leaders were subscribing to the adage "if it ain't broke, don't fix it."

The danger in maintaining the same package of threats within the deterrence policy, especially as members of the challenger configuration "drop out," is that what may have been necessary to deter others, particularly if they are major powers, may no longer be needed. In fact, these measures may be overly provocative and threatening to the remaining challenger(s). Consider the use of nuclear threats in Korea. While the Soviets and Chinese were major concerns, the integration of nuclear weapons into U.S.-ROK force planning and the inclusion of South Korea under the nuclear umbrella provided another level of cost should either of these countries initiate or actively support a war in the region. Once North Korea is the chief concern, nuclear threats were the "over kill" Peter Hayes referred to that gravely threatened Pyongyang's security, and, in turn, pushed it to acquire its own nuclear deterrent. In later years, even U.S. conventional preparations may have been far more than was necessary to deter North Korea and was based on an exaggerated threat assessment of the adversary. Insufficient attention to the changing threat configuration and continued use of nuclear threats, possibly when unnecessary, caused other problems.

The Korean case indicates that the presence of a more complex set of challenger states may not make a major difference in a defender's deterrence policy. So long as there is at least one serious threat among the challenging states, the defender's deterrence policy may not change that much, producing both positive and negative results. At the outset of the defense commitment, the defender may account for the differences in a more complex set of challenger states. Yet, as the challenger configuration changes over time, the defender is less likely to alter its deterrence policy if a significant threat remains and the policy appears to be successful.

There are two multiple challenger scenarios that do not occur in the Korean case and both point to the need for attention to changes in the challenger configuration. First, suppose again that there are three challenger states, however, as time passes, each of the challenger states "drops out," one by one, as a serious threat to the protégé. "Dropping out" may or may not entail a reduction of the challenger's military capability, but it would certainly include a decrease in hostile intent to the point that the defender concludes an attack is unlikely from any of the challengers. Deterrence would no longer be the appropriate policy and there would be an opportunity for improved relations among all of the states in the deterrence relationship. In fact, this scenario resembles the conceptualization of a single entity challenger since all three states apparently have a similar cost-benefit calculus that values improved relations over confrontation. Continued adherence to a firm deterrence policy would be counterproductive to better relations and a more lasting peace in the region.

The second scenario is largely the opposite of the previous one. Suppose the deterrence situation begins with a relatively small challenger C as the main threat with challengers A and B only reluctant supporters of C. However, after a time, A and B become more hostile and/or their military capabilities increase to the point where the defender and protégé consider all three to be a serious threat in the region. In this instance, the existing deterrence policy may be insufficient. The defender may need to bolster deterrence efforts with particular attention given to the regional military balance. In addition, the defender and protégé need to examine whether the more threatening posture of A and B are an indication of a drift from general to immediate deterrence. In that case, the defender and protégé may need to make more specific counterthreats to reinforce deterrence. Again, the defender will need to consider the possibility that each challenger may have a different cost-benefit calculus when moving to augment its deterrence policy and tailor the threats accordingly.

Indirect Restraint

Though U.S. deterrence policy did not appear to change a great deal, the shifting challenger configuration did provide another route to enhance its security commitment. By the 1970s, U.S. relations with the Chinese had improved considerably and Nixon's trip in 1972 capped a three-year effort to improve ties with China after years of strained relations. Chinese leaders hoped that contacts with the United States would aid their efforts at economic modernization and provide some leverage in their rivalry with the Soviets.

    Improved Sino-American relations placed pressure on the Soviet Union to
maintain good ties with the United States, as Moscow did not wish to become
isolated by a U.S.-Chinese friendship. In addition, the Soviets had their own
economic problems—sagging agricultural production and outmoded technology—that improved relations with the United States helped address. Arms control agreements and trade deals under Nixon's policy of detente further expanded
American contacts with the Soviets. With Sino-Soviet relations remaining tense,
neither of these nations wanted to complicate matters with a war in Korea.
Moreover, as both nations turned their attention towards economic development,
they had a greater stake in maintaining political and economic stability in Northeast Asia. Though both continued to support the North as defenders in their deterrence relationship, they did not wish to jeopardize their relations with the
United States or upset regional stability with a North Korean invasion. These
developments provided an opportunity for the United States: as Chinese and
Soviet ties with the United States improved, American leaders used these circumstances as leverage to support U.S. interests in Korea. These ties held out the
possibility that the Soviet Union and China would try to restrain North Korean
actions. Though it is not clear the degree to which the Soviets or Chinese could
exert influence over the North, the possibility was there. The Carter administration believed that China could "help prevent any military moves by North Korea" and "reduce existing tensions in that peninsula." Thus, "one of the more
interesting benefits of having China as a friend would be its ability to quietly
sway some . . . with whom it was very difficult for us to communicate."[3] These
conditions provided the opportunity for the United States to use its relations with
two of the challengers to contain the third. However, the end of the Cold War
and the tense relations that followed between North Korea, Russia, and China,
another manifestation of a shifting challenger configuration, lessened the ability
to use indirect restraint in this deterrence situation.
    These circumstances in the Korean case have broader implications for ex-
tended deterrence theory. If multiple challenging states have different cost-
benefit calculations, the defender can manipulate these and the policy goals of
one or more of the challengers to restrain the other more menacing challenging
state(s). Consider three challenger states A, B, and C where A and B are most
likely, in the defender's perception, to initiate an attack against the protégé.
Challenger C is a defender for A and B and would come to their aid if attacked.
However, the defender believes that C does not support A and B attacking first
and involving C in a war with the defender. The defender may conclude that
challenger C is lacking in military capability to initiate an attack, possesses significant military capability but not the intent to strike, or that C has neither the
military capability nor the intention of initiating an assault. In this scenario, the
defender will need to implement a deterrence policy that addresses directly the
cost-benefit calculations of A and B—declarations and deployments targeted
specifically towards the policy makers in A and B. The defender has already
concluded that C is unlikely to start a war so little direct effort is needed to deter
C. However, the defender may be able to motivate C to aid in restraining A and

B by demonstrating that an attack by A and/or B could lead to a direct confrontation between the defender and C. U.S. forces in Korea were crucial here. Recall Major General Singlaub's assessment of the removal of U.S. ground forces:

> The Chinese Communists and the Russians do not want to become directly engaged with the United States, which they would be if Kim Il Sung took off on an adventure to the south for the reunification of Korea. And they are now acting in a way that restrains him from doing this. If that force were removed, that element of constraint would also be removed—that is, Kim could launch his attack without fear of running into U.S. ground forces. And if he got in trouble, . . . there would be far less reluctance on the part of Communist China or the Soviet Union to help him "pull his chestnuts out of the fire."[4]

Not wishing a war with the defender, challenger C would use whatever influence it had over A and B to restrain them from attacking. However, this assumes that challenger C has significant influence over the actions of A and B. It is certainly possible that C's influence is minimal making this strategy less helpful in restraining A and B.

The defender might also offer positive incentives to enlist C's help in restraining A and B. These inducements could include concessions in other areas of conflict between the defender and challenger C such as trade or arms control agreements. In any case, the defender would be enhancing the chances of a deterrence success by enlisting the aid of one challenger to restrain the others. States A and B may also be aware of C's reluctance to fight the defender, raising questions about C's credibility. A and B may be reluctant to challenge the defender given the possibility that C might not come to its aid should the war go badly for them.

Beginning with the first Bush administration and throughout the nuclear crisis, the United States had similar hopes for Chinese pressure in its efforts to compel North Korea to give up its nuclear weapons programs. However, Washington often failed to see the declining influence of Beijing and the level of mistrust between these old allies. North Korean leaders believe China deserted it in favor of better relations with South Korea and it cannot depend on Beijing to support its interests. While China has been equally frustrated with Pyongyang's recalcitrance in concluding a nuclear weapons deal, Beijing has been instrumental in bringing North Korea to the bargaining table. Washington has often praised China for its efforts to start a dialogue, especially the Six Party talks and broker an agreement on this difficult issue. Yet, in the end, there have been limits to what Chinese pressure has been able to achieve.

It is interesting to note that "indirect restraint" can cut in both directions. Throughout the deterrence relationship with South Korea, U.S. leaders were often cognizant of the possibility that a conflict in Korea could lead to a direct confrontation with China and/or the Soviet Union. This awareness moderated U.S. actions to a degree. In the past few years, China was also able to exercise some restraint on U.S. policy. At many points during the Clinton and Bush II administrations, U.S. leaders came close to moving toward tighter economic sanctions on North Korea. Yet each time, China opposed sanctions believing this type of pressure was counterproductive. Beijing has also pushed for continued dialogue when the United States was reluctant to engage the North and argued for greater flexibility in U.S. policy. Chinese influence was likely one factor in Washington signing on to the proposal presented to North Korea during the June 2004 Six Party talks. While the United States has insisted the North Korea problem be handled in a multilateral forum that has also imposed some restraint on U.S. policy.

A Previous War

Another important aspect of the deterrence situation in Korea is the existence of a previous "hot" war between the adversaries. From 1950 to 1953, the United States and South Korea fought against North Korea and China, assumed by the Truman administration to be surrogates of the Soviet Union. Though no formal deterrence commitment was in place, the war acted somewhat like a deterrence failure. Not all deterrence situations, either immediate or general, experience a failure resulting in war and this brings a different dynamic to the situation helping to clarify elements of the situation, intent and capability, for example, that are uncertain in other deterrence situations. The Korean War had an important impact on U.S. assessments of North Korean, Chinese, and Soviet intent. Moreover, the war also had an important impact on the credibility of the U.S. commitment. Thus, the Korean War helped to set an important baseline for American assessments of the intent of the challenger and the degree to which the United States would support its security guarantee to South Korea.

The Intent of the Challenger

Intent is a difficult quality to assess with any degree of certainty and leaders often look to previous behavior as indicators. For U.S. policy makers, the war helped simplify those calculations; the North Korean attack was a reminder that Pyongyang placed a high value on reunification and might be willing to take big risks to achieve that goal. Though U.S. leaders believed the attack had occurred due to Soviet instigation, the war formed an important benchmark for assessing DPRK intentions as well. The passage of time diluted these judgments. However, North Korean behavior—DMZ incidents, tunneling activities, belligerent rhetoric, the *Pueblo* seizure, submarine incursions, missile tests, and the violation of the Agreed Framework—reminded American leaders of the North's uncertain intentions. In addition, U.S. concerns for North Korea's rationality added to U.S.-ROK fears. Consequently, the war, especially in the early decades of the confrontation helped, correctly or not, to simplify American assessments of North Korean intent.

The Korean War also affected American assessments of Chinese and Soviet intent. Before the war, the Truman administration concluded that the Soviet Union controlled North Korean foreign policy making the use of armed force unlikely since Moscow would not do so unless as part of a general war. Instead, Truman believed that Moscow and Pyongyang were most likely to use tactics of subversion and infiltration. The war convinced Truman that the Soviets were willing to use military force, though through a surrogate, to achieve reunification of the Koreas and subsequent Chinese intervention indicated Beijing's willingness to join the effort to advance Communism throughout the peninsula. More recent evidence indicates that China intervened to prevent a hostile, non-communist Korea on its border rather than for any aggressive intention to unify the peninsula under communist control. While this may be correct, it was *not* the U.S. perception for many years. Until the Nixon administration, the United States continued to interpret Chinese rhetoric and support for "wars of national liberation" as evidence of Beijing's aggressive intent.[5]

When relations warmed between Washington and Moscow and Beijing, the "lessons" of the Korean War were less relevant and U.S. policy makers concluded that these two adversaries were no longer interested in upsetting the status quo in Korea. However, concerning Pyongyang, the war remained a reminder to U.S. leaders that, absent a strong U.S. security guarantee and the presence of U.S. ground troops, Pyongyang might be tempted to use force as it had in 1950. However, most U.S.-ROK assessments indicated that deterrence was strong and North Korea was unlikely to test the alliance.

In recent years, the existence of a previous war became a greater issue but this time from the challenger's perspective. The Korean War ended without a formal peace treaty, only with an armistice that halted the hostilities and technically, a state of war continues to exist on the Korean peninsula. When North Korea felt relatively assured of the support of its allies, the continued absence of a peace treaty was less crucial to Pyongyang. Since the end of the Cold War and the retreat of Soviet/Russian and Chinese support, North Korea has often called for abolishing the armistice and negotiating a permanent peace treaty. This legacy of the Korean War apparently worries Pyongyang as, in their view, the armistice is an indication of continuing hostility with the United States and South Korea.

Enhancing the Defender's Credibility

The Korean War also affected the credibility of the American security commitment. Though the war occurred before a formal U.S. defense guarantee was in place, U.S. intervention was an important statement of American willingness to support South Korea. The United States had come to the ROK's aid in 1950 *without* a security guarantee in place. With a formal defense commitment beginning in 1954, it seemed likely that the United States would certainly come to South Korea's defense again should the North attack. Furthermore, U.S. policy makers believed the war occurred largely due to poor signaling of American interests in the region. U.S. intervention helped to buttress American efforts after 1953 to demonstrate its commitment to South Korea.

Threat Assessment and Credibility: Theoretical Implications

These circumstances point to some larger theoretical considerations concerning threat assessment and credibility. A deterrence situation preceded by armed conflict is likely to have some different dynamics from one that was not, having an important effect on threat assessments. At least one of the adversaries, possibly both, will believe their interests were challenged in a dramatic and violent manner. If there is no significant lessening of the animosity felt by the two sides, the war will likely act as a lesson that it might happen again. Moreover, the war may have been the result of a previous hostile relationship where deterrence had failed. If the war did not produce decisive results, a situation of general deterrence will follow. However, this time, the relationship will be more tense possibly lying somewhere between general and immediate deterrence where military preparations will be more extensive because the adversary has already shown a willingness to push the situation beyond general deterrence. For both sides, the war will be a strong influence on policy decisions. In particular, the war will add a great deal of "perceived certainty" to the threat assessments of the defender and protégé. The term "perceived certainty" is used here purposely. The war does not assure that the defender's assessments are correct. However, the defender will *perceive* that its assessment of hostile intent is more certain. If there had been doubt about the challenger's willingness to risk the costs of war, those doubts were erased. A previous war may also clarify the military doctrines, tactics, and preparations of the challenger. In all these instances, the defender will be implementing—or reimplementing if deterrence had failed—a security guarantee with greater perceived certainty than would have been the case without the war.

A previous war may also be important for the message it sends to the challenger. Whether there was a formal commitment or not, the defender has indicated its willingness to support the protégé even if the costs are high, and the defender will have a less difficult time demonstrating its resolve in the next crisis. Though the challenger may still choose to confront the defender's commitment, the previous war will send a message to the challenger that the costs of that confrontation may be high.

How does the defender react in this postwar deterrence environment? Will the defender conclude that it need not establish a vigorous defense posture—fewer troops, less economic aid, etc.—since the war demonstrated its willingness to protect the protégé? The answer to this question is still dependent on the defender's threat assessments. If a significant relaxation of tension between the adversaries follows the war, the defender may conclude that the war and other minimal actions are sufficient to establish a credible defense commitment. However, if a serious threat remains, it is likely the defender will not be content with a token defense commitment. Military planners often assume a worst-case scenario, and are unlikely to underestimate the challenger. Instead, they will undertake numerous measures to implement a credible deterrence guarantee.

Finally, during the previous war, the defender lost lives and resources in aiding the protégé. Regardless of the interests and stakes that prompted the defender to fight that conflict, the defender has now invested dearly in the future of the protégé. Pulling away from the security guarantee may be more difficult; if it was worth the effort to defend the region before, why not now? The defender may decide later that the security guarantee is no longer worth the cost. Certainly, Vietnam demonstrated that there are limits to what a defender may be willing to pay to protect a protégé. Yet, having fought in a previous war to protect an ally, and succeeding, creates some serious motivation to continue the defense commitment.

Evolving Interests

Another condition necessary for the establishment of a deterrence commitment is the presence of important national interests for the defender. If the defender has little or no interests present, there is no reason to implement a security guarantee. However, this guarantee relies on more than simply a list of interests. Interests are closely linked to assessments of what is at stake. National leaders evaluate their interests—goals and objectives—and the stakes—the costs and benefits of pursuing those goals and objectives. In the game of poker, players always wish to win the hand they are playing. However, their desire to win is much greater if the amount they could win or lose—the stakes—is higher. The greater the stakes, the more likely a defender will choose to risk implementing a security guarantee.

American perceptions of the interests and stakes in Korea have evolved considerably since 1945. These interests began primarily as a result of the Cold War when security and political concerns dominated the foreign policy agenda. The chief security interests were containment of Soviet expansion, maintenance of peace and stability in the region, and protection of Japan. Political interests included American credibility as an ally, and safeguarding the prestige of the UN.

Before 1950, the Truman administration concluded that America did have interests in Korea but the stakes were not sufficiently high nor the threat great enough to warrant establishing a formal defense commitment. On 25 June 1950, U.S. assessments of the stakes in Korea changed dramatically. The North's invasion, most certainly instigated by the Soviets in the view of the Truman administration, put Korea at the forefront of U.S.-Soviet confrontation. Korea was now inextricably linked to America's global containment policy; failure to respond in Korea could have grave repercussions elsewhere and to U.S. credibility in general. As a result, Truman decided that the United States had to respond to the North Korean invasion with a massive commitment of military power.

After the Korean War, the Eisenhower administration concluded "in the Far East, we retain our vital interests in Korea," and "we are prepared to meet any renewal of armed aggression,"[6] a far more definitive statement of U.S. interests than had preceded the conflict. Soviet expansion, whether direct or through surrogate states, had to stop. Moreover, if Soviet expansion continued it might encourage expansion elsewhere and eventually, "would have gone on to imperil the United States."[7] Coupled with the apparent willingness of the Soviets and their proxies to use force to expand the global reach of Communism, the United States implemented a formal defense commitment to protect South Korea. In particular, American leaders believed that the Korean War resulted from a U.S. failure to adequately signal its interest in South Korea. A formal guarantee would make that commitment explicit. Until U.S. relations with the Soviet Union and China improved in the late 1960s, American interests remained enmeshed in Cold War confrontation. However, these interests evolved as the Cold War climate changed. Economic growth in South Korea and Asia more generally created another set of economic interests for the United States.

Most worrisome initially was the danger to U.S. interests in Japan. To U.S. leaders, the industrial and military potential of this country made it crucial that it not fall under Soviet influence. Furthermore, a Soviet-dominated Korea would endanger Japanese security; as the adage went, "Korea was a dagger pointed at the heart of Japan." Even if no one threatened Japan, the proximity of three communist states—Korea, China, and the Soviet Union—might intimidate Japan to the point that it sought an accommodation with them.

Another concern for U.S. policy makers more generally was American credibility. Despite not having a formal security guarantee before the Korean War, U.S. leaders believed there was a commitment of sorts, albeit a poorly articulated one. During a news conference, Eisenhower stated "the Korean conflict started because of our failing to make clear that we would defend this small nation, which had just started, in a pinch."[8] The North Korean invasion challenged that perceived "commitment," putting America's reputation and credibility on the line. Moreover, the stakes were much higher now because Korea affected America's global containment strategy. Damage to U.S. credibility in Korea could affect American commitments elsewhere; if the United States did not take a strong stand in Korea, could other American allies count on the United States?

By the 1970s, American interests had evolved as U.S. relations with the Chinese and Soviets improved. No longer linked to the U.S. global strategy of containment, Korea became more of a regional concern. The United States was no less interested in preventing a war in Korea, but now the concern was for regional peace and stability in East Asia.

Most interesting here is the connection between stakes and threat perceptions. When the threat included the Soviet Union and China, the stakes were higher since U.S. interests in Korea affected America's global containment policy. When the Soviet and Chinese threat receded, American assessments of the stakes in Korea changed with an apparent reduction of the stakes for U.S. political and security interests; Korea was less connected to U.S. interests elsewhere.

Thus, when the threat changed in June 1950, the stakes for U.S. interests changed. Similarly, when the threat changed again in the late 1960s, the stakes shifted once more for U.S. political and security interests.

The post-Cold War period and the North's efforts to develop nuclear weapons and ballistic missiles brought another change to U.S. interests in the region. North Korea's weapons programs now hit other U.S. concerns—weapons proliferation and terrorism—that had both a regional and global dimension. Within the region, many worried that a North Korean nuclear weapons capability might prompt Japan and South Korea to acquire a comparable program. This would also hurt U.S. efforts globally to stem the spread of nuclear weapons, not only to so-called rogue states, but after September 11th, to terrorist groups as well. Pyongyang's missile sales to countries in the Middle East had already had an impact on regional security there; Washington did not wish to see this compounded by further sales along with nuclear weapons or material, a fear supported by the revelations of Pakistani-DPRK cooperation.

The improvement of North Korea's ballistic missile program, as demonstrated by its 1998 launch over Japan, raised an important security interest for the United States—sometime in the future, North Korea might be able to directly threaten the United States homeland with a nuclear warhead. Some have argued North Korea simply wants its own deterrent capability given its increasing isolation, loss of major-power allies, and perceived security threats. While this capability may be several years away, DPRK leaders know it could never use its missiles and nuclear weapons in an offensive manner or to threaten the United States and its allies. Others have maintained this capability complicates U.S.-ROK strategy in that North Korea could move against the South and warn the United States not to respond or it will hit the U.S. homeland. Proponents of this view maintain this as an important argument for acquiring a national missile defense system. Despite the logic of the latter argument, it seems highly implausible because it assumes North Korea might conclude it could defeat the U.S.-ROK forces already in place. However, as argued earlier, this is a highly risky proposition, and North Korean leaders know it. While Washington's response might be restrained, Seoul's would not and the result would be the same—the end of the North Korean regime. Thus, while North Korea's nuclear weapons and ballistic missile programs are serious security concerns, especially the dangers of material or technology being sold, the direct threat of the DPRK to use these weapons against the United States is less probable.

Yet, despite these concerns and the apparent progress of the North's nuclear weapons program in the past two years, the Bush administration's response has been curious at best in its efforts to downplay any crisis atmosphere and take a slow, cautious approach to addressing the problem. Based on the professed interests and stakes, the administration has not pursued a vigorous strategy of compellence either by engaging the North and offering incentives, or pursuing coercive tactics to "isolate and squeeze" the North.[9] To be sure, the administration has been preoccupied with Iraq, and officials, at times, have noted candidly that there are few good options, especially military ones in dealing with North

Korea. It is a different situation than Iraq and requires a different response. Yet, to do very little with the clock ticking as North Korea's nuclear program grows is a serious mismatch of policy with interests. The administration has been correct in its assessment of "few good options" but to not have pursued a more vigorous engagement option has been counterproductive.

The apparent strategy here has been an effort to manipulate North Korea's perception of U.S. interests and stakes to discourage Pyongyang from seeking greater concessions by downplaying U.S. urgency. However, this approach has backfired in its efforts to coax North Korean flexibility indicating the key is not Pyongyang's perception of U.S. interests but rather North Korea's views of its own interests. While U.S. efforts may have had some impact on North Korean negotiating behavior, regime survival along with Pyongyang's economic and security threats are more important to understanding and influencing its behavior.

Throughout the fifty plus years of the U.S.-ROK alliance, there has been considerable change in American assessments of the threat and the interests and stakes in the region. This demonstrates an important point: a long-term defense commitment rests on a fluid interplay of threat perception and interest/stakes assessment. Regional interests and stakes are not determined in isolation and may be closely linked to the defender's threat perception.

Growing Power of the Protégé

South Korea's economic growth along with its increasing military capabilities and international political standing is another important aspect of the evolution of U.S. interests. When the United States began its security guarantee, the South Korean economy was in difficult straits. Syngman Rhee's inept economic leadership gave few indications that South Korea would soon escape its economic paralysis. In the 1960s, under President Park, South Korea began its dramatic rise, consistently racking up GNP growth rates of 8-10 percent annually and becoming one of the leading economic forces in East Asia. The growth of ROK economic strength had several important effects on U.S. interests.

First, ROK prosperity included a significant growth in U.S.-ROK economic and trade ties. South Korea also developed important economic bonds with others in the region including Japan and the members of ASEAN, and with the European Union. The Nixon and Carter administrations saw this growth primarily in the context of burden sharing so that Seoul could provide for a greater portion of its own defense. By the 1980s, the Reagan administration recognized that South Korea's economic links to the United States and to others in Asia and Europe had also raised the stakes for U.S. economic interests. The ROK was an important component of East Asia's economic vitality that could not be disrupted by a war in Korea. This remains the case today, even to the point where trade competition is part of alliance discussions, another sign of ROK economic growth.

Second, prosperity gave South Korea the resources—military and economic—to contribute to other U.S. foreign policy goals. In the 1960s, Seoul sent two combat divisions to Vietnam. Later, the South aided American efforts in the 1990-91 Persian Gulf War and took the lead in providing the light water reactors for North Korea under the terms of the Agreed Framework. Most recently, South Korea deployed engineering and medical units along with 3,000 combat troops to support U.S. operations in Iraq, a difficult move for the Roh Moo Hyun government given the fervent domestic opposition to the war. These actions demonstrate to the United States the value of having a strong economic and military ally capable of projecting that strength to other areas.

South Korea's growth in economic and military power has had an important impact on deterrence and credibility. There is always a concern that in a crisis, the defender will not act to defend its ally. However, there is little doubt that the protégé would defend itself. South Korea's effective use of U.S. aid and subsequent growth of military capability helped to shift the deterrence situation from one that relied less on the American security guarantee—and its inherent credibility problem—and more on South Korea's primary deterrent capacity to defend itself. In fact, throughout much of the U.S. security commitment, American leaders were quite confident that if the DPRK attacked, but without substantial outside help, ROK forces were capable of defeating such an attack. As noted earlier, the success of deterrence in Korea cannot, with absolute certainty, be attributed to the presence of the U.S. security commitment. However, given South Korea's increasing military and economic prowess, it is interesting to speculate if deterrence has succeeded in the last 10 to 15 years, as much on ROK capabilities as it has on the U.S security commitment.

The increase in ROK military capabilities affected another aspect of deterrence in Korea. Despite being given a credible threat of retaliation, a challenger may attack regardless if it perceives the costs of that retaliation to be within acceptable levels. Furthermore, if deterrence relies on deterrence by defense, the challenger may conclude that the worst that can happen is a military repulse and return to the status quo. If the status quo is particularly intolerable, the challenger may be willing to take that risk. The growth of ROK military capabilities enhanced the aspect of deterrence by punishment. Indeed, ROK participation in Vietnam demonstrated that it possessed a well-trained military whose use outside Korea did not affect the regional military balance. If the North began a war and lost, South Korea might now be less likely to stop at the 38th parallel and be content with a restoration of the old borders. Another North Korean military disaster would provide an opportunity to eliminate the DPRK regime, a chance that Seoul might find difficult to pass up. For the North, this possibility is a serious threat of punishment and one that likely would enter North Korean calculations. A second failed attempt to reunify by force could bring an end to the North Korean regime.

Finally, ROK prosperity vindicated U.S. policy in the region, and American economic and political values. South Korean development occurred with the help of U.S. economic and military aid, under the protection of the U.S. security guarantee, and with a capitalist economic system advocated by Washington. In 1987, the South began a transition to democracy after years of authoritarian rule, spurred in part by its economic success. All of these demonstrated the success of U.S. policy in Korea.

South Korea's success on several fronts displays the protégé's ability to affect the defender's assessment of interests and stakes. Theorists have recognized the importance of economic aid and trade ties as a signaling device to adversaries; greater economic linkage is a way for the defender to signal its interests in the region. Yet, the protégé's own actions can also affect these economic ties and affect the defender's interest assessments. The deterrence relationship may have begun with the protégé being very dependent on the defender for economic and military support. In 1960, President Eisenhower lamented that the Korean people "have got to find a way to work themselves up the economic ladder" and that "he feared getting a bunch of mendicants on our hands." Moreover, "our aid is spread thin and it is difficult to justify disproportionate aid to a little jut on the continent of Asia."[10] As time passes, the protégé may be able to achieve a significant level of economic growth and development to increase its value to the defender. The protégé's value, namely the stakes, could take two forms. The protégé may be more valuable because of the benefits the defender receives from the economic growth of the protégé. However, it may also be the case that the protégé's value has increased because the costs of losing the protégé to an adversary have increased as well. An increase in the protégé's value is not a given, even in a long-term deterrence relationship. For example, the years of the Rhee administration along with U.S. aid to Chiang Kai-shek and to various leaders in Vietnam, demonstrate military and economic aid can be squandered, landing primarily in the pockets of government officials. If the assistance is used wisely and economic growth occurs, the protégé can push the context of the deterrence relationship from dependence on the defender to one that may resemble more of a partnership. The defender and protégé are not economic or military equals, but the growth can increase the value and power of the protégé within the deterrence relationship. If the relationship moves more towards a partnership, it may encourage closer ties and enhance the defender's commitment.

Despite the potential for enhancing deterrence, a protégé's economic development may be a double-edged sword for several reasons. First, economic growth by itself may not be sufficient to ensure the defender's commitment. A defender could use the economic growth as a justification for reducing or ending its defense commitment. If the interests are few and the stakes have waned, the defender may conclude its security guarantee is less necessary. In Korea, both the Nixon and Carter administrations viewed ROK economic progress as an opportunity to restructure the defense commitment and expected Seoul to assume a greater share of its defense. Though neither administration intended to terminate the U.S. security guarantee, ROK economic growth could have provided the justification for ending the commitment.

Second, while ROK economic and military growth has enhanced deterrence in several ways, it has also helped to complicate security relations. Throughout the U.S.-ROK alliance, the key American interest has been the maintenance of peace and stability on the peninsula. Yet, on some occasions, the United States was concerned about restraining the options of its ally, South Korea. Already in 1948, American leaders feared Rhee's pronouncements to unify the peninsula by force and refused to provide him with weapons that had offensive capabilities. During the 1970s and 1980s, the United States convinced the ROK not to retaliate against DPRK provocations, and in the mid-1970s, the Ford administration pressured the South to abandon its drive for a nuclear weapons capability. As the ROK obtained greater economic and military might, it acquired increased ability for independent action. Dominance of the Combined Forces Command also helped the United States to restrain ROK military options since an American was in overall command of all armed forces on the peninsula. In the current nuclear dispute with Pyongyang, South Korea might again be tempted to consider a nuclear option, an action that might spur a nuclear arms race in the East Asia. In the meantime, the U.S. presence in Korea continues to help convince Seoul that nuclear weapons are unnecessary for its security, as well as assure the North that the United States will not turn the South loose to pursue this option on its own. Consequently, the U.S. presence helps to assure regional stability by deterring the North and restraining the South.

Finally, the protégé's economic growth may give it greater strength and bargaining power within the deterrence relationship, creating more of partnership, but also generating some conflict within the alliance. Through the years, South Korea became less dependent on U.S. economic and military support and became a power in its own right with its own interests. This has forced greater cooperation within the alliance and more consideration of Seoul's interests and policy preferences. This has been clearly been evident as South Korea's desire for greater engagement with the North has helped to moderate U.S. policy. Moreover, the United States and South Korea have had different assessments of the severity of the North Korean nuclear threat and its implications for security in the region. However, if the goals and objectives of the protégé and defender differ, the protégé may push for greater consideration of its objectives. The result may be more friction and discord within the alliance. South Korean development and divergent policy views indicate that the alliance is struggling and in need of some attention in the areas of the U.S.-ROK Combined Forces Command, U.S. troop deployments and less tangible items such as greater U.S. understanding and consideration of ROK goals and objectives. Yet, while this dialogue between Washington and Seoul needs to occur to adjust to South Korea's new position within the alliance, it should be no surprise that an alliance of this duration will have disagreements and growing pains.

ROK economic growth did not lead to a lessening of the U.S. commitment and its prosperity alone was not most important. Rather, it was the *linkage* of ROK growth with U.S. interests that was crucial here. Since the 1970s, ROK security became increasingly connected to U.S. economic interests in the region with stakes that are high. For trade and investment with the United States, ROK economic ties with Japan and others in the region, and the overall stability of Northeast Asia, the security of South Korea became linked to the regional economic structure and U.S. interests within that structure. A war in Korea would have serious economic repercussions for the United States, Japan, and other American allies. Thus, an important dimension of U.S. interests in South Korea has been their *connectedness* to other American interests. During the first two decades, these interests were primarily linked through security and political concerns, and later, shifted more towards economic interests. The North Korean nuclear weapons dispute has rekindled concern for security issues, indicating again that interests have shifted, but the stakes have remained high.

The Korean case indicates that the protégé can have an important effect on the interest assessments of the defender. The economic value of Europe was obvious to U.S. leaders establishing the NATO commitment. Initially, Korea seemed to have very little potential, and was valuable primarily as it related to Japanese security. Deterrence theory assumes that interests remain relatively fixed, a judgment reinforced by the NATO case. Yet, in Korea, U.S. interest assessments were much more dynamic, particularly those affected by South Korea's phenomenal economic growth. By increasing its value to the defender, the protégé can encourage the defender to continue its security guarantee. Enhancing deterrence does not need to come only from the defender, and the actions of the protégé can help to "nudge" the defender into a credible security guarantee.

U.S. Extended Deterrence Policy

Since 1953, the United States has implemented a security guarantee to protect South Korea. A crucial component of this policy is the degree to which U.S. efforts created a credible guarantee based on three criteria—capability, cost, and resolve.[11] The defender must persuade the challenger that it possesses the military capability to carry out its threats and that these threats, if implemented, would raise the costs of an attack to an unacceptable level for the challenger. Finally, the defender must demonstrate the resolve to carry out the threats should deterrence fail.

There is little doubt that the United States possessed the first two requirements for a credible security guarantee, capability and cost. In addition to forces on the peninsula, American ground units stationed in Japan and Hawaii and air and naval units present throughout the Pacific provided a great deal of military power the United States could bring to a conflict in Korea. While much of this capability was not positioned on the peninsula, those forces retained crucial links to the U.S. presence there. Joint exercises such as Team Spirit and Foal Eagle that utilized U.S. forces in other locales demonstrated rapid deployment capabilities to Korea. More recently, U.S. efforts in Operations Desert Storm and Iraqi Freedom, along with the deployment of additional combat aircraft to bases in

South Korea and Guam further indicated the capacity to send large contingents of troops to trouble spots in a timely manner.

The ability to rapidly deploy U.S. forces to Korea has an important impact on capability and cost in extended deterrence situations. From time to time, situations of general deterrence may move towards a crisis of immediate deterrence where a defender believes a decision to attack its protégé is under consideration. The defender and protégé must then respond by issuing specific counterthreats to deter the possibility of attack. The defender's preparations undertaken in the context of general deterrence must have the capability to project counterthreats, should a movement towards a crisis occur. This capability can be present either in the region or redeployed in sufficient time to affect the cost-benefit calculations of the challenger. The U.S. capability to redeploy forces to Korea is an important component for meeting the requirements of capability and cost in a situation of extended general deterrence.

The most elusive requirement of a credible security guarantee is resolve. The United States has been relatively consistent in its intent to implement a credible extended deterrence policy though the means to implement that policy have changed. Washington has not always assured ROK leaders to their satisfaction, but it has, apparently, been adequate to help dissuade North Korea from attacking.

The United States has utilized four approaches in its security guarantee to demonstrate its resolve to protect the South. First, since 1954, Washington and Seoul have maintained an alliance, formalized with a mutual security treaty, and U.S. administrations, from Eisenhower to George W. Bush, have buttressed the American commitment with other public declarations of support. Even during the policy adjustments of the Nixon and Carter administrations, rhetoric for South Korea was supportive and neither president proposed scrapping the treaty. Thus, U.S. declarations of support have been consistent and an important baseline for the security guarantee.

Second, the United States has provided large amounts of economic and military aid to bolster the declarative support of the treaty. U.S. aid has acted as a signaling device of American interests in the region and helped the ROK build its own economic and military capabilities. Washington helped begin the process but South Korean economic policy and determination built a formidable economic strength that increased its value to the United States through economic integration with Asia and the construction of a strong military.

Third, the U.S. commitment has included the stationing of troops in Korea as both a tripwire and contribution to the active defense of the peninsula should deterrence fail. Though the numbers have changed, the presence of American troops has been consistent proof of U.S. willingness to accept the risks and costs of protecting the ROK. In a North Korean assault, American troops would be engaged early in the invasion and would surely incur casualties. The deaths of U.S. military personnel would raise the stakes so that the United States could not desert South Korea because it would mean deserting Americans. Credibility is further enhanced by U.S. dominance of the Combined Forces Command structure. After playing such a dominant role in planning and operations, it would be difficult to envision the United States not fulfilling its defense commitment to South Korea.

U.S. conventional forces have been an important signal of American resolve to a challenger composed of three states, sending a different message to each of the three challengers. For North Korea, U.S. forces signaled American determination to remain in Korea during a crisis and its willingness to shoulder the costs of defending the ROK should deterrence fail. Pyongyang faced a high probability that it would confront American military power should it attempt to disrupt the status quo.

For the Soviets and Chinese, the signal conveyed by U.S. conventional forces had a slightly different message. As defenders of the DPRK, Moscow and Beijing risked being dragged in should war break out in Korea. Even if they were not the instigators, the United States might conclude that the two defenders encouraged a North Korean attack, an assessment similar to that made during the Korean War. In either case, a war in Korea meant the Chinese or Soviets might become engaged with U.S. forces, including the possible use of nuclear weapons. Thus, U.S. troops helped to restrain two of the challengers—the Soviet Union and China, the big power defenders—from challenging the status quo and encouraged them to restrain the third challenger, their protégé, from taking any action that might disrupt the peace.

The final approach used by American policy makers to enhance the credibility of deterrence was the deployment of tactical nuclear weapons in Korea. The initial deployments, begun in 1958 to offset Soviet and Chinese arms shipments that violated the 1953 Korean War armistice, were intended to enhance deterrence by defense and U.S.-ROK war fighting capabilities. By the 1970s, U.S. policy makers made an explicit connection between tactical and strategic nuclear weapons, noting, "any conventional attack could set off a chain of nuclear escalation, the consequences of which would be incalculable."[12] In addition, U.S. leaders maintained that the South remained under the U.S. nuclear umbrella. In 1991, the Bush administration removed all U.S. nuclear weapons from South Korea in an effort to coax the North to fulfill inspections mandated under the North-South nuclear accord, and as part of a larger effort, particularly as the Soviet Union was disintegrating, to reign in tactical nuclear weapons. It was becoming increasingly evident that nuclear weapons based in Korea were unnecessary for deterrence.

On balance, the United States constructed a credible and consistent extended deterrence policy, though the structure of that policy varied. U.S. officials provided firm declaratory support, military and economic aid, and demonstrated American resolve by stationing ground troops and tactical nuclear weapons in Korea. U.S. forces, both conventional and nuclear, have been crucial to ensure U.S. involvement and provide for the defense of South Korea should deterrence fail.

Recall from earlier in this chapter the importance of a "multiple challenger" to a defender's threat assessment and deterrence policy. When Pyongyang's big power defenders were the main threat, U.S. policy utilized threats to use nuclear weapons against these defenders, and placed ground forces in harm's way to act as a tripwire for U.S. involvement and as a component for the active defense of the ROK. When U.S. policy makers believed that the North's big power defenders were no longer interested in provoking a war—in fact, Soviet and Chinese relations had deteriorated markedly, and over time, North Korean faith in their defenders diminished—U.S. leaders altered the means of U.S. deterrence policy. The Nixon administration removed an infantry division because it was no longer necessary to defend the South when Soviet and Chinese forces were unlikely to instigate a conflict. In addition, nuclear threats against Moscow and Beijing diminished and, in 1991, the U.S. withdrew all tactical nuclear weapons from South Korea. Thus, the alterations to U.S. deterrence policy were not so much a lessening of the security commitment as it was a recalibrating of that policy to a different threat configuration.

As the big power defenders of the challenger diminish as a threat, the defender of the protégé can lessen its role in the security relationship without jeopardizing deterrence. When this occurs, the role of economic and military aid becomes a more important component of the defender's deterrence policy. If facing all three challengers, especially when any number of these is a global adversary, there is little likelihood that the protégé can assume the major share of its defense burdens. Yet, if the global powers are no longer the chief threat, the protégé may be able to assume a significant share of its own defense. At this point, the aid provided by the defender may be a significant part of the deterrence policy, not only a signal of the defender's interests.

The Proliferation Problem

For most of the U.S.-ROK security relationship, the chief concern was a conventional attack and destabilization efforts from the North. Now nuclear weapons and the ability to deliver them over long distances greatly complicates security relations in the region. Pyongyang now likely possesses the most destructive weapons on the planet. While North Korean motives for acquiring these weapons is uncertain, their presence in this region of the world is disconcerting at best. In addition, a North Korean nuclear weapons program may prod others to pursue a similar capability and there is great concern that North Korea might sell these weapons to other states or terrorist organizations.

This is not the first time North Korean military capabilities have made worrisome improvements. In the 1970s, Pyongyang embarked on a major increase in its conventional forces, and there was little Washington and Seoul could do other than reexamine their own defense posture. While a nuclear capability is far different, in some respects, there are similarities. Deterrence could not stop the acquisitions and U.S.-ROK officials could only reaffirm their defense commitment in an effort to continue deterring and containing the North.

The goal of deterrence is to prevent an action from taking place. In pursuit of nonproliferation, this is a difficult task. It is problematic to draw lines and know when they are crossed, short of when a state actually tests the weapon and by then, it may be too late; following through on a deterrence threat could bring nuclear retaliation. Moreover, if a challenger is seeking a nuclear or ballistic missile capability for what it sees as serious security reasons, deterrence threats may worsen the insecurity making the challenger more determined to acquire the weapons. The proliferator can be punished after the fact with sanctions or possibly a military strike but it is not a certainty that this will solve the problem.

By the early 1990s, North Korea had already done substantial work on these weapons programs. The ballistic missile program made considerable progress having produced the Nodong medium-range missile and intelligence showed work on developing two new nuclear reactors and a reprocessing facility. With the North balking at inspections, U.S.-ROK leaders believed there was a serious program Pyongyang was attempting to hide.

As a result, the proliferation problem of North Korea was clearly a compellence problem. It was no longer a matter of preventing an action from occurring and instead was the dilemma of halting an endeavor already underway, a far more difficult task. With a developed program in both areas, convincing Pyongyang to give them up and absorb the related costs has been difficult for several reasons. First, if the primary motive for beginning the programs was security concerns, North Korea would be unlikely to easily abandon the programs unless their security worries had changed. Given the state of the DPRK economy, the sale of ballistic missiles and the hard currency they earn also impact its economic security. Second, North Korea had already expended considerable money and effort on these projects. To end the programs would have required a significant justification. Third, there are military and civilian bureaucracies that have interests in maintaining the program and would fight strenuously to keep it. Currently, the United States is insisting that North Korea give up its right to develop peaceful nuclear energy, a further cost to an agreement. Finally, abandoning the nuclear and ballistic missile programs would have been a very public capitulation to the demands of its adversaries. This would have been even more evident with the intrusive inspection arrangements that will be required if it relinquished its programs.

For all of these reasons, there were huge costs for North Korea to surrender its nuclear weapons and ballistic missile programs. This is especially so in the area of security; if North Korean leaders view these weapons as vital to security, giving them up carries a high price tag. To convince North Korea to relinquish something with such a high cost will require one of two things: either a process of engagement that lessens the security threat and provides incentives to offset the other costs, or threats that will impose costs greater than those incurred by giving up the programs. Concerning threats, if North Korea sees security risks as primary, especially if these risks threaten the survival of the regime, it will be very difficult to raise these costs any higher than they already are. Furthermore, even if possible to raise the threats to this level, the defender may be unwilling to impose costs of this magnitude because it may require significant economic cost or a major military action to fulfill. North Korean leaders already believe regime survival is on the line and it needs nuclear weapons and ballistic missiles to deter a hostile United States. What more could the United States threaten to convince North Korea to give these programs up?

Engagement and incentives appear to have a better chance, especially given the apparent North Korean security worries. Several possibilities exist though it is difficult to give a precise formula; this would need to be worked out in the negotiation process. The most important incentive may be offering a security guarantee, an option that is relatively low cost to the United States yet addresses some of the significant concerns for North Korea—national security and regime survival—to abandon its programs. Washington can also offer a pledge not to threaten or use nuclear weapons against the North. This provision was part of the Agreed Framework but was never implemented. The United States could establish a liaison office in North Korea and move towards full diplomatic relations while encouraging Japan to do the same. The U.S. State Department could remove North Korea from the list of states that support terrorism and remove economic sanctions, another provision that had been part of the Agreed Framework. An economic aid package would also be a significant incentive including restarting the suspended fuel oil deliveries, helping the North rebuild its dilapidated power grid, and providing increased food and development aid. The United States and others in the region will need to develop a large, package deal that provides many of these incentives, particularly addressing North Korean security, both military and economic security. Moreover, given the level of mistrust on both sides, the agreement will likely have to be phased in with interim steps of concessions and compliance. Concessions should be tied to a timeline that requires compliance and can be withdrawn should North Korea renege on its obligations.[13]

Credibility is always a crucial component of any deterrence commitment and it is equally important in compellence. The target of the compellence policy must know that the imposing state will either deliver on the threats should it not comply or receive the benefits if it does. The hostility of an on-going deterrence relationship and the uneven implementation of the Agreed Framework raised questions in the minds of North Korean leaders regarding U.S. credibility in delivering the benefits of that agreement. The construction of the LWRs was behind schedule, funding for the fuel oil shipments was often late, and the promised lifting of sanctions and movement towards normalized relations never occurred. North Korea certainly played a role in delay of the LWRs but these delays may have been the reason for Pyongyang pursuing a uranium-based program as a hedge against the apparent foot dragging of the Agreed Framework. Much evidence indicates North Korea was in full compliance with the agreement until approximately 1998, the estimated start-time of Pyongyang's uranium-based program. Because of these credibility issues and North Korea's lack of other leverage, any new agreement will likely require phased in provisions similar to the Agreed Framework. North Korea will not give up all of its cards in the early stages of a deal without assurances that the United States will follow through on its commitment. Much of the argument to this point no doubt appears overly apologetic for North Korean behavior. It is not. North Korea is a nasty regime that has brought great suffering to its people, and its behavior, including the many provocative acts and violation of the Agreed Framework, is frustrating and difficult to explain. Yet the goal of maintaining peace and preventing the spread of nuclear weapons remains, and engaging North Korea need not mean giving in to blackmail. Even as Ronald Reagan called the Soviet Union the "evil empire," he continued to engage the Soviets in hopes of moving U.S. interests forward. Though engagement may seem unsavory, it is the best route to achieving these important goals and may help lead to further changes in the North Korean regime.

What about the criticism of "buying off" North Korea and giving in to extortion? Does engaging the North and offering a package of incentives reward bad behavior? As the United States examines its policy options, it must assess the costs and benefits of each in light of its goal of a nuclear-free Korean peninsula. Since October 2002, the Bush administration has insisted that North Korea comply and will receive little else in terms of incentives lest Washington reward the North for cheating on its obligations. Holding to this position is likely to have North Korea continue on its path of developing nuclear weapons and the United States will have to face the costs of a nuclear adversary in Korea. Is this a greater threat to U.S. interests than engaging North Korea? Given the many dangers to a nuclear-armed DPRK, the costs appear to be much higher to refrain from engaging the North and attempting to craft a negotiated settlement with incentives sufficient to bring North Korean compliance. Recently, the United States has modified its approach somewhat in the proposal that preceded the third round of Six Party talks. This is a start but greater efforts at engagement will be necessary.

Other alternatives to North Korean extortion are compellence by denial and compellence by punishment. Earlier in the crisis, both under Presidents Clinton and George W. Bush, officials considered a denial strategy to take out the North's nuclear complex with a military strike. Once again, U.S. leaders believed that the costs and risks of such an action were too great and refrained from ordering the action. Except during the early years of the Clinton administration, there was little assurance all of the nuclear facilities could be located and no administration was certain a military strike would not cause North Korea to retaliate. Thus, these costs were greater than the United States and South Korea were willing to accept. Concerning punishment of North Korea, say with economic sanctions, these would likely not impose sufficient cost on North Korea to alter its cost-benefit calculus. Again, the costs of giving up two programs Pyongyang views as vital to its national security will outweigh economic sanctions, especially given that cooperation from China, South Korea, and Japan are necessary to give the sanctions teeth.

In all three of these alternatives, either the costs of imposing threats of some sort are too great for the imposing state or they will be ineffective in convincing the target to give up its weapons. In the end, the would-be proliferator continues on its path to develop nuclear weapons with little effect on its cost-benefit calculations. While a strategy of compellence with engagement and the use of incentives also has costs, it may be the best option to convince an adversary to give up its nuclear weapons capability. Certainly, this approach may not always succeed, however, in the long run, it may have costs that are more tolerable and have a better chance of achieving the desired nonproliferation goals.

Deterring Rogue States

Prior to the invasion of Iraq, the Bush administration argued that the United States had to act because Saddam Hussein and other leaders of rogue states did not understand the logic of deterrence. In the words of the 2002 National Security Strategy, "in the Cold War . . . we faced a generally status quo, risk-averse adversary. Deterrence was an effective defense. But deterrence based only upon the threat of retaliation is less likely to work against leaders of rogue states more willing to take risks, gambling with the lives of their people, and the wealth of their nations."[14] Yet critics have argued that so-called rogue states can be deterred as well as anyone else so long as the United States implements a credible deterrence strategy that threatens what the adversary values most, its survival. What input does the Korea case have for this debate?

In 1950, North Korea came very close to experiencing regime change. Without Chinese intervention, the Korean peninsula would be under one government with the capitol in Seoul. This experience etched a very important lesson in the minds of North Korea leaders—do not challenge the power of the United States directly without strong support from allies. Despite holding on to the goal of reunification, as the years passed, Pyongyang saw this possibility fade, along with the support its allies gave for any renewed hostilities. The term "rogue state" was invented in the 1990s, but that designation could have applied to North Korea much earlier, given its provocative rhetoric and behavior. Moreover, many critics characterized Kim Il Sung and his son Kim Jong Il as crazy and willing to take big risks, yet, in most respects, their behavior was quite risk-averse. Even at the height of the DPRK's efforts to destabilize the South in the late 1960s, perhaps its best attempt to earn the rogue state label, North Korean leaders were careful not to challenge the United States directly and kept their actions within certain bounds that could be turned up or down depending on the reaction of Washington or Seoul.

The more difficult question here is the danger of North Korea selling nuclear weapons, material, or technology. The U.S. security commitment has helped prevent an attack on its ally but would it prevent North Korea from selling nuclear material? Indeed, North Korea has been a prolific distributor of ballistic weapons and possibly may have sold nuclear material to Libya.[15] Yet, the United States has never firmly drawn lines regarding what behavior would be unacceptable or specified the consequences should the lines be crossed. Moreover, this points to the difficulty of using deterrence for proliferation problems.

Deterrence of a rogue state in Korea has worked for the past fifty years. Almost by default, deterring a rogue state implies a significant differential in power between the United States and a given adversary, what has been described as an asymmetric relationship. So long as the United States continues to communicate clearly the objectionable behavior it seeks to deter, issues warnings that threaten what the rogue state values, namely regime survival, and demonstrates the resolve to follow through, deterrence can be successful. As demonstrated in Korea, the United States has the capability to raise the costs should the adversary attack, and has demonstrated the necessary resolve for a credible security guarantee. Certainly, deterrence has not been successful in every instance. However, a properly implemented deterrence policy should have a similar chance for success with rogue states as against those that are not, whether it be North Korea or Iraq.

Moving from Deterrence to Engagement

Inherent in a deterrence situation is a certain level of tension and animosity existing between two or more adversaries. As each side takes the necessary military preparations and issues the proper warnings for deterrence, there seems little hope for the two sides to break out of this cycle of conflict. As a long-term deterrence situation that has flirted with engagement at several points, deterrence in Korea may provide some answers. Here are some tentative observations.

During both Bush administrations and the Clinton White House, U.S. leaders faced three broad choices in addressing the North Korean proliferation problem: coerce the DPRK into meeting U.S. demands, ignore them, or engage Pyongyang in an effort to resolve the crisis. At several points, the Clinton and George W. Bush administrations considered using coercion, either military force or the imposition of sanctions and other efforts to isolate the North. Clinton, who was predisposed to engaging the North, was spared having to make a decision due largely to Carter's trip to Pyongyang. The Bush II administration has pursued a more coercive line suspending the fuel deliveries and further construction of the light water reactors, but this is far short of the actions some in the administration wish had been taken. Regarding military action, both administrations realized there were few good options here. Both also attempted to ignore the problem from time to time, maintaining the solution was simple, live up to the agreements you signed. Yet, over time, this did little to solve the problem and North Korea moved further along in its efforts to acquire nuclear weapons. In the end, both administrations moved, though grudgingly in the case of the Bush II administration, in the direction of engagement. It is important to note here that a willingness to engage, per se, does not include a willingness to offer many incentives. While the current administration has often stated its willingness to dialogue with the North, the agenda was limited to how North Korea would fulfill its obligations.

The obstacles in moving from deterrence to engagement are several. First, states on both sides may be reluctant to engage given the hostility that underlies their deterrence relationship. If this context does not change, engagement may be viewed as a fruitless, even dangerous exercise. Second, any effort to engage the adversary may be perceived domestically as being "soft" with the leader paying a political price at home. For the United States, similar to Nixon's opening to China, a "tough" administration would have less political cost here because of its hardline credentials and would incur less domestic political cost. In Clinton's case, he was roundly criticized for any effort to engage North Korea; George W. Bush has had a far easier time moving in this direction.

How can these obstacles be overcome, if indeed engagement is the wise route? In the U.S. system, the decision to step out of deterrence and move towards engagement is largely the president's decision. Moving towards engagement takes a difficult decision by the chief executive that is part of a cost-benefit analysis that determines this path as the less costly of the various other options. Despite its initial reluctance to engage, the Bush administration has calculated that the costs of many other actions are too high to pay at this moment and is slowly moving towards engagement. However, for hawks, this may only be an effort to test North Korean intentions, a test they believe Pyongyang will fail, and will be a precursor to tougher action.[16]

Another factor to prod engagement is the views of others, particularly allies in the region. In Clinton's case, South Korea's willingness to let the United States engage the North directly opened the door to dialogue. However Kim Young Sam's abrupt reversals sometimes closed the door as fast as it opened. Pressure from South Korea, Japan, and China has also been instrumental in encouraging the Bush administration to be more flexible in its engagement policy. These circumstances point again to the interplay of policy and threat assessment in deterrence. U.S. allies in the region, particularly South Korea, have a different perception of the North Korean threat. These are the allies the United States is protecting yet they are the ones pushing for engagement. If its allies, who are much closer to the firing line, favor engagement it becomes more difficult for Washington to continue opposing such an effort. Allied pressure also gives the administration a modicum of political cover to move in this direction. Yet, in the end, it is largely an executive decision that will be taken based on an administration's assessment of interests along with the costs and benefits.

The Future

The end of the Cold War brought hope that, as Germany had done, the two Koreas would be reunited, bringing an end to one of the last legacies of that conflict. Almost 15 years since, there appears little hope that this will happen any time soon. As a result, the U.S.-ROK alliance is likely to remain in place for the foreseeable future. However, that relationship faces some serious challenges.

First and foremost, is finding a solution to the North Korean nuclear problem. The United States must work closely with its allies to develop a package that provides sufficient incentives for North Korea to give up its program while insisting on North Korean compliance and transparency. While a firm deterrence posture remains necessary for the time being, U.S. officials need to see the wisdom in providing incentives and avoiding overly provocative deterrence threats in the name of nonproliferation goals. Given the levels of mistrust, any deal will need to be phased in, requiring compliance tests on both sides to ensure neither is reneging on their end of the bargain. It will also be important that the process leading up to the agreement and the agreement itself help lessen the overall level of hostility between the United States and North Korea.

Second, relations within the U.S.-ROK alliance will need attention. The relationship has suffered over issues such as Washington's approach to North Korea, the failure to fully consult with Seoul on important policy matters, ROK opposition to the war in Iraq, the location and overall levels of U.S. troops in South Korea, and revisions to the command structure. Some in South Korea have questioned the need for a strong relationship and have called for a shift away from the U.S.-ROK alliance to one that aligns South Korea with China based on the growth of shared economic and strategic interests. There are serious challenges ahead to maintaining and redefining the alliance.

The U.S. security guarantee and the American presence in South Korea will continue to be an important stabilizing influence in the region. Yet, the previous fifty years have shown that the means used by that policy may change—indeed, should change—as threat assessments, the capabilities of the protégé, and the overall global context changes. Korea remains a difficult and complex region for U.S. policy makers to navigate, but one that deserves great care and attention to ensure continued peace and stability in the region.

Notes

1. Morgan, *Deterrence: A Conceptual Analysis*, 27-46.
2. Huth, *Extended Deterrence and the Prevention of War*, 15-20.
3. Carter, *Keeping the Faith: Memoirs of a President*, 195.
4. *Review of the Policy Decision to Withdraw United States Ground Forces from Korea* (1978), "Testimony of Major General John K. Singlaub," 31.
5. Seth Faison Jr., "Mao's '50 Cable Gives Evidence of Korea Plan," *New York Times*, 26 February 1992.
6. Dwight D. Eisenhower, "Annual Message to the Congress on the State of the Union," *Public Papers, 1954*, 8.
7. John Foster Dulles, *Department of State Bulletin*, 14 September 1953, 339.
8. Dwight D. Eisenhower, "The President's News Conference of February 2, 1955," *Public Papers, 1955*, 236.
9. Roehrig, "One Rogue State Crisis at a Time!" 169-170.
10. Eisenhower, "Memorandum of Conference With President Eisenhower," 14 September 1960, *FRUS, 1958-1960*, XVIII, Japan; Korea, 691-693.
11. Kaufmann, *The Requirements of Deterrence*, 19.

12. Harold Brown, *Department of Defense: Annual Report, Fiscal Year 1979*, (Washington, D.C.: Government Printing Office, 1979), 68.

13. For more detailed treatments of these issues, see Cha and Kang, *Nuclear North Korea: A Debate on Engagement Strategies*, and O'Hanlon and Mochizuki, *Crisis on the Korean Peninsula: How to Deal with a Nuclear North Korea*.

14. *National Security Strategy*, September 2002, 15.

15. David E. Sanger and William J. Broad, "Evidence is Cited Linking Koreans to Libya Uranium," *New York Times*, 23 May 2004, A1.

16. Victor Cha makes a similar argument in "Hawk Engagement and Preventive Defense on the Korean Peninsula," *International Security* 27, no. 1 (Summer 2002): 40-78.

Selected Bibliography

Books and Articles

Acheson, Dean. *Present at the Creation*. New York: W. W. Norton, 1969.

Alves, Dora, ed. *Change, Interdependence, and Security in the Pacific Basin: The 1990 Pacific Symposium*. Washington, D.C.: National Defense University Press, 1991.

———. *Pacific Security Toward the Year 2000: The 1987 Pacific Symposium*. Washington, D.C.: National Defense University Press, 1988.

Ahn, Byung-joon. "South Korean-Soviet Relations." *Asian Survey* 31, no. 9 (September 1991): 816-825.

An, Tai Sung. *North Korea in Transition*. Westport: Greenwood Press, 1983.

Armacost, Michael H. and Daniel I. Okimoto, eds. *The Future of America's Alliance in Northeast Asia*. Stanford, CA: Asia-Pacific Research Center, 2004.

Arquilla, John and Paul K. Davis. *Extended Deterrence, Compellence and the "Old World Order."* N-3482-JS, Santa Monica, CA: Rand Corporation, 1992.

Art, Robert J. "The Defensible Defense: America's Grand Strategy After the Cold War." *International Security* 15, no. 4 (Spring 1991): 5-53.

Art, Robert J. and Patrick M. Cronin, eds. *The United States and Coercive Diplomacy*. Washington, D.C.: U.S. Institute of Peace Press, 2003.

Bacevich, A. J. *The Pentomic Era*. Washington, D.C.: National Defense University Press, 1986.

Bandow, Doug. "Leaving Korea." *Foreign Policy*, no. 77 (Winter 1989-90): 77-93.

Barilleaux, Ryan J. and Andrew Ilsu Kim. "Clinton, Korea, and Presidential Diplomacy." *World Affairs* 162, no. 1 (Summer 1999): 29-40.

Bazhanov, Eugene and Natasha Bazhanov. "The Evolution of Russian-Korean Relations." *Asian Survey* 34, no. 9 (September 1994): 789-799.

Bermudez, Joseph S. Jr. "North Korea's Light Infantry Brigades." *Jane's Defence Weekly* (15 November 1986): 1176-1178.

———. *The Armed Forces of North Korea*. London: I.B. Tauris, 2001.

Betts, Richard K. *Surprise Attack: Lessons for Defense Planning*. Washington, D.C.: Brookings Institution, 1982.

Blackburn, Robert M. *Mercenaries and Lyndon Johnson's "More Flags": The Hiring of Korean, Filipino, and Thai Soldiers in the Vietnam War.* Jefferson, NC: McFarland, 1994.

Blackwill, Robert D and Paul Dibb, eds. *America's Asian Alliance.* Cambridge, MA: MIT Press, 2000.

Brownell, George A. *The Origin and Development of the National Security Agency.* Laguna Hills, CA: Agean Park Press, 1981.

Bundy, McGeorge. "The Bishops and the Bomb." *The New York Review of Books* (16 June 1983): 62-66.

Buss, Claude A. *The United States and the Republic of Korea: Background for Policy.* Stanford: Hoover Institution Press, 1982.

Byers, R. B. *Deterrence in the 1980s: Crisis and Dilemma.* London: Croom Helm Ltd., 1988.

Carter, Ashton B. and William J. Perry. *Preventive Defense: A New Security Strategy for America.* Washington, D.C.: Brookings Institution, 1999.

Carter, Jimmy. *Keeping the Faith: Memoirs of a President.* New York: Bantam Books, 1982.

Cha, Victor D. *Alignment Despite Antagonism: The United States-Korea-Japan Security Triangle.* Stanford: Stanford University Press, 1999.

————. "Hawk Engagement and Preventive Defense on the Korean Peninsula." *International Security* 27, no. 1 (Summer 2002): 40-78.

Cha, Victor D. and David C. Kang. *Nuclear North Korea: A Debate on Engagement Strategies.* New York: Columbia University Press, 2003.

Chay, John. "The First Three Decades of American-Korean Relations, 1882-1910: Reassessments and Reflections." Pp. 15-33 in *U.S.-Korean Relations, 1882-1982,* edited by Tae-hwan Kwak. Seoul: Kyungnam University Press, 1982.

Chung, Chong-Shik, ed. *Korean Unification: Source Materials with an Introduction,* Volume II. Seoul: Research Center for Peace and Unification, 1979.

Chung, Chong-Wook. "Chinese Foreign Policy in East Asia: Trends and Implications." Pp. 59-72 in *The Future of South Korean-U.S. Security Relations,* edited by William J. Taylor, et al. Boulder, CO: Westview Press, 1989.

Cimbala, Stephen J. *Nuclear Strategizing: Deterrence and Reality.* New York: Praeger Publishers, 1988.

————. *Extended Deterrence: The U.S. and NATO Europe.* Lexington: Lexington Books, 1987.

————. *Strategic Impasse: Offense, Defense and Deterrence Theory and Practice.* Westport: Greenwood Press, 1989.

————. *NATO Strategy and Nuclear Escalation.* London: Pinter Publishers, 1989.

Clark, Donald, ed. *The Kwangju Uprising: Shadows over the Regime in South Korea.* Boulder: Westview Press, 1988.

Clough, Ralph N. *Deterrence and Defense in Korea: The Role of U.S. Forces.* Washington, D.C.: The Brookings Institution, 1976.

————. "The Soviet Union and the Two Koreas." Pp. 175-199 in *Soviet Policy in East Asia,* edited by Donald S. Zagoria. New Haven: Yale University Press, 1982.

Commager, Henry Steele, ed. *Documents in American History*, 7th ed., Volume II. New York: Appleton-Century-Crofts, 1962.

The Communist Bloc and Western Alliances. London: International Institute, 1961-1963.

Conroy, Hilary and Wayne Patterson. "Duality and Dominance: A Century of Korean-American Relations." Pp. 1-10 in *Korean-American Relations, 1866-1997*, edited by Yur-Bok Lee and Wayne Patterson. Albany, NY: State University of New York Press, 1999.

Cossa, Ralph A., ed. *U.S.-Korea-Japan Relations: Building Toward a "Virtual Alliance."* Washington, D.C.: Center for Strategic and International Studies, 1999.

Crowe, William J. and Alan D. Romberg. "Rethinking Pacific Security." *Foreign Affairs* 70, no. 2 (Spring, 1991): 121-140.

Cumings, Bruce. *The Origins of the Korean War: Liberation and the Emergence of Separate Regimes, 1945-1947*, Volume I. Princeton: Princeton University Press, 1981.

———. *The Origins of the Korean War: The Roaring of the Cataract, 1947-1950*, Volume II. Princeton: Princeton University Press, 1990.

———, ed. *Child of Conflict: The Korean-American Relationship, 1943-1953*. Seattle: University of Washington Press, 1983.

———. *Korea's Place in the Sun*. New York: W.W. Norton, 1997.

———. "The Conflict on the Korean Peninsula." Pp. 103-121 in *Asia: Militarization and Regional Conflict*, edited by Yoshikazu Sakamoto. London: Zed Books, 1988.

Cumings, Bruce, Ervand Abrahamian, and Moshe Ma'oz. *Inventing the Axis of Evil: The Truth about North Korea, Iran, and Syria*. New York: New Press, 2004.

Curtis, Gerald L. and Han Sung-joo, ed. *The U.S.-South Korean Alliance*. Lexington: D.C. Heath and Company, 1983.

Destler, I.M. and Michael Nacht. "Beyond Mutual Recrimination: Building a Solid U.S.-Japan Relationship in the 1990s." *International Security* 15, no. 3 (Winter 1990/1991): 92-119.

Detrio, Richard T. *Strategic Partners: South Korea and the United States*. Washington, D.C.: National Defense University Press, 1989.

Dong, Joon Hwang. "An Evaluation of U.S. Security Assistance to the ROK and Some ROK-U.S. Defense Cooperation Issues." *The Korean Journal of Defense Analysis* 2, no. 2 (Winter, 1990): 195-217.

Dorff, Robert H. and Joseph R. Cerami. "Deterrence and Competitive Strategies: A New Look at an Old Concept." Pp. 109-123 in *Deterrence in the 21st Century*, edited by Max G. Manwaring. London: Frank Cass, 2001.

Drennan, William M. "Nuclear Weapons and North Korea: Who's Coercing Whom?" Pp. 157-223 in *The United States and Coercive Diplomacy*, edited by Robert J. Art and Patrick M. Cronin. Washington, D.C.: U.S. Institute of Peace Press, 2003.

Eberstadt, Nicholas. "Can the Two Koreas be One?" *Foreign Affairs* 71, no. 5 (Winter 1992/93): 150-165.

———. *Korea Approaches Reunification*. Armonk, New York: M.E. Sharpe, 1995.

———. *The End of North Korea*. Washington, D.C.: American Enterprise Institute, 1999.

Eberstadt, Nicholas and Richard J. Ellings, eds. *Korea's Future and the Great Powers*. Seattle: University of Washington Press, 2001.

Eckert, Carter J., Ki-baik Lee, Young Ick Lew, Michael Robinson, and Edward W. Wagner. *Korea Old and New: A History*. Cambridge: Harvard University Press, 1990.

Elliott-Batem, Michael. *Defeat in the East: The Mark of Mao Tse-tung on War*. London: Oxford University Press, 1967.

Ellison, Herbert J. "Russia, Korea, and Northeast Asia." Pp. 164-187 in *Korea's Future and the Great Powers*, edited by Nicholas Eberstadt and Richard J. Ellings. Seattle: National Bureau of Asian Research, 2001.

Endicott, John. "Japanese Security Policy: Stability in an Era of Change." *The Korean Journal of Defense Analysis* 2, no. 2 (Winter 1990): 97-114.

Freedman, Lawrence. *The Evolution of Nuclear Strategy*. London: The International Institute for Strategic Studies, 1989.

————. *Deterrence*. Cambridge, UK: Polity Press, 2004.

Gabriel, Richard, ed. *Fighting Armies*. Westport: Greenwood Press, 1983.

Gantz, Nanette C., ed. *Extended Deterrence and Arms Control*, R-3586-FF. Santa Monica, CA: RAND Corporation, 1988.

Garnham, David. "Extending Deterrence with German Nuclear Weapons." *International Security* 10, no. 1 (Summer 1985): 96-110.

George, Alexander L. *Forceful Persuasion: Coercive Diplomacy as an Alternative to War*. Washington, D.C.: United States Institute of Peace Press, 1991.

George, Alexander L. and Richard Smoke. *Deterrence in American Foreign Policy: Theory and Practice*. New York: Columbia University Press, 1974.

Gilinsky, Victor. *Nuclear Blackmail: The 1994 U.S.-Democratic People's Republic of Korea Agreed Framework on North Korea's Nuclear Program*. Stanford: Stanford University Press.

Gleysteen, William H. Jr. *Massive Entanglement, Marginal Influence: Carter and Korea in Crisis*. Washington, D.C.: Brookings Institution, 1999.

Godwin, Paul H.B. "China's Asian Policy in the 1990s: Adjusting to the Post-Cold War Environment." Pp. 118-147 in *East Asian Security in the Post-Cold War Era*, edited by Sheldon W. Simon. Armonk, NY: M.E. Sharpe, 1993.

Gray, Colin. *Nuclear Strategy and National Style*. Lanham, MD: Hamilton Press, 1986.

Gregor, A. James. *Land of the Morning Calm: Korea and American Security*. Washington, D.C.: Ethics and Public Policy Center, 1990.

Gregor, A. James and Maria Hsia Chang. *The Iron Triangle*. Stanford: Hoover Institution Press, 1984.

Grinker, Roy Richard. *Korea and Its Futures: Unification and the Unfinished War*. New York: St. Martin's Press, 1998.

Haig, Alexander M. Jr., *Caveat: Realism, Reagan, and Foreign Policy*. New York: Macmillan, 1984.

Han Sung-joo. *The Failure of Democracy in South Korea*. Berkeley: University of California Press, 1974.

————. "South Korea's Participation in the Vietnam Conflict: An Analysis of the U.S.-Korean Alliance." *ORBIS* (Winter 1978): 893-912.

Harrington, Fred Harvey. "An American View of Korean-American Relations, 1882-1905." Pp. 35-51 in *Korean-American Relations, 1866-1997*, edited by Yur-Bok Lee and Wayne Patterson. Albany, NY: State University of New York Press, 1999.

Harris, Stuart and James Cotton, eds. *The End of the Cold War in Northeast Asia*. Boulder: Lynne Rienner Publishers, 1991.

Harrison, Selig S. *Korean Endgame: A Strategy for Reunification and U.S. Disengagement*. Princeton: Princeton University Press, 2002.

———. "The Missiles of North Korea." *World Policy Journal* 17, no. 3 (Fall 2000): 12-24.

———. "Time to Leave Korea?" *Foreign Affairs* 80, 2 (March/April 2001): 62-78.

Hayes, Peter. *Pacific Powderkeg: American Nuclear Dilemmas in Korea*. Lexington: Lexington Books, 1991.

———. "American Nuclear Hegemony in Korea." *Journal of Peace Research* 25, no. 4, (December 1988): 351-364.

Henderson, Gregory. *Korea: The Politics of the Vortex*. Cambridge: Harvard University Press, 1968.

Henriksen, Thomas H. and Jongryn Mo, eds. *North Korea after Kim Il Sung*. Stanford, CA: Hoover Institution Press, 1997.

Heo, Uk and Shale A. Horowitz, eds. *Conflict in Asia*. Westport, CT: Praeger, 2003.

Heo, Uk and Chong-Min Hyun. "The 'Sunshine' Policy Revisited: An Analysis of South Korea's Policy toward North Korea." Pp. 89-103 in *Conflict in Asia,* edited by Uk Heo and Shale A. Horowitz. Westport, CT: Praeger, 2003.

Hinton, Harold C., Donald Zagoria, Jung Ha Lee, Gottfried-Karl Kindermann, Chung Min Lee and Robert L. Pfaltzgraff Jr. *The U.S.-Korean Security Relationship: Prospects and Challenges for the 1990s*. Washington, D.C.: Pergamon-Brassey's Inc., 1988.

Hopmann, Terrence and Frank Barnaby, eds. *Rethinking the Nuclear Dilemma in Europe*. London: Macmillan, 1988.

Hunt, Michael H. "Beijing and the Korean Crisis, June 1950-June 1951." *Political Science Quarterly* 107, no. 3 (Fall 1992): 453-478.

Huth, Paul. *Extended Deterrence and the Prevention of War*. New Haven: Yale University Press, 1988.

———. "Extended Deterrence and the Outbreak of War." *American Political Science Review* 82, no. 2 (June 1988): 423-443.

———. "The Extended Deterrent Value of Nuclear Weapons." *Journal of Conflict Resolution* 34, no. 2 (June 1990): 270-290.

Huth, Paul and Bruce C. Russett. "What Makes Deterrence Work?" *World Politics* 36, no. 4 (July 1984): 496-526.

———. "Testing Deterrence Theory." *World Politics* 42 (April 1990): 466-501.

Hwang, In Kwan. *The United States and Neutral Reunited Korea*. Lanham, MD: University Press of America, 1990.

Hwang, Dong Joon. "An Evaluation of US Security Assistance to the ROK and Some ROK-US Defense Cooperation Issues." *The Korean Journal of Defense Analysis* 2, no. 2 (Winter 1990): 195-217.

Jervis, Robert. *The Meaning of the Nuclear Revolution: Statecraft and the Prospect of Armageddon*. Ithaca: Cornell University Press, 1989.

———. *The Illogic of American Nuclear Strategy.* Ithaca: Cornell University Press, 1984.

———. "Deterrence Theory Revisited." *World Politics* 31, no. 2 (January 1979): 289- 324.

Jervis, Robert, Richard Ned Lebow, and Janice Gross Stein. *Psychology and Deterrence.* Baltimore: The Johns Hopkins University Press, 1985.

Johnson, Stuart E. and Joseph A. Yager. *The Military Equation in Northeast Asia.* Washington, D.C.: The Brookings Institution, 1979.

Joo, Seung-ho. "The New Friendship Treaty between Moscow and Pyongyang." *Comparative Strategy* 20, no. 5 (December 2001): 467-481.

Jordon, Amos A., William J. Taylor Jr., and Lawrence J. Korb, *American National Security,* 4th ed. Baltimore: The Johns Hopkins University Press, 1993.

Kang, David C. "International Relations Theory and the Second Korean War." *International Studies Quarterly* 47, no. 3 (September 2003): 301-324.

Kaufmann, William W. *The Requirements of Deterrence.* Princeton: Center for International Studies, 1954.

Keitaro, Oguri. "In Search of Rapprochement: Tokyo and Pyongyang." *Japan Quarterly* (July-September, 1991): 262-271.

Kelleher, Catherine McArdle, Frank J. Kerr, and George H. Quester, eds. *Nuclear Deterrence: New Risks, New Opportunities.* New York: Pergamon-Brassey's, 1986.

Kennan, George F. *Memoirs: 1925-1950.* Boston: Little, Brown, 1967.

Khrushchev, Nikita, translated and edited by Strobe Talbott. *Khrushchev Remembers.* Boston: Little, Brown, 1970.

———. translated and edited by Strobe Talbott. *Khrushchev Remembers: The Last Testament.* Boston: Little, Brown, 1974.

Kihl, Young Whan. "South Korea in 1989." *Asian Survey* 30, no. 1 (January 1990): 67-73.

———, ed. *Korea and the World: Beyond the Cold War.* Boulder, CO: Westview, 1994.

Kihl, Young Whan and Lawrence E. Grinter, eds. *Security, Strategy and Policy Responses in the Pacific Rim.* Boulder: Lynne Rienner Publishers Inc., 1989.

Kim, Hakjoon. "U.S.-South Korean Security Relations: A Challenging Partnership." *The Korean Journal of Defense Analysis* II, no. 1 (Summer, 1990): 149-160.

Kim, Hong Nack. "Japan's Relations with North Korea." *Current History* (April 1991): 164-167, 180.

Kim, Ilpyong, ed. *Korean Challenges and American Policy.* New York: Paragon House, 1991.

Kim, Samuel S. and Tai Hwan Lee. "Chinese-North Korean Relations: Managing Asymmetrical Interdependence." Pp. 109-137 in *North Korea and Northeast Asia,* edited by Samuel S. Kim and Tai Hwan Lee. Lanham, MD: Rowman & Littlefield, 2002.

Kim, Se-Jin, ed. *Documents in Korean-American Relations.* Seoul: Research Center for Peace and Unification, 1976.

Kim, Sunhyuk. *The Politics of Democratizaton in Korea: The Role of Civil Society.* Pittsburgh: University of Pittsburgh Press, 2000.

Kissinger, Henry. *For the Record: Selected Statements, 1977-1980.* Boston: Little, Brown, 1981.

Knaack, Marcelle Size. *Encyclopedia of US Air Force Aircraft and Missile Systems*, Vol. 1. Washington, D.C.: Government Printing Office, 1978.

Koh, Byung Chul. "The Korean War as a Learning Experience for North Korea." *Korea and World Affairs* 3, no. 3 (Fall 1979): 366-384.

———. "The Pueblo Incident in Perspective." *Asian Survey* (April 1969): 264-280.

———. "North Korea in 1987." *Asian Survey* 28, no. 1 (January 1988): 62-70.

———. "Confrontation and Cooperation on the Korean Peninsula: The Politics of Nuclear Proliferation." *The Korean Journal of Defense Analysis* 6, no. 2 (Winter 1994): 53-83.

———. *The Foreign Policy Systems of North and South Korea*. Berkeley: University of California Press, 1984.

———. "Unification Policy and North-South Relations." Pp. 264-308 in *North Korea Today: Strategic and Domestic Issues*, edited by Robert A. Scalapino and Jun-Yop Kim. Berkeley: Institute of East Asian Studies, University of California, 1983.

Korean Overseas Information Service. *Tunnels of Aggression*.

Kreisberg, Paul H. "The U.S. and Asia in 1990." *Asian Survey* 31, no. 1 (January 1991): 1-13.

Kwak, Tae-Hwan, ed. *The Two Koreas in World Politics*. Seoul: Kyungnam University Press, 1983.

———. "The Reduction of U.S. Forces in Korea in the Inter-Korean Peace Process." *The Korean Journal of Defense Analysis* 2, no. 2 (Winter 1990): 171-194.

Kwak, Tae-Hwan, John Chay, Soon Sung Cho, and Shannon McCune. *U.S.-Korean Relations, 1882-1982*. Seoul: Kyungnam University Press, 1982.

LaFeber, Walter. *The American Age: U.S. Foreign Policy at Home and Abroad*. New York: W.W. Norton, 1994.

Laney, James T. and Jason T. Shaplen. "How to Deal With North Korea." *Foreign Affairs* 82, no. 2 (March/April 2003): 16-30.

Lebow, Richard Ned. *Between Peace and War*. Baltimore: The Johns Hopkins University Press, 1981.

———. *Nuclear Crisis Management: A Dangerous Illusion*. Ithaca: Cornell University Press, 1987.

———. "Correspondence: Deterrence Failure Revisited," *International Security* 12, no. 1 (Summer 1987): 197-213.

———. *Nuclear Crisis Management: A Dangerous Illusion*. Ithaca: Cornell University Press, 1987.

Lebow, Richard Ned and Janice Gross Stein. "Deterrence: The Elusive Dependent Variable," *World Politics* 42 (April 1990): 336-369.

Lefever, Ernest W. *Nuclear Arms in the Third World*. Washington, D.C.: Brookings Institution, 1979.

Lee, Chae-Jin. "China and North Korea: An Uncertain Relationship," Pp. 193-209 in *North Korea after Kim Il Sung*, edited by Dae Sook Suh and Chae-Jin Lee. Boulder, CO: Lynne Rienner, 1998.

Lee, Chae-Jin and Hideo Sato. *U.S. Policy Toward Japan and Korea: A Changing Influence Relationship*. New York: Praeger, 1982.

Lee, Chong-Sik. *Japan and Korea: The Political Dimension*. Stanford: Hoover Institution Press, 1985.

Lee, Manwoo, Ronald D. McLaurin, and Chung-in Moon. *Alliance Under Tension: The Evolution of South Korean-U.S. Relations*. Boulder: Westview Press, 1988.

Lee, Manwoo and Richard W. Mansbach. *The Changing Order in Northeast Asia and the Korean Peninsula*. Seoul: IFES, Kyungnam University, 1993.

Lee, Manwoo. "The Two Koreas and the Unification Game." *Current History* 92 (December 1993): 421-425.

Lee, Suk Bok. *The Impact of U.S. Forces in Korea*. Washington, D.C.: National Defense University Press, 1987.

Lee, Yur-Bok and Wayne Patterson, eds. *One Hundred Years of Korean-American Relations, 1882-1982*. University, AL: University of Alabama Press, 1986.

———. *Korean-American Relations, 1866-1997*. Albany, NY: State University of New York Press, 1999.

Levin, Norman D. "Global Detente and North Korea's Strategic Relations." *The Korean Journal of Defense Analysis* 2, no. 1 (Summer 1990): 33-53.

Lho, Kyongsoo. "The Military Balance in the Korean Peninsula." *Asian Affairs* (February 1988): 36-44.

Mack, Andrew. "North Korea and the Bomb." *Foreign Policy*, no. 83 (Summer 1991): 87-104.

Manwaring, Max G., ed. *Deterrence in the 21st Century*. London: Frank Cass, 2001.

Marantz, Paul. "Moscow and East Asia: New Realities and New Policies." Pp. 28-43 in *East Asian Security in the Post-Cold War Era*, edited by Sheldon W. Simon. Armonk, NY: M.E. Sharpe, 1993.

Matray, James Irving. *The Reluctant Crusade: American Foreign Policy in Korea, 1941-1950*. Honolulu: University of Hawaii Press, 1985.

May, Ernest R. *Lessons of the Past: The Use and Misuse of History in American Foreign Policy*. New York: Oxford University Press, 1973.

Mazarr, Michael J. *North Korea and the Bomb*. New York: St. Martin's Press, 1995.

———. "Going Just a Little Nuclear." International Security 20, no. 2 (Fall 1995): 92-122.

Mazarr, Michael J., John Q. Blodgett, Cha Young-koo, and William J. Taylor Jr., eds. *Korea 1991: The Road to Peace*. Boulder: Westview Press, 1991.

McGlothen, Ronald L. *Controlling the Waves: Dean Acheson and U.S. Foreign Policy in Asia*. New York: W.W. Norton, 1993.

McLaurin, Ronald D. and Chung-in Moon. *The United States and the Defense of the Pacific*. Boulder: Westview Press, 1989.

McNamara, Robert S. "The Relationship of Strategic and Theater Nuclear Forces." *Foreign Affairs* 62, no. 1 (Fall 1983): 59-80.

Mearsheimer, John J. *Conventional Deterrence*. Ithaca: Cornell University Press, 1983.

Military Balance. London: International Institute, 1965-2003.

Miller, Merle. *Plain Speaking: An Oral Biography of Harry S. Truman*. New York: Berkley Publishing, 1973.

Morgan, Patrick. *Deterrence: A Conceptual Analysis*, 2nd ed. Beverly Hills: SAGE Publications, Inc., 1983.

————. *Deterrence Now*. Cambridge, UK: Cambridge University Press, 2003.

Morgenthau, Hans J. *In Defense of the National Interest*. New York:Alfred A. Knopf, 1951.

Morrison, Elting E., John M. Blum, and John J. Buckley, eds. *The Letters of Theodore Roosevelt*, Volume II. Cambridge: Harvard University Press, 1951.

Nahm, Andrew, ed. *The United States and Korea: American-Korean Relations, 1866-1976*. Kalamazoo: The Center for Korean Studies, Western Michigan University, 1979.

————. *Korea: Tradition and Transformation—A History of the Korean People*. Elizabeth, NJ: Hollym International Corp., 1988.

Nam, Joo-Hong. *America's Commitment to South Korea: The First Decade of the Nixon Doctrine*. Cambridge: Cambridge University Press, 1986.

————. "The Entangling Conflict in Korea." *The Journal of International Affairs* (Summer/Fall 1987): 91-107.

Natsios, Andrew S. *The Great North Korean Famine*. Washington, D.C.: US Institute of Peace, 2001.

Niksch, Larry. "North Korea." Pp. 103-126 in *Fighting Armies*, edited by Richard A. Gabriel. Westport: Greenwood Press, 1983.

————. "South Korea." Pp. 127-151 in *Fighting Armies*, edited by Richard A. Gabriel. Westport: Greenwood Press, 1983.

Nitze, Paul. "The Relationship of Strategic and Theater Nuclear Forces." *International Security* 2, no. 2 (Fall 1977): 122-132.

Noland, Marcus. *Avoiding the Apocalypse: The Future of the Two Koreas*. Washington, D.C.: Institute for International Economics, 2000.

Nixon, Richard. *The Memoirs of Richard Nixon*. New York: Grosset & Dunlap, 1978.

————. *U.S. Foreign Policy for the 1970's: A New Strategy for Peace*. Washington, D.C.: Government Printing Office, 1970.

————. *U.S. Foreign Policy for the 1970's: Building for Peace*. Washington, D.C.: Government Printing Office, 1971.

Oberdorfer, Don. *The Two Koreas*. New York: Basic Books, 1997.

Oh, Kongdan. "North Korea in 1989." *Asian Survey* 30, no. 1 (January 1990): 74-80.

Oh, Kongdan and Ralph C. Hassig. *North Korea Through the Looking Glass*. Washington, D.C.: Brookings Institution, 2000.

Oh, Kwan-Chi. "The Military Balance on the Korean Peninsula." *The Korean Journal of Defense Analysis* 2, no. 1 (Summer 1990): 95-109.

O'Hanlon, Michael. "Stopping a North Korean Invasion." *International Security* 22, no. 4 (Spring 1998): 135-170.

O'Hanlon, Michael and Mike Mochizuki. *Crisis on the Korean Peninsula: How to Deal with a Nuclear North Korea*. New York: McGraw-Hill, 2003.

Olsen, Edward A. *U.S. Policy and the Two Koreas*. Boulder: Westview Press, 1988.

————. *Toward Normalizing U.S.-Korea Relations: In Due Course?* Boulder, CO: Lynne Rienner, 2002.

Orme, John. "Deterrence Failures: A Second Look." *International Security* 11, no. 4 (Spring 1987): 96-124.

Ow-Taylor, Chwee Huay. "Korea's Economic Performance in 1990." *Korea Economic Update* 2, no. 1 (Spring 1991): 2.

Paige, Glenn D. *The Korean Decision.* New York: The Free Press, 1968.

Pape, Robert A. Jr. "Coercive Air Power in the Vietnam War." *International Security* 15, no. 2 (Fall 1990): 103-146.

Park, Tong Whan. "From Extended Deterrence to Global Interdependence: The Future of U.S. South Korean Security Relations." Pp. 133-157 in *Korea 1991: The Road to Peace,* edited by Michael J. Mazarr, et al. Boulder, CO: Westview Press, 1991.

Paul, T.V. *Power versus Prudence: Why Nations Forgo Nuclear Weapons.* Montreal: McGill-Queen's University Press, 2000.

Perry, John Curtis. "Dateline North Korea: A Communist Holdout." *Foreign Policy* 80 (Fall 1990): 172-191.

Pollack, Jonathan D. and Young Koo Cha. *A New Alliance for the Next Century: The Future of U.S.-Korean Security Cooperation.* Santa Monica, CA: RAND, 1995.

Quester, George H. *Deterrence Before Hiroshima: The Airpower Background of Modern Strategy.* New York: Wiley, 1966.

———. *The Future of Nuclear Deterrence.* Lexington: D.C. Heath, 1986.

Rhee, Sang-Woo. "North Korea in 1990." *Asian Survey* 31, no.1 (January 1991): 71-78.

Rhee, Taek-hyung. *U.S.-ROK Combined Operations: a Korean Perspective.* Washington, D.C.: National Defense University, 1986.

———. *Security and Unification of Korea.* Seoul: Sogang University Press, 1984.

Roehrig, Terence. "Assessing North Korean Behavior: The June 2000 Summit, the Bush Administration and Beyond." Pp. 67-88 in *Conflict in Asia,* edited by Uk Heo and Shale A. Horowitz. Westport, CT: Praeger, 2003.

———. "One Rogue State Crisis at a Time!: The United States and North Korea's Nuclear Weapons Program." *World Affairs* 165, no. 4 (Spring 2003): 155-178.

Rosenau, James N., ed. *International Politics and Foreign Policy.* New York: The Free Press, 1969.

———. *Encyclopedia of the Social Sciences.* New York: Crowell, Collier and MacMillan, 1968.

Roy, Denny. "North Korea's Relations with Japan." *Asian Survey* 28, no. 12 (December 1988): 1280-1293.

Rusk, Dean. *As I Saw It.* New York: W.W. Norton, 1990.

Russett, Bruce M. "The Calculus of Deterrence." *Journal of Conflict Resolution* 2, no. 2 (June 1963): 97-109.

———. "Extended Deterrence with Nuclear Weapons: How Necessary, How Acceptable?" *The Review of Politics* 50, no. 2 (Spring 1988): 282-302.

Sagan, Scott D. "Why Do States Build Nuclear Weapons." *International Security* 21, no. 3 (Winter 1996/97): 54-86.

Sakamoto, Yosikazu, ed. *Asia: Militarization and Regional Conflict.* London: Zed Books, 1988.

Sarantakes, Nicolas Evan. "In the Service of Pharaoh? The United States and the Deployment of Korean Troops in Vietnam, 1965-1968." *Pacific Historical Review* 68, no. 3 (August 1999): 425-449.

Sawyer, Robert K. *Military Advisors in Korea: KMAG in Peace and War.* Washington, D.C.: Government Printing Office, 1962.

Scalapino, Robert A. and Chong-Sik Lee. *Communism in Korea, part II*. Berkeley: University of California Press, 1972.

Scalapino, Robert A. and Jun-Yop Kim, eds. *North Korea Today: Strategic and Domestic Issues*. Berkeley: Institute of East Asian Studies, University of California, 1983.

Scalapino, Robert A. and Hongkoo Lee, eds. *Korea-U.S. Relations: The Politics of Trade and Security*. Berkeley: Institute of East Asian Studies, 1988.

Schaller, Michael. *The United States and China in the Twentieth Century*, 2nd ed. New York: Oxford University Press, 1990.

Schrader, John Y. and James A. Winnefeld. *Understanding the Evolving U.S. Role in Pacific Rim Security*. Santa Monica, CA: RAND Corporation, R-4065-PACOM, 1992.

Schram, Stuart, ed. *Selected Works on Mao Tse-tung*, Volume II. Peking: Foreign Language Press, 1965.

Schelling, Thomas C. *Arms and Influence*. New Haven: Yale University Press, 1988.

————. *The Strategy of Conflict*. New York: Oxford University Press, 1960.

Shultz, George P. *Turmoil and Triumph: My Years as Secretary of State*. New York: Macmillian, 1993.

Sigal, Leon V. *Disarming Strangers: Nuclear Diplomacy with North Korea*. Princteon: Princeton University Press, 1998.

Sills, David L., ed. *International Encyclopedia of the Social Sciences*. PLACE: Crowell, Collier and MacMillan, 1968.

Simon, Sheldon W., ed. *East Asian Security in the Post-Cold War Era*. Armonk, New York: M.E. Sharpe, 1993.

Snyder, Glenn. *Deterrence and Defense*. Princeton: Princeton University Press, 1961.

Snyder, Scott. *Negotiating on the Edge: North Korean Negotiating Behavior*. Washington, D.C.: U.S. Institute for Peace, 1999.

Solomon, Richard H., ed. *Asian Security in the 1980s*. Cambridge: Oelgeschlager, Gunn & Hain, 1979.

Spector, Leonard S. *The Undeclared Bomb*. Cambridge: Ballinger, 1988.

————. *Nuclear Ambitions*. Boulder: Westview Press, 1990.

Speed, Roger. *Strategic Deterrence in the 1980s*. Stanford: Hoover Institution Press, 1979.

Stebbins, Richard P. and Elaine P. Adams, eds. *Documents on American Foreign Relations, 1968-69*. New York: Council on Foreign Relations, 1972.

Stern, Paul C., Robert Axelrod, Robert Jervis, and Roy Radner. *Perspectives on Deterrence*. New York: Oxford University Press, 1989.

Stueck, William. *Rethinking the Korean War: A New Diplomatic and Strategic History*. Princeton: Princeton University Press, 2002.

Suh, Dae-Sook. *Kim Il Sung: The North Korean Leader*. New York: Columbia University Press, 1988.

Suh, Dae-Sook and Chae-Jin Lee, eds. *North Korea After Kim Il Sung*. Boulder, CO: Lynne Reinner, 1998.

Suk, Chin-Ha and James L. Morrison. "South Korea's Participation in the Vietnam War: A Historiographical Essay." *Korea Observer* 18, no. 3 (Autumn 1987): 270-316.

Sunoo, Harold Hakwon. *America's Dilemma in Asia: The Case of South Korea*. Chicago: Nelson-Hall, 1979.

Takesada, Hideshi. "Korean Security and Unification in the Detente Era." *The Korean Journal of Defense Analysis* 2, no. 1 (Summer 1990): 179-189.

Tarr, David W. *Nuclear Deterrence and International Security: Alternative Nuclear Regimes.* New York: Longman Publishing Group, 1991.

———. "Coercive Diplomacy in the Gulf Crisis: Deterrence vs. Compellence." *The Jerusalem Journal of International Relations* 13, no. 3 (September 1991): 45-62.

———. "The American Military Presence Abroad." *ORBIS* 9, no. 3 (Fall, 1965): 630-654.

Taylor, William J., Young Koo Cha, John Q. Blodgett, and Michael Mazarr, eds. *The Future of South Korean-U.S. Security Relations.* Boulder: Westview Press, 1989.

Tow, William T. *Encountering the Dominant Player: U.S. Extended Deterrence Strategy in the Asia-Pacific.* New York: Columbia University Press, 1991.

———. "Reassessing Deterrence on the Korean Peninsula." *The Korean Journal of Defense Analysis* 3, no. 1 (Summer 1991): 179-218.

Truman, Harry S. *Memoirs.* Garden City, NJ: Doubleday, 1956.

Truman, Margaret. *Harry S. Truman.* New York: William Morrow, 1973.

U.S.-Korean Security and Relations: New Challenges and Opportunities. Proceedings of the Third Annual Conference, 29 November-2 December 1987 of the Council on U.S.-Korean Security Studies.

Waltz, Kenneth N. "Nuclear Myths and Political Realities." *American Political Science Review* 84, no. 3 (September 1990): 731-745.

Weathersby, Kathryn. *Cold War International History Project.* < http://wwics.si.edu/index.cfm?topic_id=1409&fuseaction=topics.home>.

Weede, Erich. "Extended Deterrence by Superpower Alliance," *Journal of Conflict Resolution* 27, no. 2 (June 1983): 231-253.

Weinberger, Caspar. *Fighting for Peace: Seven Critical Years in the Pentagon.* New York: Warner Books, 1990.

Weinstein, Franklin B. *U.S.-Japan Relations and the Security of East Asia: The Next Decade.* Boulder: Westview Press, 1978.

Whelan, Richard. *Drawing the Line: The Korean War.* Boston: Little, Brown, 1990.

Wishnick, Elizabeth. "Russian-North Korean Relations: A New Era?" Pp. 139-162 in *North Korea and Northeast Asia,* edited by Samuel S. Kim and Tai Hwan Lee. Lanham, MD: Rowman and Littlefield, 2002.

Wit, Joel S., Daniel B. Poneman, and Robert S. Gallucci. *Going Critical: The First North Korean Nuclear Crisis.* Washington, D.C.: Brookings Institution, 2004.

Woodward, Bob. *Bush at War.* New York: Simon & Schuster, 2002.

Wu, Samuel S.G. "To Attack or Not to Attack." *Journal of Conflict Resolution* 34, no. 3 (September 1990): 531-552.

Yon, Hyon-sik. "The Russian Security Interests in Northeast Asia." *The Korean Journal of Defense Analysis* 6, no. 1 (Summer 1994): 155-174.

Zagoria, Donald S., ed. *Soviet Policy in East Asia.* New Haven: Yale University Press, 1982.

———. "North Korea: Between Moscow and Beijing." Pp. 351-371 in *North Korea Today: Strategic and Domestic Issues,* edited by Robert A. Scalapino and Jun-Yop Kim. Berkeley: Institute of East Asian Studies, University of California, 1983.

Zhang, Shu Guang. *Deterrence and Strategic Culture: Chinese-American Confrontations, 1949-1958.* Ithaca: Cornell University Press, 1992.

Zinner, Paul E., ed. *Documents on American Foreign Relations, 1957.* New York: Council on Foreign Relations, 1958.

Government Documents

1996 South Korea Defense White Paper. <www.mnd.go.kr>.

Clinton, William J. *Weekly Compliation of Presidential Documents.* Washington, D.C.: Government Printing Office, 1993.

Documents on American Foreign Relations. New York: Council on Foreign Relations.

National Security Strategy of the United States, September 2002   <www.whitehouse.gov/nsc/nssintro.html>.

OECD Economic Surveys, 1993-1994: KOREA. Washington, D.C.: OECD Publications and Information, 1994.

Public Papers of the President.

Tenet, George. *The Worldwide Threat,* various years. <www.cia.gov>.

U.S. Department of Defense. *Annual Report*

———. *Military Posture.*

———. *A Strategic Framework for the Asian Pacific Rim: Looking Toward the 21st Century,* April 1990.

———. *A Strategic Framework for the Asian Pacific Rim: Looking Toward the 21st Century: Report to Congress,* 28 February 1991.

———. *Soviet Military Power, 1989.*

———. *2000 Report to Congress: Military Situation on the Korean Peninsula,* 12 September 2000. <http://www.dod.gov> (June 2002).

U.S. Department of State. *Department of State Bulletin*

———. *Foreign Relations of the United States.*

———. *American Foreign Policy: Current Documents.* Washington, D.C.: Government Printing Office.

Treaties and Other International Agreements of the United States of America, 1776-1949, Volume 9. Washington, D.C.: Government Printing Office, 1972.

U.S. Arms Control and Disarmament Agency. *Fact Sheet—U.S.-Democratic People's Republic of Korea Agreed Framework,* 21 October 1994.

U.S. Congress. *Military Situation in the Far East.* Hearings before the Committee on Armed Services and the Committee on Foreign Relations, 82nd Congress, 1st Session, to Conduct an Inquiry into the Military Situation in the Far East and the Facts Surrounding the Relief of General of the Army Douglas MacArthur From his Assignments in that area. Washington, D.C.: Government Printing Office, 1951.

U.S. House of Representatives. *Deaths of American Military Personnel in the Korean Demilitarized Zone.* Hearings before the Subcommittees on International Political and Military Affairs and International Organizations of the Committee on International

Relations. 94th Congress, 2nd Session, 1 September 1976. Washington, D.C.: Government Printing Office, 1976.

———. *Developments in United States-Republic of Korea Relations.* Hearing before the Subcommittee on Asian and Pacific Affairs of the Committee on Foreign Affairs. 101st Congress, 1st Session, July 26, 1989. Washington, D.C.: Government Printing Office, 1990.

———. *Impact of Intelligence Reassessment on Withdrawal of U.S. Troops from Korea.* Hearings before the Investigations Subcommittee of the Committee on Armed Services. 96th Congress, 1st Session, June 21 and July 17, 1979. Washington, D.C.: Government Printing Office, 1979.

———. *Korea: North-South Nuclear Issues.* Hearing before the Subcommittee on Asian and Pacific Affairs of the Committee on Foreign Affairs. 101st Congress, 2nd Session, July 25, 1990. Washington, D.C.: Government Printing Office, 1991.

———. *Korean Aid.* Hearings before the Committee on Foreign Affairs. 81st Congress, 1st Session, June 8, 9, 14, 15, 16, 17, 20, 21, and 23, 1949. Washington, D.C.: Government Printing Office, 1949.

———. *North Korean Military and Nuclear Proliferation Threat: Evaluation of the U.S.-DPRK Agreed Framework.* Joint Hearing before the Subcommittees on International Economic Policy and Trade and Asia and the Pacific of the Committee on International Relations.   104th Congress, 1st Session, February 23, 1995. Washington, D.C.: Government Printing Office, 1995.

———. *Policy Implications of North Korea's Ongoing Nuclear Program and Markup of H. Con Res. 179, H. Con. Res. 189, and H. Con. Res. 240.* Hearing and Markup before the Subcommittee on Asian and Pacific Affairs of the Committee on Foreign Affairs. 102nd Congress, 1st Session, November 21, 1991. Washington, D.C.: Government Printing Office, 1992.

———. *Review of the Policy Decision to Withdraw United States Ground Forces from Korea.* Hearings before the Investigations Subcommittee and the Committee on Armed Services. 95th Congress, 1st and 2nd Sessions, May 25, July 13, 14, August 1, September 3, 1977, January 4, 5, 6, 10, 11, 12, 13, 14, 1978. Washington, D.C.: Government Printing Office, 1978.

———. *Review of the Policy Decision to Withdraw United States Ground Forces From Korea.* Report of the Investigations Subcommittee of the Committee on Armed Services. 95th Congress, 2nd Session, April 26, 1978. Washington, D.C.: Government Printing Office, 1978.

United States Senate. *Implications of the U.S.-North Korea Nuclear Agreement.* Hearing before the Subcommittee on East Asian and Pacific Affairs of the Committee on Foreign Relations. 103rd Congress, 2nd Session, December 1, 1994. Washington, D.C.: Government Printing Office, 1995.

———. *Inquiry into the Military Situation in the Far East and the facts surrounding the relief of General of the Army Douglas MacArthur from his assignment in that area,* Part 4. Hearings before the Committee on Armed Services and Committee on Foreign Relations. Washington, D.C.: Government Printing Office, 1951.

———. *Mutual Defense Treaty With Korea*, Hearings before the Committee on Foreign Relations. 83rd Congress, 2nd Session, January 13 and 14, 1954. Washington, D.C.: Government Printing Office, 1954.

———. *Statement of General Thomas A. Schwartz, Commander in Chief United Nations Command/Combined Forces Command and Commander, United States Forces Korea, testimony before the Senate Armed Services Committee*, 106th Congress, 2nd Session, 7 March 2000 and 107th Congress, 2nd Session, 5 March 2002.

———. *Statement of General John H. Tilelli Jr., Commander in Chief, United Nations Command/U.S. Forces Korea/Combined Forces Command Korea*, testimony before the Senate Armed Services Committee, 106th Congress, 1st Session, 4 March 1999.

———. *Statement by General Louis C. Menetrey, Commander in Chief, United Nations Command/U.S. Forces Korea statement before the Subcommittee on Defense Appropriations*, 23 February 1989.

———. "Statement of Hon. Thomas Hubbard, Deputy Assistant Secretary of State for East Asian and Pacific Affairs," *North Korean Military and Nuclear Proliferation Threat: Evaluation of the U.S.-DPRK Agreed Framework*, 104th Congress, 1st Session, 23 February 1995. Washington, D.C.: Government Printing Office, 1995.

———. *United States Security Agreements and Commitments Abroad: Republic of Korea*. Hearings before the Subcommittee on U.S. Security Agreements and Commitments Abroad of the Committee on Foreign Relations. 91st Congress, 2nd Session, Part 6, February 24, 25, and 26, 1970. Washington, D.C.: Government Printing Office, 1970.

———. *U.S. Troop Withdrawal From The Republic of Korea*. A Report to the Committee on Foreign Relations by Senators Hubert H. Humphrey and John Glenn, 95th Congress, 2nd Session, January 9, 1978. Washington, D.C.: Government Printing Office, 1978.

———. *The Vandenberg Resolution and the North Atlantic Treaty*, Hearings before the Committee on Foreign Relations, 81st Congress, 2nd Session, May 11, 12, 19, June 3, 1948, February 18, March 8, April 5, 12, 19, 21, June 2, 6, 1949. Washington, D.C.: Government Printing Office, 1949.

Index

Acheson, Dean, 30, 36, 120-122, 124-128, 130, 150
Ackermann, Rep. Gary, 208
Agreed Framework, 8, 86, 99-100, 143-144, 146, 183, 222-223, 227, 192, 201, 208-210, 214-217, 255
Airland battle doctrine, 191
Albright, Madeline, 91, 96, 144, 213
Art, Robert, 23
Association of Southeast Asian Nations (ASEAN), 96, 139
axis of evil, 24, 79, 95, 98, 145-146, 218, 223

Baker, James, 138, 203
Bermudez Jr., Joseph, 53, 83, 92, 94
Bolton, John, 79
Bradley, Gen. Omar, 123, 127
Brown, Harold, 51, 60-61, 136, 171
Brezhnev, Leonid, 50
Bundy, McGeorge, 179-180
Bush, George H. W., 138-142, 172, 186, 192, 203-205
Bush, George W., 14, 24, 79, 91, 144-147, 172-173, 175, 245, 256; and North Korea policy, 172-173, 175, 215-227

Cairo Conference, 115
Carter, Jimmy, 16, 57, 135-136, 170-171, 174, 176, 180-181, 189, 194, 232; meeting

with Kim Il Sung, 207, 214; plan to remove ground troops, 60, 135-136, 149
Cimbala, Stephen, 12
Clinton, Bill, 79, 91, 96, 142-144, 172, 201, 205-215, 226-227, 256
Cha, Victor, 97
Cheney, Richard, 61, 138, 172, 177, 204, 218, 221
Chiang Kai-shek, 115, 119-120, 248
China, 17, 30-33, 35-38, 41-46, 232-240; treaty with North Korea, 43-44, 76-77
Christopher, Warren, 205-206
Chun Doo Hwan, 64, 137-138, 171
Churchill, Winston, 115
Cold War, 1-2, 29, 60, 76, 92, 112, 116, 139, 142, 161, 182, 191, 233, 243, 245, 257
Combined Forces Command, 81, 184-186, 249, 251,
compellence, 6, 11, 22-26, 203, 224-226, 232, 234
credibility, 17-22, 24, 162, 182, 231, 247, 255
Cuban Missile Crisis, 44, 50-51, 191
Cushman, Lt. General John, 191

demilitarized zone (DMZ), 1, 39, 46-47, 50, 57-59, 81, 84, 101, 133-134, 142, 148, 176-177, 181, 190, 194, 240

Democratic People's Republic of
   Korea. *See* North Korea
Deng Xiaoping, 181
deterrence, 11-22, 26; definition
   of, 12; by denial, 12, 179;
   existential, 179-180; extended,
   8, 16-17, 21, 231, 234; general,
   14-16, 18-19, 21, 64, 231;
   immediate, 14-16, 21, 231;
   literature, 3-5; primary, 16-17,
   79; by punishment, 12-13, 179,
   247; by reward, 12-13;
   troops as a tripwire, 179-182,
   251
Dulles, John Foster, 32, 121-122,
   130, 150, 165-168, 187

Eisenhower, Dwight, 31-33, 37,
   130, 148, 150, 166-168, 173,
   187-188, 244, 248; and the
   New Look, 188
engagement, 6, 258-259

Foal Eagle exercises, 182, 250
Ford, Gerald, 170

George, Alexander, 21, 24-25, 111,
   123-124
Gilman, Rep. Benjamin, 211
Gorbachev, Mikhail, 60, 192
Greater Sanctions declaration, 32,
   165-166
Gregg, Donald, 95, 98

Haig, Alexander, 137
Harrison, Selig, 97
Hayes, Peter, 188
Hollingsworth Line, 55
Honest John missiles, 40, 173, 186
Hussein, Saddam, 98, 147, 217,
   223-224, 257
Huth, Paul, 20-21

interests: and effect on deterrence,
   20-22, 111-113, 243-246

International Atomic Energy
   Agency (IAEA), 85, 141-142,
   177, 204-206, 217, 227
Iraq, 24, 87, 99, 145, 147, 152, 218,
   223, 246, 257

Japan: occupation of Korea, 3, 115,
   234; and North Korean missile
   test, 89-90, 205, 245; U.S.
   interests in, 130-131
Jervis, Robert, 13, 21
Johnson, Louis, 123
Johnson, Lyndon, 16, 38, 42, 45,
   47, 131-132, 169
Joint Denuclearization agreement,
   85, 205, 217, 225
Jo, Gen. Myong Rok, 96, 98, 144,
   214
Joo, Seung-Ho, 78
juche, 38, 58, 92
June 2000 Summit, 96, 144, 212

Kanter, Arnold, 204
KATUSA, 38
Kaufmann, William, 17-18, 162
Kelly, James, 221
Kennan, George, 118, 129
Kennedy, John, 37
Khrushchev, Nikita, 33-34
Kim Dae Jung, 96, 144, 172, 212,
   216, 219
Kim Il Sung, 14, 22, 34-36, 38, 43-
   51, 56-57, 59, 64, 75-76, 86,
   88, 92, 116, 124, 164, 169, 257
Kim Jong Il, 14, 22, 59, 75, 78, 89-
   91, 96-97, 99-100, 144, 183,
   210, 221, 257
Kim Yong Nam, 210-211
Kim Young Sam, 86, 172, 183,
   206, 215, 259
Kissinger, Henry, 19
Koh, Byung Chul, 35, 99
Kojong, King, 113-114
Koreagate, 135-136, 174
Korean Military Advisory Group
   (KMAG), 122

Korean Peninsula Energy
    Development Organization
    (KEDO), 86-87, 217, 220, 225
Korean War, 17, 30-34, 50, 54,
    101, 112-113, 150, 162, 167-
    168, 176, 243; and
    appeasement, 127-129; and
    armistice, 32, 35, 186; and
    effect on deterrence, 240-243
Krauthammer, Charles, 208
Kumgang, Mt., 93-94, 212
Kwangju Massacre, 137-138

LaPorte, Gen. Leon, 185
Lebow, Richard Ned, 13, 18
Lee Hoi Chang, 212
Libya, 221, 257
Livsey, Gen. William, 185
Luck, Gen. Gary, 185

MacArthur, Gen. Douglas, 118,
    120, 131
Mao Zedong, 36, 45, 119
massive retaliation, 32, 162, 188
Mazarr, Michael, 99, 204-206, 208-
    209
McCain, Sen. John, 208
Mearsheimer, John, 12, 19
Menetrey, Gen. Louis, 151, 185,
    190-191
Missile Technology Control
    Regime (MTCR), 90, 92, 212
Morgan, Patrick, 13-16, 18, 22-23
Murkowski, Sen. Frank, 208

National Security Review 28, 203
National Security Strategy, 77, 257
Natsios, Andrew, 93
Nixon, Richard, 133-135, 148, 169-
    170, 173, 176, 259; and Nixon
    doctrine, 133, 151, 169-170
Nodong missiles, 88-89, 92
North Atlantic Treaty Organization
    (NATO), 3, 19, 77, 149, 166,
    168, 193, 250
North Korea: ballistic missiles,

1, 65, 75, 79, 88-92, 96-98;
    biological weapons, 79, 87-88;
    chemical weapons, 79, 87-88;
    conventional forces, 34-36, 38-
    41, 51-56, 61-64, 80-84, 101-
    103; economic reforms; 93-
    94; food crisis, 92-95;
    kidnapping Japanese, 100-101;
    nuclear weapons, 75, 79, 84-
    88, 98, 145; relations with
    China, 43-44, 50-51, 59-61,
    76-77; relations with Japan,
    100-101; relations with
    Russia/Soviet Union, 43-44,
    50-51, 59-61, 77-78; relations
    with South Korea, 49;
    terrorism, 64, 223-224
NSC 8, 116-118, 120, 122, 150
NSC 13, 135
NSC 68, 30, 112, 126
NSC 73/4, 31, 129
NSC 118/2, 31
NSC 5702/2, 188
Nuclear Nonproliferation Treaty
    (NPT), 25, 85-87, 141-143,
    146,149, 202-206, 218
Nuclear Posture Review, 77

Oberdorfer, Don, 204-205
O'Hanlon, Michael, 84
Operation Everready, 167-168
OPLAN 5026, 183;
    5027, 183, 207;
    5029, 183;
    5030, 184

Paige, Glenn, 123
Pak Gil Yon, 222
Pakistan, 87, 101
Park Chung Hee, 16, 38, 43, 45, 50,
    56-58, 133, 169, 171, 232
Perry, William, 86, 206-207, 213
    214; Perry Review, 97, 211-
    212
Porter, William, 14, 42, 46-48, 134,
    148

Powell, Colin, 79, 146-147, 215
    216, 218-219
Proliferation Security Initiative,
    177
Putin, Vladimir, 78, 90

Ranjin-Sonbong free trade zone,
    93-94
rationality, 13-14
Reagan, Ronald, 137-138, 141,
    171-172, 174, 176, 256
Republic of Korea. *See* South
    Korea
Rhee, Syngman, 3, 34, 36-37, 42-
    43, 120, 148, 150, 165-167,
    188, 248
Richardson, Bill, 218
RisCassi, Gen. Robert, 185
Robb, Sen. Charles, 208
rogue states, 2, 95, 146-147, 223
    224, 257-258
Roh Moo Hyun, 177, 219
Roh Tae Woo, 138, 192
Roosevelt, Franklin D., 115
Roosevelt, Theodore, 115
Rumsfeld, Donald, 146, 178-179,
    184, 192, 219; Rumsfeld
    Commission, 89
Rusk, Dean, 30-31, 40-41, 47, 116,
    121
Russett, Bruce, 20-21, 173, 175
Russia/Soviet Union, 17, 29-34,
    36-37, 59-61, 112, 232-240;
    treaty with North Korea, 43-
    44, 49-51, 77-78, 90
Russo-Japanese War, 114-115

Schelling, Thomas, 18, 20, 22-23,
    175-176
Schlesinger, James, 170
Schwartz, Gen. Thomas, 81, 95,
    185
Scowcroft, Brent, 192
Scud missiles, 88, 92
Sennewald, Gen. Robert, 185
September 11th, 2, 98, 112, 145,

    151-152, 218, 223, 245
Shufeldt Treaty, 113-114
Shultz, George, 138
Sigur, Gaston, 202
Singlaub, Gen. John, 180
Sino-Japanese War, 114-115
Six-Party talks, 100, 219-222
Smith, Walter Bedell, 30, 122
Smoke, Richard, 21, 25, 111, 123-
    124
Snyder, Glenn, 12
Sokolski, Henry, 99
South Korea: armed forces, 35, 38-
    41, 52-56, 61-64, 80-84;
    nuclear weapons, 149; Persian
    Gulf War, 140-141; role in
    deterrence, 6-7, 131-135, 139-
    141, 149-150, 175, 246-250;
    Vietnam War, 131-133, 247
Stalin, Joseph, 36, 150
Stein, Janice Gross, 13
Suh, Dae-Sook, 46
sunshine policy, 212, 216, 219

Taepo Dong missiles, 89-90, 211
Taft-Katsura agreement, 115
Team Spirit exercises, 171, 182,
    191, 205-207, 250
Tenet, George, 79, 86, 90, 92, 98
threat assessment, 5-6, 29-30, 48-
    49, 232-234, 242-243
Tilelli, General John, 81, 183, 185
Trilateral Coordination and
    Oversight Group (TCOG), 212
Truman, Harry, 30, 116-120, 122-
    127, 243

Ulchi Focus Lens exercises, 182
United Nations, 24, 113, 117, 120,
    125-126, 128, 130-131, 169,
    206, 243
United Nations Command (UNC),
    57
United States: concerns about a
    nuclear North Korea, 142-143;
    economic aid to South Korea,

173-175, 246, 251; forces in
East Asia, 163-164;
conventional forces in South
Korea, 163-164, 169-170, 175-
184, 252; nuclear weapons in
South Korea, 164, 186-193,
252; security treaty with South
Korea, 1, 8, 165-170, 193-194,
251
USS *Pueblo*, 16, 25, 40, 47, 49,
134, 169, 231, 240

Vessey, Gen. John, 51-52, 57, 185
Vietnam War, 25

Waltz, Kenneth, 12
Wickham Jr., Gen. John, 185
Weinberger, Caspar, 137
Wolfowitz, Paul, 140

Yeltsin, Boris, 77-78

About the Author

Terence Roehrig is Associate Professor and Chair of the Department of Political Science at Cardinal Stritch University in Milwaukee, Wisconsin. He received his PhD from the University of Wisconsin-Madison and his MA from Marquette University. He has published a book titled *The Prosecution of Former Military Leaders in Newly Democratic Nations: The Cases of Argentina, Greece, and South Korea* that addresses how military leaders can be held accountable for past human rights abuses without subverting the transition to democracy. He has also written numerous articles and book chapters on North Korea's nuclear weapons program, Korean security issues, human rights, and transitional justice.

9 780739 105603